INSECT
ECOLOGY

INSECT ECOLOGY

PETER W. PRICE

Department of Entomology
University of Illinois
Urbana

A WILEY-INTERSCIENCE
PUBLICATION

JOHN WILEY & SONS

New York • London • Sydney • Toronto

Library of Congress Cataloging in Publication Data:

Price, Peter W
  Insect ecology.

  "A Wiley-Interscience publication."
  Bibliography: p.
  Includes index.
  1. Insects—Ecology. I. Title.
QL463.P73   595.7'05   75-12720
ISBN 0-471-69721-4

Printed in the United States of America

10 9 8 7 6 5 4 3 2

PREFACE

This book is written as a text for a course for advanced undergraduates and graduate students in entomology. In selecting material for this book it has been difficult to decide how much general ecology and how much entomological material to incorporate. A guiding principle has been to familiarize the reader with the general ecological literature while emphasizing the important role that studies on insects have played in ecological thought, the significance of insects as members of communities, and their potential value in resolving many debates in ecology. Since insects have been herbivores probably longer than any other terrestrial animals, and since they are the most important herbivores in many communities, they offer an ideal opportunity for integration of plant and animal ecology. I have attempted this integration in various chapters, since the ecology of plants, as a food source for many insects, is necessarily involved in the understanding of insect ecology.

The content of each chapter has been determined to some extent by the availability of other texts. Because methods in insect ecology have been expertly covered by Southwood (1966), these are not emphasized in this text. Andrewartha and Birch (1954), Clark et al. (1967), and Varley et al. (1973) provide good introductions to studies on insect population dynamics. The experimental approach to insect ecology is treated by Lewis and Taylor (1967). Several excellent books on biological control of insects and weeds are mentioned in Chapter 12, and pest management is covered in Metcalf and Luckmann (1975), therefore applied aspects of insect ecology are not treated in detail in this book. Apart from the deemphasis on areas of insect ecology mentioned above I have aimed at a comprehensive treatment of the subject. Such a treatment has not been attempted since Chapman's (1931) *Animal ecology with special reference to insects,* and Andrewartha and Birch's (1954) *The distribution and abundance of animals.* I hope that the contents of this text will offer some measure of the extent to which the subject has grown since these two books were published. This text also diverges from those mentioned above in using in several chapters an evolutionary approach to ecology. This approach seems appropriate for dealing with a group of animals that, because of their large numbers, high mortality per generation, and short generation time, evolve very rapidly.

PETER W. PRICE

Urbana, Illinois
March 1975

ACKNOWLEDGMENTS

Literally hundreds of people have contributed to this book. I have drawn heavily from the scientific literature, and I am indebted to all those authors who are cited for making ecology interesting to me. I have been constantly stimulated and challenged by my graduate students, by other students in the Department of Entomology and the Ecology Program, and by those students taking my insect ecology course at the University of Illinois. I wish my teaching efforts were as educational for them as they have been for me. My colleagues in the Department of Entomology have taught me a lot about insects. I am sincerely grateful to them all.

I must continue to acknowledge the profound influences that R. B. Root has had on my ecological thinking as adviser for my dissertation, collaborator in research, comrade on field trips, and at all times my friend. My gratitude to him runs deeper than is possible to express. My wife, Maureen, has sustained me in many ways. I have benefited during the preparation of this book from the advice of colleagues who read drafts of chapters. They provided many helpful suggestions and pointed out errors of fact, relevant sources of information, and areas of insect ecology that required more attention. I am particularly indebted to R. W. Matthews who reviewed an early plan, subsequently read a complete draft of the book, and made many constructive criticisms. Several students, especially C. Bouton, K. McCarthy, M. Mayse, and J. Thompson read most of a draft and improved the manuscript by their helpful comments. I have also gained from advice given by colleagues who read the chapters indicated in parentheses: G. O. Batzli (9), A. Beattie (20), D. Culver (18), L. M. Dill (5), L. E. Gilbert (3), E. R. Heithaus (20), D. J. Horn (12), J. Mann (21), R. L. Metcalf (11), R. A. Metcalf (16), R. W. Poole (7, 14, 19), B. R. Rathcke (2, 9, 17), R. B. Root (13, 15, 16), A. M. Shapiro (10), D. S. Simberloff (21), J. N. M. Smith (4), W. W. Steiner (10), R. G. Wiegert (6), and M. F. Willson (3, 8, 16). I am also grateful for preprints and for the permission to use them from H. Caswell, R. G.

Cates, L. R. Fox, L. E. Gilbert, M. S. McClure, G. H. Orians, and R. L. Trivers. Mrs. Alice Prickett supervised the drafting of the majority of figures and personally created Figs. 3.4, 14.2, 15.4, 20.2, and 20.3. I thank her and M. Paulson, G. Glende, F. Chu, D. Wallace, and J. Hipskind for their care and patience with the seemingly endless art work. The copious quantities of typing, copying, and mailing involved with the several drafts of the book were executed with dispatch by R. Plymire, J. Michael, J. Alexander, B. MacMillan, and S. Morisette. During most of the book preparation I was supported through U.S. Public Health Training Grant PH GM 1076 for which I am most grateful.

I appreciate permission from authors and publishers to reproduce figures and tables from the following sources: L. R. Clark et al. 1967. *The ecology of insect populations in theory and practice*. Methuen and Co., Ltd. (Fig. 1.1); Duke University Press, publishers of *Ecology and Ecological Monographs* (Figs. 2.1, 2.2, 3.3, 5.7, 7.8, 8.2, 8.3, 9.10, 13.2, 13.6, 14.3, 16.2, 17.4, 17.6, 18.1, 18.12, 18.13, Table 6.4); A. Watson (ed.) 1970. *Animal populations in relation to their food resources*. By permission of Blackwell Scientific Publications (Fig. 2.3); Chicago Academy of Sciences, publishers of *Bulletin of the Chicago Academy of Science* (Fig. 2.4); National Academy of Sciences (Fig. 2.7); The University of Chicago Press (Figs. 2.8, 3.5, 5.1, 8.8, 9.8, 19.4, 19.5); By permisison of P. P. Feeny. 1968. Effect of oak leaf tannins on larval growth of the winter moth, *Operophtera brumata. Journal of Insect Physiology* 14. Pergamon Press Ltd. (Fig. 3.1); Reproduced from the *Canadian Entomologist* (Figs. 4.4, 4.6, 4.7, 4.8, 5.10, 5.13, 9.14, 11.3, 12.3); Reproduced from *Journal of Animal Ecology* by permission of Blackwell Scientific Publications (Figs. 4.9, 4.10, 4.11, 4.12, 5.2, 8.11, 8.12, Tables 14.2, 14.4, 14.5, Figs. 18.3, 18.10, 18.11); Croze, H. 1970. Searching image in carrion crows. Suppl. 5 to *Journal of Comparative Ethology*. Verlag Paul Parey (Fig. 4.13, 4.14); E. C. Pielou. 1969. *An introduction to mathematical ecology*. John Wiley and Sons, Inc. (Fig. 5.3); Macmillan Journals Ltd., publishers of *Nature* (Figs. 5.4, 5.5, Table 7.5); G. F. Gause. *The struggle for existence*. Williams and Wilkins Co., © 1934. The Williams and Wilkins Co., Baltimore (Figs. 5.6, 14.5); University of California Division of Agricultural Sciences (Fig. 5.8, 5.9); J. B. Cragg (ed.). *Advances in ecological research*. Academic Press, London (Fig. 6.1, Table 14.3); Edward Arnold (Publishers) Ltd. (Fig. 6.2); R. B. Root (Fig. 6.3); G. O. Batzli. 1974. Production assimilation and accumulation of organic matter in ecosystems. *Journal of Theoretical Biology* 45. Academic Press, London (Fig. 6.4); W. H. Freeman and Co., for *Scientific American* (Figs. 6.5, 11.4); J. D. Durand. 1967. The modern expansion of World population. *Proceedings of the American Philosophical Society* 111:136–145 (Fig. 7.1); Dover Publications, Inc. (Figs. 7.5, 7.6); Reproduced by permission of the National Research Council of Canada from the *Canadian Journal of Zoology* **32** (1954): 283–301 (Tables 7.2, 7.3); Reprinted with permission of Macmillan Publishing Co., Inc. from *Ecology of populations*, A. S. Boughey. Copyright © 1968 by Arthur S. Boughey (Figs. 7.7, 21.11); Plenum Press (Fig. 7.9); Used with the permission of the *Quarterly Review of Biology* (Figs. 7.10, 7.11); H. G. Baker and G. L. Stebbins (eds.). 1965. *The genetics of colonizing species*. Academic Press (Figs. 7.12, 7.13, 7.14); The Society for the Study of Evolution, publishers of *Evolution* (Figs. 8.1, 8.9, 8.10, 20.4, 21.17); Dr. Henry Townes, and the American Entomological Institute (Fig. 8.5); From M. E. Solomon. 1969 and 1973 (reprint). *Population dynamics. Studies in Biology*, No. 18, Edward Arnold, London (Fig. 9.1); *The Journal of Mammalogy* (Fig. 9.2); Wisconsin Department of Natural Resources *Conservation Bulletin* (Fig. 9.3); E. J. Brill, Publishers of *Arch. Neerl. Zool.* (Fig. 9.6); Reproduced from *Insect Abundance* by permission of Blackwell Scientific Publications (Table 9.2); The Systematics Association (Fig. 10.4); A. J. Cain. 1954. *Genetics* **39** (Fig. 10.5); B. Clarke. 1962. *Heredity* **17**, published by Longman Group Ltd. (Fig. 10.6); Entomological Society of America (Figs. 11.1, 11.2); C. H. Lindroth and Munksgaard International Booksellers and Publishers, Ltd. (Fig. 13.12); *Australian Journal of Zoology* (Fig. 14.5, 14.8); F. J. Ayala. Competition between species: Frequency dependence. *Science* **171** (February 26, 1971):820–824. Copyright 1971 by the American Association for the Advancement of Science (Fig. 14.14); Brookhaven National Laboratory (Figs. 15.5, 18.2); P. Weygoldt. *The biology of pseudoscorpions*. Harvard University Press. Copyright © 1969 by the President and Fellows of Harvard College (Fig. 17.2); E. P. Odum. The strategy of ecosystem development. *Science* **164**(April 18, 1969):262–270. Copyright 1969 by the American Association for the Advancement of Science (Fig. 17.7, Table 17.3); From Robert H. MacArthur and Edward O. Wilson, The theory of island biogeography (copyright © 1967 by Princeton University Press), Fig. 2, p. 8, Fig. 7, p. 21, Fig. 8, p. 22, Fig. 9, p. 23, and Fig. 10, p. 24. Reprinted by permission of Princeton University Press (Figs. 18.9, 21.13, 21.14, 21.15, 21.16); R. H. Whittaker. Dominance and diversity in land plant communities. *Science* **147**(January 15, 1965):250–260. Copyright 1965 by the American Association for the Advancement of Science (Fig. 18.14); L. E. Gilbert and P. H. Raven (eds.). *Coevolution of animals and plants*. University of Texas Press. 1975 (Fig. 18.15); Reprinted with permission of Macmillan Publishing Co., Inc., from *Communities and ecosystems*, R. H. Whittaker. Copyright © 1970 by R. H. Whittaker (Fig. 19.1); R. W. Cruden. Pollinators in high-elevation ecosystems: Relative effectiveness of birds and bees. *Science* **176**(June 30, 1972):1439–

1440. Copyright 1972 by the American Association for the Advancement of Science (Table 20.2); New York Botanical Garden (Table 20.3); the National Geographic Society which kindly provided negatives for the figures (Figs. 21.2, 21.3, 21.4); W. L. Brown, Jr. (Fig. 21.6); *Bulletin of the American Museum of Natural History* (Fig. 21.7); H. H. Ross, and W. E. Ricker. 1971. The classification, evolution, and dispersal of the winter stonefly genus *Allocapnia*. *Illinois Biological Monographs* 45, published by the University of Illinois Press (Figs. 21.8, 21.9, 21.10); Reprinted with permission from L. R. Holdridge et al. *Forest environments in tropical life zones.* 1971. Pergamon Press Ltd. (Fig. 21.12).

I appreciate permission from authors and publishers to quote from the following sources: G. G. Simpson. 1964. *This view of life.* Harcourt, Brace, Jovanovich, Inc. (p. 21); C. S. Elton. 1927. *Animal ecology.* Sidgwick and Jackson, Ltd. (p. 18); The Society for the Study of Evolution, publishers of *Evolution* (p. 30); E. Sondheimer and J. B. Simeone (eds.). *Chemical ecology.* Academic Press, New York (p. 32); C. H. Muller and Torrey Botanical Club (p. 33); L. Tinbergen. 1960. *Arch. Neerl. Zool.* 13. E. J. Brill, Publishers (p. 50, 60); H. Caswell, F. Reed, S. N. Stephenson, and P. A. Werner. Photosynthetic pathways and selective herbivory: A hypothesis. *American Naturalist* 107:465–480. ⓒ 1973 by the University of Chicago. All rights reserved (p. 45, 46); G. F. Gause. *The struggle for existence.* Williams and Wilkins Co. ⓒ 1934. The Williams and Wilkins Co., Baltimore (p. 86); University of California Division of Agricultural Sciences (p. 90); D. F. Westlake. 1963. Comparisons of plant productivity. *Biological Review* 38. Cambridge University Press (p. 105); Reproduced by permission of the National Research Council of Canada from the *Canadian Journal of Zoology* 39(1961):697–753 (p. 235); E. B. Ford. 1964. *Ecological genetics.* Methuen and Co. Ltd. (p. 187); R. R. Askew. 1971. *Parasitic insects.* American Elsevier Publishing Company (p. 233); P. DeBach (ed.). *Biological control of insect pests and weeds.* Chapman and Hall Ltd., and Halstad Press (p. 234); Entomological Society of America (p. 236); The Royal Society, publishers of the *Proceedings of the Royal Society*, London, Series B (p. 243); From E. P. Odum. *Fundamentals of ecology*, 3rd ed. Published by W. B. Saunders Company, Philadelphia. 1971 (p. 270); J. B. Cragg (ed.). *Advances in ecological research.* Academic Press, London (p. 290); Reproduced from *Journal of Animal Ecology* by permisison of Blackwell Scientific Publications (p. 313); Brookhaven National Laboratory (p. 315); W. D. Hamilton. 1964. *Journal of Theoretical Biology.* Academic Press, London (p. 320); Duke University Press, publishers of *Ecology* and *Ecological Monographs* (p. 344).

                                                                          P. W. P.

CONTENTS

Chapter outlines are provided at the beginning of each chapter. They identify important aspects of the subject to be considered.

INSECT
ECOLOGY

Chapter I

INTRODUCTION: ELEMENTARY CONCEPTS

I t is hard to define ecology. "The science of relationships of organisms to their environment" means essentially the study of almost everything that involves living things, and does not help to define its limits. Perhaps the older definitions of Haeckel (quoted in Shelford 1907) and Shelford (1907) are more helpful. Haeckel defined ecology as the domestic side of organic life. Shelford's definition, "life needs and housekeeping habits of organisms," reflects a similar attitude toward this science. An alternative approach might be suggested by defining ecology as the study of "theories of natural history," which emphasizes that we are looking for explanations of natural phenomena, and the reasons for patterns in nature. Haeckel (1870) certainly subscribed to this view.

One fascinating aspect of ecology is summed up by the title of Hutchinson's (1965) book, *The ecological theater and the evolutionary play.* In other words, the ecological setting acts as a stage for evolutionary processes. Simpson (1964a) puts ecology in its place more precisely: "Given an existing population structure and an existing ecological situation, and given the genetic variation of the population as it moves through time, the action of selection seems to be fully deterministic." Therefore, the approach adopted in this book treats ecology as "the study of environments for evolutionary processes." This definition focuses attention on the dynamics within a given environment, the functional relationships between organisms, and the analysis of control mechanisms in the ecosystem. Dynamics, functional relationships, and control mechanisms are key words in an evolutionary ecology. Descriptive ecology only permits the asking of one question "What?". An analytical ecology based on these words permits further and vastly more interesting questions, "How?" and "Why?". It is safer to assume that everything in an ecosystem is changing all the time than to treat the system as a static unit. Descriptive ecology is a dry subject unless it is related to the underlying mechanisms that produced the situation described.

Since ecology is a relatively young science, few fundamental principles go unchallenged. Ecology is really a debate. Therefore it is vital to know the debaters, the proponents, and the critics, the data supporting their views, and the organisms they studied and how they studied them. This book is intended to help the reader to compile a "who's who in ecology," both for the humans involved and the organisms that have been studied.

Several levels of organization must be studied in ecology. The individual is the basic unit for study, although to understand how the individual is adapted to its environment, it is often necessary to look at parts of individuals. Hamilton (1967) emphasized that the reproducing individual is the primary unit of natural selection.

A group of individuals can be called a population and may be defined in two ways. In the first, the word population merely denotes all the individuals in a given area. A more precise definition is given by Mayr (1963) who defines the local population or deme as the group of potentially interbreeding individuals at a given locality. Thus all members of a local population share in a single gene pool, and such a population may be defined as "a group of individuals so situated that any two of them have equal probability of mating with each other and producing offspring," provided that they are sexually mature, of opposite sexes, and equivalent with respect to sexual selection (Mayr 1963).

Groups of populations that actually or potentially interbreed with each other constitute a species. This concept of the species, known as the multidimensional species concept (see Mayr 1963), helps the ecologist to regard the individual as a unique member of a population or species just as we do in human populations. One is tempted to think that individuals are one of a type that can be described by the study of one specimen or of very few. Now that the evolutionist and taxonomist have discovered the error of this typological thinking, the ecologist should make every effort to regard populations as collections of individuals, each contributing a unique property to the population and thus deserving of study. The species is the unit of evolution, and speciation "is the method by which evolution advances" (Hamilton 1967).

Higher levels of organization include the community, which consists of coexisting interdependent populations, and the ecosystem, or the community and its physical environment. Regional ecosystem types, such as grassland, desert, and deciduous forest, are called biomes. The biosphere is the biological system that includes all of the earth's living organisms interacting with the physical environment (Odum 1971).

Another useful ecological unit that cuts across this hierarchical classification is the life system, first used explicitly by Clark et al. (1967). It is defined as the part of an ecosystem that determines the existence, abundance, and evolution of a particular population. The life system is composed of a subject population and its effective environment which includes the totality of external agencies influencing the population. For each member of a population the environment also includes the other members (Clark et al. 1967). In the light of the life system concept the ecosystem can be redefined as interlocking life systems.

In the life system (Fig. 1.1) the phenotypes of individuals are molded by the interaction between their genetic makeup (genotype) and the environment. Since individuals constitute the population genotype, the environment will also influence the population, and the gene pool of the population. Therefore the sum total of the genetic material in the population, will have a profound influence on the population performance,

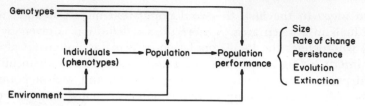

Fig. 1.1 The interacting factors in the life system that influence population phenomena. After Clark, Geier, Hughes, and Morris 1967.

such as its size, rate of change, persistence, evolution, and extinction. This performance will be greatly modified also by environmental factors. The genotype of the individual is permanently set when the male and female gametes fuse. However, expression of the genotype is molded by the environmental conditions in which it finds itself. This environmental influence is constantly changing, perhaps more rapidly in temperate than in tropical latitudes, perhaps more rapidly in exposed than in protected sites.

Environmental change will seldom favor one genotype all the time so that population survival depends on the presence of a diversity of genotypes. This diversity of the genotypes in the population is maintained by two factors. The first is mutation or the production of new genes, and the second is recombination or the regrouping of genes. These are more or less random elements of change in the gene pool of the population.

The phenotypes in populations are influenced by two constantly changing, interacting processes—the genotypes and the environment. The genotypes represent a random mixture of genes from the gene pool although the gene pool does have an important historical element that has been molded by natural selection, which has tended to reduce this randomization. Those genotypes that are expressed as vigorous phenotypes will be favored in the environment that cannot support all individuals produced, and this selection will provide a directional element to the change in the gene pool of the population. Thus the population is constantly molded by the changing genetic and environmental elements.

This molding of the population by means of natural selection is one of the basic concepts in ecology. A brief review of factors leading to the formulation of this concept follows. King George III of England reigned for 60 years from 1760 to 1820. He was on the throne during the early stages of the industrial revolution, a revolution that also necessitated an agrarian revolution to feed the masses of people that were flocking to the towns. George's reign saw an increase in population in England from

$7\frac{1}{2}$ million to 14 million, a near doubling in 60 years, whereas it had taken 3000 years or more to reach $7\frac{1}{2}$ million. Malthus, who wrote his classic essay in 1798, was the first to recognize the population explosion, within 40 years of its priming. Malthus pointed out that, unchecked, populations increase at a geometric rate; the environment cannot possibly support the resulting populations so that in "plants and animals its effects are waste of seed, sickness and premature death." The essay by Malthus provided Darwin with the answer to his nagging problem of how to explain the transmutation of species, and Darwin (1859a, b) realized that of the huge potential populations of organisms only the fittest survived. Since there is no way of measuring fitness except by survival, Darwin's "survival of the fittest" through natural selection and adaptation leads to circular arguments; thus adaptation is usually described as any quality of an organism, population, or species that increases its chances of leaving viable progeny. Fitness may be defined as the ability of an individual or population to leave viable progeny in relation to the ability of others. Thus the variety of genotypes in a population produced by mutation and recombination is reduced by the mortality of maladapted types caused by an environmental factor. This is why Mayr (1963) has called natural selection "the differential perpetuation of genotypes."

Further insight into the process of natural selection can be gained by considering the additional basic concepts of feedback and homeostasis. No species can survive if it becomes so abundant that it outstrips its food supply. Extinction is then inevitable, and selection will root out such organisms. Thus, in general, there are feedback loops and control mechanisms that lead to a pervading homeostasis in the environment—"The Balance of Nature." Pimentel (1968) sums up a brief review on change in population numbers by stating, "Stability and constancy are characteristics of natural populations." This does not seem to agree with an earlier statement that much in an ecosystem is changing most of the time. Pimentel's statement does not discount the possibility of change; it emphasizes that natural populations change less than we might expect them to. His concept of genetic feedback helps us to understand this balance (Fig. 1.2). This feedback may be either positive or negative, so that adaptations are improved and deleterious traits are suppressed.

Feedback leading to stability may involve only short-term adjustments in the community. For example, when a particular prey species becomes scarce, a predator may change its behavior by searching and eating another prey species. This adjustment will relieve predation pressure on the former species which then increases in density, while the new species

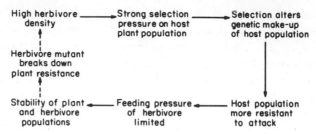

Fig. 1.2 An example of a genetic feedback mechanism that acts negatively to reduce herbivore density. The dashed lines show the beginning of a second phase in the feedback loop where a gene mutation permits an individual to overcome the plant's resistance. Natural selection for progeny of this individual leads again to high herbivore densities. See also Fig. 3.2.

to which the predator has switched is more heavily preyed upon and declines in density. The prey populations become balanced and the predator population fluctuates little.

Evolutionary, or long-term, adjustments in populations may be induced through a feedback mechanism where the selective agent is sufficiently severe or persistent to change the population permanently. For example, myxomatosis, a disease of rabbits, is carried by fleas in Europe. Before the disease was introduced, the rabbits normally bred in burrows or warrens in the ground. This behavior brought rabbits constantly into contact with the vectors of the disease which reproduced in the nest litter and resulted in a strong selection for those rabbits that sheltered and bred above ground. Here the fleas were less likely to come into contact with new hosts, and the disease-vector-host cycle was effectively broken. There are, however, other factors involved in the epidemiology of myxomatosis, and this represents only one of the feedback loops in the evolutionary change of the rabbit populations infected.

Thus the action of a pathogen and an insect vector changed the ecology of the rabbit, and through selection—genetic feedback—the pathogen and the insect were reduced in numbers both by behavioral changes in the rabbit population and by increased resistance to the pathogen. Both quantitative factors (population size) and qualitative factors (behavioral change) are involved in these control mechanisms. The lurking question behind such a case history is "Could we determine the reason for rabbits breeding above ground had we not seen the selection for this behavior taking place?" Another example is given in Chapter 3 (p. 50) and it remains an unsettling question.

Another fundamental concept in ecology is that energy flows through the ecosystem, and this is contrasted with the cycling of chemicals in the

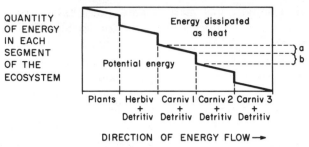

Fig. 1.3 Use of energy as it flows through an ecosystem. It assumes that all potential energy is consumed either while alive or when dead; that is, none is stored. At each trophic level maintenance energy is lost as heat (*a*), and energy is lost as heat in each transformation from one trophic level to the next (*b*). Ultimately all energy in the system is dissipated as heat. Thus the system can be maintained only by an outside supply of energy. Herbiv—herbivore, Carniv—carnivore, Detritiv—detritivore.

system. The first law of thermodynamics states that energy can be neither created nor destroyed. The second law states that in every energy transformation potential energy is reduced because heat energy is lost to the system in the process. Thus as food passes from one organism to another the potential energy contained in the food supply is reduced step by step until all the energy in the system becomes dissipated as heat (Fig. 1.3). Therefore, there is a unidirectional flow of energy through a system, with no possibility for any recycling of energy.

In contrast, chemicals are not dissipated and remain in the ecosystem indefinitely (Fig. 1.4) unless erosion from the system occurs. Erosion includes natural movement out of the system in water, on land, and in the air, and induced movement by man. Lacking erosion chemicals constantly circulate or recycle in the system.

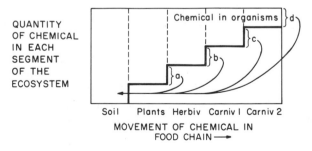

Fig. 1.4 The cycling of a chemical in the ecosystem assuming no erosion. Chemicals in organisms not consumed by the higher trophic level (*a* to *d*) slowly return to the soil as they are released through decay.

Ecology as a subject has many stimulating characteristics. First, it demands a synthesis of biological sciences. Ecology forms a natural union with evolutionary theory, population biology and genetics, behavior, and ethology. All these subjects increase interaction between the sciences defined by taxa such as zoology, botany, and entomology. There is a certain relief in the discovery that ecology permits an escape from tax-onomically oriented disciplines. In insect ecology, for example, plants that act as food and shelter for insects must be studied, and birds and mammals that feed on insects must be understood. The many facets to understanding the insectan way of life makes much of what we see on a field trip pertinent to our own interests.

Second, a comparative ecological approach permits a rational com-parison of a lion with a louse, for example, in their strategies for gain-ing food or for leaving viable offspring. Also the comparison of form and function or activity of species provides a much more powerful tool for interpreting observations than the observation of one species at a time. Seeing an organism in its ecological setting permits a very perceptive analysis of its natural history.

Finally, thinking ecologically enables a holistic concept of the organism in the ecosystem. It permits insight into the forces impinging on an organism in a natural setting. The pressures that animals and plants species are exposed to, and to which they must adapt and evolve can be appreciated. Therefore, it is not forgotten that the food plant and the insect coevolved for thousands of years, so that there are many historical factors that have led to the present visible relationship. We are merely the transient observers of the perpetual motion in nature.

Entomologists have much to be proud of since studies of insects have contributed greatly to the development of thinking in ecology. Insect population dynamics has always received much attention. More recently studies on energetics of insect populations has contributed significantly to the development of concepts on energy flow. Predator-prey and com-petitive relationships are better understood because of contributions by entomologists, and studies on biological control of plant and insect pests by insects have been major stimuli in these areas. The ecology of coevo-lutionary interactions between plants and herbivores and the area of chemical ecology have received considerable stimulus from insect studies. Other areas of ecology could be added.

Entomologists also have much to offer in the further development of ecological thought. Because insects are numerous in species and individuals per species so large, samples are relatively easy to obtain. Short life cycles and small size permit simple rearing techniques. Specimens can be collected usually without severe depletion of local populations. Thus insects enable research hardly possible on vertebrates, and many areas of ecology will benefit from use of these organisms. Coevolution of plant and herbivore, chemical ecology, pollination ecology, community ecology, and reproductive strategies are all rapidly developing areas in which entomologists can make major contributions. The theory of island biogeography was originally tested experimentally using insects and other arthropods, and the application of the theory to mainland situations offer almost endless scope for the entomologist. The opportunities awaiting insect ecologists to contribute to the science of ecology are immense.

Part I
TROPHIC
RELATIONSHIPS

S ince food is essential to all organisms, feeding relationships have been a central focus among ecologists, and a theme that runs throughout the science. Ecologists who looked for patterns in nature regarded food as an organizing influence in communities. They saw that the types of food and feeding lead to predictable relationships between trophic levels, in relative numbers of organisms, foraging strategies (Chapter 2), coevolution (Chapters 3 and 4), and energy flow (Chapter 6). In many communities insects play a key role as herbivores and predators (Chapter 5), and in turn form an important source of food for other organisms. The interactions between insects and their plant food (Chapter 3), and insects and their predators (Chapters 4 and 5) thus influence profoundly the amount of energy that passes from one trophic level to another (Chapter 6).

Food is a recurring theme throughout the other parts of this book. Food may limit population growth; it influences dispersion of the population and the timing and extent of dispersal. The ability of insects to eat man's pests has made some insects his allies (Part II). As food becomes limiting, competition for it increases, and coexistence of species is threatened unless they coadapt by partitioning this resource (Part III). Thus food and competition for it influence the distribution and abundance of species, and consequently the structure of communities (Part IV).

Chapter 2

TROPHIC
STRUCTURE
OF COMMUNITY

We can expect food to be an important or even central issue in ecology because food shortage will limit population increase if nothing else prevents population growth before this ultimate factor. Therefore in looking for simple patterns in nature, it is natural to focus attention first on the production and consumption of food, that is, what organisms eat, and what eats these organisms in turn. These are trophic relationships, and by analyzing these relationships within a community a picture may be obtained of the trophic structure of that community. Usually the relationships become exceedingly complex; nevertheless the pattern is still visible.

Elton (1927) was the first to coin the phrase "food-chain" signifying the feeding links between organisms as food passes from the plant to the herbivore to the carnivore, and perhaps to higher carnivores. This concept can be illustrated with one of Elton's examples:

pine trees → aphids → spiders → chicadees → hawks

This example also illustrates where insects and other arthropods commonly fit into the food chain, and how they are important links in the movement of energy in the community. For less wooded areas the food chain may be based on corn as follows:

corn → corn-earworm → ichneumonid parasite → warbler → hawk

or

corn seed → corn-seed → carabid → vole → owl
             beetle   beetle
             (carabid (eats eggs
             herbivore) and larvae of
                         corn-seed beetle)

Insects frequently fit into the second and third links in the food chain. There are exceptions but the majority of cases fit this position. Therefore, insects must be considered as vital to practically any terrestrial community, and to many aquatic ones.

What provides the original source of energy that passes through the community? It cannot be produced, according to the first law of thermodynamics, so there must be a vast store available that supports the biosphere. This store is the sun. Radiant energy from the sun is used to drive the photosynthetic process that manufactures carbohydrates from oxygen and carbon dioxide which is mediated by chlorophyll contained in green plants. Therefore, the sun must figure prominently in any food chain:

$$\text{sun} \rightarrow \text{corn} \rightarrow \text{corn-seed} \rightarrow \text{carabid} \rightarrow \text{vole} \rightarrow \text{owl}$$

            beetle   beetle

                          predator

The trophic level concept categorizes these links in the food chain into the following heirarchy of levels:

Producers	Plants produce food (some bacteria produce food also)
Consumers	All other organisms consume food
Primary consumers	Herbivores
Secondary consumers	Carnivores
Tertiary consumers	Carnivores

If the herbivore is a plant such as a parasitic fungus then the secondary consumer could be a herbivore also, but this is of minor concern.

While this organization provides a valuable framework for thinking about feeding relationships, there are difficulties to fitting actual examples into the system:

1. Where do omnivores fit? They feed at two trophic levels at least, and a large number of animals are omnivorous during their life span. Three examples follow: (*a*) Foxes on Spitsbergen (borders Arctic Ocean east of Greenland) are saprophagous in the winter and eat seal remains and bear dung, while in the summer they eat birds, insects, and plant matter. To add to the confusion, during the summer they are part of the terrestrial food chain, whereas in the winter, when they are forced to seek food on the ice, they become a part of the food chain of the sea! (*b*) Fraser Darling (1937) in his book *A herd of Red Deer* described how deer, during the period in which they are in velvet (growing their antlers before the fall rutting season), not only eat the usual grasses and herbs but also supplement their diet with frogs, insects, and other animal protein. (*c*) Insects perhaps provide the best examples of omnivores. Many holometabolous insects (insects that have a larval stage that is radically different in shape from the adult) have larvae that feed at one trophic level and adults that feed at another. Three examples are given on page 16. In example i the adult steps down a trophic level to feed and in examples ii and iii the adults feed on a higher trophic level. Since food is frequently in short supply, holometabolous insects that feed on different foods in their larval and adult stages avoid any chance of competition for food within a species. This is an adaptation that

Family or superfamily	Larval food	Adult food
i. Parasitic hymenoptera, e.g., Ichneumonidae	Insect host	Nectar, honeydew
ii. Mosquitoes, e.g., *Culex* and *Anopheles* spp.	Plankton and bottom algae (aquatic)	Blood of vertebrates and invertebrates (terrestrial)
iii. Many flies, e.g., Muscidae (stable fly)	Animal and plant food in cow dung	Blood of vertebrates

contributes to the abundance and success of these species. They constitute 85% of all insects. Not only is competition between parents and young reduced, but also larvae can become specialized as feeders and adults as dispersers and gamete producers. The remaining 15% of insects are hemimetabolous, where the immature stages (nymphs) are similar to the adult in morphology and ecology.

2. Another difficulty is in the placement of species where sexual differences in feeding occur, actually another type of omnivory. In several species of biting flies (e.g., blackflies and mosquitoes) only the female takes a blood meal. In some parasitic Hymenoptera the females feed upon the host on which they lay an egg while the males are herbivorous and feed on nectar and honeydew (e.g., Ichneumonidae, Calcidoidea).

It becomes evident that few orders of insects have a preponderance of feeders in one trophic level, but at the family level general feeding patterns are more prevalent (Table 2.1). Even at this level of classification many trophic levels are frequently represented and the size of the taxon must be further reduced to get better fits into the trophic level system. Ultimately, as with the omnivores mentioned above, even single species sometimes cannot be placed in a single trophic level.

Darnell (1961) used the ultimate solution to this problem by charting the complete feeding or trophic spectrum of each species. Unfortunately detailed studies are necessary, and the useful generality of the trophic level concept is lost. However, both approaches are useful. Darnell studied the estuarine community in Lake Pontchartrain in Louisiana. He found that most consumer species do not conform precisely to specific trophic levels. For example, adult blue catfish included in their diet 12% molluscs, 17% macrocrustacea, 30% fishes, 26% vegetation, and 15% miscellaneous material. The atlantic croaker divided its attentions between animals and detritus and changed its feeding habits with age (Fig.

Table 2.1   Examples of insect taxa that contain species that are predominantly either herbivores or carnivores. Taxa in parentheses are the orders to which the suborders and families belong.

Taxon	Herbivores		Carnivores	
Order	Homoptera		Odonata	
	Isoptera*		Anoplura	
	Psocoptera*		Strepsiptera	
	Lepidoptera		Mecoptera	
Suborder	(Hymenoptera)	Symphyta	(Hymenoptera)	Apocrita†
Family	(Coleoptera)	Cerambycidae	(Coleoptera)	Coccinellidae†
		Chrysomelidae		Carabidae†
		Curculionidae		Staphylinidae†
	(Hemiptera)	Miridae	(Hemiptera)	Anthocoridae
		Lygaeidae†		Reduviidae
		Tingidae		Phymatidae
		Corimelaenidae		Nabidae

* Some members of taxon may be classed as saprophages as they eat predominantly dead organic matter.
† Important exceptions exist in these taxa.

2.1). By placing species at the top of columns (usually adults) the trophic spectrum of many species can be directly compared (Fig. 2.2). Although details in the trophic spectrum indicate omnivory in many species, frequently there is a preponderance of feeding at one trophic level that would justify its placement at this level.

When the top animal of a food chain is considered and feeding habits are followed back toward the producers, there is seldom a simple linear linkage in feeding relationships. The top predators, usually large animals, have social restraints on how close they can exist in an area. Elton quotes the Chinese proverb "One hill cannot shelter two tigers," which illustrates the point well. The top predator needs large amounts of animal food; it cannot afford to specialize on its food, which is usually small mammals, birds, or fish, as these prey populations are fluctuating and some species become temporarily rare. Also, all food items are either fleet of foot or have other effective defense mechanisms. The top predator must be an opportunist—it must get what it can when it is available: for an owl, a sickly rat now, a young mouse later, a snake preoccupied with eating a toad the next day, and so on. Lions will actually hunt and kill zebra, wildebeests, and hartebeests, but they will also pick the carcasses of animals that hunting dogs have hunted and killed, and take over water buffalo killed by crocodiles.

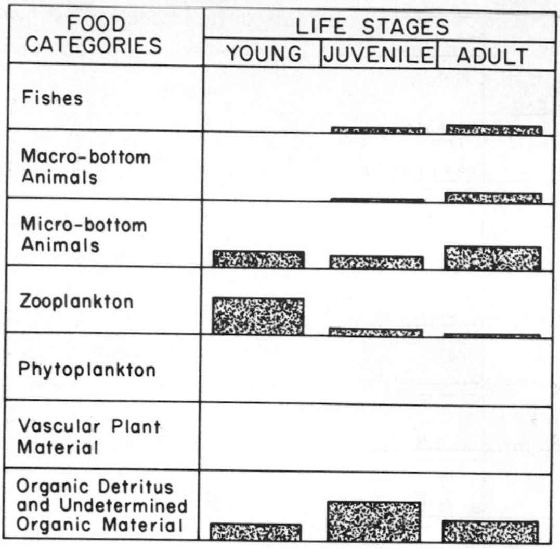

FOOD CATEGORIES	LIFE STAGES		
	YOUNG	JUVENILE	ADULT
Fishes			
Macro-bottom Animals			
Micro-bottom Animals			
Zooplankton			
Phytoplankton			
Vascular Plant Material			
Organic Detritus and Undetermined Organic Material			

Fig. 2.1 Trophic spectrum for young, juvenile, and adult stages of the Atlantic croaker (*Micropogon undulatus*) from Lake Pontchartrain. Each bar represents the percent volume of food observed in a particular food category. Thus the sum of the heights of all bars within a life stage equals 100% and this is the height of each food category. Note how the spectrum changes with age from predominance of zooplankton, to detritus to bottom-dwelling animals and fish. After Darnell 1961.

Top predators feed on a diversity of prey and this prey also feeds upon a diversity of other organisms. These latter organisms can be more specialized as food is probably more abundant, and lower still herbivores tend to be comparatively specific in their choice of food. Rather than food chains, food webs exist, with many feeding links in the community. Top predators are rather large and sparsely distributed and herbivores are rather small (with notable exceptions) and common (Fig. 2.3). Elton (1927), calling this the pyramid of numbers, gave an example: "In a small pond, the numbers of protozoa may run into millions, those of *Daphnia* and *Cyclops* into hundreds of thousands, while there will be far fewer beetle larvae and only a very few small fish." It is clear that Elton was thinking of relative numbers in a set of convergent food chains, that each of these organisms had a trophic relationship—a functional relationship—with others. Because Elton was not explicit on this point, his idea has been misinterpreted, particularly in North America (Macfadyen 1963). Elton's idea was radically simplified into the statement, "Large animals are rare in a community, small animals are common." An example was used by Lindeman (1942), from Williams' (1941) study of the floor-fauna invertebrates of the Panama rain forest (Fig. 2.4). At

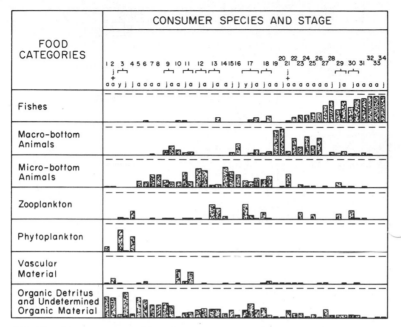

Fig. 2.2 Trophic spectra of 34 major consumers in the Lake Pontchartrain community. Note that many species feed predominantly at one trophic level: y = young, j = juvenile, a = adult. Dashed line indicates height of column if 100% of feeding occurred in that food category. After Darnell 1961.

least here is an actual example that supports Elton's general point, but Elton (1966) has since clarified the Eltonian pyramid concept by calling it a "Pyramid of consumer layers," a name that points out the trophic relationships between the size classes that is lacking in Williams' study.

Paine (1966) studied a rocky intertidal community and found 38 species of herbivore, 6 species of primary carnivore, and 1 species of secondary carnivore. Since all feeding links were identified, this represents a pyramid of consumer layers.

Robinson's (1953) example illustrates an Eltonian pyramid well (Fig. 2.5). He studied the fauna of a brown slime flux of an elm tree in England. A branch of the tree was torn off and the ooze that formed in the scar supported eight arthropods: one phytophagous mite in the flux material, six dipterous larvae in the flux material (three phytophagous, three carnivorous), and one carnivorous staphylinid beetle on the flux surface. Robinson's paper illustrates how difficult it is just to establish a few feeding relationships in a very simple community. Particularly for entomologists, it illuminates the magnitude of the task in seeking pat-

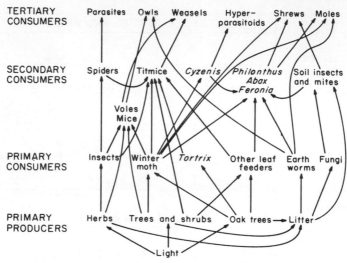

Fig. 2.3 Feeding links between some components of the community in Wytham Wood, Oxfordshire, based on studies by Elton, Varley, and others (see Elton 1966). Note that some links refer to species, others to groups of species in order to conserve space. *Cyzenis* is a tachinid parasitoid of the winter moth, *Philonthus* is a staphylinid beetle and *Feronia* and *Abax* are carabids, and *Tortrix* is a caterpillar (Lepidoptera). Note that parasites and parasitoids share the same trophic positions as predators. In these cases reduced size occurs at successive trophic levels. After Varley 1970, by permission of Blackwell Scientific Publications.

terns and order in communities that are composed of hundreds of species. There are nevertheless interesting approaches to this problem which are covered in Part IV.

There are some glaring exceptions to the Eltonian pyramid. If the elm

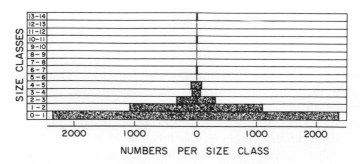

Fig. 2.4 A pyramid of numbers representing size relationships in the forest floor fauna in a Panama rain forest. The trophic relationships were infered from size relationships (in millimeters) and were not observed directly. After Williams 1941.

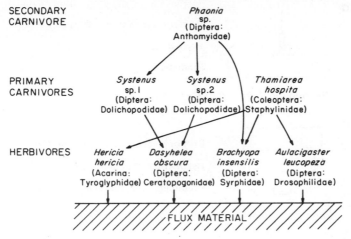

Fig. 2.5 An Eltonian pyramid of numbers seen in a brown slime flux from an elm tree in Sheffield, England. The feeding relationships are indicated. After each scientific name the order and family of the animal follows. After Robinson 1953.

tree is included in Robinson's study there is only one producer, four herbivores, and so on, and there is an inversion of the base of the pyramid. This will commonly be seen when the herbivore is small in relation to its food plant, or where parasitic organisms are concerned.

The next best way to quantify the amount of protoplasm in each trophic level is to weigh it. The weight of living organisms is called biomass. Then the problem appears to be solved. The elm tree may weigh 27 metric tons, herbivores on the elm tree may weigh 5 g, and predators on the tree may weigh 0.5 g. Odum (1957) studied an old field community in Georgia and found the following biomass relationships: Producers—500 g dry wt/m², herbivores—1 g dry wt/m², and primary carnivores, 0.01 g dry wt/m² (Fig. 2.6a). This example fits the pyramid concept perfectly, but there are still many exceptions (e.g., Fig. 2.6b), and a better way must be found to estimate the available food in one trophic level that is consumed by the organisms in the higher level.

Consider the sequence of biomass relationships between the carcass of a mouse and that of a carrion beetle (*Necrophorus*). At an early stage in the relationship, with eggs on the carcass, biomass is arranged pyramidally, but when feeding is completed most of the biomass is in the form of large carrion beetles. The shape of the pyramid changes rapidly during the course of feeding. Inverted pyramids can also occur when biomass is used. A good example is the biomass of phytoplankton in the English Channel that supports a larger biomass of zooplankton (Fig. 2.6b) be-

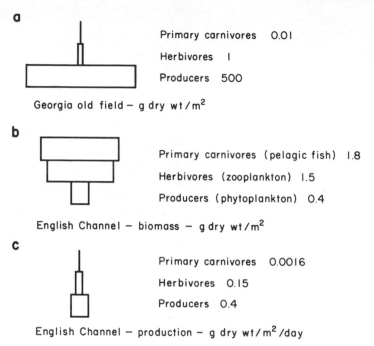

a

Primary carnivores   0.01

Herbivores   1

Producers   500

Georgia old field − g dry wt/m²

b

Primary carnivores (pelagic fish)   1.8

Herbivores (zooplankton)   1.5

Producers (phytoplankton)   0.4

English Channel − biomass − g dry wt/m²

c

Primary carnivores   0.0016

Herbivores   0.15

Producers   0.4

English Channel − production − g dry wt/m²/day

Fig. 2.6 (a) A pyramid of biomass seen in an old field in Georgia (Odum 1957). (b) An inverted pyramid of biomass in the English Channel—phytoplankton has a lower standing crop than the zooplankton and the zooplankton biomass is less than that for the fish (Harvey 1950). This inversion is possible because of the high production rates of small organisms seen in c (Harvey 1950).

cause the production rate of the phytoplankton is so much higher and a relatively small standing crop (the biomass that exists at any one point in time) processes large amounts of energy (Harvey 1950) (Fig. 2.6c).

Lindeman provided ecology with a more or less completely new approach to trophic relationships in a single classic paper, "The trophic-dynamic aspect of ecology," published in 1942. He stated: "The basic process in trophic dynamics is the transfer of energy from one part of the ecosystem to another," and he emphasized the efficiency of the transfer of energy between trophic levels. As seen in Chapter 1 potential energy is lost at every transfer so, in fact, there can never be more energy in the herbivore layer than in the producer layer, and energy, expressed as calories produced, per area per unit time, is the one measure that can provide realistic pyramids of trophic relationships which cannot become inverted. Lindeman studied the productivities of trophic levels in Cedar Bog Lake in Minnesota and obtained results that are compared with Juday's (1940)

Table 2.2   Pyramids of energy production in Cedar Bog Lake and Lake Mendota. Units are gram calories per square centimeter per year.

	Cedar Bog Lake	Lake Mendota
Tertiary consumers	—	0.7
Secondary consumers	3.1	6.0
Primary consumers	14.8	144.0
Producers	111.3	428.0

SOURCE.   From Lindeman 1942 and Juday 1940.

from Lake Mendota, Wisconsin (Table 2.2). Odum and Smalley (1959), who studied energy flow in a salt marsh on Sapelo Island, Georgia, indicate clearly that numbers and biomass bear little relationship to the energy flow through a population of grasshoppers (Fig. 2.7). Energetic relationships in communities are treated in Chapter 6.

There are four major methods of studying trophic relationships. The first is to use direct observation as birdwatchers do from a blind (e.g., Tinbergen 1960). In some cases it may be possible to use a camera for recording feeding events as Royama (1970) did while studying Great tits (see Chapter 4, p. 65).

A second method is gut analysis. Samples of potential food are collected in the field and compared with fragments of food in the gut of the animals under study. This can be done with birds and bats that utilize insect food (e.g., Whitaker 1972) and small mammals (e.g., Hansson 1970) and large insects that utilize plant food. For example, Bernays and Chapman (1970) extracted grass fragments from the foregut of the grasshopper *Chorthippus parallelus* captured in the field in the adult or fourth instar stage. Preparations were also made of the abaxial and adaxial surfaces of leaf blades of all the grasses in the field. Thus they were able to find the percentage of each grass species in the diet of *C. parallelus*. Accuracy of identification was usually over 80% and reached 100% for some species of grass.

Radionuclide tracer analysis is a third important method. In many insects and other arthropods it is impossible to identify fragments of food; either the fragments are too small, the insect has fed on relatively amorphous food, or the insects have taken a liquid meal. Thus radionuclide tracer studies become valuable. Plants may be labeled with ^{32}P by using a stem well (e.g., Shure 1970, 1973). A well is made around the base of a plant and filled with water. Slits in the stem are made at the

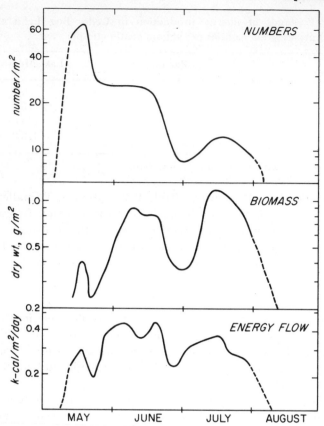

Fig. 2.7 A comparison of numbers, biomass (dry weight), and energy flow per square meter in a population of the salt marsh grasshopper, *Orchelimum fidicinium*, feeding on salt marsh grass *Spartina alterniflora* on Sapelo Island, Georgia. From Odum and Smalley 1959.

bottom of the well, and then the isotope is added and ^{32}P-water solution is drawn into the plant by the negative transpiration pressure. Then the wells are sealed. With time the ^{32}P spreads throughout the plant, and can be counted on a detector. Also organisms around the tagged plants can be collected over the course of time and those that are tagged have obviously eaten plant parts. The relative amount of feeding can be obtained by expressing the counts per minute per milligram dry weight. Once the herbivores are labeled, the predators can be identified in the same way.

Finally serological techniques may be used. Use of the precipitin test gives an extremely sensitive indication of trophic relationships, but it can usually be used only as a positive or negative record; relative quantities of food taken cannot be estimated. As with the radionuclide method, only one food source can be tested at a time, and the feeding spectrum cannot be studied simultaneously. Thus there are serious limitations to the method, although sensitivity is an asset. Basically an antigen is prepared from the prey species under study (e.g., Frank 1967). It is injected into a rabbit to produce a specific antibody. The antibody is then used to test the gut content of potential predators. A positive precipitin reaction demonstrates that the predator had prey parts (antigen) in its gut. This method has been used successfully by Frank (1967) for predators of winter moth pupae, by Dempster (1960) for predators of eggs and larvae of the broom beetle, and by Young, Morris, and Reynoldson (1964) in lake-dwelling triclad trophic relationship studies.

By taking a closer look at organisms, trends in characteristics of progressive trophic levels become evident. These trends are generally applicable but there are certainly notable exceptions. Many characteristics are closely related; for example, increased body size, higher powers of dispersal, lower reproduction rate, and longer life expectancy are all qualities set by any one quality. Given one quality, the others more or less have to follow. From herbivores to top carnivores, the following tends to be true:

1. Fewer species.
2. Lower population levels.
3. Lower reproductive rates.
4. Increased body size.
5. Increased food-searching area, increased diversity of habitats utilized [called an inverse pyramid of habitats by Elton (1966)]. [Trends 1–5 were described by Elton (1927).]
6. Higher powers of dispersal.
7. Higher searching ability.
8. Higher maintenance cost (energy).
9. Utilization efficiency of food higher.
10. Food of higher calorific value.
11. Reduced feeding specialization.
12. More complex behavior.
13. Longer life expectancy.

Elton's (1966) "inverse pyramid of habitats" is a good way to emphasize how top predators must search extensively and diversely to find enough of the dispersed food resources that they are able to consume.

McNab (1963) has provided a survey of vertebrate animals that support some of these generalizations; notably, animals of large size utilize large areas of land in their search for food, and "hunters" (predators of animals, seeds and fruits) utilize more area than do "croppers" (grazers and browsers) (Fig. 2.8).

The trends of fewer species (trend 1) and reduced feeding specialization (trend 11) with progressive trophic levels seem to be supported by the sizes of families of insects. Many families of herbivores are large and contain species that are specific in their food preferences: for example, Cicadellidae (Jassidae), Aphididae, Chryomelidae, Cerambycidae, Curculionidae, Scolytidae, Cecidomyiidae, and Mycetophilidae. Families with predatory insects are frequently much smaller: for example, Reduviidae, Nabidae, Chrysopidae, Coccinellidae, and Asilidae (cf. lists of insects such as that of Kloet and Hincks 1945). The large family Carabidae, members of which are well known as predators, may seem to be an exception to this trend. However, many species are omnivorous or facultative saprophages (eating dead organic matter).

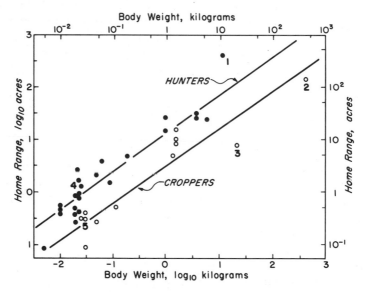

Fig. 2.8 Relationship between body weight and home range size for hunters (closed circles) and croppers (open circles). Note that although the racoon (*Procyon lotor*) (1) is smaller than the moose (*Alces alces*) (2), the hunter has a larger home range than the cropper. (3) Beaver, *Castor canadensis*, (4) deer mouse, *Peromyscus maniculatus*—granivore, (5) Meadow vole, *Microtus pennsylvanicus*—grass feeder. After B. K. McNab. Bioenergetics and the determination of home range size. *Amer. Natur.* 97:133–140, published by the University of Chicago Press. © 1963 by the University of Chicago. All rights reserved.

There are exceptions to these trends. Large herbivores in Africa usually weigh more than their predator, the lion. Social hunting behavior has evolved which enables exploitation of these large herbivores, and if the hunting group is regarded as a corporate body, perhaps the generality is still valid. This argument is less valid for wolves and their prey where a pack of six wolves will not weigh the same as the moose or caribou they hunt on occasion. This is probably true also for African hunting dogs, which prey on zebra and other grazing animals, and ants, which are able to transport huge loads to their nest. These exceptions do illustrate a further point—intelligence and cooperation through social organization are really valuable adaptations!

Another set of trends worth considering are in feeding strategy with increasing animal size. In general the progression is:

$$\text{herbivory} \rightarrow \text{carnivory} \rightarrow \text{omnivory} \rightarrow \text{herbivory}$$

as animals get larger and larger. As stated already, in general, carnivores tend to be larger than the herbivores they eat. As carnivores get larger it becomes more and more difficult to find enough food, especially as speed and agility are reduced; thus an omnivore strategy is the only answer. Finally, with very large organisms that are now relatively sluggish, animal food cannot be caught and the organism must specialize on the most abundant source of food—the plants. Among the vertebrates small birds and mammals are herbivores, canids and felids are predators, bears are omnivores, and elephants, for example, are herbivores.

Insects are particularly likely to illustrate this trend as large size causes slow oxygen diffusion to cells, weight increases dramatically, and sluggish movement becomes inevitable. The heaviest insect is a scarabaeid beetle, *Goliathus goliathus*, which feeds on plant material, and the largest insect in the British Isles is the plant-feeding stag beetle, *Lucanus cervus*. The largest predatory insects are considerably lighter in weight than goliath beetles: e.g. preying mantids and the carabids such as *Calosoma sycophanta*. Small insects are frequently herbivores such as leafhoppers, aphids, beetles, and fly larvae. Small insects can be predators but very large insects cannot.

These trends are probably most applicable to terrestrial and freshwater food relationships as baleen whales are prominent exceptions in the ocean. They feed on krill, shrimp-like Euphausiidae, and other zooplankton. This exception is made possible by the abundance of plankton in the ocean and an adaptation for straining its very small food items (krill are 4 to 6 cm long) through the baleen strainers. If a large and reliable source of food permits a species to specialize then it can become an exception to any generalities.

The role of organisms in the community is closely tied to their feeding relationships, and thus the niche a species occupies has been defined traditionally in terms of food requirements and how these relate to the needs of other species (e.g., Elton 1927, but see Chapter 13 on the niche concept). Because species with very different taxonomic affinities may be very closely related ecologically in terms of trophic relationships, the need exists to consider such ecologically similar groups as units in the analysis of communities. Root (1967) has defined such a unit, or guild, as a group of species that exploit the same class of environmental resources in a similar manner. In his (Root 1973) community study of arthropods on collards (*Brassica oleracea*), he identified the following guilds associated with collard leaves.

1. Pit feeding guild—flea beetles, weevils (total of 18 species)—which eat small patches of leaf, usually without perforating both surfaces.
2. Strip feeding guild—caterpillars (Lepidoptera) and Orthoptera (total of 17 species)—which chew down the side of a leaf in strips.
3. Sap feeding guild—aphids, frog- and leafhoppers, treehoppers, mirid bugs, psyllids, tingids (total of 59 species)—feeders on sap using piercing-sucking mouth parts.

Many guilds of insects may exist on a single plant. In addition to the three above, there may be stem boring, root feeding, seed eating, and pollen and nectar gathering guilds. This diversity of feeding types is possible largely because of the small size of many insects and the possibility for specialized morphological adaptation in the larval stages of holometabolous insects.

Guilds may be much smaller than those above: there were six species of bird in the foliage gleaning guild in oak woodlands (Root 1967); six species of cocoon parasitoid on the jack pine sawfly (Price 1971a), and four species of herbivores in the slime flux of an elm tree (Fig. 2.5). In the next two chapters the relationships between adjacent trophic levels are examined more closely.

Chapter 3

COEVOLUTION
OF PLANTS
AND HERBIVORES

A t the end of their paper, "Butterflies and plants: A study in coevolution," Ehrlich and Raven (1964) said, "Probably our most important
overall conclusion is that the importance of reciprocal selective responses
between ecologically closely linked organisms has been vastly underrated
in considerations of the origins of organic diversity. Indeed, the plant-
herbivore interface may be the major zone of interaction responsible for
generating terrestrial organic diversity" (see also Ehrlich and Raven
1967). Brues (1924) had gone a considerable way to reaching this conclusion 40 years earlier.

There is a constant warfare. Acquiring sufficient energy to enable reproduction is the essential preoccupation of every member of a species. Even
worker ants that never reproduce possess this drive (but that paradox is
explained in Chapter 16). An individual would certainly be maladapted
if it maintained a trait that permitted easy access by other species to the
energy store represented by the protoplasm of its body. The only exception to this statement can be seen in relationships for mutual benefit
where the energy store, or usually prescribed parts of that store, are left
available for a species in the higher trophic level, provided that the
organism receives a significant gain by doing so. This aspect of coevolution is covered briefly in various parts of this chapter. Individuals must
defend their collected energy against all would-be consumers. If another
organism higher in the trophic system can break down the defense it has
access to a lucrative energy source, and furthermore this food will not
have to be shared among other species until others are able to break
down the defense mechanism also. The winner of this arms race receives
a double advantage. As plants are the producers, the first organisms in
the food chain because they manufacture organic chemicals, these are the
first that must defend themselves—against the herbivores. An attack by
a herbivore selects an adaptation for defense in the plant, or even a
counterattack. This cycle of attack and counterattack between organisms
of adjacent trophic levels is the essence of the coevolutionary process.
Plants and insects have been at it for millions of years so some very
refined results may be expected in this age-old interaction.

The basic components required by a plant, and manufactured by the
plant, can be classified into three biochemical groups: (1) those that
catalyze biochemical reactions; (2) those that participate in building
processes in the plant organism; and (3) those that supply energy. All
plants require inorganic ions and must produce enzymes, hormones, carbohydrates, lipids, proteins, and phosphorus compounds for energy transfer. These compounds are all intimately involved in the growth and
reproduction of the plant.

However the plant kingdom contains a vastly greater variety of chemicals than those involved in these primary functions. Presumably the other chemicals are by-products in the synthesis of primary metabolic products, and, lacking a means of excreting them, the plants store them in any convenient place within the plant structure. Some plants manufacture a particular chemical and others do not; this phenomenon suggests that this chemical is not an essential ingredient in plant metabolism. These kinds of substances have been called secondary metabolic products.

The fact that these products are very common in plants is supported by the large volume of literature on the chemical taxonomy of plants, which is based primarily on secondary metabolic products. Closely related plants are likely to share similar metabolic pathways for primary products, with the simultaneous production of similar secondary metabolic products. A single gene mutation, which may change a single enzyme, may be reflected in a change in the type of secondary metabolic product produced. Therefore chemical taxonomy tends to be a more precise analytical test for determining phylogeny in evolution than morphology, with the pleiotropic effects that may occur in the phenotype as a result of gene mutation.

Insects keyed into this system of chemical relationships between related plant species very early in their evolution. For example, several families of plants contain mustard oils—Capparidaceae, Cruciferae, Tropaeolaceae, and Limnanthaceae and certain insects will feed only on members of these families, for example, the flea beetles *Phyllotreta cruciferae* and *Phyllotreta striolata* (Feeny, Paauwe, and Demong 1970). Mustard oils are irritants, capable of causing serious injury to animal tissue, and are also among the most potent antibiotics known from higher plants. For proof of their potency a teaspoonful of horseradish or mustard should be tasted.

The family Solanaceae is well known for the alkaloids members contain. For example, green parts of the potato, *Solanum tuberosum*, contain solanine; tobacco, *Nicotiana* spp., contains nicotine; and the deadly nightshade, *Atropa belladonna*, produces atropine, and some insects are restricted to members of this family in their feeding habits. Examples are the Colorado potato beetle, *Leptinotarsa decemlineata*, certain flea beetles, and tobacco and tomato hornworms, *Manduca sexta* and *M. quinquemaculata*.

Two closely related families of plants, Asclepiadaceae and Apocynaceae, include members that have a milky sap and cardiac glycosides. Each family has two specific insect herbivores from the arctiid genera, *Euchaetias* and *Cycnia* as follows:

Genus	Asclepiadaceae (milkweeds)	Apocynaceae (dogbanes)
Euchaetias	*egle*	*oregonensis*
Cycnia	*inopinatus*	*tenera*

Closely related plants support closely related insects. In the evolution of specific differences in insects, slight but permanent changes in digestive or other enzymes permitted the exploitation of closely related plants. This permitted the rapid speciation within a group once the early members had become tolerant to, or able to break down, the toxic substances in these plants. This is the gist of Ehrlich and Raven's (1964) paper. Fraenkel (1959, 1969) has emphasized the important role of secondary plant substances in host selection of herbivorous insects.

Characteristics of secondary metabolic products may be summarized as follows (mostly from Whittaker 1970a):

1. They are not essential to the basic protoplasmic metabolism of the plant.
2. There is no evident reason, if the plant is considered by itself without reference to other organisms, why the plant should produce them at all.
3. They are of irregular or sporadic occurrence, appearing in some plants or plant families and not in others; this fact reinforces the view that they are not essential to plant metabolism.
4. The occurrence of the same or related secondary compounds in related plant species makes these compounds important concerns of chemical taxonomy of plants, although some compounds have often been independently evolved.
5. Many of these products are produced in large quantity and are metabolically expensive; they must be serving a valuable purpose.
6. Many of these products are toxic to animals and other plants, or at least repellent. Whittaker (1970a) states, "The view has developed through observations of Dethier (1954), Fraenkel (1959), Ehrlich and Raven (1964) and others, that the secondary plant substances have their primary meaning as defenses against the plant's enemies." Enemies include pathogens, herbivores, or competitors, and this biochemical inhibition of feeding by animals or plants is called "allelopathy."

Allelopathic chemicals affecting plant-plant interactions have been studied by Muller (1966) who has worked extensively on chemical interactions in the chaparral vegetation in California. He has emphasized their importance: "The significance of allelopathy to ecological theory is very great. Small quantities of toxins may be responsible for massive reductions in plant growth and in water or mineral absorptions and thus strongly influence microclimate. Traditional theories of competition, reaction, biomass proportions, energy flow, mineral cycling, and ecosystem organization are all liable to reevaluation when allelopathy is demonstrable."

Muller demonstrated that *Salvia leucophylla* (Labiatae), which is one of the aromatic shrubs typical of chaparral, contains phytotoxic terpenes that volatilize and inhibit the establishment of a variety of plants within 2 m. Under the shrubs, and 2 m beyond the perimeter of the plant patch, there may be a completely bare zone and only at about 6–10 m do the grassland herbs show full and vigorous growth. This is a remarkable method for reducing competition from other plants for space, and particularly water, during the hot dry summers of the mediterranean climate. Muller's findings have been disputed by Bartholomew (1970, 1971) and the discussion is still underway (Muller and del Moral 1971). However there is so much evidence for allelopathic interactions between plants (e.g., Pickett and Baskin 1973) that the outcome of this controversy will not undermine their importance.

Other species such as *Helianthus anuus* and *Leptilon canadense* produce autotoxic chemicals. In the early growth of these plants the toxins probably reduce viability of younger and smaller members of the same species and so reduce competition. As the toxins accumulate in the soil, however, they contribute to the plant's own demise, and the occupied space becomes available for a tolerant species to colonize.

These competitive interactions illustrate how important chemicals are in plant succession and competition, and in the production of predictable results in community analysis. Important use of allelopathy may also be made in agriculture. For example, some strains of the cucumber, *Cucumis sativus*, may inhibit weed growth by 87% whereas others have almost no inhibitory quality. Incorporation of the allelopathic agent in cucumber cultivars would give the plants a competitive advantage over coexisting weeds (Putnam and Duke 1974).

Similar chemicals are at least of equal importance in the plant's defense against herbivores. The production, by the tobacco plant, of nicotine is an obvious example where the toxin is so effective in reducing insect attacks on the plant that it has been employed as an insecticide by humans. The pyrethrins in pyrethrum flowers have been used for the same purpose. Sinigrin, a mustard oil glucoside in Cruciferae, protects plants from a large array of potential herbivores (e.g., Erickson and Feeny 1974). Indeed herbivores may have exerted the primary selective pressure for the production of toxic chemicals that subsequently became effective in plant-plant interactions (L. E. Gilbert, personal communication). An ovipositing female insect can locate the majority of progeny of a reproducing plant, which leads to heavy mortality of seeds or seedlings and strong selection for defense. Allelochemicals that reduce competition are usually effective only after the plant is well established, with correspondingly weaker reinforcement for production of the chemicals.

Feeny (1968) tested the effect of tannins produced in oak leaves on the growth rate and pupal weight of the winter moth, *Operophtera brumata*, which is a serious pest of oak in Europe and Eastern Canada. He extracted condensed tannins (not hydrolysable) from old (September) oak leaves where the tannin content was 2.4% of the fresh weight of the leaf. The tannin was mixed with casein in an artificial diet so the protein became tanned, just as it would when a caterpillar chewed up an oak leaf. He used third and fourth instar larvae to start the experiment, and the results are shown in Fig. 3.1. One may imagine how the tannins in oak leaves reduce the fecundity of the resulting adults, if the larvae grow to about half the size of those without tannin in their diet. Also the larvae eat less of the leaf because they are much smaller, and the populations are reduced because of lower fecundity. A similar role to tannins

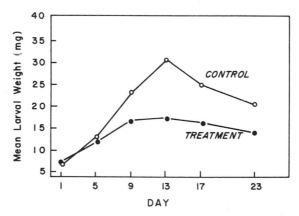

Fig. 3.1 The change in mean larval fresh weights of winter moth, *Operophtera brumata* with time, for larvae fed on a casein diet (control) and a casein complexed with tannin diet (treatment). The mean larval fresh weight increments (initial to peak weight) were 25.2 mg on the control diet and only 11.7 mg on the treatment diet. From Feeny 1968.

may be played by endopeptidase inhibitors in legume seeds that reduce digestion of nitrogen compounds (Applebaum 1964).

At the applied level the problems of manipulating secondary metabolic products in food plants become complex. This type of chemical is frequently responsible for the attractive taste of the plant (e.g., mustard oils in crucifers), but the same chemical may act as a feeding or oviposition cue to a specific pest species and an antibiotic to nonspecific pests. This dilemma was found in the cucumber by Da Costa and Jones (1971). The bitter gene, *Bi*, is dominant and is responsible for the production of the antibiotic cucurbitacins and the bitter taste. These tetracyclic triterpenoids stimulate feeding by the specific cucumber beetle so plants homozygous for the recessive gene, *bi*, lacking cucurbitacins, would offer a means of beetle control. However, *bibi* gene plants lack resistance to general pests such as two-spotted mites. The stepwise coevolutionary process is clearly seen here (Fig. 3.2).

There are so many plants, in such an array of taxonomic groups that produce chemicals with insect hormone activity, that the possibility of

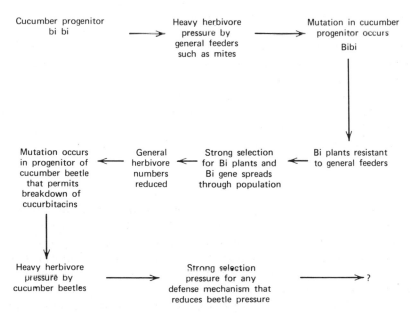

Fig. 3.2 The possible stages in stepwise coevolution between the cucumber and its herbivores. From information in DaCosta and Jones 1971 (cf., Fig. 1.2, p. 6).

chance occurrence is almost certainly ruled out. This situation must surely indicate convergence of armament strategies in the coevolutionary warfare. The hormone mimics may be of the juvenile hormone type that maintain the immature condition, or of the moulting hormone type that synchronize moulting activity, both vital processes in insect development.

Juvenile hormone activity has been found in the firs (*Abies*) and Douglas fir (*Pseudotsuga*) (Sláma 1969). Interest was generated in these chemicals by the discovery that certain North American paper products contained juvenile hormone activity for the European bug, *Pyrrhocoris apterus* (see Sláma 1969, Sláma and Williams, 1965, 1966). When reared in contact with these papers the bugs did not mature but developed into giant nymphs. The hormone mimic, now named "juvabione," was found to be present in the wood of balsam fir, *Abies balsamea*, the preferred constituent of paper pulp.

Moulting hormone activity has been found in *Podocarpus, Polypodium*, and *Vitex* (Sláma 1969). Screening of plant species in Japan revealed that 40 provided active extracts or 4% of the 1056 species tested (Williams and Robbins 1968). Bracken fern is known for its high yield of ecdysone derivatives and these are very active when injected into locusts. However, locusts can eat the foliage with impunity as they break down the hormone (Carlisle and Ellis 1968), no doubt a counterattack evolved after the ecdysone-like chemicals in bracken had been effective defensive chemicals for a few thousand years. They may still be active for many invertebrate herbivores. In fact, insects feeding on vascular cryptogams are so rare that examples are newsworthy items (e.g., Singer, Ehrlich, and Gilbert 1971). These ecdysterols are also found in members of the family Amaranthaceae although activity differs greatly from one insect species to another and from one ecdysterol to another. Some are certainly insecticidal when applied topically and others do inhibit normal development (Hikino and Takemoto 1972).

It is to be expected that plants put more energy into protecting reproductive organs than into vegetative parts (cf., McKey 1974). Reproductive organs are usually smaller and so more easily damaged, they are richer in nutrients and so a greater prize for the herbivore, and indeed they are the basis for the whole existence of the plant. For example, the psychoactive ingredient in marijuana, *Cannabis sativa*, is concentrated in flowers and seeds of the plant. Hypericin, a toxic agent in *Hypericum* species of which the Klamath weed is one (see Chapter 12), is present at a concentration of 30 $\mu g/g$ wet weight in the lower stem, 70 $\mu g/g$ wet weight in the upper stem, and 500 μg/g in the flower (Rees 1969). The pyrethrum plant *Chrysanthemum cinerariaefolium* produces pyrethrins known to have a high insecticidal activity. This is the compound that gives the startling "knock down" effect in household insecticides that persuades the housewife to spray a little more and to buy another can because it is so effective. The pyrethrins are concentrated in the flower heads of this composite and most of the chemical is in the seeds. The very rapid action of this chemical will prevent extensive damage to plant parts that could be very rapidly destroyed but for this protection. Many members of the family Rosaceae produce seeds with cyanogenic activity (e.g., apple, almond, and peach).

In the same vein, long lived plants should be expected to have better chemical protection than more ephemeral species have. Cates and Orians (1975) have found this expectation to be justified in a large sample of plants (see Chapter 17 for more details).

Herbivore pressure may also result in polymorphism in plant populations or differential allocation of chemical defense between populations. Cates (1975) shows that wild ginger, *Asarum caudatum*, has two morphs. Where numbers of general herbivores such as slugs are very low, a morph that allocates much energy to growth rate and seed production is common. However where slugs are abundant, a morph with reduced growth rate and seed production exists, but more energy is channelled into a potent chemical defense.

More than 90% of species of the genus *Acacia* in Central America are protected from herbivores by cyanogenic chemicals in the leaves (Rehr, Feeny, and Janzen 1973). The remainder lack chemical defense but have gained a more potent defense. Belt (1874) discovered that some species, Bull's-horn acacias (e.g., *A. cornigera*), act as host to colonies of ants (genus *Pseudomyrmex*). The ants act as allelopathic agents for the plant (Brown 1960, Janzen 1966, 1967a,b). The ants gain protection from the plant by living in the swollen stipular thorns, and food in the form of sugars is secreted by petiolar nectaries, and proteins in small "Beltian bodies" are produced at tips of new leaves. The aggressive ants patrol the plant and ward off herbivores and suppress potentially competitive plants by chewing the growing tips (Janzen 1967b). Similar relationships exist between ants and *Cecropia* plants (Janzen 1969b) in which the precision of coevolution can be seen in the production of animal sugar (glycogen) in the extrafloral nectaries of the host plant, the only known case in the higher plants (Rickson 1971).

Another case where plants provide insects with food is seen in their mutualistic relationship with pollinators. The original pollinators may have been typical herbivores that fed upon pollen and happened to carry it from plant to plant. From this casual beginning some of the most remarkable coevolved systems have developed (see Chapter 20 on pollination ecology).

Many plant chemicals are also used in the mutualistic relationships developed with other organisms. For example, it appears that lectins may act to bind nitrogen-fixing bacteria to roots of soybeans (Bohlool and Schmidt 1974) and thus initiate root nodule formation typical of leguminous plants.

The copious literature indicating that the plants' enemies are the primary selective agents for the production of toxic chemicals is very convincing. However these chemicals may be used in primary processes in the plant. Many toxic chemicals exist in a state of dynamic equilibrium, with a half life of a few hours in some cases (e.g., Loomis 1967, Burbott and Loomis 1969, Croteau et al. 1972). When ^{14}C and ^{15}N labeled nicotines were fed to tobacco plants the label appeared in amino acids, sugars, and organic acids (Tso and Jeffrey 1959, 1961), all of primary importance to the plant. Although about 12% of fixed carbon per day in a tobacco plant is used in nicotine biosynthesis, almost 40% of the nicotine in a plant is degraded in a 10-hour photoperiod (Robinson 1973). These findings, which are representative of many others, should prompt the search for adaptive roles of toxic chemicals that are independent of selection pressure from the plant's enemies. They may act as storage for essential chemical ingredients, or as regulators in biochemical processes.

The insect herbivores can clearly withstand the many chemical defenses of plants or they would not be so successful in terms of numbers of species and population sizes. Vertebrates contain enzymes in the liver, their detoxifying center, that promote a metabolic attack on a variety of drugs and pesticides (Krieger, Feeny, and Wilkinson 1971, see also Freeland and Janzen 1974). Similar enzymes have been found in invertebrates, and in lepidopterous larvae they are concentrated in the midgut tissues. These microsomal mixed-function oxidases catalyze a huge diversity of reactions and are often instrumental in the development of insecticide resistance in insect populations. Thus although the pyrethrins in *Chrysanthemum* were once probably a potent defense, and although they still protect the flowers from many herbivores, they are unable to counter those insects with high microsomal oxidase production. An almost incredible twist to this coevolutionary race, as Whittaker and Feeny (1971) mention, is that perhaps *Chrysanthemum* has delivered a winning blow, a temporary one at least, by manufacturing sesamin, an inhibitor of `mixed-function oxidases! And so the step-by-step coevolutionary process continues.

Rather than do battle with plant toxins, herbivores may also avoid them. There exists a paradox in an earlier statement about caterpillars feeding on oak leaves. The winter moth is a serious pest on oaks, and yet the tannins in the leaves are very effective in reducing individual growth rates, fecundity, and population growth. The answer to this paradox lies in the temporal avoidance by the winter moth caterpillars of the condensed tannins in oak leaves. Feeny (1970) actually set out to find why winter moth larvae hatch from their eggs so early in the season, sometimes even before leaves are available to feed upon, and thus risk tremendous mortality. Later there is an apparent abundance of food for a period that would allow two generations of winter moth to succeed, although there is only one generation per year. He studied many different factors and the results, among others, are given in Fig. 3.3. Feeding early in the season makes best use of the protein available, and the selection pressure to feed early is sufficiently strong to modify the whole life history of the moth. This has also been noticed by Drooz (1971) in the elm spanworm.

Avoidance of toxins is also possible for other insects. Numerous insects such as some aphids (e.g., Way and Cammell 1970) feed on dying foliage and so avoid toxic compounds (as well as for nutritional reasons) or other defensive strategies on the part of the plant. The very fine piercing mouthparts of the true bugs, Hemiptera and Homoptera, enable them to feed between pockets or ducts of toxin in the host plant and thus they achieve a spatial avoidance.

Secondary metabolic products can be utilized by insects as cues to identify the plant for feeding and breeding purposes, once the insect species has evolved a mechanism for tolerating or detoxifying the plant's defense (Fraenkel 1959, 1969). If an insect species is able to utilize a toxic plant for food, by some physiological adjustment, the advantages are at least fourfold.

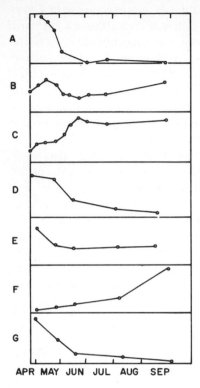

Fig. 3.3 General trends in (*a*) number of Lepidoptera larvae feeding on oak leaves (including winter moth larvae), (*b*) reducing sugar content of oak leaves (percent dry weight as glucose), (*c*) sucrose content, (*d*) water content, (*e*) protein content, (*f*) tannin content, (*g*) protein–tannin ratio of oak leaves. The two variables that correlate well with decline of winter moth numbers are water content and protein content. Feeny suggests that, since some Lepidoptera larvae feed on oak leaves late in the season, sufficient water is available for insect growth. Protein availability is reduced by the quantity of nonhydrolysable tannin in the leaf. The protein–tannin ratio gives an estimate of the available protein and just as available protein becomes limiting so the feeding stage of the winter moth is completed. After Feeny 1970.

1. The herbivore gains a source of food that cannot be utilized by any other herbivore, or very few other herbivores, and competition for food is minimized.
2. This food is very easily recognized by its secondary compound label.
3. Feeding on this food may also impart a toxic or unpalatable characteristic to the herbivore (e.g., Brower and Brower 1964). Predation pressure on this herbivore will therefore be reduced.
4. The antibiotic properties of many toxic chemicals may protect the herbivore against pathogens (e.g., Frings et al. 1948 demonstrated the antibacterial action in the blood of the large milkweed bug that ingests heart poisons in its diet).

Eisner, Kafatos, and Linsley (1962) suggest the possibility that a predaceous cerambycid beetle has taken this process one step further, so that the predator gains at least temporary protection by eating an "unpalatable" prey—unpalatable, that is, to most other predators. The tachinid parasite, *Zenillia adamsoni,*· of monarch butterfly larvae that feed on poisonous milkweeds, also contains active poisons in its body (Reichstein et al. 1968).

Some plant products are merely eaten by the herbivore, stored, and regurgitated in defense against predators. These are not really secretions but sequestered substances. Eisner et al. (1974) show that a diprionid sawfly uses the resin it obtains from pine needles, stores it in diverticula of the gut, and regurgitates it as a sticky blob at the mouth. This is distasteful to vertebrate predators such as chickadees and finches, and gums up the mouthparts of invertebrate predators and the ovipositors of hymenopterous parasites.

Eisner, Hendry, Peakall, and Meinwald (1971) discovered that incorporated in the defensive secretion of the grasshopper *Romalea microptera*, there is a repellent herbicide derivative presumably obtained by feeding upon plants sprayed with herbicide. This surely indicates that insects may use to their advantage any chemical that is available, manmade or natural.

If it is so advantageous to specialize in feeding on toxic plants, why are some species monophagous (feeding on one species of food) and others polyphagous (feeding on many species of food)? Also, why do some species feed on apparently innocuous hosts? There are many solutions to any given problem in nature and the evolutionary process ensures that many possible avenues are tested. Some species have never had the evolutionary chance to crack potent plant defenses because the gene pool has not produced the necessary combination of enzymes. Others have evolved to specialize by dealing with a few potent plant chemicals, and yet others evolved to generalize by utilization of many less toxic plants. These seem to be the two basic alternatives and both require quite an expensive metabolic commitment on the part of the insect. The monophagous species must produce large quantities of an enzyme to detoxify their food, or they must evolve storage mechanisms, as in the case of diprionid sawfly larvae. Conversely Krieger, Feeny, and Wilkinson (1971) have shown that the polyphagous species of insects usually produce much more of the microsomal mixed-function oxidases in their midguts to deal with the very diverse array of plant chemicals in their potential diet.

As far as finding food goes, the monophagous species will have to search harder, but it can become highly specialized in its search and it has those chemical markers to cue in on. The polyphagous species has a more abundant food source but its chemical cues are less distinctive, or produced in lesser amounts, and the insect cannot afford to specialize on any one of the variety of chemicals in its diet. The monophagous species will usually have to share its food source with few other herbivores, whereas the polyphagous species may be faced with many potential

competitors. There are no outright winners in nature and every avenue
for adaptive gain sets rather precise limits on how far this advantage can
be exploited.

It becomes clear that if either the monophagous or polyphagous feeding strategies are metabolically costly, the cost of gaining this energy
must reduce the amount of energy that can be channeled into reproduction. That is, even the food source of herbivores contains an environmental resistance factor in the form of toxic chemicals. Presumably
insects fed on a bland (nontoxic) diet would show their real biotic potential and those fed on natural foods would show their biotic potential
minus the environmental resistance contained in food (rather like Feeny
did with winter moths on artificial diets). In the comparison of the
growth parameters r and r_{max} this factor should be calculated for (see
Chapter 7).

If several evolutionary lines of insects adapt to feeding upon a toxic
plant, and use these toxins as cues for their behavior, as frequently happens, the result will be a unique insect fauna on each set of plants that
are chemically related. This makes the study of the insect fauna of poisonous plant families very interesting and valuable for understanding
community organization (e.g., see Gilbert 1975).

The family Asclepiadaceae, the milkweeds, contains some species that
manufacture cardiac glycosides that are emetic when ingested by vertebrates at half their lethal dosage (e.g., Brower 1969). This is an important
point for the herbivore that sequesters these glycosides because, if the
predator is killed, there is no chance of the predator population learning
to avoid feeding on an aposematic species (one that advertizes its distasteful nature by being brightly colored). There is only a small group
of insects in four insect orders that feed consistently on *Asclepias* in
temperate North America, and they are found almost exclusively on
milkweed (Table 3.1, Fig. 3.4). All are aposematically colored, suggesting
that they all are chemically protected. Contrary to this expectation
Brower (1969) has claimed that monarch butterflies that have fed in
northeastern North America are palatable because their food plants lack
cardiac glycosides. However, Duffey (1970) showed that the species of
milkweed mentioned by Brower do contain glycosides. It now appears
that there is a great variation in glycoside content in monarch butterfly populations, from zero to concentrations sufficient to cause emesis
(Brower et al. 1972). Thus there exists a palatability spectrum for the
butterfly's predators (Brower et al. 1968). Scudder and Duffey (1972, see

Fig. 3.4 Two members of the milkweed fauna, the large milkweed bug, *Oncopeltus fasciatus* (*a*), and a milkweed longhorn beetle, *Tetraopes femoratus* (*b*), on swamp milkweed, *Asclepias incarnata*. Both species are red on the lighter areas of the body and black on the remainder. Thus the insects contrast strikingly with the green leaves of the host plant and they sit prominently on upper foliage, a behavior that differs considerably from that of cryptic species.

43

Table 3.1 The insect community on milkweeds (Asclepiadaceae) in temperate North America which are mostly aposematic species. The one exception is placed in parentheses (personal observations). Other insects feed sporadically on milkweeds but are not found predominantly on these plants.

Order	Family	Species	Aposematic coloring
Coleoptera	Cerambycidae	*Tetraopes tetraophthalmus*	Red with black spots
		Tetraopes femoratus	Red with black spots
		Tetraopes quinquemaculatus	Red with black spots
	Chrysomelidae	*Labidomera clivicollis*	Red and black pattern
	(Curculionidae	*Rhyssomatus lineaticollis*	Black)
Lepidoptera	Danaidae	*Danaus plexippus*	Adult—orange and black
			Larva—black, yellow, and white stripes
	Arctiidae	*Euchaetias egle*	Adult and larva— white, yellow, and black
		Cycnia inopinatus	Adult—white, yellow, and black
			Larva—orange with grey hairs
Hemiptera	Lygaeidae	*Oncopeltus fasciatus*	Red and black
		Lygaeus kalmii	Red and black
Homoptera	Aphididae	*Aphis nerii*	Yellow and black

also Feir and Suen 1971) found cardiac glycosides in aposematic lygaeids feeding on milkweeds, and these chemicals were also incorporated into the insects' defensive secretions. Beetles, such as *Tetraopes* spp., that are specific to milkweeds also contain glycosides (Duffey and Scudder 1972). We must infer from the studies above that the majority of milkweeds of the genus *Asclepias* contain cardiac glycosides and that most insects that feed on these plants are protected by ingesting and sequestering these toxic chemicals.

The production of sesamin in the pyrethrum flower that inhibits mixed function oxidase activity has been mentioned. A more extensive set of counter responses may be seen in leguminous plants presumably in response to herbivore pressure by bruchid (pea and bean) weevils that oviposit on legume pods. A summary provided by Janzen (1969a) and Center and Johnson (1974) covers physical and chemical defense:

1. Some species produce gum when the seed pod is first penetrated by a newly hatched larva—this may push off the egg mass, or drown the larvae, or hamper their movements.
2. Pods may dehisce, fragment, or explode, scattering seeds to escape from larvae coming through the pod walls and from ovipositing females.
3. Some species have pods free of surface cracks as some bruchids cannot glue eggs on a smooth surface.
4. Some species have indehiscent pods and thus exclude those species that oviposit only on exposed seeds.
5. Some species have a layer of material on the seed surface that swells when the pod opens and detaches the attached eggs.
6. Many species have poisonous or hallucinogenic compounds such as alkaloids, saponins, pentose sugars, and free amino acids (primary response).
7. Some are rich in endopeptidase inhibitors, making digestion of the bean by the bruchid very difficult.
8. Some have a flaking pod surface that may remove eggs laid on it.
9. In *Acacia* spp. the immature seeds remain small throughout the year and abruptly grow to maturity just before being dispersed.
10. In a species of *Cassia* the seeds are so thin that a bruchid could not mature in one.
11. In many wild herbaceous legumes the seeds are so small that bruchids cannot mature in them. Janzen (1969a) lists many other examples.

On a much broader scale that cuts across families and even higher taxa there exists the possibility that plant species have fundamentally different nutritional values that are correlated with the types of photosynthesis in the plant. Caswell et al. (1973) have proposed a hypothesis:

"As a general rule, plants possessing the C_4-dicarboxylic acid pathway of carbon fixation (hereafter 'C_4 species') are a poorer food source for herbivores than those possessing only the C_3-Calvin cycle pathway ('C_3 species'), and that this difference is reflected in a tendency for herbivores to avoid feeding on C_4 species."

The most important differences between C_3 and C_4 species that affect their ecology are (see Black 1971 for details):

1. C_4 species have a higher photosynthetic capacity than do C_3 species. The rate of net photosynthesis is two to three times higher than in C_3 species, particularly at high temperatures (30–40°C) and high light intensities (3000–5000 ft candles and higher).
2. C_4 species require about half as much water as C_3 species to produce one unit of dry matter.

These characteristics must have profound importance in the ecology of these species, in energetics and systems ecology and in agriculture, as well as for the herbivores that utilize them. Table 3.2 gives some examples.

To return to the hypothesis, the authors present an impressive list of data from studies on (1) diet of herbivores; (2) preference experiments in the laboratory; (3) survival and reproduction of herbivores on different plant species, on both vertebrates and invertebrates, particularly insects. This led them to conclude, "There is a general, but not universal, tendency for herbivores to avoid C_4 species, and that C_4 species are generally inferior food sources in terms of survival and reproduction of herbivores." Not only do C_4 plants have a competitive advantage through greater net production but they are likely to have a lesser herbivore load. This should be examined more closely in terms of pest management strategies on crops.

There are several possible reasons for this nutritional inferiority of C_4 species. They have most starch stored around the vascular bundles and so it is less available to herbivores, or it takes more effort to eat it. In C_3 plants starch tends to be spread throughout the mesophyll. Also the veins of grasses usually are overlaid with short cells containing silica or cork bodies and thus the most nutritive parts of the leaf are best protected in C_4 plants. Other aspects of nutritional status, such as lower nitrogen content of C_4 plant leaves, and on average twice as much nondigestible lignin in C_4 as C_3 forage crops, reinforce the impression that C_4 plants are a relatively poor food source. Caswell and Reed (1975) have since confirmed the inferior nutritional value of C_4 species to grasshoppers. For example, when *Melanoplus biliteratus* nymphs were reared on a C_4 species, survival to the adult stage was only 27% whereas with six C_3 species survival ranged from 37–53%. Fecundity was also greatly reduced from 97–256 eggs per female fed on C_3 species to only 22 eggs per female fed a C_4 species.

This new hypothesis should be kept in mind in all considerations of plant-herbivore interactions at the community and ecosystem level. For example, it may be predicted that under heavy grazing pressure C_4 species will be favored and increase in abundance. Evans and Tisdale (1972)

Table 3.2   **Examples of C$_3$ and C$_4$ species and genera with notes on their ecological or agricultural status. C$_4$ species are important crops, weeds, and components of plant communities in desert and saline conditions where water stress is severe. C$_3$ plants also include important crops and weed species. Notice that genera may contain species that are C$_3$ or C$_4$, such as Atriplex.**

	C$_4$ species	C$_3$ species

Monocotyledons	*Setaria*—important weed
	 Sorghum—important crop
	 Saccharum officinarum—
	   sugar cane—net primary
	   production very high
	 Spartina—very high net
	   primary production in
	   estuaries
	 Zea mays—corn or maize,
	   important crop
	 Andropogon—important
	   grass in dry areas
		Avena Oats ⎫ important
		 Hordeum Barley ⎬ grain
		 Triticum Wheat ⎭ crops
		 Poa pratensis—Kentucky
		   blue grass, important
		   in hay crops and as a weed

Dicotyledons	*Amaranthus*—serious weed
	 Atriplex 2 sp.—dry and saline
	   areas
	 Portulaca—desert plant
	 Salsola—dry and saline areas
		Ambrosia—serious weed
		 Atriplex 1 sp.—saline areas
		
		 Beta—root crop
		 Brassica—cabbage crops
		 Chenopodium—weed
		 Datura—weed
		 Daucus—weed
		 Glycine max—soybean,
		   important crop
		 Gossypium—cotton, important
		   crop
		 Helianthus—sunflower

SOURCE.   From Black 1971.

have found this to be the case in Idaho where heavy grazing by cattle, sheep, and mule deer is changing the composition from dominance by *Agropyron spicatum* (a C$_3$ species) to dominance by *Aristida longiseta* (a C$_4$ species).

Physical interactions in coevolution are more obvious than chemical ones, and the prevalence of mechanical defenses of plants indicates how fierce the interactions with their herbivores have been. Examples of mechanical defenses of plants in the form of spines, pubescence, and toughness of texture may be seen commonly, so only two examples are given here.

Gilbert (1971) argues that in coevolution chemical defenses may well evolve before mechanical defenses. The chemical defenses act as a filter and as these increase so the number of herbivores decreases until it is evolutionarily more expedient for the plant to develop some rather specific mechanical defenses against the few serious herbivores that remain. This is the case in *Passiflora adenopoda*, which is preyed upon by heliconiine butterflies. The plant is covered with hooked trichomes (hairs) that catch in the integument of the caterpillar, immobilize the herbivore, and puncture it so it starves and dessiccates at the same time.

Cook, Atsatt, and Simon (1971) have studied an interesting case of polymorphism in seeds of dove weed, *Eremocarpus sitigerus*, which are the preferred food of doves. That polymorphism has been selected by these granivores is clear from the following relationships: Mojave Desert —doves not observed—no polymorphism; Coastline California—doves in large numbers—weed populations often with five seed-coat morphs. Five morphs are determined genetically and a sixth morph phenotypically as more grey seeds are produced in senescent plants. These grey seeds are chemically protected from dove predation as they are unpalatable. In Chapters 4 and 10 the effective defense resulting from polymorphism is discussed. It is interesting that a compromise has had to be made by the plant, and an idea of the cost of evolving chemical defenses may be better appreciated. The grey seeds are inferior to other morphs on practically all grounds except survival during predation. Grey seeds are more susceptible to fungal attack, they have a thinner moisture-holding sheath, they germinate less well after soaking in water, they are smaller, and they give rise to smaller plants. The cost of having the chemical defense is considerable.

Another method of avoiding predation is to disperse seeds or fruits rapidly and extensively with the resultant greater difficulty in discovering food for species that are seed specialists. The multitude of seed-dispersal mechanisms among plants obviously accomplish this aim. Adaptations for wind dispersal and for attaching to animals take many forms. Animals carry fruits and seeds in the mouth or gut and feed on the palatable part of the fruit or seed coat, and the seed is dispersed and may be buried by small mammals, harvester ants, and wood ants, or seed caching beetles (see Harper, Lovell, and Moore 1970, Sudd 1967, Alcock 1973a, Kirk 1972, 1973, Manley 1971). Many seeds have oily coats or appendages (caruncles and elaiosomes) that are eaten by ants and other insects (Sudd 1967), while the seed remains intact and is dispersed. Some seeds improved germination after passing through the gut of animals (Krefting and Roe 1949). This advantage can be obtained at the cost of producing a palatable fruit.

The further the seeds are dispersed the less rewarding will predation be on these seeds and a pattern such as that proposed by Janzen (1970) may be observed that relates seed density to the probability of survival of seed (Fig. 3.5). There is a minimum distance between parent and progeny where survival is likely. The population recruitment curve is clearly the product of seed density and probability of survival. Thus if a species does not evolve an effective dispersal mechanism to make seeds unprofitable, the only alternatives are to make them unpalatable, or very small.

The selection pressures on plants to avoid herbivore attack may be difficult to observe, but sometimes plant populations being dramatically influenced by herbivores can be seen. These instances may be extremely rare, even in evolutionary time, as heavy herbivore pressure will produce the strong selection pressure that causes a new defense in the plant. A stable equilibrium may follow for many years, and we may be led to

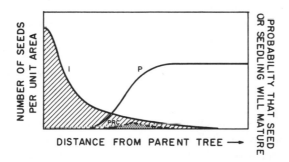

Fig. 3.5 The relationship between density of seeds (*I*) and probability of escaping from a seed or seedling predator (*P*) relative to the distance of seeds from the parent tree. The product of *I* and *P* values gives the population recruitment curve (*PRC*) where progeny are most likely to survive at some distance from the parent. From D. H. Janzen. Herbivores and the number of tree species in tropical forests. *Amer. Natur.* **104**:501–528, published by the University of Chicago Press. © 1970 by the University of Chicago. All rights reserved.

assume that the herbivore is innocuous. The plant may also lose vigor when developing the new defense, as during production of the grey unpalatable seeds of dove weed. A price must be paid for extra defense, and it would be valuable to know some quantitative estimates. In the case of *Passiflora adenopoda* perhaps 1% of its energy goes to the manufacture of trichomes. A much larger percentage would go into resin production in pines or latex in milkweeds, but in these cases it is hard to know how to apportion the costs between protection and storage of useful chemicals and waste products. Many studies are needed to elucidate the costs of coevolutionary processes.

Some examples of heavy herbivore pressure may help appreciation of the possible brevity of the selection process. In 1966 a European flea beetle, *Psylloides napi*, that fed on yellow rocket, *Barbarea vulgaris*, was discovered new to New York state. Adults fed on leaves while larvae burrowed in the petioles. By 1969 it had reached infestation proportions and was killing off whole local populations of its host and exerting a strong selective pressure. The whole episode would probably have gone unnoticed but for a detailed study on crucifer communities being undertaken by Root, Tahvanainen, and others at that time (Tahvanainen and Root 1970). Now it appears that *P. napi* may act as a valuable biological control agent on yellow rocket.

Only a few reports of an apparently rare sawfly, *Monostegia abdominalis*, existed on its occurrence in North America before 1970. Then it was found in high numbers in remote areas of Quebec killing relatively large areas of a loosestrife *Lysimachia terrestris* (Price 1970a).

Perhaps the most dramatic example of herbivore pressure has been witnessed in the control of Klamath weed by the introduced beetle, *Chrysolina quadrigemina* (see Huffaker 1967, Huffaker and Kennett 1969 for an account). Selection of plants by the beetles has not been random but has concentrated on plants in unshaded spots, so the pattern seen in Fig. 3.6 has emerged (see also Harper 1969). *Chrysolina* populations were so high in exposed sites that *Hypericum* populations crashed, and *Chrysolina* numbers fell too because of lack of food. Because this leaf beetle cannot breed well in the shade it might be concluded that (1) *Hypericum* is a shade adapted species and (2) *Chrysolina* is a rare insect. Both conclusions are very misleading. The question should be posed again, as it was with the rabbit-flea-myxomatosis situation, "Could the ecology of these species be properly understood if this interaction had not been witnessed?" and also, "How many other plant species have distributions dictated by herbivore pressure?"

Where this sort of herbivore pressure acts on some populations and not on others the process of evolution is accelerated tremendously, speci-

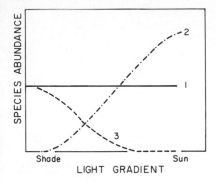

Fig. 3.6 Schematic representation of abundance of plant host, *Hypericum*, and herbivore, *Chrysolina*, on a light intensity gradient from shade to full sunlight. (1) *Hypericum* before introduction of *Chrysolina*. (2) *Chrysolina on Hypericum* soon after introduction. (3) Resultant distribution of *Hypericum* with *Chrysolina* rare throughout the gradient.

ation may result, and both plant species diversity and herbivore diversity, and thus biotic diversity in general, must be strongly influenced by the coevolutionary process (see also Ehrlich and Raven 1964, Gillett 1962, Krieger, Feeny, and Wilkinson 1971).

The ecology of the plant-herbivore interaction is a rapidly developing field involving extensive use of chemical ecology, another area that has gained tremendous impetus in the past decade. For further reference some recent symposia in these areas include Insect and Host Plant (de Wilde and Schoonhoven 1969), Chemical Ecology (Sondheimer and Simeone 1970), Insect/Plant Relationships (van Emden 1972a), Phytochemical Ecology (Harborne 1972), and Coevolution of Animals and Plants (Gilbert and Raven 1975).

Chapter 4

COEVOLUTION
OF PREY
AND PREDATOR

I n Chapter 3 some aspects of the interaction between the first and second
trophic levels were covered. Moving up the feeding chain one step, we
must now consider coevolution (or coadaptation) between the second
and third trophic levels. After the herbivores, all other members in the
food chain of living organisms are either predators or parasites, so predation is an important subject in ecology. Parasites are usually bathed in
their food, or intimately associated with it; thus they become less interesting as a group for study of ways of obtaining food, although there is
much to learn from their dispersal strategies. Added to the importance
of general predators many people regard the total consumption of any
organism, plant or animal, as predation. Therefore predation is a central
issue in understanding how energy moves through the food chain, and in
understanding both the adaptive strategies for getting food, and for the
avoidance of becoming food. Since food is a critical resource for all
organisms, predation must be considered to be at the heart of ecological
thinking, and this explains why so many researchers have been fascinated
by the subject. These factors justify the space devoted to this subject in
this book.

The importance of predation as an exploitation strategy may be summarized under four main categories. First, predators play a prominent
role in the flow of energy through the community. Examples of predation can be seen at the feeding links between every trophic level. Second,
predators and parasitoids have been repeatedly singled out as regulators
of the animal populations upon which they feed. The biological control
of insects, until recently, has relied upon this notion, and in Chapter 9
on population dynamics it is seen how predation rates as a factor in
regulation. It is certainly one of the most visible aspects of mortality.
Third, predators play a role in maintaining fitness of the prey population. This statement is axiomatic when fitness is defined in terms of survival and the leaving of viable progeny. Those organisms eaten by predators are unfit. Those organisms best able to defend themselves or otherwise escape predation survive. Predation is therefore heavy on old and
decrepit individuals, those that are diseased or malformed, and those
young whose parents are sufficiently unfit not to make adequate arrangements for the survival of their progeny. This may range from a delin-
quent giraffe mother who does not defend her calf sufficiently to prevent
lion predation, to a moth that lays its eggs in a position that makes them
vulnerable to attack by parasitoids. Predation is one of the chief mortalities to which organisms are exposed and tends to maintain a healthy and
vigorous breeding population of prey. Finally predators act as selective
agents in the evolution of their prey. Any severe mortality factor is likely

to change the population permanently, and this is certainly true of predation. Some of the very diverse evolutionary trends are listed at the end of
this chapter. Their diversity and commonness attests to the prevalence
of predation as a selective factor in nature. Practically every insect species
can be fitted into one or more of the categories listed, indicating that at
some stage in its evolutionary development every insect species has been
exposed to either heavy or prolonged predation. Perhaps predation pressure has produced one of the most visible evolutionary forces in the
whole animal kingdom.

In the insects there is a large group of species that parasitize others.
In spite of Reuter (1913) making a clear distinction between these insects
and true parasites they are still commonly called parasitic insects, although since about 1960 the more precise term parasitoid has been used
more frequently in the literature. A predator is defined as an organism
that kills and consumes many animal-food items in its life span, although
if plants are completely consumed such as seeds or seedlings, predation
may also cover these forms of feeding. In contrast, a parasitoid can be
defined as an insect that requires and eats only one animal in its life
span, but may be ultimately responsible for killing many. Here an egg
is laid on or in a host (or prey), a larva hatches and consumes the host,
and becomes a free living adult, which, if female, proceeds to oviposit on
many other hosts that will nourish its progeny. This is where a single
female may be ultimately responsible for the death of many individuals.

Some would argue that both types of food exploitation should be
called predation. Certainly, the fact that both predator and parasitoid
kill many food items makes them exactly comparable as far as effects on
prey populations go. The only difference is that the predator kills food
for itself and the parasitoid kills or paralyzes food for its progeny. However, predators such as insectivorous birds also collect prey for their
young, and as far as population dynamics are concerned the results are
the same! Therefore parasitoids must be considered under predation, and
in fact a great deal of predation theory has been developed with parasitoids in mind. Only Nicholson (1933) and Nicholson and Bailey (1935)
need be mentioned to show how important parasitoids have been in
stimulating the development of ecological theory, but their work is discussed in Chapter 5, which considers predator populations rather than
individuals. The ecology of parasitoids is treated also in Chapter 12 on
biological control.

By looking at a single species of predator some general ideas may be obtained on how a predator exploits a given environment most efficiently, when prey species are most likely to be vulnerable to predation, and how they reduce this vulnerability. An example is the vertebrate predator, the great tit, *Parus major*. This bird is a large relative of the chickadees in North America—the black-capped, Carolina, and brown-capped chickadees. They are all insectivorous. By studying the great tit in some detail one may catch a glimpse of how this vertebrate predator views its insect food supply.

The great tit occurs throughout the palearctic region, and has been intensively studied in England, continental Europe, and Japan. In southern Holland, Luuk Tinbergen from the University of Groningen studied the great tit feeding its nestlings in a scots pine plantation called the Zwarte Berg. He wrote the manuscript of his 1960 paper during the winter of 1954 to 1955 and continued his field work in the summer of 1955. At the end of that year he died, so although the paper was published in 1960 the author could not have been aware of Holling's work in Canada which began to appear in print in 1959 (see p. 61), and which has also added significantly to the understanding of predation.

Tinbergen argued in his "probability of encounter hypothesis" that if a very simple view of predation is adopted, and random movements of the predator and random dispersion of the prey are assumed, the number of a particular prey N_A captured by a predator can be expressed simply as

$$N_A = R_A D_A t$$

where N_A = total number of species A prey captured by predator in time interval t; D_A = population density of prey; and R_A = risk index of prey species A for a particular predator.

Several factors influenced the risk index. For example, prey size was important. Very few small insects were collected and in the case of larvae of the pine noctuid moth (*Panolis flammea*) none less than 18 mm were taken although they represented 20% of the species available (Fig. 4.1). Each prey species also was subjected to a typical intensity of predation in relation to that of *Panolis* at any one time. Tinbergen took *Panolis* larvae (over 2 cm long) and gave them a risk value of 100, and then compared the relative risk of many other insects. For example, if species A was twice as abundant as *Panolis* in the environment, but formed the same percentage of the food brought to the nest by the great tits, its relative risk would be 50% of *Panolis*. In this way Tinbergen could quantify the relative palatability, and ease in finding the important food items, in the great tits' diet (Table 4.1). In fact Tinbergen found that R_A, or the probability of a prey item being discovered and eaten by the predator,

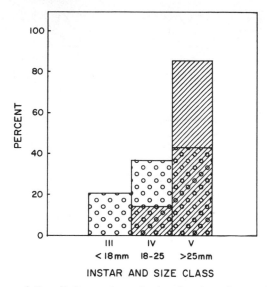

Fig. 4.1 Percentage of *Panolis* larvae in each size class in twig samples (dotted), and in food of great tits (hatched). Data from Tinbergen 1960.

varies radically and depends on a number of factors: prey size, density of prey, availability of other food, developmental stage of prey (larva, pupa, or adult), and learning processes in the predator.

It is clear that as far as the survival of the insect is concerned, its abundance, defensive, and palatability characteristics relative to the other prey species in the community will influence actual mortality enormously. One example from Tinbergen's work is given in Fig. 4.2. Even within a species, its density had a dramatic influence on the success of the predator in finding its food (Fig. 4.3). Here, at the lowest densities the percentage

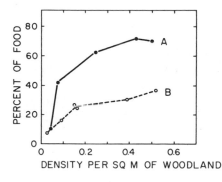

Fig. 4.2 Percentage of total food taken by great tit represented by *Panolis* larvae in relation to their density in the trees, and the availability of alternative prey (*A*) during periods in which large *Panolis* caterpillars occurred together with prey of low risk index only, (*B*) when appreciable populations of high or moderate risk index species were present (e.g., *Lymantria, Acantholyda,* or *Diprion* cocoons). After Tinbergen 1960.

Table 4.1   Risk index for insect species in the Zwarte Berg in relation to predation by the great tit, Parus major.

Taxonomic group or common name	Species	Risk index	Important characters in relation to risk index
Lymantriid moth	*Lymantria monarcha* 20 mm (larva)	225.0	Cryptic but large (6 cm)
Pine noctuid moth	*Panolis flammea* 20 mm (larva)	100.0	Cryptic but large
Pine looper moth	*Bupalus piniarius* (adult)	95.0	Moths on ground but cryptic
Pamphiliid sawfly	*Acantholyda nemoralis*	49.0	Web easily seen but larva smaller than *Panolis*
Tortricid moth	*Cacoecia piceana*	10.0	Same as for *Acantholyda*, difference not understood
Diprionid sawflies	*Diprion nemoralis* and *D. simile*	3.1	Solitary but conspicuous
Diprionid sawflies	*Diprion virens* and *D. frutetorum* (larvae)	2.2	Solitary and cryptic (green)
	Diprion virens (prepupae and pupae)	16.0	Solitary, pupae non resinous
Diprionid sawflies	*Diprion pini* and *D. sertifer* (larvae)	0.1	Very conspicuous, colonial, resinous taste
	Diprion pini (prepupae and pupae)	22.0	Solitary, pupae nonresinous

SOURCE.   From Tinbergen 1960.

of a species in the food was relatively low. At higher densities the percentage showed a much steeper rise than in the expectation curve, and reached a high value at medium densities. At the highest densities the slope of the curve was much less steep than the slope of the expectation curve. Also the palatability and other risk factors affected the quantity of a species taken. For example, leveling off occurred at about 29% in *Panolis*, 25% in *Acantholyda*, and 12% in *Diprion sertifer*.

These points indicate the sorts of selective pressures under which prey populations change. It emphasizes that to avoid predation evolutionary change relative to the other species present may be just as important as absolute changes. These relative changes are difficult to evaluate as it is hard to choose an adequate baseline on which to measure change.

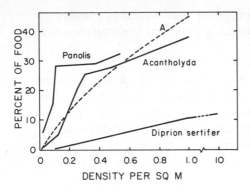

Fig. 4.3 Percentage of a prey species in the great tit diet in relation to the density of the prey. Density figures refer to larvae over 20 mm long in *Panolis*, and over 10 mm in the other species. Data for *Acantholyda* were collected in the presence of large *Panolis* larvae, and for *Diprion sertifer* before the appearance of *Panolis*. (*a*) Expectation curve for *Acantholyda* derived from the probability of encounter hypothesis and the density of other species present. After Tinbergen 1960.

Tinbergen explains the change in risk of a species with density as follows. Tinbergen's own words are used to explain low risk at low densities as these are the words that have created a controversy that is unlikely to be settled for a long time. His statement has strong supporters and vehement critics with very keen and observant biologists on both sides.

The remarkably low risk at low densities is perhaps most easily explained by the hypothesis of searching images. We have assumed that specific searching images are adopted only when the species in question has exceeded a certain density. Accordingly the birds would make only a limited number of chance encounters when density is below the critical level, while predation would become more efficient at higher densities. The observations on *Acantholyda*, *Cacoecia* and *Panolis* (without alternative [food]) suggest that the critical density is rather sharply defined, for the increase in risk seems to be restricted to a rather narrow range of densities. The observations, however, are too few to warrant a definite conclusion on this point.

Tinbergen makes the point that search images for palatable prey are "accepted" at much lower densities than those for unpalatable prey (cf., Fig. 4.3). And to quote further:

Finally, we may ask why specific searching images are not used at low densities. From a functional point of view, this can be understood if we assume that the birds can adopt only a limited number of searching images. Under these circumstances it will be more profitable to search for abundant than for rare prey. Moreover, it may be supposed that a certain number of encounters is required for the acceptance and maintenance of a searching image.

Tinbergen was trying to assess the mental ability of the great tit, although he was aware of the importance of the profitability of search (cf., Royama's concept of profitability discussed later in this chapter, p. 66). Tinbergen went on to explain the low risk at high density by saying that the great tit has a preference for a mixed diet. Therefore an individual bird will not take more than 50–60% of its total diet in the form of a single species.

Tinbergen summarizes his hypothesis as follows: ". . . the intensity of predation depends to a great extent on the use of specific searching images. This implies that the birds perform a highly selective sieving operation on the visual stimuli reaching their retina." This is "a kind of learning process." Dawkins (1971a,b) showed that chicks do learn to see cryptic food and thus supports Tinbergen's hypothesis. However, she argues cogently that the term adopting a search image has been used in conflicting ways and is not helpful. The term learning to detect may be preferable. Alcock (1973b) defined the concept as "hunting for certain visual cues associated with relatively cryptic food while ignoring or overlooking others."

There is also something to learn from a brief summary of the criticisms of, and difficulties with, the hypothesis.

1. All prey species densities were not measured; therefore, the proportion of one prey in the total available could not be determined. The following ratio is needed:

$$\frac{\text{proportion of species } A \text{ present in total food available}}{\text{proportion of species } A \text{ taken by predator}}$$

2. The density of prey does not reflect the proportion of individuals that are unpalatable through disease and such. (Tinbergen recognized this important variability within a population).
3. He does not consider that within a species some individuals may be more readily discovered than others. If most favorable parts of niches are occupied first, and parts in which individuals are more vulnerable later (cf., Errington's work on muskrats discussed in Chapter 5), then this could produce the same change in prey risk that Tinbergen documented. This applies to low risk at low density changing to high risk at moderate density. This would certainly be in accord with current concepts on predation covered in Chapter 5.

4. Within the bird's defended territory the density of prey may be very
    much reduced by predation so that locally, profitability of searching
    for that prey, and probability of finding it are very low even though
    "average density" estimates indicate that only 30–40% of prey is
    taken. This may account for the apparent low risk at high density.
5. Tinbergen does not consider the distance of the prey from the nest,
    an important part of prey profitability.
6. Tinbergen makes three assumptions to explain the change in prey
    risk that are hard to test. First, he assumes that the bird uses a
    searching image. Second, he assumes that only a limited number of
    such images can be stored at one time, and third, he assumes a
    preference for a mixed diet.

In general the problem of discovery of prey must be considered on a
microenvironmental level and the situation is much more complex than
it appears at first sight. These are all surmountable difficulties and Tinbergen's paper has stimulated a great deal of good research. Some is
discussed later under the concept of profitability proposed by Royama
in 1970 (p. 66).

Clearly, a detailed study of the feeding rate of a predator in a simple
environment was needed to avoid the difficulties that arise in interpreting
Tinbergen's data. The essential components of a predator's life, and the
act of predation, must be understood. Holling, then at the Sault St. Marie
laboratory of the Canadian Forest Service, championed the component
analysis approach to predator–prey interactions. He asked a simple question, "What are the parameters that are universal in the act of predation?" By examining the components experimentally, using various animals, he was able to develop models predicting results that are still
proving to be true for real situations.
    The simplicity in the concept of the component analysis approach
can be seen by one of his early experiments (Holling 1959a). He placed
a blindfolded human subject in front of a table. On the three foot square
table he thumb-tacked sand paper disks 4 cm in diameter. The subject
was then asked to tap the table until she found a disk, remove the disk,
and set it aside and then continue tapping, and so on. She tapped for
one minute. For each density of disks eight replicates were made. The
disk density ranged from 4 to 256 per 9 ft^2.
    The results can be seen in Fig. 4.4. Why should there be a curvilinear
response? Why should there not be a linear relationship in which the

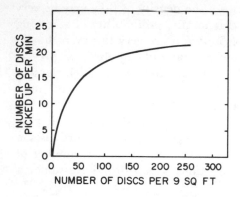

Fig. 4.4 A graphical representation of Holling's disk equation showing the rate of discovery by a human "predator" in relation to the density of sandpaper disk "prey." After Holling 1959a.

doubling of disk density doubled the rate of discovery? Here the number of disks picked up increased at a progressively decreasing rate as disk density rose. Holling pointed out that at low densities the majority of time was spent searching. Efficiency rose rapidly with increasing density until so many disks were found that most time was spent picking them up and laying them aside. The human "predator" could only handle a certain maximum number of "prey" disks per unit time.

Many of these curves have been described by Holling himself and subsequent workers for diverse real situations, and thus support Holling's functional response curve. The general, so-called disk equation is

$$N_A = \frac{a T_T N_o}{(1 + a T_H N_o)}$$

where N_A = number of disks removed, N_o = density of disks, T_T = time interval available for searching, T_H = handling time, and a = rate of discovery (rate of search times. probability of finding a given disk). It is taken for granted that the predator is hungry, but hunger is an additional important component of the functional response. The curve is representative of many cases of predation by invertebrates so far studied and fits many functional responses of parasitoids to host density. It was called a type 2 response curve by Holling. (Holling's type 1 curve represents a rather specialized example which is not dealt with in this book. See Holling 1961, 1965.) But at the moment our concern is how a vertebrate predator such as the great tit might react to prey density.

Holling (1959b) found from his own experiments that an s-shaped functional response curve could be expected for vertebrates, and cited Tinbergen's data and that of a former student of Tinbergen, Mook (1963), which had been obtained in Canada, as other examples of the vertebrate functional response model (Fig. 4.5). Holling's explanation

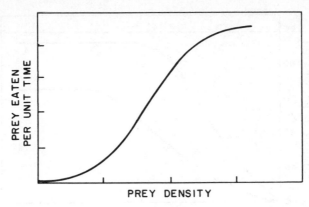

Fig. 4.5 The sigmoid functional response, or type 3 response, showing the change in capture rate by an individual predator in terms of prey density.

for this response is much simpler than Tinbergen's. Given the four essential components in the type 2 functional response, rate of successful search, time predator and prey are exposed, handling time, and hunger (not incorporated into the disk equation, but see Holling 1966), which must also be shared by vertebrate predators, only one new component need be added to describe adequately the sigmoid response—learning. The predator, with sufficiently frequent contact with particular items, will learn to find and recognize them and handle them more rapidly. At a given density its efficiency or rate of capture will increase rapidly. Ultimately handling time will become the dominant component in the time available and the rise will decelerate to a plateau, just as Tinbergen had found. Since invertebrates may also show a sigmoid response [e.g., *Nemeritis canescens*, a parasitoid of moth larvae (Hassell 1970, Takahashi 1968)] it is best to refer to the two functional responses simply as type 2 and type 3 responses without using the terms invertebrate and vertebrate response. Some vertebrates show a type 2 response (Holling 1965).

Holling (1965) also found that the s-shaped functional response (or Holling's type 3 response) changed markedly with the strength of the stimulus from the prey just as Tinbergen had (Fig. 4.6). Sawfly survival was much greater (30%) in the presence of a palatable prey—sunflower seeds. Tinbergen's comparative risk R_A can change radically as associated species change.

Concerning selection by avian predators it is therefore maladaptive to be associated in space and time with a less palatable species, as predation pressure is greatly increased. Some of the ways to avoid this situation are to be temporally and/or spatially separated, or to mimic the unpalatable

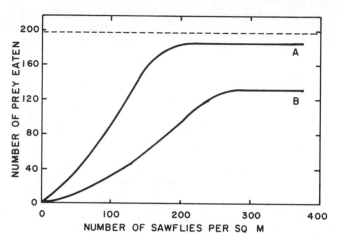

Fig. 4.6 Change in the functional response of the deer mouse, *Peromyscus leucopus*, to the density of prey sawflies in cocoons in the presence of alternate foods (*a*) dog biscuits, a low palatability alternate food, and (*b*) sunflower seeds, a high palatability alternate food. Dashed line indicates the total food eaten, sawflies plus alternate food. The number of dog biscuits eaten was expressed in "sawfly-units" of approximately equivalent nutritive value. After Holling 1965.

species. With such strong selective pressures as 30% advantage, evolution will be rapid and probably quite precise.

From the sawfly and dog biscuit situation in the laboratory it is possible to extrapolate to the field where the sawfly coexists with another species of dog-biscuit-like palatability. Here the sawfly may evolve to look like its less palatable sympatriot, and thus form a Batesian mimicry complex where the model is relatively unpalatable and the mimic is palatable. [Batesian mimicry is defined as the result of evolutionary advergence in shape, patterning, color, or behavior of an edible "mimic" toward (close?) resemblance of a less palatable, and distantly related "model."] The levels of palatability have to change only little so that both species are relatively unpalatable and provide an example of Müllerian mimicry—the result of evolutionary convergence in shape, patterning, and color of distantly related unpalatable species.

Other ways of avoiding predation are crypsis or defense. The effect of crypsis would be to alter the slope of the functional response, which has the same effect on survival as being in the presence of a more palatable species. If a prey species evolves a defensive mechanism the shape of the response will change radically as the species essentially becomes strongly repellent or distasteful. Holling's computer model predicted this change without any information on real situations. As prey density increases the number taken increases initially and then the predator learns to avoid them (Fig. 4.7). Even with an invertebrate predator feeding on a prey with a defensive behavior, as the prey density increases so the defense becomes more potent, which results in reduced predation.

Tostowaryk (1972) was the first to demonstrate this experimentally using the invertebrate predator *Podisus modestus* (Pentatomidae) on the colonial sawflies *Neodiprion swainei* and *Neodiprion pratti banksianae*. The defensive regurgitate of the prey larvae was described in Chapter 3 (p. 41). As the "colony" size increases so predation decreases (Fig. 4.8). The normal colony ranges in size from 60 individuals at the beginning of the season to 20 to 40 at the end of the season. One of the determinants of colony size may well be the efficiency with which this collective defense can operate. These sawfly species are North American representatives of the diprionid family to which those that Tinbergen studied belong. Tostowaryk's studies help us to understand why the colonial diprionids had such a low prey risk in the presence of great tit predation.

In the light of Holling's work another look at the great tit is worthwhile, this time through the camera lens and eye of Royama, who studied the species in Japan and at Wytham Wood near Oxford, England, while at Oxford University in the Edward Grey Institute. He set up cameras at the back of tit nesting boxes so that each time an adult brought prey to the nest a photograph could be taken automatically of the bird face and prey item. The precision of the photography was so great that each item could be identified, usually to species. A total of 29,000 photographs

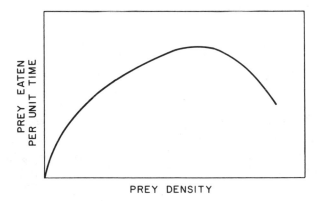

Fig. 4.7 The functional response of a predator to a distasteful prey illustrated by the change in rate of predation with increasing prey density. After Holling 1965.

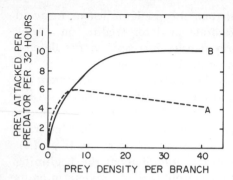

Fig. 4.8 The functional response of third instar nymphs of the pentatomid bug, *Podisus modestus*, to (*a*) normally active second instar larvae of the sawfly, *Neodiprion pratti banksianae*, that showed a defensive behavior in response to predator attack (*b*) larvae of the same age and species immobilized by treatment in hot water and thus incapable of defense. Note that initially the active larvae are more heavily preyed upon as they are more visible to the predator, but as the prey density increases the colonial defensive behavior lowers the predation to less than 50% of that on the defenseless larvae. After Tostowaryk 1972.

on 97 nestling days were collected in 3 years, representing by far the largest and most accurate body of data on the food items of an insectivorous bird so far collected. At the same time Varley and Gradwell, whose work is discussed in Chapter 9, supplied the insect abundance data from field sampling.

Royama (1970) found that the number of prey taken by great tits was not related to the number present in the tree canopy (Fig. 4.9). How could these rather unexpected results be explained? Royama proposed a new model based on (1) the action of natural selection, (2) the principle involved in the evolution of clutch size in birds [Lack (1954) states that the clutch size in nidicolous species, i.e., that rear young in a nest, is adapted to the largest number of young for which the parents can provide enough food], and (3) the hunting efficiency of an individual predator in relation to the density of the prey (i.e., the disk equation of Holling 1959a). These are three widely accepted ideas.

Royama also makes three assumptions: (1) Great tits have developed as efficient a method of hunting as their physiological capacity and their environmental conditions permit; (2) Composition of prey species in the habitat is constantly changing; and (3) Different prey species occupy different niches.

A predator would, therefore, have to search for different prey species in different niches, and so must allocate its hunting time between them. As Royama assumed that the predator tries to maximize its hunting efficiency, the problem is to discover the most productive way for it to allocate its hunting time between the different prey species in different niches. To do this Royama proposed the concept of "profitability" of a prey-species in its niche, where profitability may be measured as the

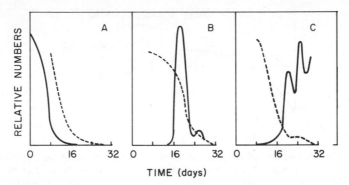

TIME (days)

Fig. 4.9 The abundance of some prey species in oak foliage (dashed line) and the number brought to the nest by great tits (solid line) during the spring in Wytham Wood. The vertical scales are not equivalent for the different sets of data. (*a*) Predation is reduced over 4 days before prey abundance is low; (*b*) predation increases dramatically as the prey larvae mature and pupate. (*c*) Predation is greatest after the abundance of prey has declined. After Royama 1970.

biomass (or calorific or nutritional values) that the predator can collect in a given time in hunting this prey species.

Suppose there are two alternative prey of the same biomass and so on. Then the profitability of the prey species is N_A/T_T in Holling's disk equation terminology—the number caught per unit time. The profitability increases as the density of the prey species in its niche increases, but gradually flattens off (Fig. 4.10). Then suppose that the predator can move freely between two distinct niches A and B where prey species A and B live. In niche B the density of prey B is fixed at N_{oB} and the density of prey A (N_{oA}) is the only variable.

If N_{oA} is much smaller than N_{oB} (see $N_{oA}<N_{oB}$ in Fig. 4.10) there would be comparatively large differences between the profitability of A and B (cf., difference between P_A and P_B). However, the difference would be much less, although niche A would now be the more profitable, if the density of prey A increased to $N_{oA'}$ at which density the profitability becomes only as high as $P_{A'}$ as compared with P_B. If the predator tries to increase its hunting efficiency more time should be spent in niche B when $N_{oA}<N_{oB}$. If, however, N_{oA} increased to N_{oB} then P_A increases to P_B and the predator can take equal profits out of niches A and B. Allotment of time would be a matter of chance, and on average equal. If N_{oA} increased further to $N_{oA'}$ ($>N_{oB}$) and so does profitability P_A to $P_{A'}$ the difference between $P_{A'}$ and P_B is much smaller than that between P_A and P_B. Although more time should naturally be spent in niche A rather than in niche B, the total gain by doing so would be much smaller than

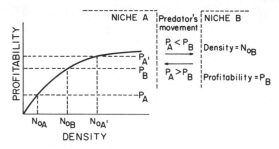

Fig. 4.10 The profitability of niche A in relation to the density of prey species A and species B, and the predator's movements between insect niches. Note that the density of species A changes $(N_{oA} \rightarrow N_{oA'})$ in relation to the fixed density of species B (N_{oB}). The profitability changes, as N_A changes, according to Holling's disk equation. It is assumed that species A and B have the same biomass, palatability, visibility, and defensive reactions. After Royama 1970. Reproduced from *Journal of Animal Ecology* by permission of Blackwell Scientific Publications.

it was when $N_{oA} < N_{oB}$, and more time was spent in niche B. For further increase in N_{oA} there would be hardly any substantial increase in the profitability in niche A, and so a further increase in time spent in niche A would yield no increased profit. Clearly, from the predator's point of view, it is not the density of prey, but its profitability that is important (cf., Fig. 4.9).

As the composition of prey frequently changes the predator has to pay attention to every potential niche to keep itself informed about profitable niches and to reject poor ones. It will stay a short time in poor niches, and a longer time in good ones. However, as no substantial differences in profitability would be appreciated by a predator among niches where the prey density is above a certain level, no further increase in time spent hunting would be observed. Royama concludes that the time spent hunting in a niche (T_T) will be an increasing function of prey density (N_o) but must flatten off (Fig. 4.11). From these curves the relationship of N_A to N_o is developed by substituting values of N_o and T_T in the disk equation, and the curves are all sigmoidal (Fig. 4.12).

If N_A is expressed as a percentage of the prey species concerned in the total number of prey taken by the predator, under Tinbergen's assumption that all other species are put in a single category whose density does not vary, it will yield the trend that Tinbergen in fact observed in his great tits. Therefore the model proposed generates the trend that Tinbergen found, and fits Royama's own data. If the Law of Parsimony, the principle that no more causes should be assumed than will account for the effect, is followed, then Royama's explanation of the sigmoidal response by vertebrate predators, being the more frugal in its assumptions,

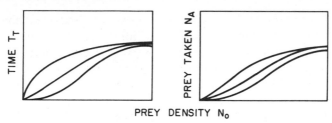

Fig. 4.11   The time spent hunting by a predator in relation to prey density. The three examples are the possible shapes of curves representing T_T as an increasing function of N_o. After Royama 1970. Reproduced from *Journal of Animal Ecology* by permission of Blackwell Scientific Publications.

Fig. 4.12   Relationship between the number of prey taken and prey density calculated from Fig. 4.11 using the disk equation. After Royama 1970. Reproduced from *Journal of Animal Ecology* by permission of Blackwell Scientific Publications.

may seem more appealing than Tinbergen's. However, Alcock (1973b) showed that redwinged blackbirds can learn where they are likely to find food and what food they are likely to find and these complementary processes support Royama's and Tinbergen's hypotheses respectively. Even parasitoids may learn to use a similar pair of clues in searching for hosts (Taylor 1974).

Croze also studied at Oxford University under the direction of Niko Tinbergen, Luuk Tinbergen's younger brother. Croze (1970) was critical of Royama's thesis and his comments supporting Tinbergen's search image hypothesis should be consulted. But Croze, who studied the searching behavior of the carrion crow (*Corvus corone*), provided some interesting additional information. He found that there were two important aspects to the crow's searching behavior, area restriction and reward rate. Once a crow found prey it tended to search more closely and in a more closely defined area, and as long as it was rewarded fairly frequently it would stay in the vicinity. Similar behavior has been observed by Smith (1974) in blackbirds and in thrushes searching for earthworms. This compares with Royama's ideas on niche searching and profitability, and the behavior will have an impact on prey populations. One response of the prey population is that a well-spaced dispersion pattern evolves (Fig. 4.13). As the prey population became more scattered the intercatch distance increased disproportionately to the interprey distance. Increased distance between prey increases the searching time and so reduces the predator's functional response.

Then Croze asked what happens in terms of predator behavior and prey survival when the predator looks for more than one thing at a time? The question arose from the observation that many camouflaged animals are polymorphic for color and pattern (Sheppard 1958) and that visual polymorphism may cause a reduction of mortality due to predation (see references for polymorphism in Table 4.2, and Chapter 10 on ecological genetics). Croze tested experimentally the idea that polymorphism increased survival of crow prey. Trimorphic populations suffered far less predation than monomorphic. A mean of 10.5 shells in polymorphic populations and only 3.5 shells in monomorphic populations were left by the crows searching among 27 regularly arranged shells; that is, a morph had a threefold selective advantage when occurring as one third of a polymorphic population. In another experiment it took a crow 2.5 minutes to find the ninth shell in a monomorphic population and 5 minutes to find the ninth shell in a polymorphic population (Fig. 4.14). The crow gave up the search when it took longer than 5 minutes to discover a shell. This occurred after the thirteenth shell in the monomorphic population, and after the ninth shell in the polymorphic population.

Croze's conclusions on the ecological consequences of predation were as follows: (1) the first line of defense is camouflage, (2) area-restricted search increases the selection pressure for a prey behavior that scatters their population, and (3) the specificity of the searching behavior (search image) selects for (a) polymorphism within a camouflaged prey species and (b) divergent coloration and behavior of sympatric species.

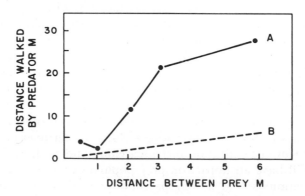

Fig. 4.13 The relationship between the distance walked between prey items by a carrion crow (a) and the distance between the prey (b). As the prey distance increases the crow spends disproportionately more time searching for prey. After Croze 1970.

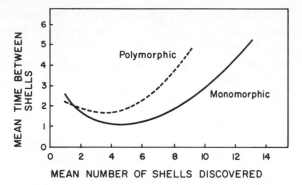

Fig. 4.14 Mean time taken between the discovery of successive shells when a crow searched in a population of 27 shells, each shell set 12 m from the next. Each experiment was concluded when the crow gave up the search when it took more than 5 minutes to discover the prey item. After Croze 1970.

There are some cases in which a good estimate of the adaptive advantage to protective devices can be obtained. In Tinbergen's study, *Panolis* filled 33% of the great tit's diet and *Diprion frutetorum* 3% at a certain time in the year. For every one *D. frutetorum* taken, 11 *Panolis* were taken; thus *Panolis* was 11 times more vulnerable to great tit predation than was the sawfly. If it is assumed that the populations of these two species were equal and that the great tit ate the equivalent of one complete population, it follows that 97% of the sawfly population survived and 67% of the *Panolis* population survived. Or for every 100 surviving sawfly about 70 *Panolis* survived, a 30% advantage to the sawfly. In the case of *Diprion pini* larvae, with colonial defense and distasteful nature, only 0.1% of the diet was filled by this species. For every one *D. pini* taken, 330 *Panolis* were taken, and conversely, using the same assumptions as for *D. frutetorum*, for every 100 *D. pini* that survived 67 *Panolis* survived. In Croze's work an individual in a trimorphic population had a threefold advantage over one in a monomorphic population. For every 100 individuals in a trimorphic population that survived, 33 in a monomorphic population survived. In Holling's example given earlier (p. 63) the same prey in the presence of a more palatable species (sunflower seeds) survived 30% better than in the presence of a less palatable species (dog biscuits).

Blest (1957a) provides an interesting example of how predators differ in their response to prey defense. The nymphalid butterfly, *Aglais urticae*, has the underside of the wings cryptic and the dorsal surface with a bright brown and orange pattern. At rest the butterflies sit with their wings closed, and when disturbed they suddenly open their wings which elicits an escape response on the part of the predator. Blest gently removed the scales of some butterflies so that their pattern was gone and then tested the difference in predation. The normal butterflies had a 32% advantage over the treated butterflies when yellow buntings were the predator and a 63% advantage with reed buntings. The butterfly, *Nymphalis io,* also responds to predation by rapidly lowering its wings, but this species exposes four eyespots on its wings that mimic the vertebrate eye rather closely. Blest (1957a) removed spots from some of these individuals and tested the predation by yellow buntings. The number of overt escape responses by the predator was 31 for spotless and 128 for normal individuals, or a 76% advantage to the spotted individuals.

For the melanic peppered moth *Biston betularia* in industrial areas, Kettlewell (1956) found that the advantage over the normal white moth with black spots was about 52%, and in the unpolluted country the survival of the nonmelanic was 66% better than that of the melanic form. These figures were calculated from release and recapture data. Where actual bird predation was observed in unpolluted areas the typical form had a six to one advantage over the melanic form, or an 86% advantage.

Finally Roeder and Treat (1961) found that noctuid moths detect the ultrasonic chirps of the searching bat and perform a protean display, so escaping predation. They studied 402 field encounters between bats and moths and recorded the survival of reactors and nonreactors to the bats' chirps. The advantage to evasive action proved to be 40% (meaning for every 100 reacting moths that survived, there were only 60 surviving nonreactors).

The frequency of very high selective advantages for defense in insects is noteworthy. This helps in understanding how so many incredibly intricate defenses have evolved. The speed of selection and adaptation can be particularly rapid in insects where fecundities are frequently high, with correspondingly high mortalities, and populations are large with high variability between individuals. In Table 4.2 are listed some of the responses to predation pressure that can be seen in insects. These are grouped according to how their defense is likely to influence population dispersion. Unpalatable or noxious species will benefit from a situation where the avoidance reaction of the predator is reinforced before enough time elapses for its learned response to be forgotten. Thus dense populations are likely to be an advantage. Conversely, as Croze points out, any palatable species should be dispersed widely to prevent a predator from forming a search image for these species or from increasing its efficiency in finding prey by any means at all. Likewise if a species is palatable but has an intimidation display, the prey should also be well dispersed. Here

Table 4.2 Some responses to the high selection pressure of predation—particularly vertebrate predation. (References provide some background for each type of protection, not necessarily support for this ecological classification of protection).

---

1. Protective strategies that result in selection for contagious distribution of prey—distasteful or otherwise noxious species.
    (a) Aposematic or warning coloration—advertizing distasteful nature (Cott 1940).
    (b) Chemical defenses (Eisner 1970).
    (c) Müllerian mimics (Remington 1963, Rettenmeyer 1970).
    (d) Intimidation displays and chemical defense, for example, colonial sawflies (Prop 1960, Tostowaryk 1972).
2. Protective strategies that result in selection for increased inter-prey distances —palatable species.
    (a) Crypsis and catalepsis (frozen posture usually with appendages retracted) (Thayer 1909, de Ruiter 1952, 1956, Hinton 1955, Cott 1940, Portmann 1959, Keiper 1969, Sargent and Keiper 1969, Robinson 1969).
    (b) Intimidation displays (Blest 1957a, b).
3. Protective strategies that permit, but do not necessarily select for contagious distribution of prey—palatable species.
    (a) Polymorphism (Cain and Sheppard 1954a, b, Clarke 1960, 1962a, Sheppard 1952).
    (b) Batesian mimicry (Remington 1963, Rettenmeyer 1970).
    (c) Protean displays (Humphries and Driver 1970)
    (d) Phenological separation of prey from predator (Waldbauer and Sheldon 1971).
    (e) Cellular defense reactions (against internal parasitoids only) (Salt 1970).

---

there is no factor that will reinforce the predator's escape response, so that each defensive action must come to the predator as a completely unexpected stimulus. If the predator can learn to expect the response and learns the prey is palatable, the local population is doomed. A third group of defenses exists where selection may work in either direction, but here the direction does not depend on the type of defense the prey species had. Robinson (1969) proposed an alternative and valuable scheme of classification based on the primary defenses evolved by visually hunted prey.

Thus the density of insect populations may well depend on the predation pressure they are exposed to and the defensive mechanism that has evolved in this coevolutionary process. But this statement must be re-examined in Chapters 5 and 9, when the effect of predation on the regulation of prey populations is discussed.

Chapter 5

PREDATOR AND PREY POPULATION DYNAMICS

The characteristics of a general predator have been reviewed by Salt (1967) and a verbal description summarizes predator characteristics discussed in Chapter 4 and expands concepts about predation. Note that although Salt worked on *Woodruffia*, a protozoan predator, his review refers to predation in general. Pimlott and Errington, whose insights I also refer to, worked on vertebrates, and their general concepts interlock well with those of Salt.

1. Hunting is usually initiated by hunger and stopped by satiation.
2. Hunting site is determined primarily by inherited behavioral characteristics although past experience on high concentrations of prey may modify these reactions.
3. Searching rate is a product of the rate of movement of the predator relative to that of the prey, and the reactive perceptual field of the predator. Both values may be influenced by internal physiological states such as hunger, by external physical conditions, by prior experience of capture, and by prey characteristics such as size and color.
4. When selection of an individual prey animal is made from a group, the different or conspicuous individual is usually attacked. (One might wonder, then, how warning coloration can evolve; see Chapter 10 for discussion.)
5. Predators do not attack all age or size classes of a prey species with equal frequency. Usually some size or age classes of the prey are immune. Pimlott (1967) explains that wolf predation is not the result of random contacts but that the wolves actually test the ability of the prey to escape by driving an ungulate herd and singling out the least mobile animals. This is probably true of many predators, both vertebrate and invertebrate, that test the defensive reaction of their prey. Thus among ungulates, wolves prey primarily on the young of the year and on animals in older classes. Predation is heaviest on the young during the summer, but is less intensive in the winter when old animals are vulnerable. Thus predation pressure reduces the reproductive capacity of the prey very little.
    Errington (1946, 1967) found that Norway rats, California ground squirrels, rabbits, mice, and muskrats are heavily preyed on by certain predators. This predation tended to be centered on individuals or parts of populations forced to live at a disadvantage. Rats may overflow good habitats into inhospitable habitats—into places poor in food where they may be forced to resort to hazardous routines to stay alive. For this reason, after a life spent studying predation in vertebrates, Errington (1967) wrote: "I believe that the population

effect of predation is often greatly overrated." However, it should not be forgotten that his studies were mostly on territorial prey; that is they probably had the following characteristics:

(*a*) General intolerance to crowding.
(*b*) Obvious habitat selection of the most favorable areas.
(*c*) Older, dominant males defend the best territories and younger males must occupy marginal areas, thus supporting Salt's general statement.

6. Although some predator species attack only one prey species, most predators subsist on several kinds of prey. Frequency of individuals in a diet is determined by the following factors, in order of importance:

(*a*) Frequency of species in the environment.
(*b*) Innate preferences of the predator.
(*c*) Competition with other kinds of predators.
(*d*) Profitability of prey, or the inverse of Tinbergen's prey risk.

7. Rate of capture by an individual predator is a product of the following:

(*a*) All of the disk equation components (see Chapter 4).
(*b*) Percentage of attacks that are successful. For most predators the degree of success is lower than usually supposed. One success in two attacks is a high value, and the average is about one in ten.

8. Responses by the predator to changes in prey density are determined by food habits of the predator:

(*a*) If it is an obligate feeder on a single species of prey, the numbers of each population oscillate with predator highs following prey highs (cf., arctic cycles mentioned in Chapter 9). Emigration and immigration by the predator and exemption from attack of certain life history stages or size classes of the prey contribute to the stability in the oscillations. (See also discussion of Nicholson and Bailey, and Leslie and Gower models later in this chapter).
(*b*) If the predator feeds on more than one species of prey, changes in density of one prey species bring about a shift in the per-

centage composition in the diet of the predator. (Later in this chapter and in Chapter 19 the importance of predation in maintaining stability of populations and diversity in communities is discussed.)

9. Predators react to changes in their own density in the same fashion as other animals by competing for a common requisite. This has been largely forgotten in discussions on biological control, for example, but see Chapter 12. In social predators, moderate densities increase the efficiency of hunting. Cannibalism is a highly effective density regulating mechanism in predators (see Chapter 16).
10. Competition between predators of two or more species for a common prey reduces the efficiency of both and may cause shifts in the percentage composition of the diet of both. This competition assumes its most extreme form when one of the competing species also consumes the other for food. However, Pimlott (1967) mentions that intensive utilization of prey animals that are captured is a characteristic of wolf predation, suggesting an essential economy on the part of predators that would tend to reduce competition.

A consideration follows of how predator and prey populations interact with each other numerically. Royama's (1971) comparative study of predation models shows how the various models discussed here are related.

Lotka (1925) and Volterra (1926) were the first to make any concrete predictions on predator–prey population interactions and reached the same conclusion independently. Their assumptions are as follows:

1. Animals move at random.
2. Every encounter with a prey results in a capture (cf., Salt 1967 above), and every prey that is captured is eaten. This is irrespective of densities of populations of predators and prey.
3. The populations of both predator and prey have all the qualities necessary for them to conform to the logistic theory—growth rate accelerates until a limiting factor causes deceleration.

Logistic theory is described in Chapter 7 but part of the theory uses the Malthusian exponential growth formula. The rate of increase of a single species of prey living by itself in unlimited space is

$$\frac{dN'}{dt} = r'_m N'$$

where r_m' = maximum rate of increase per individual (birth rate), and N' = density of prey population. In the absence of prey, predators would die of starvation. Therefore, the rate of decrease of a population by deaths—or the negative rate of increase—is

$$\frac{dN''}{dt} = d''N''$$

where d'' = death rate, which is negative, and N'' = density of predator population. If both predator and prey are living together in a limited space, r_m' will be reduced by an amount that depends on the density of the population of predators [i.e., $(r_m' - ?)N'$]. Also the negative coefficient d'' will be increased by an amount dependent on the density of the population of the prey species [i.e., $(d'' + ?)N''$]. Because of the assumptions made by Lotka and Volterra the changes in r_m' will be proportional to N'' [i.e., $(r_m' - ?N'')N'$] and those in d'' will be proportional to N' [i.e., $(d'' + ?N')N''$]. Therefore the two equations become

for prey populations $\qquad \dfrac{dN'}{dt} = (r_m' - C'N'')N'$

and

for predator populations $\qquad \dfrac{dN''}{dt} = (d'' + C''N')N''$

where C' = constant: Volterra regarded it to be a measure of the ability of the prey to defend itself (cf., R_A' of Tinbergen), and C'' = constant: Volterra regarded it as a measure of the effectiveness of offense of the predator (also included in R_A' of Tinbergen). The equations provide a "periodic solution" in that the trends in densities of populations of prey and predator change direction in a systematic way (Fig. 5.1). Volterra called it the law of periodic cycle.

Quite small quality changes in animals result in the curve cutting either the abscissa or ordinate (in the phase diagram Fig. 5.1b) after several oscillations of increasing amplitude, that is, extermination of one species, leaving the other in complete possession of the field. If this happens to be the predator it must switch food or die out also. Gause (1934) called this a relaxation oscillation to distinguish it from the classical oscillation in which the closed loop indicates that both predator and prey live together indefinitely.

Nicholson and Bailey (1935) criticized the Lotka-Volterra equations on three major points:

1. Lotka and Volterra assumed the "population reaction" when pred-

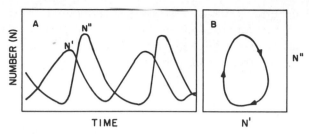

Fig. 5.1 The population oscillations of prey (N') and predator (N'') predicted by the Lotka-Volterra equations. (*a*) Numbers plotted against time. (*b*) Phase diagram indicating perpetual coexistence of prey and predator. From H. G. Andrewartha and L. C. Birch. *The distribution and abundance of animals*, published by The University of Chicago Press. Copyright 1954 by the University of Chicago Press. All rights reserved.

ator encounters prey is instantaneous. This is not so and the time that elapses before the result of the "encounter" is evident may in some cases be as long as a generation of the predator. This is particularly true of parasitoids where oviposition of an egg on the prey does not show a population effect—in terms of adult predators—until that egg has hatched and the larva has fed, pupated, and emerged as an adult. Therefore there is an important lag effect between prey and predator populations.
2. They assumed that each individual in prey and predator populations is exactly equivalent to every other individual of the same species. No allowance was made for different age groups; for example, egg, larva, pupa, and adult.
3. Lotka and Volterra used calculus in their arguments that describe continuous changes in populations.

Nicholson and Bailey proposed a new model, with parasitoids in mind; that is, there is a 1:1 ratio between predator and prey numbers. Their assumptions should be compared with the qualities of predators and prey discussed in Chapter 4, earlier in this chapter, and in Chapter 12.

1. Prey is distributed uniformly in a uniform environment.
2. Ease with which prey can be found does not vary with density of population.
3. Predator population searches at random.
4. Appetites of predators (i.e., capacity for oviposition) are insatiable, irrespective of prey population density.
5. Predator has an "areal range" = constant = distance traveled during lifetime while searching times twice the distance from which it can

perceive a prey. That is the predator can see in both directions as it hunts; thus areal range is equivalent to the area searched in a life-time.

6.   Predator has an "area of discovery" = constant =

$$\frac{\text{number of prey found by predator during lifetime}}{\text{number of prey in "areal range" of the predator}}$$

This measures the proportion of prey found in the total area searched, or the efficiency of the predator in finding its prey.

With this information the number of prey in the next generation can be calculated using the formula

$$pa = \log_e \frac{u_i}{u_{i+1}}$$

where p = parasitoid population density, a = area of discovery, u_i = initial host density, and u_{i+1} = host density in next generation.

For a parasitoid species with a given area of discovery there is a par-ticular density at which it effectively searches a fraction of the environ-ment equal to the fraction of hosts that are surplus, that is, the interest from the population not the capital, and at this density exactly the sur-plus of hosts is destroyed. Also there is a particular density of a host-species (capital) that is just sufficient to maintain this density of para-sitoids from generation to generation. When the densities of the inter-acting animals have these values they must remain constant indefinitely in a constant environment—the steady state.

The slightest departure on either side of the steady state produces oscillations. When age distribution, or the lag in predator response, is ignored, oscillations continue indefinitely with a constant amplitude just as Volterra and Lotka predicted. When age distribution is taken into account oscillations increase in amplitude with time as in a relaxation oscillation (Fig. 5.2). If the density of the host is slightly above the steady-state value and is in the process of being reduced by a parasitoid, when the host reaches its steady density, the density of the parasitoid is the result of the host density in the preceding generation, when it was above the steady state. This is where age distribution is important. There are more than sufficient parasitoids to destroy the surplus hosts, and the host density is still further reduced in the following generation. As a result the densities of the interacting animals should oscillate about their steady values—with increasing amplitude.

This does not actually appear in nature. Nicholson and Bailey con-cluded that the probable ultimate effect of increasing oscillations is the breaking up the species population into numerous small widely sep-

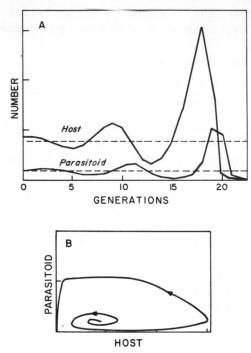

Fig. 5.2 The population oscillations of host and parasitoid numbers predicted by the Nicholson-Bailey equation. (*a*) numbers plotted against time. (*b*) Phase diagram indicating increasing oscillations. Steady densities are represented by dashed lines. After Nicholson 1933, by permission of Blackwell Scientific Publications.

arated groups that wax and wane and then disappear, to be replaced by new groups in previously unoccupied situations. While this idea is currently an important one in evolutionary theory, Nicholson and Bailey could hardly justify this deduction from a mathematical model that assumes at the beginning that animals are distributed evenly over a uniform area.

Tinbergen and Klomp (1960) took a more pragmatic approach to the Nicholson and Bailey model by testing how variable factors would change the response of the populations from one of increasing oscillation amplitude. Some of their conclusions follow:

1. If it is assumed that the reproductive rate of the host is sensitive to density and decreases with density increase, naturally the oscillations cannot be so violent. The result is regular fluctuations or slight damping of oscillations depending on the extent of the sensitivity of fecundity to density.

2. Egg production of parasitoids is likely to be finite. Therefore, the area of discovery is likely to decrease with host density at values above a critical one at which eggs cannot be produced rapidly enough. Therefore, the amplitude of oscillations will increase.
3. If mortality is dependent on the density (see also p. 78) of the population the same result may occur in two ways:

    (a) If parasitoid mortality is dependent on parasitoid density and increases with density then oscillation amplitude is decreased.
    (b) If host mortality is dependent on host density and increases with density this also leads to damped oscillations.

4. Where percent predation increases with host density in a sigmoidal fashion, damped oscillations are generated, provided that at intermediate densities more than 25% of the prey is taken. Their major conclusion is that the type 3 functional response (although they did not use this term) can cause damping of the oscillations that are inherent in the host-parasitoid model of Nicholson and Bailey. Therefore, birds and small mammals appear to be important factors in the balance of herbivorous insect and parasitoid populations (for further discussion see the population regulation effect of Holling's type 3 functional response later in this chapter). It has been found since, however, that parasitoids may also show a sigmoid response (see p. 63).

The two models so far considered are deterministic, and yet random processes obviously affect the predator–prey relationship in nature; thus a stochastic model may be more realistic. Leslie and Gower (1960) have developed such a model. They determined that, given large populations of prey, although all prey individuals were accessible to predators, the two populations would fluctuate irregularly around the stable state once the equilibrium level had been reached. Extinction of either species was extremely unlikely (a mean of once in every 1.4×10^{11} units of time). As numbers were reduced, extinction became more likely, although if a certain proportion of the prey was unavailable to predation (optimally around 20%) then stability of the system was very much increased. Prey may become unavailable because of heterogeneity of the environment (cf., Errington 1946, 1967, and the critique of Tinbergen's work in Chapter 4) or because of predator characteristics (Salt 1967, where *Woodruffia* encysts when prey reaches a certain low, unprofitable density).

Finally, if the rate of change of the predator population increases with increasing density (see p. 91), a very realistic possibility, so that predator

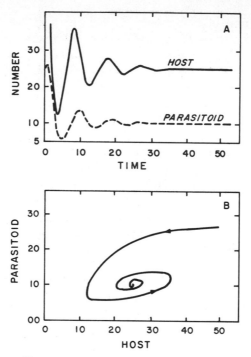

Fig. 5.3 Damping oscillations predicted by the Leslie-Gower model when the rate of change of the parasitoid is density dependent (see p. 85 for definition). (*a*) Numbers plotted against time. (*b*) Phase diagram indicating decreasing oscillations. After Pielou 1969.

populations respond more slowly at low prey populations than at high prey populations, using the Leslie-Gower model, a damping of oscillations toward equilibrium results (Fig. 5.3, see also Pielou 1969). Holling and Ewing (1971, see Holling 1968, for similar discussion) have also presented models that predict damping of predator–prey oscillations where "a variety of behavioral mechanisms are included that tend to tune the system more to existing conditions than to the past. By so doing, the instability produced by the memory of the system is counteracted." That is, lag in predator response is compensated for by behavioral adjustments.

Hassell and Varley (1969) were familiar with the biology of parasitoids. From several published accounts of the efficiency of parasitoids in finding their hosts, they showed that Nicholson and Bailey's "area of discovery" (*a*) was far from constant for real parasitoid situations (Fig. 5.4), as Andrewartha and Birch (1954) had done before them. For several species

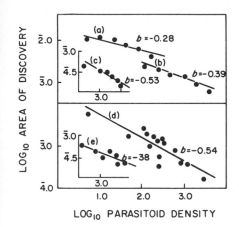

Fig. 5.4 Relationships between searching efficiency ($\log_{10}$ area of discovery) and density ($\log_{10}$ parasitoid density) of five species of parasitoid. After Hassell and Varley 1969.

and over several orders of magnitude, log a was linearly related to parasitoid density (p) in the following manner:

$$\log a = \log Q - (m \cdot \log p)$$

where a = area of discovery, p = parasitoid density, Q = "quest constant" and m = "mutual interference constant." Both Q and m are calculated empirically from the regression line. Therefore the factor $m \cdot \log p$ would increase with density and a would decline with density. Thus a in the Nicholson and Bailey model should be replaced by the density sensitive Q/p^m. The new "parasite quest" theory model becomes, by substitution

$$\log_e \frac{u_i}{u_{i+1}} = Q p^{1-m}$$

where u_i = initial host density and u_{i+1} = host density in next generation.

In this new model the parasitoid population has a direct density-dependent factor built into its behavior. [A density-dependent factor is discussed in Chapter 9 (p. 170)—it is any factor the effect of which increases as a percentage of the population as the population increases in density.] The greater the value of the mutual interference constant m, the greater will be the tendency for the host-parasitoid model to stabilize (Fig. 5.5). As m approaches Q, the parasitoid's behavior conforms more and more closely to the Nicholsonian system and the more unstable the interaction becomes. The more that is learned about parasitoids the more it is realized how sensitive they are to the presence of others, but this topic is treated in Chapters 9 and 12 on population dynamics and biological control.

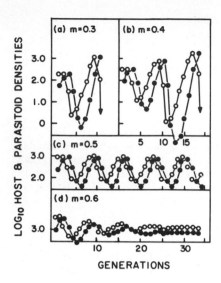

Fig. 5.5 Population oscillations of host (○) and parasitoid (●) predicted by the Hassell-Varley model with the mutual interference constant, m, increasing from 0.3 in (a) to 0.6 in (d). After Hassell and Varley 1969.

Gause (1934) was the first to test the Lotka-Volterra model experimentally. He used two protozoa: *Didinium nasutum*, the predator, and *Paramecium caudatum*, its prey. Reproduction is by binary fission; thus Gause made a clever choice, since the response of the predator to feeding is close to being instantaneous. Thus the food chain was bacteria → *Paramecium* → *Didinium*.

In his first experiment Gause used a homogenous microcosm without immigration of prey or predator. The predator rapidly discovered all the prey and *Paramecium* and *Didinium* went extinct, but the bacteria remained abundant (Fig. 5.6a). The Lotka-Volterra model was not supported.

Next Gause left a refuge present in the form of a sediment in the medium where *Paramecium* were safe from attack by predators. Here the result was more unpredictable. In some microcosms all prey were devoured; in others the prey escaped from the predator and the predator went extinct (Fig. 5.6b); and in others the populations of predator and prey coexisted for several days. Gause then resorted to a final effort to obtain oscillations in predator and prey populations. He did not use a refuge but artificial immigration, one of each species every third day. The result was oscillations that lasted variable lengths of time (Fig. 5.6c), But Gause pointed out that at the low population levels between peaks definite prediction on the outcome could not be made because in his words "multiplicity of causes acquires great significance. . . . As a result it

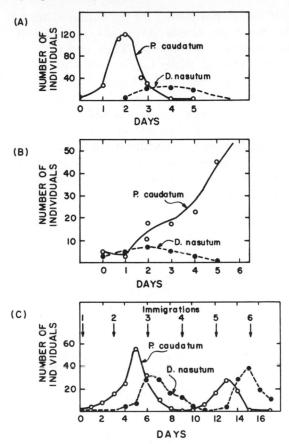

Fig. 5.6 Gause's three experiments testing the Lotka-Volterra equations, (a) in a homogeneous microcosm, (b) in a microcosm with a refuge from predation, (c) with immigration of one of each species at times indicated. After Gause 1934.

turns out to be impossible to forecast exactly the development in every individual microcosm and we are again compelled to deal only with the probabilities of change." That is, a stochastic model is needed, not a deterministic model. Thus the Lotka-Volterra model was not supported by Gause's experiments. Luckinbill (1973) examined a similar system and obtained coexistence for about 100 generations of prey by maintaining food of prey as a limiting factor at peak prey densities.

Probably DeBach and Smith who published in 1941 were the first to test the Nicholson-Bailey model experimentally (Note, Gause did not test a parasitoid-host situation so that although Gause knew of Nicholson's 1933 paper, he was not testing the Nicholsonian model). They used as subjects the house fly *Musca domestica* and a chalcid parasitoid *Nasonia* (=*Mormoniella*) *vitripennis*. They compared what was predicted by the Nicholson and Bailey model with what they found in their own cultures over seven generations (Fig. 5.7). The fit was remarkably good as far as it went, but it is not powerful evidence in support of the model. However the experiment does show that oscillations appear to be an inherent component of the predator-prey interaction although Wangersky and Cunningham (1957) predicted from the results that by the tenth generation the fluctuations would settle into a limit cycle rather than continue in oscillations of increasing magnitude (see also Andrewartha and Birch 1954 for further discussion of this experiment). Burnett (1958) studied a similar system and observed increasing oscillations until extinction occurred in the twenty-first generation (see Varley et al. 1973, for discussion).

Varley (1947) claimed from his field data on the knapweed gallfly (*Urophora jaceana*) that he had good supporting evidence for the Nicholson-Bailey model. He was the first to test the model in the field. He asked: "What factors control the population density of the knapweed gallfly in nature, and how do they operate?" Varley argued that controlling factors must be density dependent—that is, they must act more severely when the population density is high, and less severely when the population density is below the average. He discounted crowding as a factor as populations were never high enough in the flower heads of the knapweed. This left as factors two parasitoids *Eurytoma curta* and

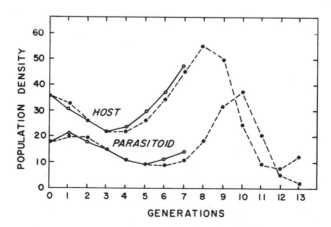

Fig. 5.7 The predictions of the Nicholson-Bailey model (dashed lines) tested with populations of the host *Musca domestica* and the parasitoid *Nasonia vitripennis* (solid lines). After DeBach and Smith 1941.

Habrocytus trypetae, although the second parasitoid was hardly numerous enough to be very effective. Thus Varley paid most attention to *Eurytoma curta.*

Although Varley claimed a striking agreement between calculated values using the Nicholson-Bailey model and those observed in the field, the data leave doubt in one's mind. For example under certain conditions (92% density independent mortality) the calculated density of gall flies was 3.3 and observed values were 6.9 and 2.0/m² in adjacent years. Likewise, the calculated number of available larvae was 60 and the observed values were 147 and 28/m² in adjacent years. By using a fixed area of discovery for the parasites Varley actually countered his own argument that regulation is achieved by density-dependent mechanisms. Because of Hassell and Varley's study, the changing area of discovery is recognized now as a crucial element in the stability of the parasitoid-prey interaction. Andrewartha and Birch (1954) have made an incisive criticism of Varley's data in relation to the Nicholson-Bailey model.

Although we should not accept Varley's claim of validation of the Nicholson-Bailey model in his field studies, we must not deny him the credit for leading insect ecologists into a new way of looking at insect populations. It is hard to find a field study of insect populations that predates Varley's (studies on German forest insects provide examples, e.g., Schwerdtfeger 1941). It is still harder to find a study with so much attention to detail, and so much understanding of the organisms involved. Varley championed the quantitative approach to field studies on insect populations and has remained prominent in the field to this day.

Huffaker (1958) at the University of California at Berkeley resorted to laboratory studies to evaluate the basic relationships between predator and prey populations. He employed the six-spotted mite *Eotetranychus sexmaculatus* which feeds on oranges and its predator mite, *Typhlodromus occidentalis.* By setting out oranges and rubber balls on a tray he could alter the absolute amount of food and the dispersion of that food. In the simplest universe he had 4 large areas of food for prey (1/2 orange area each) grouped at adjacent, joined positions—a 2-orange feeding area on a 4-orange dispersion. Predators were introduced 11 days after the prey. The predator could discover the prey so easily that the prey were reduced in numbers to such a low level that the predators starved and became extinct, and the prey slowly increased (Fig. 5.8). Huffaker therefore increased the complexity of the environment by reducing the size of each food item and diluting their density in the universe. Even with small areas of food (1/10 orange area) for prey, alternating with 20 foodless positions, a 2-orange feeding area on a 20-orange dispersion, the predator and prey did not coexist. Finally, he used 120 oranges, each

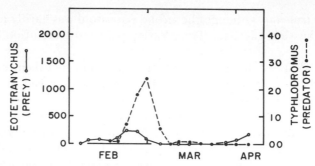

Fig. 5.8   The results of Huffaker's test of the coexistence of a predator and a prey using a 2-orange feeding area on a 4-orange dispersion. After Huffaker 1958.

with 1/20 orange area available as food, a 6-orange feeding area on a 120-orange dispersion. Around the oranges he made a complex maze of petroleum jelly partial barriers so there was no easy access from one orange to another. He introduced one 6-spotted mite on each of 120 oranges and the 27 female predators were added 5 days later, one on each of 27 oranges dispersed evenly throughout the universe. He also added little posts from which prey would disperse by silken thread and a fan was supplied to produce a small air current. The predator was unable to disperse in this way.

Huffaker actually obtained three oscillations of predator and prey when finally the predator went extinct because of a shortage of prey (Fig. 5.9). Huffaker says, "However, by utilizing the large and more complex environment so as to make less likely the predator's contact with the prey at all positions at once . . . , it was possible to produce three waves or oscillations in density of predators and prey. That these waves represent a direct and reciprocal predator-prey dependence is obvious." Even in this elegant experiment, coexistence was not achieved simply by increasing environmental heterogeneity. The food quality of the prey de-

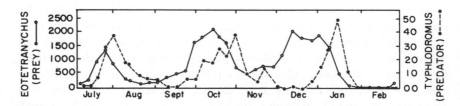

Fig. 5.9   Results of Huffaker's final experiment when the prey and predator coexisted for three oscillations in a complex environment. After Huffaker 1958.

teriorated with increasing mite density, and acted in a density-dependent manner.

Luckinbill's (1973) studies identify food limitation of the prey as an important factor in producing limit cycles in predator and prey populations which may be achieved even in the absence of spatial heterogeneity or greater prey dispersal ability. However, Huffaker's work demonstrates the importance of four factors that may contribute to the stability of predator–prey interactions:

1. Environmental heterogeneity.
2. Spatial relationships of predator and prey.
3. Relative dispersal rates of predator and prey.
4. The influence of the change in quality of prey food.

Type 2 and 3 functional responses were introduced in Chapter 4 and describe the response of a single predator to changes in prey density. However, this individual response also has a population effect. As prey density increases, each individual increases its consumption of food; food gathering becomes less expensive energetically and more energy can be channeled into reproduction. The reproductive rate increases and, therefore, the numbers in the population increase—a numerical response. Also, migrating predators will tend to stay longer in areas of high prey density, and this will result in population aggregations in relation to prey density—another aspect of the numerical response. In addition, Murdoch (1971) has argued that predators may show a developmental response because they eat more prey at higher densities and grow more as a result, and then kill more prey because of their larger size.

Therefore, the total response of predators to increasing prey density involves five factors: (1) individual functional response; (2) increased reproduction in the population; (3) increased immigration; (4) developmental response; and (5) predator functional response to predator density. Evaluating the relative importance of each of these factors in field populations of predators and prey should prove to be challenging.

The population regulation effects of Holling's type 2 and type 3 functional responses should now be considered (see Holling 1965) to discover which type of predation is likely to produce the greatest prey population stability. The percent mortality necessary to stabilize the prey popula-

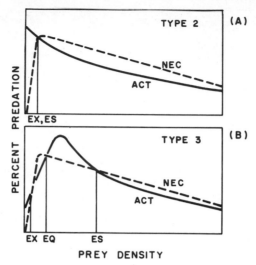

Fig. 5.10   Population regulation effects of Holling's type 2 (*a*) and type 3 (*b*) functional responses. *NEC* = percent mortality necessary to stabilize populations (cf., Lewontin's (1965) reproductive function in Chapter 7), *ACT* = actual percent predation, *EX* = threshold density for population extinction, *EQ* = equilibrium density, *ES* = threshold density for population escape. After Holling 1965.

tion (*NEC*) will vary considerably with prey density. It is equivalent to the potential for reproductive success of the population, or the mortality needed to counteract this potential. Reproduction will be very low when mates are too far apart for a high mating rate, and high at moderate densities—declining as shortages of resources increase (Fig. 5.10).

In Holling's type 2 response the percent mortality will constantly decline as prey density increases (cf., Fig. 5.11). Therefore, the result of the functional response can be superimposed on the reproductive potential curve (*NEC*) (Fig. 5.10a). An unstable equilibrium is developed at *EX*, *ES*. At prey densities below *EX* predation will always be greater than the prey can support, and extinction results. At prey densities above *EX* predation is never sufficient to stabilize the prey population, and the population can escape from the controlling influence of predation and can erupt. This is the escape equilibrium (*ES*). Here no feedback mechanism is likely to stabilize the population.

The situation is different however where the type 3 response is involved. The percent predation begins to increase as the prey density increases (Fig. 5.12). When this response is superimposed on the *NEC* curve (Fig. 5.10b) we see that a stable equilibrium (*EQ*) is developed. Below *EX*, the prey population goes to extinction because of the high predation rate, higher than that needed to stabilize the population.

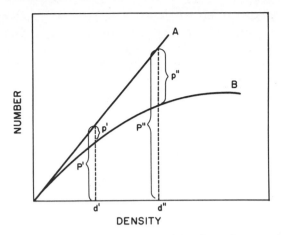

Fig. 5.11 The decline in percent mortality resulting from the type 2 functional response. At low prey densities (d') the percentage of prey not taken $(p' \times 100)/P'$ is small,
but as prey density increases (d'') the percentage not taken $(p'' \times 100)/P''$ increases. A =
number of prey available, B = number of prey taken.

Above *ES*, actual predation is too low to stabilize the population so that
the prey escapes from the influence of predation and erupts. Above *EX*,
however, the prey population will increase because predation pressure
is lower than necessary but it can only increase to *EQ* when predation
becomes a controlling influence. And below *ES* the population can de-

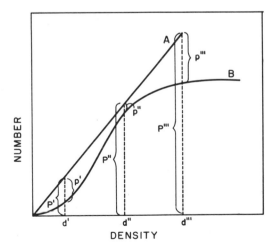

Fig. 5.12 The change in percent mortality resulting from the type 3 functional
response. Percent predation is low at low densities (d'), high at moderate densities (d'')
and low at high densities (d'''). Notation as in Fig. 5.11.

cline only as far as *EQ*. So the point *EQ* represents a stable equilibrium density. Below it, reproduction is greater than predation; above it, predation is greater than reproduction.

Therefore it appears that the type 3 response is more likely to improve the stability of a prey population than is the type 2 response. Tinbergen and Klomp (1960) also concluded that vertebrate predation (i.e., birds), which exhibited the type 3 response in their example, could cause the damping of oscillations inherent in the host-parasitoid model of Nicholson and Bailey. More recently avian predators of the fall webworm, *Hyphantria cunea* (Morris 1972), and of the scolytid beetle, *Phloeophthorus rhododactylus* (Waloff 1968a), have been shown to respond as predicted by Holling's model.

Holling (1965) used the same type of reasoning to show the population effects of Batesian mimicry. Here he simplified the situation by having *NEC* (percent mortality necessary to stabilize populations) constant for the nonmimetic and mimetic population (Fig. 5.13). He assumed that if mimetic and nonmimetic populations were equal when predation was present, without predation the nonmimetic species must have a higher reproductive rate. Therefore the percent mortality necessary to stabilize the population must be higher (cf., NEC_X and NEC_Y in Fig. 5.13).

Holling's computer model showed that the development of mimicry lowers the proportion of prey destroyed and shifts the peak of the domed predation curve to a higher density (cf., P_X and P_Y in Fig. 5.13). Holling concluded that despite the marked drop in the line of necessary mortality, the change is great enough to raise the equilibrium density of the mimics (EQ_Y) significantly above that of the nonmimics (EQ_X). Therefore, the equilibrium density of a prey population can be increased by mimicking an unpalatable species.

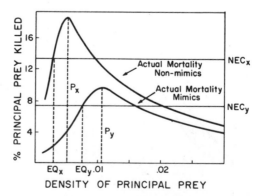

Fig. 5.13 The effect of Batesian mimicry on population regulation predicted by use of the functional response model. After Holling 1965.

In spite of the apparent instability of the interaction between prey and a predator exhibiting a type 2 response, some factors may promote stability. Some predators (e.g., the snails *Thais emarginata* and *Acanthina spirata*) may show a type 2 response in the presence of a single prey species. However, when several prey species exhibit a patchy dispersion predators may become trained to the more abundant prey, which is attacked disproportionately by individuals and the predator population as a whole (Murdoch 1969). Predators may then "switch" to another prey as relative population sizes change. This behavioral switching probably operates with a short time lag and has a potential stabilizing effect on the predator–prey interaction. Coccinellid beetle predators did not show this switching behavior when given a choice of aphid species (Murdoch and Marks 1973). Also, the type 3 response may be observed when refuges from predation exist, but as the prey population increases, a smaller percentage of it can occupy the refuge (Murdoch 1973, see also criticism of Tinbergen's work p. 60). Stability of the host-parasitoid interaction also increases when adult parasitoids interfere with each other's search and when they tend to aggregate at relatively high host densities (Hassell and Rogers 1972, Hassell and May 1973, and Rogers and Hassell 1974).

At the beginning of this chapter it was stated that wolves tend to optimize the yield of their prey by concentrating predation on young and old members of the prey population. The breeding individuals are almost immune from predation. Given the fact that mortality in the prey population must occur, or prey populations would overeat their food supply, wolf predation has as little detrimental effect on the prey as is possible.

Wynne-Edwards (1962) used a human example to illustrate the advantages of optimization. Man is essentially a predator of sea fish. The effort in catching fish can be increased with a corresponding increase in the total catch, but only up to a certain critical maximum. If the fishing intensity is stepped up beyond this level, the stock begins to suffer depletion and the annual catch starts getting smaller. Increasing effort produces a smaller total return supporting the old maxim "Fish more and catch less." Payne (1968) has documented how man has been too blind in this way with the whaling industry. His recordings, "Songs of the humpback whale," convinces one that man is destroying a series of articulate animals that few people have had the chance to appreciate.

This critical level of fishing intensity that Wynne-Edwards describes gives the greatest possible sustained yield, both in absolute terms and in terms of unit effort expended, and also the greatest cumulative total catch. Wynne-Edwards also argues that in natural populations there must also be "the need for restraint in the midst of plenty." This must apply to all animals whose numbers are ultimately limited by food. It must be highly advantageous to survival, and thus strongly favored by natural selection for animal species (1) to control their own population-densities and (2) to keep them as near as possible to the optimum level for each habitat they occupy.

How do the populations maintain this homeostasis? Briefly Wynne-Edwards argues in his Chapter 1 as follows. If selection worked only on the individual in the population, and since survival of the population or species depends on leaving viable progeny, there would be strong selection for increase of fecundity ad infinitum. He argues this is not actually seen in nature and restrictions on fecundity are imposed in a number of ways: females lay fewer eggs than their potential when populations are high, they eat more of their eggs, or fewer females breed. All are adaptations that cut directly across the interests of fecundity in the individual. The extreme case is when social insects have sterile castes so that selection has actually removed the reproductive ability of individuals completely. Wynne-Edwards concludes that this "could only have evolved when selection had promoted the interests of the social group, as an evolutionary unit in its own right." At first sight it seems that selection may work for the benefit of the group and to the detriment of the individual. This Wynne-Edwards called group selection.

Clearly, it is an advantage to a population to remain at a stable level: large declines may lead to extinction; large increases may lead to food shortage. Now if selection can work at the group or local population level, it will usually work toward homeostasis in the group, and this will occur at the highest population level that can be constantly maintained by the food population. Therefore, group selection will operate to optimize exploitation of a food resource. The concept of group selection is discussed in more detail in Chapter 16 on social systems and behavior. It must be stated that the idea of group selection as conceived by Wynne-Edwards has not been generally accepted (e.g., see Lack 1966) but the hypothesis has generated some important developments in our concepts on natural selection.

The relevance of predation to general concepts on exploitation is clear. By treating predation in small, simplified, segments one can begin to understand the complexity of the food gathering processes. As a mental exercise it is interesting to think of two situations that have been covered to see how they interact. For example how is the population regulation effect of the type 3 functional response confused by the situation in which the predator feeds on three-prey species with changing populations? Predation also illustrates that there are an enormous number of ways of achieving a necessary result: gaining food or avoiding being food (see also Schoener 1971 on feeding strategies). Surely only a process with a built in random element, such as natural selection, could furnish so many answers to a single pair of problems. The study of predation also shows that there is no winner in the evolutionary contest between food and feeder. Every adaptation carries with it an evolutionary commitment to either a smaller array of foods (specialization) or a less efficient exploitation of foods (generalization). In fact by studying predation alone one could expand into studying the whole of ecology (as defined in this book) without much difficulty.

Chapter 6

ENERGY FLOW

E nergy studies are of great importance in ecology. As seen in Chapter 2
study of energetic relationships between trophic levels provides the
most useful and most easily interpreted data. Hairston, Smith, and Slobodkin (1960) argued that energy-rich organic sediments (coal, oil, peat,
etc.) accumulate at a very low rate compared to the energy fixation by
green plants. This implies that the biosphere as a unit is energy limited.
Phytoplankton is frequently depleted by herbivores so that the herbivores
are obviously limited by energy. It has been shown that herbivore population size is dependent on the rate of energy fixation by food plants in
an aquatic community. They also argued that in terrestrial situations
living vegetation is not usually depleted by herbivores. Many of the
cases of depletion are by exotic herbivores, that is, herbivores without
the population check of their natural predators. Therefore usually herbivores are predator limited and thus food or energy limits predator
numbers. Therefore only terrestrial herbivores are not limited by energy
availability and all other organisms must adapt to apportioning the
energy supply as efficiently as possible. This view of nature has been
challenged (see p. 175) on the grounds that not all plant material is
available to herbivores, as seen in Chapter 3. However the simplicity and
generality of the argument carries a message worthy of careful consideration.

Slobodkin (1962) provides another interesting insight to energy allocation by organisms. He burned a series of whole animals in a microbomb
calorimeter. The observed calorific values formed a skewed normal distribution with relatively low variance (Fig. 6.1). The distribution was
skewed toward the lower energy values, and was explained by Slobodkin
on the grounds that in general, "energy is limiting to almost all populations almost all of the time and that this limitation has been the case
throughout evolutionary history." Since selective advantage is gained by

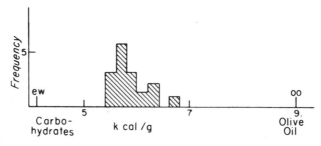

Fig. 6.1 The frequency distribution of the calorific value per gram (ash-free) of 17
species of animals in five phyla. The lines EW (egg white) and OO (olive oil) indicate
the calorific extremes found in organisms. From Slobodkin 1962.

leaving many viable progeny, it is clear that there is a selective advantage to reproduction—"but no clear advantage to adiposity." Excess calories will, therefore, be converted to offspring, and not to fat, throughout evolutionary history. If energy were not limiting, a normal distribution of calorific values in organisms might be expected. "The limitation of energy would imply that animals usually maintain the lowest possible set of biochemical components consonant with survival." That is, they put a minimum of energy into maintenance and growth and a maximum into reproduction. Therefore the availability of energy, its movement in the community, and the allocation of energy within an organism are important factors in trying to understand evolutionary strategies in plants and animals. More recently Paine (1964, 1971), although agreeing with this general argument, found that the scatter of calorific values of animals is greater than that in Slobodkin's data. He suggests that this is so because the opportunity, capability, and need for storage of fats varies greatly from one species to another. Even within a single species there are considerable changes in calorific value during a season according to the stage of development of the organism. Animals about to go into a nonfeeding stage are generally high in calorific value. For example, the prepupal larvae of the fly *Sarcophaga bullata* had 5.914 kcal/g, 11-day pupae 5.399 kcal/g, and the newly emerged adults 5.079 kcal/ash-free g (Slobodkin 1962). The energy per gram of animal declines showing that the high energy store is used up.

Although the acquisition and allocation of energy are important in ecology, energy need not be the most limiting factor in the food supply, nor the most important organizing influence in the community. Nutrients are also essential to organisms although many studies underemphasize their ecological importance. The limiting factor in the food of aphids is not energy but the level of amino nitrogen (Dixon 1970a), and aphids may excrete 90% of the energy they obtain from the plant host to obtain adequate nutrients (Llewellyn 1972). Much of the energy in a plant may not be available to herbivores because microclimate is unsuitable (e.g., Dixon 1970a), or some parts cannot be reached because of plant and herbivore morphology (Way and Cammell 1970) or because of chemical protection (e.g., Feeny 1970), as discussed in Chapter 3. Chew (1974) has argued that, although some animals may consume insignificant amounts of the primary production, their roles in the community are nevertheless important. Especially for herbivores the nutrient status of the food is at least as important as its energy content (see also Paine 1971). Carnivores and their prey have nutrient requirements that are more nearly similar, and carnivores tend to feed on a more diverse array of foods, possibly making the study of energy relationships in these species more valuable.

Since all energy (with very minor exceptions) is ultimately derived from the sun, the extent of this energy source must be known first. The quantity of solar energy entering the earth's atmosphere is approximately 15.3×10^8 cal/m² per year. A large part of this is scattered by dust particles or is used in the evaporation of water. The average amount of radiant energy actually available to plants varies with geographical location:

Georgia (latitude 33°N) 6.0×10^8 cal/m² per year
Michigan (latitude 42°N) 4.7×10^8 cal/m² per year
Britain (latitude 53°N) 2.5×10^8 cal/m² per year
                                       (from Phillipson 1966)

More than 95% of this energy is immediately lost from the plants in the form of heat and heat of evaporation. The remaining 1–5% is used in photosynthesis and is transformed into plant tissues, with the energy stored in the chemicals in these tissues. The energetic relationships of the first trophic level are shown in Fig. 6.2. The energy values balance as far as methodology would allow, and the laws of thermodynamics are supported.

At first sight it is remarkable that the photosynthetic efficiency (see Table 6.1) is so low. In the example given in Fig. 6.2 it is 4.95/4.71 or 1.05%. Other examples are given in Table 6.2, and the range of efficiencies appears to be 1.9 to 3.2% efficiency in agricultural crops and 2.2 to 3.5% in mature forest when estimated over a growing season (Hellmers 1964).

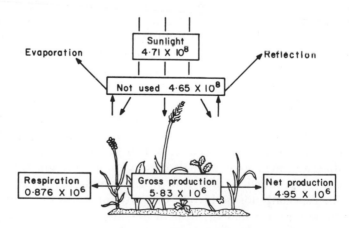

Fig. 6.2 Energetic relationships at the primary producer level in a perennial grass and herb community of an old-field in Michigan. Data from Golley 1960, from Phillipson 1966.

Table 6.1 Ecological efficiencies of energy transfer expressed as percentages (see Odum 1971 and Kozlovsky 1968 for additional relationships).

Photosynthetic efficiency (e.g., Hellmers 1964).

$$\frac{\text{net production} \times 100}{\text{visible light energy available}}$$

Assimilation efficiency (e.g., Odum 1971)

$$\frac{\text{assimilation at trophic level } t \times 100}{\text{ingestion at trophic level } t}$$

Production (tissue growth) efficiency

$$\frac{\text{production at trophic level } t \times 100}{\text{assimilation at trophic level } t}$$

Trophic level (Lindeman's) efficiency (Lindeman 1942)

$$\frac{\text{ingestion by trophic level } (t+1) \times 100}{\text{ingestion by trophic level } t}$$

However these low figures grossly underestimate the ability of chloroplasts to fix energy. Individual plants synthesize organic matter by use of chemical energy, and this energy is released by oxidation (or respiration) of organic substances. Therefore the gross production is reduced by respiration and the net primary production is usually 50 to 90% of the gross primary production. Although calculations may allow for cloud cover reducing available light, no correction is made for light absorbed by nonphotosynthesizing parts of the plant, or for reflected light (e.g., Hellmers 1964). Actually the efficiency of chloroplasts to convert light energy into work has been estimated by Spanner (1963) to have a maximum value of 80% in bright light and 60% in low light intensity.

Table 6.2 Photosynthetic efficiencies of some plants.

Plant	Location	Efficiency
Sugar cane	Java	1.9
Rice	Japan	2.2
Scots pine	Britain	2.2–2.6
Beech	Denmark	2.5

SOURCE.   From Hellmers 1964 and Ovington 1962.

Individual heterotrophs do not assimilate all of the food they consume. Up to 90% of the total food intake may pass through the body and out as feces, giving an assimilation efficiency of 10% (see Table 6.1). At the other extreme some organisms may have an assimilation efficiency of 75% (Phillipson 1966), with carnivores tending to have higher efficiencies than herbivores. It is not surprising then that trophic level (or Lindeman's) efficiency (see Table 6.1) is low, ranging from 5 to 20%.

Lindeman felt that there was evidence in 1942 that trophic level efficiency tends to increase as the food passes up the food chain. However Slobodkin (1962) concluded that trophic level efficiency—what he called ecological efficiency—ranged from 5–20% and that at present there is no evidence to indicate a taxonomic, ecological, or geographic variation in ecological efficiency.

Clearly the number of trophic levels is limited by the amount of radiant energy reaching the biosphere or a part of the biosphere, the efficiency with which it is converted to organic material, and the efficiency with which each subsequent trophic level uses this energy. Since efficiencies are generally very low, we can expect very few links in the chain before all available energy is dissipated. Four or five trophic levels seem to be the maximum. As the energy source becomes smaller, more and more energy must be utilized to find this food until ultimately the energy is so sparse that more is expended in its exploitation than is gained from the food so that another trophic level cannot exist. Wiegert and Owen (1971) argue convincingly that basic differences in life histories of primary producers in terrestrial versus aquatic systems influence the length of food chains in these systems. Trees have a long generation time and a low biotic potential. The percentage of net production of a mature deciduous forest taken by herbivores is as low as 1.5 to 2.5 (see also Golley 1972, Reichle et al. 1973, Van Hook and Dodson 1974); thus little energy is passed up the food chain involving living organisms (biophages) and these chains are typically short, with three trophic levels. In consequence much living material dies and becomes available to saprophages, making the saprophage-based food chains relatively important in deciduous forests. By contrast, in ocean water, phytoplankton have a high biotic potential and a short generation time. Sixty to 90% of net primary production may pass to the primary biophages. A large proportion of fixed energy passes along the biophage food chain, which consists typically of four trophic levels, and the saprophage-based food chain is relatively insignificant.

Since radiant energy varies so much with latitude some latitudinal differences should also be expected in the length of food chains, and adaptations to exploit large and small energy supplies of organisms living in tropical rain forest and arctic tundra.

Photosynthetic production is the primary source of organic matter and potential energy, on which nearly all forms of life, including man, are dependent. The only known exceptions to complete dependence on green plants are certain bacteria, which can synthesize organic matter using only chemical energy and inorganic materials, and man, who can obtain some of the energy he requires from wind and water power, atomic energy, and direct solar energy conversions. The bacteria contribute a minute amount to the total supply of organic energy. Man is completely dependent on photosynthesis for most of his nutritional requirements and the energy he obtains from fossil fuels, such as coal and oil, was produced by photosynthesis during earlier ages. Westlake (1963) says, "The ecologist who is interested in the dynamics of communities, rather than their description, is deeply concerned with the magnitude of this primary photosynthetic production, and the factors influencing it, for the rate of primary production is ultimately one of the main factors controlling the rates of multiplication and growth of the organisms in a community." Table 6.3 provides some data on production by plant communities at various latitudes.

Table 6.3   Net primary production (biomass) on fertile sites at different latitudes, in metric tons per hectare per year.

Ecosystem	Climate	Organic productivity
Desert	Arid	1
Deciduous forest	Temperate	12
Agriculture—annual plants	Temperate	22
Coniferous forest	Temperate	28
Agriculture—annual plants	Tropical	30
Rain-forest	Tropical	50
Agriculture—perennial plants	Tropical	75

SOURCE.   From Westlake 1963.

Even at a given latitude the annual primary net productivity varies tremendously. Ovington, Heitkamp, and Lawrence (1963) give figures for central Minnesota (Table 6.4). In natural vegetation productivity increases as the woody component increases. Apparently woody growth permits efficient utilization of time available for production because photosynthesis can start early in the spring and continue late into the fall. Oakwood production is very efficient as no nutrients or cultivation energy are supplied by man.

Table 6.4   Net primary production (biomass) in different ecosystems in central Minnesota, in metric tons per hectare per year.

Vegetation sample	Ecosystem			
	Prairie	Savanna	Oakwood	Maize-Corn
Herbaceous layer	0.920	1.886	0.182	9.456
Shrub layer	0.010	0.041	0.389	—
Tree layer				
Current year	—	2.833	4.046	—
Older	—	0.503	3.575	—
Total for aerial parts	0.930	5.263	8.192	9.456

SOURCE.   From Ovington, Heitkamp, and Lawrence 1963.

Viewing production in this way, one can make predictions on the relative sizes of the herbivore biomass, and the relative numbers of species of herbivores that can be supported by each ecosystem type. Herbivore biomass might be about 10% of the plant biomass, and since the latter are different by an order of magnitude, equivalent differences in the herbivores can be expected. Even on the basis of biomass alone more insect problems on corn than in the prairie should be anticipated, particularly since corn is a monoculture whereas biomass in the prairie is divided between 10–20 plant species. Corn production is high. Here a large part of the plant contains photosynthetic tissue, and much human effort goes into this production—cultivation and fertilizer. It would be interesting to compare the biomass of insects and other herbivores in corn that had no insecticide treatment with the biomass in an oakwood.

Not only will production change the character of the herbivore community, but the storage of energy by plants will also. In the savanna and oakwood ecosystems a large amount of energy is stored as woody tissue. Insects adapted to feed on this supply are not faced with an ephemeral food source and life histories can be prolonged. Prolonged life histories lead to slower population changes and increase the chances of stability of populations. The character of the community may be strongly influenced by energy storage. Some well known examples of long lived insect species that feed on woody tissues are the long-horn beetles (Cerambycidae), metallic wood-boring beetles (Buprestidae), and many other beetles, wood wasps (Siricidae), carpenter moths and leopard moths (Cossidae), some crane flies (Tipulidae), and the cicadas (Cicadidae), including the 13- and 17-year periodical cicadas. Typical prairie species that overwinter in the egg or adult stage, and have an annual or multivoltine life cycle include grasshoppers (Acrididae), crickets (Gryllidae), leafhoppers (Cicadellidae or Jassidae), flea beetles (Chrysomelidae), and a great number of plant-feeding flies.

Just as plants vary in their energy storage capacity, the herbivores have adapted many different ways of allocating assimilated energy. Allocation depends on the type of energy source they exploit for food (whether it is ephemeral or long lasting), the physiological stresses to which they are exposed (weather, seasonal change), and the reproductive strategy evolved (many small progeny, few large; few large clutches of eggs, many small clutches). The possibilities that a herbivore or carnivore has available to adjust its energy utilization in evolutionary time and in a single life cycle are numerous (Fig. 6.3). Selection will normally work toward increasing the harvest, ingestion, and assimilation. But there is an obvious evolutionary choice between being sluggish and docile and expending little maintenance energy, and being highly mobile and utilizing much maintenance energy. At every ramification from here on there is an evolutionary choice between alternatives that affect the whole life of organ-

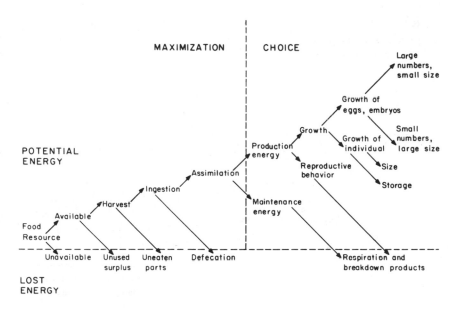

Fig. 6.3   An energy flow chart for a population or individual of a consumer species. Adapted from R. B. Root, personal communication.

isms, and a choice within a life history according to the needs of each life stage. Insects are remarkable in showing diverse strategies in energy utilization from stage to stage. If the selection pressures that influence the apportionment of energy in animals and plants were fully understood, several major questions in ecology could be answered (e.g., see Chapter 8 on strategies in reproduction).

To better understand energy allocation, it helps to have a compartment model of energy flow in an organism to focus attention on the factors that need to be measured (Fig. 6.4). Batzli's (1974) model is conceptually rigorous and is used here. Energy does not become part of the organism until it is captured as reduced carbon. In heterotrophs this is when it has been assimilated through the gut wall. Egested material passes through the alimentary canal without entering the biochemical pool of the individual. Excretory products are lost from the biochemical pool of the organism and should be considered a cost of maintenance of that pool which is comparable to respiratory energy. Once energy (reduced carbon) has been fixed or assimilated by an organism, it becomes gross production and can travel through several pathways:

1. Respiratory metabolism with ethanol, lactic acid, or CO_2 produced.
2. Nitrogenous compounds excreted as waste products.
3. Organism may perform work by moving a weight.
4. Reduced carbon may be incorporated into new molecules. When net production is positive, new tissues are produced more rapidly than old tissues are broken down.

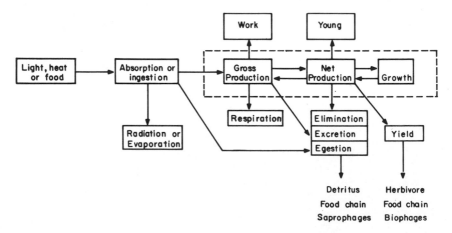

Fig. 6.4 Model of energy flow through individual organisms (autotrophs or heterotrophs). Dashed line represents boundary of organism. From Batzli 1974.

From the model gross production can be calculated by the formula:

$$GPP = AR + NPP + AEX + AW$$

for autotrophs where GPP is gross primary production, AR is auto-trophic respiration, NPP is net primary production, AEX is autotrophic excretion, and AW is autotrophic work. When $AEX \simeq AW \simeq 0$, which is usually true, the equation simplifies greatly.

For heterotrophs

$$GSP = HR + NSP + HEX + HW$$

where GSP is gross secondary production, and NSP is net secondary production, and other symbols are as for autotrophs with H designating heterotrophic activity. Here HEX and HW will often be significantly greater than zero.

Tissue, or net production, may be lost in four ways:

1. Reproductive propagules (young).
2. Portions of individuals may be sloughed off as dead material (elim-ination). This is very important in insects as cast skins represent a considerable loss in energy. The total dry weight of exuviae during the life of one aphid was 30% of the total dry weight of growth. In aphids this represents 14% of net production. A population of aphids on one tree may lose 300–360 kcal/year on exuviae (Llewellyn 1972).
3. Another type of "sloughing" is in the form of secretions (elimination). Again this is an extremely important energy drain in insects when one considers the production of pheromones and defensive secretions.
4. Portions of an individual may be consumed by other organisms (yield). In this regard it is important to remember that biophages do affect the rate of production of their food; they essentially feed inside the organism box, whereas saprophages cannot affect the rate of pro-duction of their food and feed outside the organism box. This major difference must surely lead to fundamental differences in exploitation strategies of biophages and saprophages.

When an individual dies it becomes either elimination or yield, and all rates of energy flow become zero. Thus net production can be calcu-lated by the formulae:

Autotrophs (A)	$NPP = AG + ARP + AEL + AY$
Heterotrophs (H)	$NSP = HG + HRP + HEL + HY$

where G is growth, RP is reproduction, EL is elimination, and Y is yield. Productivity of the population is obtained by summing GPP's *and* GSP's for individuals and *NPP* and *NSP* is obtained by summing *NPP*'s and *NSP*'s for individuals omitting the term for reproduction in the equation.

In Chapter 3 it was seen that a good deal of energy is put into reducing yield, which must reduce net production. This is done by manufacturing toxins and storing them, or eliminating them at the appropriate time, growing spines or hairs for mechanical protection, or actively escaping an attack. All are drains from the energy pool of the organism. Then the choice between using energy for maintenance during care of young or for producing more young and taking less care of them can be made. It would be valuable to be able to partition the energy drains on the organism between the various elements of the total life strategy of the organism. Using such data comparatively for closely related organisms as well as for very different organisms would help tremendously in resolving debates on latitudinal gradients of clutch size, r- and K-selection, and reproductive strategies in general. However, more is needed than quantities for the compartments in the energy flow diagram. We need to subdivide respiration (R) into R for basic maintenance, and R for foraging, R for care of young, and R for competition. We would like to know how elimination is partitioned between caste skins in insects, sex pheromones, allelochemicals for competitive purposes, and defensive secretions. Thus to understand fully a reproductive strategy many more details than the model implies must be known (see also Chapter 8, and Price 1974b).

Locomotion is a major drain from the gross production of many insects. Tucker (1969) and Schmidt-Nielsen (1972) have provided valuable summaries on energetic cost per unit body weight per unit distance traveled. These enable ready comparison of cost of walking and running with that of swimming and flying. In Fig. 6.5 walking and running are seen to be much more energetically costly than is flying for any given weight of animal. A gull is far more economical in its locomotion than is a rat of the same size. Also, within a certain type of locomotion, the smaller an organism, the more costly is its transport. If the trend for walkers and runners is extrapolated upward to include body weights of insects (e.g., 10^{-4}–10^{-6} kg) the cost of transport is energetically very expensive. Possibly insects that jump, a common form of locomotion, have a transport system that is relatively cheap. However insects that fly may have an even cheaper system. The rate of loss of efficiency with decreasing size of organism is much less steep for flyers than for walkers. A bee travels at no greater cost per unit weight than a rat over 1000 times its size. It may cost a fruit fly 1000 times more energy to walk a certain distance than to fly it.

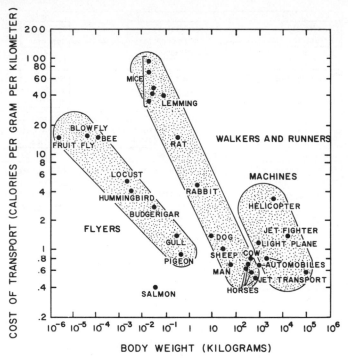

Fig. 6.5 The relationship between the size of an animal or machine and the energetic cost of movement by means of walking or running, flying, or swimming (salmon only). From the energetics of bird flight by V. A. Tucker. Copyright © 1969 by Scientific American, Inc. All rights reserved.

Insects have been limited in size by an exoskeleton that becomes less and less efficient with increasing size, and a respiratory system using movement of air down tracheae that becomes slower and slower with size. With small size goes the very high cost of locomotion by walking, and we can begin to understand the tremendous selective pressure on insects to become efficient fliers. The least change in morphology resulting in increased performance in the air would be very strongly reinforced. There seems to be a set of interacting factors that promoted the probability of flight evolving in insects, which can be derived from three basic insect characteristics (Fig. 6.6). This hypothetical set of interacting forces on the evolution of insects merely shows that flight was likely. It does not conflict with any of the present theories on the evolution of flight (see Alexander and Brown 1963), nor does it explain why other terrestrial arthropods, or immature insects, have no wings. It must be realized, however, that the evolution of flight has been an exceedingly rare event. Only

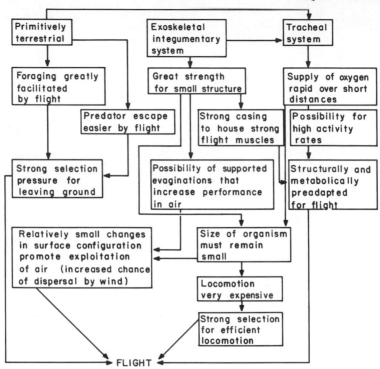

Fig. 6.6 Interacting forces bearing on the development of wings in insects, given their three basic characteristics—their primitively terrestrial evolution, an integument of skeletal tissue and a tracheal system (actually dependent on the exoskeleton, and the insects' origin on land.)

four groups of organisms have been involved. A great diversity of insects had wings 340 million years ago, and had the air to themselves for at least 150 million years. Pterodactyls were abundant between 70–150 million years ago, birds appeared 130–180 million years ago, and bats about 60 million years ago. It is significant that small organisms have shown the most dramatic adaptive radiation ever seen on this earth for exploitation of air space.

What is the role that insects play in energy flow and how do they utilize their food energy? Odum, Connell, and Davenport (1962) studied the population energy flow of the three major primary consumer groups living in early stages of old-field succession at the Atomic Energy Commission Savannah River area, South Carolina. These were the seed eaters, the Savannah sparrow, *Passerculus sandwichensis* and the old field mouse, *Peromyscus polionotus*, and the foliage eating Orthoptera, grasshoppers, *Melanoplus femur-rubrum* and *Melanoplus biliteratus*, and a tree cricket, *Oecanthus nigricornis*. At average density levels energy flow was estimated to be 3.6 kcal/m² per year for sparrows, 6.7 kcal/m² per year for mice, and 25.6 kcal/m² per year for Orthoptera. Insects are very important members of the herbivore trophic level. Wiegert and Evans (1967) calculated that in an old field the Orthoptera and harvester ant populations together accounted for 81% of the total energy flow (assimilation) through the secondary producer trophic level.

Although the Orthoptera utilized a smaller part of the food available to them (2–7%) than the seed eating sparrows and mice (10–50%) they channeled more into production than did the seed eaters. Maintenance costs of homeotherm vertebrates are much higher than for invertebrates, so actual production figures showed even greater differences than did the energy flow values (Table 6.5). Production by Orthoptera was 100 times greater than sparrows and 33 times greater than mice. Therefore the insect herbivores not only consume more energy (in absolute terms) in the primary producer trophic level than did the vertebrates, but they also make much more energy available to the carnivore trophic level. They therefore play a major role in the energy flow of a community. If insects were not a part of the community we would expect a significant drop in the possible number of trophic levels, and a gross simplification of feeding links in the food-web.

Wiegert and Evans (1967) have summarized energy flow data for old-field situations in Michigan and South Carolina (Table 6.6), and the following points are worthy of note. Ingestion rates in insects are very high in some cases. Even spittlebugs, which appear to be quite insignificant in the field, ingest more than the mice in the same field. Golley and Gentry (1964) report that the seed eating harvest ant, *Pogonomyrmex badius*,

Table 6.5   Production in an old field by populations of herbivores at average densities (kilocalories per square meter per year).

Herbivore	Production	Percent of assimilation channeled into production
Sparrows	0.04	1
Mice	0.12	2
Orthoptera	4.00	15

SOURCE.   From Odum, Connell, and Davenport 1962.

Table 6.6 Summary of annual energy utilization of primary consumers in old field communities in South Carolina (S.C.) and South Michigan (S.M.) (kilocalories per square meter per year).

	Ingestion		Assimilation		Secondary production	
	S.C.	S.M.	S.C.	S.M.	S.C.	S.M.
Sparrows	4.0	2.6	3.6	2.3	0.04	0.05
Mice	7.4	1.1	6.7	0.6	0.12	0.01
Orthoptera	76.9	3.7	25.6	1.4	4.00	0.51
Spittlebugs	—	1.5	—	0.9	—	0.08
Other herbivorous insects	7.7	0.7	2.6	0.3	0.40	0.10

SOURCE.   From Wiegert and Evans 1967.

consumed more energy than did either sparrows or mice in the South Carolina old field. Assimilation efficiencies (Table 6.1) vary considerably, but the vertebrates are very efficient in assimilating their food. Well over 50% is usually assimilated, but seeds are a richer source of nutrients than are leaves. Insects are much less efficient in assimilation as less than 50% of the ingested material is assimilated (except in the sedentary spittlebug). Even so the unassimilated plant material that passes out as feces is considerable and is important to the decomposer-based trophic system. During an insect infestation frass becomes an important litter component. Cow dung may seem prominent in a meadow, but insect frass may be much more abundant! When secondary production is considered, again insects are seen to be a very important component of the community. In every case they produce more than vertebrates in the same area. For most people it is unexpected to find that spittlebugs in a field contribute more to secondary production than sparrows or mice. When the large numbers of mature Orthoptera in a field late in the growing season are considered perhaps it is less surprising that these insects contribute more than the vertebrates. For comparison, secondary production by elephants in Uganda was estimated to be 0.34 kcal/m² per year, less than that of Orthoptera in an old field in South Carolina and Southern Michigan.

The great importance of insects in secondary production depends on their large populations and the efficiency with which they convert assimilated material into secondary production. Note the large differences between insects and vertebrates in production efficiency (see Table 6.1)

Table 6.7   The production/assimilation efficiencies of insects and mammals.

	Efficiency (%)	
Hemimetabolous insects		
Salt marsh grasshoppers	36.73	
Old field grasshoppers	36.22	
Alfalfa field spittlebugs	41.45	
	Laboratory (%)	Field (%)
Holometabolous insects		
Lepidoptera		
Operophtera brumata	40.5	59
Hydriomena furcata	41.8	47
Erannis spp.	43.3	64
Cosmia trapezina	46.2	56
Harvester ant	0.7	
Mammals		
Old field mouse	1.79	
Meadow vole	2.95	
Uganda cob	1.46	
African elephant	1.46	

SOURCE.   From Wiegert and Evans 1967 and Smith 1972.

given by Wiegert and Evans (1967) and Smith (1972) (Table 6.7). For the fairly sedentary mirid bug, *Leptoterna dolabrata,* efficiency ranged from 50–58% over a 5-year period (McNeill 1971). Waldbauer (1968) has reviewed much literature on insect metabolism and efficiency. The reason for the extremely low value for harvester ants is not clear at present, but an investigation of the literature on biology and methods of study may provide some clues. It seems that the harvester ant converted most assimilated energy into maintenance and little into net production (Engelmann 1966, see also Hadley 1972).

The importance of aphids in community energetics is not generally realized although the significance of honeydew as a food for numerous animals and fungi is better understood. The large number of specialized feeders on aphids—lacewings, syrphids, geocorids, braconids, chalcids, cynipids, and fungi—rival in diversity the many insects that feed on honeydew. Llewellyn (1972) studied the lime aphid, *Eucallipterus tiliae,* which feeds on lime trees in England. He found that these aphids consume 3672 kcal/m² per year. This rate is impressive when compared to that of other organisms. Beef cattle at 0.18/ha consume 730 kcal/m² per

year and oak tree caterpillars 154 kcal/m² per year. Of this energy consumed by aphids only 5% went into production but 90% was excreted
as honeydew. In this light it is hardly surprising that honeydew is utilized
by so many organisms, and that ants domesticate them. Energy turnover
equivalent to standing crop was 482 times per annum and the energy
drain on a tree was 28,055 kcal/year.

Aphids do not destroy the photosynthetic machinery of the plant. They
can therefore extract much larger amounts of energy per square meter of
vegetation than do conventional grazers, without destroying their food
source. Indeed, aphids may even increase fixation of carbon in the host
plant by removing accumulated nutrients that, if not utilized in this
way, would depress the rate of photosynthesis (Way and Cammell 1970).
This parasitic habit is a great advantage to the Hemiptera and Homoptera and should stimulate more attention to this group in energetic
studies and community organization in general (see also Wiegert 1964a).
In fairness to leaf cutter ants it must be stated that they may also increase
production by their activities. Although a nest may reduce gross production of forest in Costa Rica by 1.76 kcal/m² per day, activity accelerated
net production by at least 1.80 kcal/m² per day by returning material
rich in nutrients to the forest floor (Lugo et al. 1973).

The impact that an insect population has on the primary producers
depends on the type of damage they cause. If insects feed on leaves, then
a 5–20% consumption concentrated on these leaves is usually insignificant as many crops can withstand a 30–40% defoliation without serious
loss in harvest. However if the 5–20% of plant production is taken by
insects in the form of flowers and/or seeds this is likely to be catastrophic
to the plant population. There is a great deal of data on the effect of
insects on crop production, or conversely how crop production increases
with the application of insecticide. Unfortunately this method of assessing
the impact of insects has rarely been used to look at natural situations.
A brief look at agricultural experiment station reports, such as that from
the Rothamsted Experiment Station Annual Report for 1970 (Johnson
1971), indicate what should be expected in agricultural situations. In the
second year of insecticide treatment of an old pasture the production
was 30% greater than in unsprayed areas. In newly sown rye grass in the
second year of treatment production was increased 25%. The production
of a field bean crop increased from 1.07 metric tons/hectare to 1.61
metric tons/hectare when sprayed against bean aphids—an increase in
production of 50%. When spray was applied to the roots of field beans,

to kill the weevil, *Sitona* sp., production increased from 0.63 metric tons/hectare to 0.82 metric tons/hectare—a 30% improvement. Thus insects can exert a tremendous pressure on their plant food populations, particularly in agricultural situations.

In natural situations the calculation of herbivore impact is more difficult as primary production and secondary production must be measured and, by detailed studies on consumption, assimilation, and production efficiencies of herbivores in the laboratory, the consumption of herbivores in the field can be estimated. Therefore impact is usually underestimated in these situations as there is no estimate of production of primary producers in the absence of herbivores. Some examples will aid in comparing agricultural and natural situations. Stockner (1971) found that the aquatic stratiomyid fly, *Hedriodiscus truquii*, the dominant herbivore on the algal mat that grows in thermal springs in Mount Rainier National Park, only consumed 0.5–1.0% of the primary production. Grasshoppers ingested 0.5% of net primary production in old field vegetation but 2.5% in an alfalfa field (Wiegert 1965). McNeill (1971) studied the mirid bug, *Leptoterna dolabrata*, in an unmown grassland and found that the resource utilization by this herbivore was only 0.06–0.23% of the primary production. Impact on the plants was increased by damage to plant tissue by the piercing mouth parts, and the injected toxins from the salivary secretions. Andrzejewska (1967) calculated that plant losses were 26–36% greater than plant consumption by the cicadellid, *Cicadella viridis*, in Poland. But even then the impact is very low compared to the agricultural situation. However spittlebugs in alfalfa fields were calculated by Wiegert (1964b) to reduce photosynthetic fixation of energy by five times the total energy ingested by the insects (ingestion was 38.6 kcal/m² per year, cf., value in Table 6.6 for spittlebugs in an old field). This highly significant reduction, both for plant survival and crop yield, was due to removal of amino acids from the host plant.

The differences between the agricultural and natural settings raise the questions:

1. Why don't herbivores in natural environments eat more of the available resources?
2. What makes agricultural crops particularly vulnerable to herbivore pressure?
3. How do agricultural crops differ from natural communities?

They may be resolved by an understanding of community organization (Chapter 18) and diversity and stability (Chapter 19).

Another example that illustrates the importance of insects, and in this case arthropods and other invertebrates, involves the breakdown of leaf litter and the subsequent release of nutrients in forests. As already mentioned (p. 104), Wiegert and Owen (1971) consider the saprophage-based food chains relatively important in forest ecosystems. The role of arthropods in litter breakdown may be studied by placing fallen leaves in mesh bags, and after a period of time extracting the arthropods and measuring the loss of litter weight (e.g., Crossley and Hoglund 1962) or area (e.g., Edwards and Heath 1963). Other methods are described by Edwards et al. (1970) who also provide much of the information discussed below. Collembola and oribatid mites are usually the most abundant arthropods in litter although diplopods contribute significantly to decomposer metabolism. Nematodes and oligochaet worms are as important as these arthropods in litter breakdown. All these taxa are more abundant in less acid mull organic matter of oak litter than in mor derived from beech and coniferous litter.

Soil animals increase the speed of litter breakdown by disintegrating tissue, increasing surface area, changing the physical and chemical nature of the litter in other ways, and mixing it with inorganic matter (Edwards et al. 1970). All activities increase availability to bacteria and fungi. Much of the litter ingested by animals is egested as feces. In some soils most of the plant remains consist of feces. Larvae of a single species of terrestrial caddis fly, *Enoicyla pusilla*, consumed from 4.5 to 19% of litter produced in a stand of coppiced oak (van der Drift and Witkamp 1960). Of the ingested material 7% was assimilated and 93% egested. The fecal pellets had a larger exposed surface, better aeration and water-holding capacity, and a higher pH than did the original litter. Microbial activity in the feces was much higher than in whole leaves, and on average was slightly higher than in mechanically ground leaves. Using litter bags of different sizes Edwards and Heath (1963) showed that in 9 months 60% of leaf litter area was removed by earthworms; in the absence of these, mites, collembolans, enchytraeid worms, and other small invertebrates removed 30% of the leaf area and when these were excluded no visible breakdown of leaves occurred. Witkamp (1971) has stated that litter breakdown, or fragmentation, is due to the litter fauna whereas litter decomposition, or chemical deterioration, occurs through microbial action. As Edwards et al. (1970) conclude, soil invertebrates contribute significantly to leaf degradation although total energy flow may be small compared to that through bacteria and fungi. Wallwork (1970) should be consulted for the role of specific taxa in the soil system.

Efficiency has been discussed frequently in this chapter, but is it necessarily realistic to think of organisms in terms of their efficiency? Is there an adaptive advantage to being efficient? Slobodkin (1961) talks about the prudent predator and the efficient prey. Actually the predator must be prudent and exploit its prey efficiently, and the prey must efficiently compensate for this predation. Thus high efficiency is selected for. Slobodkin says that in a grain → mouse → cat situation "the efficiency of the mice in the mouse-cat case depends not only on the physiology of the mice but on the behavior of the cat, and the kind of grain provided for the mice. Efficiency, in this sense, although it is referred to as the efficiency of mice, is actually a function of three different species." But consider the situation where three species are on the same trophic level and compete for the same food source. Then, however efficient a species is, if another species eats more rapidly and consumes all the food, the efficient species will be outcompeted and die of starvation. It is easy to think of such a situation in plant populations where nutrients or water are in limited supply and all plants must compete for these resources. Those plants that grow early and rapidly may well gain an advantage and here rapid growth rather than maximum efficiency would clearly be of selective advantage.

Odum and Pinkerton (1955) suggested that natural systems tend to operate at the efficiency that produces a maximum power output (see also Odum 1956), and there may therefore be selection for producing a wastage of energy. The question of "maximum efficiency" versus "maximum power output" clearly depends on many factors and raises some questions:

1. Is energy in short supply for all organisms?
2. Can a species afford to be inefficient?
3. Can competition produce an advantage to wastage of energy?

It appears that high efficiency is not always selected for and fitness can be improved by apparent waste of energy. One example is the strategy of some plants that make large numbers of seeds irregularly so the seed predator population is swamped with food whenever seeds are produced (Janzen 1969a). It has been argued by Lloyd and Dybas (1966) that the same strategy is involved with the massive synchronized emergences of periodical cicadas. Since they take 13 or 17 years to develop, this seems to be a very wasteful way of using time and energy when the dog-day cicadas can grow much larger in much less time.

Many problems in ecology require data from energetic studies, and can hardly be resolved without them. Reproductive strategies of organisms involve the adaptive allocation of energy to progeny (see Chapter 8). How much energy is allocated to total reproduction, how much is allocated per progeny, and what molds this allocation are still unanswered questions for most organisms. The major unifying theme in systems ecology has been energy flow, and yet much work on energetics remains to be done in this field. In studies on pollination ecology (see Chapter 20) we need to understand the selective pressures that influence the arrangement of flowers providing energy-rich nectar, and the energetic costs to foraging pollinators. As in most areas of ecology the opportunities for contributing to this field of energetics are enormous.

Part II
POPULATIONS

Many qualities of individuals and interactions between them are expressed ultimately as population phenomena. The quantity and quality of progeny a female produces, influenced by the evolutionary strategy for reproduction (Chapter 8), affects the demography (Chapter 7) of the population and its dynamics (Chapter 9). The genetic constitution of individuals and populations (Chapter 10) and their relative fitness under changing conditions affect demography, dynamics, and persistence of populations. Man's efforts in manipulating populations, by use of insecticides (Chapter 11) and natural control agents (Chapter 12), have contributed significantly to the understanding of population phenomena.

Population distribution, abundance, and persistence depend also on the quantity and location of resources available for exploitation and the manner in which individuals integrate into the trophic system. Refuges from competition and adequate resources permit coexistence within the community and persistence of the population (Part III). The relative availability of these attributes for coexisting species determines population abundance and the dominance and diversity characteristics of communities. Ultimately the genetic constitution and resultant persistence, size, and dispersion of populations influences speciation, and the geographic patterns seen in populations and species (Part IV).

Chapter 7

DEMOGRAPHY: POPULATION GROWTH AND LIFE TABLES

W e have a vested interest in population growth. With our own population increasing at an ever increasing rate it is of more than academic interest to discuss how populations of other animals change with time. With ignorance and worse, misconception, rife in the lay public and among many community, state, and federal leaders, it is an obligation for us to be well informed and vocal on matters relating to population growth. Deevey (1960) and Durand (1967) both show the long-range trend of world population growth (Fig. 7.1). Durand states that the accelerated growth probably began somewhat before 1750 in parts of Europe, Russia, and America, and possibly before 1700 in China. Whenever it started, there is no sign of it leveling off.

Many people, even in high office, rest in the balmy complacency of assurance that science can solve everything. Even de Castro, Chairman of FAO's policy-making executive council wrote in 1952: "The empty sleeve of the Malthusian scarecrow has flapped in the winds of prejudice for a century and a half, but science and history have finally shown that no one need take it seriously." Brody (1952), whose paper includes this quote, restates Malthus' (1798) principal argument that the human population has the capacity and will for indefinite exponential growth whereas the population-supporting capacity of the earth is limited. What is the prognosis for the human population? Detailed discussion of the subject would be out of place here but there are four very sober and

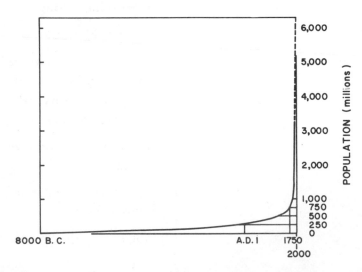

Fig. 7.1   Trend in human world population over 10,000 years. Note the exponential growth that marks the human species as unique, since no other species has ever maintained this growth form for such an extended period of time. From Durand 1967.

informative books of readings on the human population: Detwyler (1971), Ehrlich and Ehrlich (1970), Hardin (1969), and Shepard and McKinley (1969).

Malthus in his famous essay of 1798 was rather more explicit about the nature of this will in the human population for indefinite exponential growth: "I think I may fairly make two postulata. First, that food is necessary to the existence of man. Secondly, that the passion between the sexes is necessary and will remain nearly in its present state." Here he was arguing against a strange man, Godwin, who felt that such a passion might in time be extinguished. Malthus pointed out that a population can increase in a geometric ratio, and subsistence only increases in an arithmetic ratio; thus population is bound to outgrow food supply. So Malthus concludes: "And that the superior power of population cannot be checked without producing misery or vice, the ample portion of these too bitter ingredients in the cup of human life and the continuance of the physical causes that seem to have produced them bear too convincing a testimony."

Geometric growth, or exponential growth, when a population increases by a constant factor per unit time, can be expressed by the equation

$$\frac{dN}{dt} = rN$$

where N is the number in a population, and r is the rate of change per individual, or the instantaneous rate of population increase. This very rapid growth (Fig. 7.2a) is usually checked by factors that cause mortality —predators, parasites, severe weather, and aggression—or reduced fecundity, and ultimately by food shortage if all else fails. In a given environment a certain amount of food is available to a population. If the population exploits less than this amount of food it can continue to increase; if it exploits more than this amount of food it is bound to decline; and if it eats precisely that amount of food a steady state will be reached.

Verhulst recognized in 1838 that there had to be a maximum amount of food available and therefore a limit to the human population. The closer the population came to this limit the slower would its increase be until there was no increase at all. The rate of population increase, r,

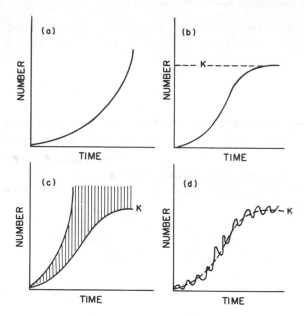

Fig. 7.2 (*a*) Exponential growth; (*b*) logistic growth to the carrying capacity *K*; (*c*) the difference between exponential growth and logistic growth caused by one environmental factor, competition for the resource that cannot support more than *K* individuals; (*d*) irregular growth of an insect population toward the carrying capacity.

must be modified therefore by a factor that decreases growth rate with increasing population density until a maximum population is reached that can be sustained by the resources. This maximum has been called the carrying capacity, *K*, and the factor can be written $(K-N/K)$, so the population growth formula becomes:

$$\frac{dN}{dt} = rN\left(\frac{K-N}{K}\right)$$

which describes a sigmoidal or logistic curve (Fig. 7.2*b*). When $N=K$, $dN/dt=0$, so unless *K* is depleted the population levels off at the carrying capacity, and a steady state is maintained. As *N* approaches *K*, $(K-N/K)$ will decrease and the rate of population growth will decline.

Other factors besides shortage of food are likely to be limiting and these will reduce the maximum population below the carrying capacity determined by food availability alone. Thus the difference between the exponential growth and logistic growth represents the interaction between the "biotic potential" of the population, and the food supply (Fig. 7.2*c*). Some authors have stated that the difference between these curves defines the "environmental resistance" or the effect of all factors that limit the biotic potential. But clearly the difference is the result of only one type of environmental factor—competition—either for food, space, or other resources in limited supply. Many other factors may reduce population growth and keep populations well below the carrying capacity and these are all a part of "environmental resistance." This term and "biotic potential" were first used by Chapman in 1928. Since complete destruction of a food supply is rarely seen in nature, it seems that environmental resistance usually keeps the population below the carrying capacity. Pearl and Reed (1920) developed the same equation as Verhulst independently so the logistic growth model is frequently referred to as the Verhulst-Pearl equation.

As might be expected there are several limitations to the logistic growth model because of the following assumptions:

1. Individuals are all equal in their reproductive potential. Clearly immatures contribute nothing and matures will vary considerably in their productivity. The logistic model assumes an even age distribution so that the same proportion of individuals in a population are breeding all the time.
2. Reproduction is constant irrespective of climate and other variations.
3. Responses are instantaneous and there is no allowance for time lags.
4. The carrying capacity, K, is constant; K cannot be reduced by excessive feeding or changing influences on the trophic level below.
5. Environmental resistance through competition is a linear function of density.

These assumptions may be acceptable for laboratory populations of insects under constant conditions such as *Tribolium* flour beetles where the generation time is also short and the food resources are maintained. In natural insect populations there is usually (1) a distinct breeding season—a season of population increase, (2) a feeding period during which the population decreases due to predation, disease, and such, and (3) unfavorable climatic conditions that interrupt activity and during which further mortality occurs. The very closest approximation to the Verhulst-Pearl model under these circumstances is an irregular climb in numbers to the carrying capacity (Fig. 7.2d). Thus the model is useful in formulating ideas about population regulation and stability but is not very helpful in predicting population change. The model has stimulated a great deal of research, but as it usual with the simplest and therefore most helpful models, this deterministic model has failed to describe many real situations. Mertz (1970) gives an excellent account of population growth and the use of models.

The exponential and logistic equations describe continuous population increase. However population increase must be described in a different way when reproduction is seasonal, as it is in the great majority of insects and plants in temperate and desert conditions, and frequently also in the tropics. If the initial population size is N_o, and exactly one year, or one generation, later each individual has died and has been replaced on the average by λ offspring, then the population size (N_1) after one season will be:

$$N_1 = \lambda N_o$$

In the second (N_2) and subseqeunt ($N_3 \ldots N_t$) seasons it will be:

$$N_2 = \lambda N_1 = \lambda(\lambda N_o) = \lambda^2 N_o$$
$$N_3 = \lambda^3 N_o$$
$$N_t = \lambda^t N_o$$

Geometric growth is again evident and if the population at any particular time in each generation is plotted, for example, the population at the start of each generation, an exponential growth curve results. If the whole population is figured through several generations the pattern ,shown in Fig. 7.3 emerges. For seasonal breeders such as plants and insects this growth model is more helpful. For example even with a rate of increase of two there are large differences between population levels at N_3 and N_4. Considering that the fecundity of insects is frequently 100–200 eggs, then these differences will be exaggerated, and it can be understood why in 1 year an insect species is quite inconspicuous and, apparently "all of a sudden," the following year, it is in epidemic proportions doing considerable damage. No other explanation than this model for seasonal breeders needs to be invoked, although there may be many other factors that come into play.

The description of population growth where generations overlap is more complex. We must know (1) how many offspring an average female will produce at each age interval in her life and (2) the number of individuals that are present at each age interval, or in each age class. To do this the approach is simplified by following only the females in a population. When the female population size and the sex ratio are known, it is simple to calculate the male and total populations. Other assumptions remain the same as in the model for seasonal breeders without overlapping generations:

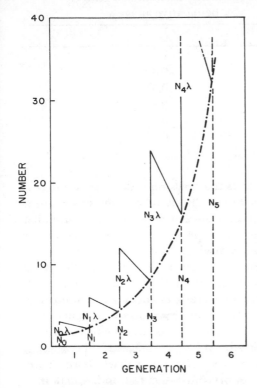

Fig. 7.3 Population growth of seasonal breeders where $N_o = 1$ and $\lambda = 2$ and all breeders die before the next breeding season. This model is therefore applicable to many insect populations. Note that if all points at a certain time in each generation are joined they demonstrate exponential growth (see dash and dot line joining successive generations prior to breeding).

1. Each season the population acts in exactly the same way—no evolutionary or environmental changes occur.
2. Population birth and death rates do not vary in response to crowding.

With overlapping generations the effects of aging on birth and death rates must be known. The life span of an insect cohort may be 5 months, which can be divided equally into 1-month periods. If x gives the age of individuals at the beginning of each period, and for each age the proportion of females that have survived to that age is designated as l_x—the age specific survivorship—the statistics of the cohort can be tabulated as on page 130.

Only at certain ages will females be capable of breeding and producing progeny. Much of the time they are immature or too old. By direct observation an estimate can be made of the number of daughters a female can be expected to leave each month, m_x—the expected number of daughters that will be produced at age x by a female who is still alive at age x—and each month can be considered as a breeding season (Table

Age at beginning of interval	Probability at birth of a female being alive at age x
x	l_x
0	1.0
1	0.8
2	0.5
3	0.3
4	0.1
5	0

7.1). The total of the m_x column gives the gross reproductive rate that is the expected total number of births produced by a female who lives through all age groups. But population growth depends on the number of surviving females and their individual production of progeny, or the product of l_x and m_x. This gives the reproductive expectation of a female at age x for a female entering the population (Table 7.1). The total progeny left by an average female in the population in this example will be 2.1, designated R_o, the net replacement rate, defined as the number of daughters that replace an average female in the course of a generation. One female on average produced 2.1 females. Therefore there was a population increase. A stable population would have an $R_o = 1$. The simplest way to obtain this information is to select a group of newly born organisms and follow the life of this cohort until the last individual dies. However, population change can be calculated also by knowing the age distribution of a total population (see p. 131 and Fig. 7.4) and the

Table 7.1 A hypothetical life table for an insect population in which maximum longevity is 5 months. R_o = net replacement rate.

Age at beginning of interval x	Age specific survivorship l_x	Expected daughters m_x	Reproductive expectation $l_x m_x$
0	1.0	0	0
1	0.8	0	0
2	0.5	3	1.5
3	0.3	2	0.6
4	0.1	0	0
5	0	0	0
	Gross reproductive rate $= \overline{5}$		$R_o = \overline{2.1}$

parameters for each age interval as in Table 7.1. This is the method used for calculating human population growth and other populations that can be adequately censussed (see Poole, 1974, for further discussion).

Once R_o is known, the instantaneous rate of population increase, r, can be calculated by the approximation

$$r = \frac{\log_e R_o}{T}$$

or the number of progeny produced per unit time, and T, the mean generation time, is the mean of the period over which progeny are produced, estimated by the formula

$$T = \frac{\Sigma l_x m_x x}{\Sigma l_x m_x}$$

Birch (1948) provides a more accurate calculation of r.

Since R_o is the net replacement rate per generation it is not a useful statistic for comparison between species as generation times vary tremendously. Thus r is a much more useful statistic for comparing growth rates of populations of different species, or growth rates of populations of the same species under different environmental conditions. Under optimal conditions r is designated r_m or r_{max}, the innate capacity for increase, or the rate of increase in a population growing under optimal conditions (i.e., a population expressing its biotic potential). This value can be useful in comparing species strategies in reproduction. A very high r_m may mean that under natural conditions the populations suffer a high mortality (Smith 1954). A low r_m may indicate low mortality in nature and would lead to a search for adaptive methods for avoiding mortality.

Because at each interval of time new members are added and present members disappear by death, natural populations with overlapping generations are a complex of individuals representing all possible age groups. It is therefore essential to know the age distribution in the population. This is normally presented as an age pyramid, and by the shape of the pyramid it is possible to identify young, stable, and senescent populations (Fig. 7.4).

Numerical changes in a population can be described completely by knowing the birth rate, the death rate, and the migration rate in that population. Life tables provide a way to tabulate births and deaths, and entomologists modified life tables so that migration could also be included.

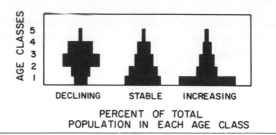

Fig. 7.4 Age pyramids indicating the idealized pattern for declining, stable and increasing populations. Note the differences between relative numbers of young in each population.

Thus the life table is really a summary statement on the life of a typical individual of a population or a cohort of individuals. From these data the expected life remaining to an individual can be calculated, whatever its age, and included in the table. This is the substance of an actuary's professional diet. Deevey (1947) states that a table showing the expectation of life at birth, at age 20 and at 5-year intervals after that, was in use by the Romans in the third century. Life insurance rates depend on life expectation in the population, and by insuring many people a company can calculate its commitments from the expectation of life column, e_x, in a life table, which tabulates the mean life remaining to those attaining a certain age interval.

From the study of human populations we obtained a valuable method for looking at animal populations. The pioneers in this change were Pearl and Parker (1921); Pearl and Miner who wrote their paper, "The comparative mortality of certain lower organisms" in 1935, and Deevey in 1947. Deevey's paper provides many examples of the life table format, and a method for the calculation of e_x.

If l_x gives the number in a cohort, or a proportion in that cohort, that survives to age x, these values can be plotted to obtain a survivorship curve. Lotka (1925) gave some survivorship curves for man (Fig. 7.5). Although maximum longevity was hardly increased the mean longevity was greatest for the United States population. This difference was largely due to infant mortality, but even in middle age the mortality was higher in England. Survivorship may also be very different at the same time in different parts of the world. For example, survivorship curves for the United States and India in 1910 show practically the same characteristics as Fig. 7.5, with India similar to the Northampton population in 1780.

As Lotka pointed out it is probably more informative to plot the survivors, l_x, on a logarithmic scale. Then a straight line indicates a constant rate of mortality throughout life, or no greater probability of dying

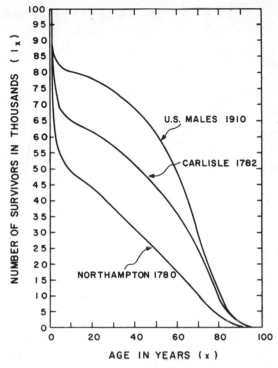

Fig. 7.5 Survivorship curves for U.S. males in 1910, a population in Carlisle, England, in 1782 and another in Northampton, England, in 1780. Note that l_x is on an arithmetic scale. From Lotka 1925.

at one age than another. Thus variation in slope measures what Lotka called the force of mortality. The survivorship curve for males in the United States in 1910 is given in Fig. 7.6. At first the slope is very steep, it decreases at about the fourth year of life when it reaches a minimum, and then increases continuously to the end of life. In fact different organisms show different survivorship curve characteristics, and it is possible to determine the vulnerable stages in a life history by comparing survivorship curves. There seem to be three general shapes to the curve (Fig. 7.7). The type I curve shows a very low death rate of young and high mortality in old age. Seldom do natural populations actually show this type of curve exactly but some are close to it; for example, the present human population, some *Drosophila* populations, the rotifer *Proales*, and Dall mountain sheep. The type II survivorship seems to apply to *Hydra* and many species of birds after the end of their first summer, although juvenile mortality must be high. Examples are the

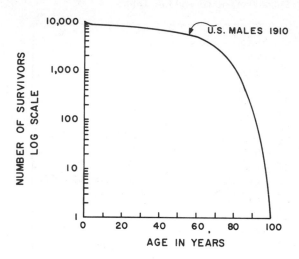

Fig. 7.6 Survivorship curve for U.S. males in 1910 with l_x on a logarithmic scale. The slope of curve indicates directly the "force of mortality" at that age interval. From Lotka 1925.

blackbird, song thrush, American robin, starling, and lapwing (Deevey 1947, but see Botkin and Miller 1974). The Type III curve is less often observed but, if they were studied, many parasitic organisms would show this survivorship where huge mortalities occur in early stages. Other examples are some fish populations and organisms with pelagic eggs and larvae such as oysters. Many examples of survivorship curves show char-

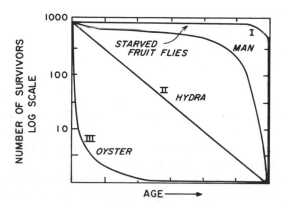

Fig. 7.7 Generalized survivorship curves of type I, II, and III plus the curve for a human population represented by U.S. males in 1910. Reprinted with permission of Macmillan Publishing Co., Inc. from Ecology of Populations by A. S. Boughey. Copyright © 1968 by Arthur S. Boughey.

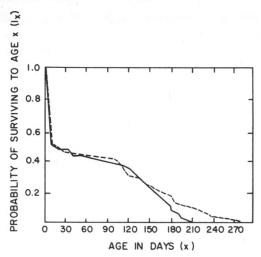

Fig. 7.8 Survivorship curves for *Oncopeltus fasciatus* (solid line) and *O. unifasciatellus* (dashed line), showing lack of fit to any of the generalized trends. From Landahl and Root 1969.

acteristics of two or more types combined during a life cycle, for example, the large milkweed bug, *Oncopeltus fasciatus*, and its tropical congener, *O. unifasciatellus* (Fig. 7.8).

The typical life table has the following columns (see Deevey 1947):

x = age of cohort.

d_x = number dying in age interval (the usual basic data from which the life table is constructed). The number in a cohort is usually 1000 individuals.

l_x = number surviving at beginning of age interval (usually out of 1000 born).

$1000q_x$ = mortality rate (per thousand) alive at beginning of age interval, or d_x as a percentage of l_x.

e_x = expectation of life, or mean life-time remaining to those attaining age interval.

Morris and Miller (1954) were the first to adapt the life table format for the study of natural insect populations. They were not so interested in the life expectancy of an individual as they were in the cause of mortality at a particular age interval. By quantifying these causes the population dynamics of the insect could be better understood. They studied the spruce budworm, *Choristoneura fumiferana*, in New Brunswick, Canada. Not only could births (i.e., eggs) be counted, and deaths due to parasites, predators, disease, and winter weather, but also dispersal to and from the site could be estimated. So all the important determinants of population size were quantified (see Table 7.2).

The age interval x was not divided up into equal lengths of time but into life stages—Eggs, Instar I, Hibernacula, Instar II, Instars III–VI, pupae, and adults, and an additional column d_xF was added, the factor responsible for d_x. This d_xF column listed all the mortality factors that could be quantified and the d_x and $1000q_x$ columns contained actual values for each of these factors. The effect of an insecticide such as DDT on the population could also be included (Table 7.3).

Since their development for natural populations life tables have been used widely in insect population studies (see Harcourt 1969). There are now sufficient life tables from natural populations of insect herbivores (see Table 7.4) to make some tentative generalizations about the shape of survivorship curves. From the 22 life tables examined it appears that there are two basic types although intermediates occur (Fig. 7.9). Type A shows very high mortality in early stages with more than 70% occurring by the midlarval stage. An extreme case is seen in the homopteran *Lepidosaphes ulmi* in which the crawler stage suffers heavy mortality (Samarasinghe and LeRoux 1966). Many of the species showing heavy early mortality are free living and exposed, although some are apparently protected by buds or webs. In the latter case establishment of early larvae is probably difficult. Members of type B have a convex survivorship curve with 40% or less mortality by the midlarval stage. The majority of species are protected apparently by their burrowing habit, or colonial defense behavior. The only exception is *Pieris rapae* on cultivated cabbages (Harcourt 1966) where natural mortality factors may have been ameliorated. Survivorship curves for both *Coleophora serratella* and *Leucoptera spartifoliella* suggest that types A and B will prove to be extremes in a continuum of types between them.

The shapes of insect survivorship curves are of interest in understanding the reproductive strategies of parasitoids that attack these insects (see Chapter 8) and in applied control. Control methods should aim at reducing survival to less than two progeny per female on average, rather than obtaining a certain percentage kill without regard to the fecundity of the females. For example even a 98% mortality after insecticide application, in a species where females lay 200 eggs, would still result in a doubling of the population in the generation. The survivorship curve indicates the vulnerable stages of each species and may lead to emphasis of control efforts on this stage. For example, application of insecticide

Table 7.2 Life table for the 1952–1953 generation in a relatively low population of spruce budworm in the Green River watershed, New Brunswick. Note that the cohort studied (l_x) is the mean number in an egg mass, and the age intervals (x) are not equal but are defined by the developmental stages of the insect. The original publication should be consulted for details of the calculations involved.

x Age interval	l_x No.* alive at beginning of x	$d_x F$ Factor responsible for d_x	d_x No.* dying during x	$100\,q_x$ d_x as percentage of l_x
Eggs	174	Parasites	3	2
		Predators	15	9
		Other	1	1
		Total	19	11
Instar I	155	Dispersion, etc.	74.40	48
Hibernacula	80.60	Winter	13.70	17
Instar II	66.90	Dispersion, etc.	42.20	63
Instars III–VI	24.70	Parasites	8.92	36
		Disease	0.54	2
		Birds	3.39	14
		Other—inter.†	10.57	43
		Total	23.42	95
Pupae	1.28	Parasites	0.10	8
		Predators	0.13	10
		Other	0.23	18
		Total	0.46	36
Moths (SR = 50 : 50)	0.82	Sex	0	0
Females ×2	0.82	Size	0	0
		Other	0	0
		Total	0	0
'Normal' females ×2	0.82	—	—	—
Generation	—	—	173.18	99.53
Expected eggs	62	Moth migration, etc.	−513	−827
Actual eggs	575			

Index of population trend: Expected 36%
Actual 330%

* Number per 10 ft² of branch surface.
† Other factors minus mutual interference among all factors.
SOURCE. From Morris and Miller 1954.

137

Table 7.3 Life table for the 1952–1953 generation in a high population of spruce budworm in the Green River watershed, New Brunswick. Starvation was a serious mortality factor, due to death of new foliage caused by late frosts, and an aerial application of an insecticide, DDT, inflicted additional, but relatively minor mortality.

x	l_x	$d_x F$	d_x	$100\, q_x$
Age interval	No.* alive at beginning of x	Factor responsible for d_x	No.* dying during x	d_x as percentage of l_x
Eggs	2176	Parasites	1	< 1
		Predators	174	8
		Other	21	1
		Total	196	9
Instar I	1980	Dispersion, etc.	1148	58
Hibernacula	832	Winter	141	17
Instar II	691	Dispersion, etc.	484	70
Instars III–VI	207	Parasites	2.90	1
		Disease	0.30	< 1
		Birds	1.70	1
		Starvation	165.30	80
		DDT	8.30	4
		Other—inter.†	26.70	13
		Total	205.20	99
Pupae	1.80	Parasites	0.13	7
		Predators	0.11	6
		Other	0.27	15
		Total	0.51	28
Moths (SR = 54 : 46)	1.29	Sex	0.10	8
Females ×2	1.19	Size	0.57	48
		Other	0.00	0
		Total	0.57	48
'Normal' females ×2	0.62	—	—	—
Generation	—	—	2175.38	99.97
Expected eggs	47	Moth migration, etc.	−199	−423
Actual eggs	246			

Index of population trend: Expected   2%
Actual   11%

* Number per 10 ft² of branch surface.
† Other factors minus mutual interference among all factors.
SOURCE. From Morris and Miller 1954.

Table 7.4 Sources for life tables of natural populations of insect herbivores which provide survivorship data used in construction of Fig. 7.9 (except those in Group C).

Group	Insect species	Insect order	Habit	Reference
A—70% or more of mortality by midlarval stage.				
1.	*Choristoneura fumiferana*	Lepidoptera	In bud or web	Morris and Miller 1954
2.	*Bupalus piniarius*	Lepidoptera	On foliage	Klomp 1966
3.	*Plutella maculipennis*	Lepidoptera	On foliage	Harcourt 1963
4.	*Spilonota ocellana*	Lepidoptera	In bud	LeRoux et al. 1963
5.	*Archips argyrospilus*	Lepidoptera	In leaf roll	LeRoux et al. 1963
6.	*Rhyacionia buoliana*	Lepidoptera	In bud and shoot	Miller 1967
7.	*Operophtera brumata*	Lepidoptera	On foliage	Embree 1965
8.	*Recurvaria starki*	Lepidoptera	In needle mine	Stark 1959
9.	*Sitona regensteinensis*	Coleoptera	On root nodules	Waloff 1968b
10.	*Lepidosaphes ulmi*	Homoptera	On branches	Samarasinghe and LeRoux 1966
11.	*Arytaina genistae*	Homoptera	On foliage	Waloff 1968b
B—40% or less of mortality by midlarval stage.				
1.	*Ostrinia nubilalis*	Lepidoptera	In stems	LeRoux et al. 1963
2.	*Coleophora serratella*	Lepidoptera	In case	LeRoux et al. 1963
3.	*Lithocolletis blancardella*	Lepidoptera	In leaf mine	Pottinger and LeRoux 1971
4.	*Pieris rapae*	Lepidoptera	On foliage (cultured environment)	Harcourt 1966
5.	*Neodiprion swainei*	Hymenoptera	On foliage, colonial	McLeod 1972
6.	*Scolytus scolytus*	Coleoptera	Under bark	Beaver 1966
7.	*Scolytus ventralis*	Coleoptera	In twig mines	Berryman 1973
Between A and B				
	Leucoptera spartifoliella	Lepidoptera	In twig mines	Waloff 1968b
C—Probably in Group A but uncertain as no data are provided for midlarval stage.				
1.	*Bruchidius ater*	Coleoptera	In pod	Parnell 1966
2.	*Apion fuscirostre*	Coleoptera	In pod	Parnell 1966
3.	*Phytodecta olivacea*	Coleoptera	On foliage	Richards and Waloff 1961

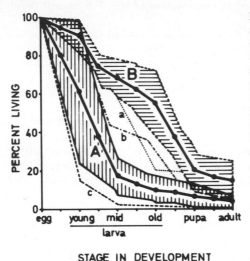

Fig. 7.9 General trends in survivor-ship curves for 19 species of herbiv-orous insects listed in Table 7.4. Shaded areas indicate the zones that include all survivorship curves in the group indicated, the species of which are listed in Table 7.4. Dots are mid-points between limits of the shaded areas, on the vertical scale, and the heavy lines joining these indicate the general characteristics of type *A* and *B* survivorship curves. Part of the sur-vivorship curves for three species not included in the shaded areas are given separately: (*a*) *Coleophora serratella*; (*b*) *Leucoptera spartifoliella*; (*c*) *Lep-idosaphes ulmi*. Reproduced from *Evo-lutionary strategies of parasitic insects and mites*, edited by P. W. Price, pub-lished by Plenum Publishing Com-pany Limited, 1975.

before the midlarval stage on group A species may frequently be very effective, since high natural mortality indicates exposed and vulnerable immatures.

If the age at which an animal dies can be observed directly, then it is a relatively simple matter to construct a life table. A classic case of this was studied by Murie (1944) in his monograph "The wolves of Mount McKinley." Murie was interested in the mortality of Dall Mountain sheep caused by wolf predation. He collected skulls of sheep that had accumulated over a period of years and determined the sheep's age at death from the annual rings on the horns. Thus Deevey (1947) was able to construct a good life table for the sheep.

For insects, this method is not available and we are forced (1) to observe a cohort very closely, usually therefore in unnatural conditions, or (2) to take successive population samples to see how the population declines through a generation. Morris has probably been the most influential worker in the development of insect sampling techniques with a view to developing life tables (e.g., Morris 1955). Points mentioned here refer to the spruce budworm but the principles can be readily applied to other species, especially herbivores. First, the detailed life history must be known so that all stages of the species can be readily found in the trees. This includes eggs, mining larvae, larvae in webbed foliage, and pupae that are about 2-cm long. Good life history data also enable accurate timing of samples of the different life stages. To obtain this information a full scale study is usually necessary as life histories of so few insects are adequately known, and phenology changes from place to place.

Second, a sampling unit must be selected so that it is easily collected in the field, and subject to as little variation as possible, which might be caused by defoliation in the case of herbivore populations. The unit should also be reasonably small so that many can be collected, and finally the sampling unit must be quantifiable in terms of numbers per tree, and numbers per unit area. For herbivorous insects a part of the host plant usually serves as the sample unit. Morris (1955) selected a lateral half of a whole branch of balsam fir so that insects could be expressed per unit area of branch surface. The balsam fir has a triangular growth pattern on branches, with all side branches more or less in one plane, so the area of a sample could be calculated quite accurately from two measurements, length and maximum width. By measuring the diameter at breast height of the tree from which the sample was taken tables could be consulted to find the total branch area per unit area of ground. Thus populations could be expressed in absolute terms.

Third, one must determine the best location of the sample. Since budworm density varies tremendously with height in the crown, sampling could become very complicated and laborious. For survey work when rapid sampling was necessary only branches from the midcrown, representing mean population levels, were taken.

Fourth, mid-crown in tall stands may be 40–50 feet above ground so ladders and pole pruners, or trucks equipped with hydraulically operated platforms as for telephone line repairs, are essential. And so the technical difficulties are gradually surmounted. The technical details of sample collection, the difficulty with creating statistically rigorous techniques, and the length of time required before meaningful data are accumulated have all conspired to limit to very few the studies on forest insect populations (see Chapter 9).

Relative abundances are easier to obtain by means of trapping techniques (see Southwood 1966) and for studies of insects as food for vertebrates these methods provide a much greater return per unit effort.

Before the reader is mislead into the conclusion that the instantaneous rate of increase, r, remains constant for a population or species over long periods of time, the possible effects of natural selection in changing r must be explored, and also how a certain r may be achieved by different means (r must be constant within a generation however). How is population growth altered by changes in life history and differences in reproduction between populations and species? Do we have any insight into how selection works to define the most propitious time for reproduction? First, major differences in life history are examined. For example, some ideas in Cole's (1954b) classic paper, "The population consequences of life history phenomena," are worth careful scrutiny.

One of the factors that Cole examined was how breeding once in a lifetime (semelparity) compared to breeding several times (iteroparity) influenced population growth (Fig. 7.10). This is a choice that the evolutionary process has made for organisms. From the figure the number of eggs a semelparous female would have to lay to achieve the same r as an iteroparous species can be calculated. For example, females of an iteroparous species may start to reproduce at 30 days and lay 100 eggs in each clutch. How many eggs would a female of another species have to

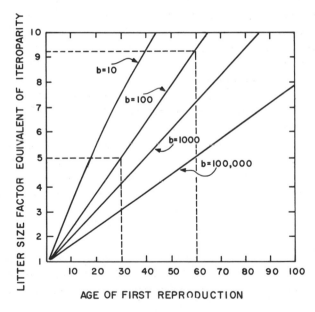

Fig. 7.10 The factor by which litter size must be increased to achieve in a single reproduction the same intrinsic rate of increase, r, that would result from indefinite iteroparity; b = brood size of an iteroparous species and the ordinate gives the factor by which this must be multiplied. From Cole 1954b.

lay, if she laid one batch of eggs, to have the same population consequences? ($100 \times 5 = 500$ eggs). If reproduction occurs at 60 days, then if an
iteroparous species lays 100 eggs per clutch, a semelparous species must
lay 925 eggs to produce the same population growth rate. Cole's paper
should be consulted to see how selection is likely to work on these two
basic differences in reproductive strategy.

With respect to many insect and plant species having annual life
cycles and high fecundities, Cole argues that any selective pressure for
iteroparity as a means of increasing r must be negligible. For example
an iteroparous insect that produces 30 eggs in each annual reproductive
period would have to produce only 31 eggs in a single clutch if it were
semelparous to achieve the same r. Even with only 30 eggs per clutch the
gain in becoming iteroparous is less than a 1% increase in r. With fecundities commonly ranging from 60 to 200 eggs per female insect the
iteroparous habit will usually be maladaptive. For the other extreme
consult Goodman (1974) who considers iteroparous species with very
small clutch sizes.

Cole looked at another factor that influences population growth, the
age at first reproduction, or the effect of delayed maturity on the rate
of population increase (Fig. 7.11). For example, when the brood size is 10
the rate of increase is more than doubled by breeding at age 2 rather

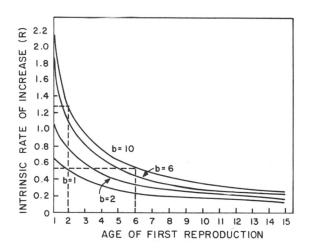

Fig. 7.11   The effect of changing the time of first reproduction on the intrinsic rate of
increase, r, of a population; $b =$ brood size for an indefinitely iteroparous species
where a brood is produced at every time interval after first reproduction. From Cole
1954b.

than at age 6 ($r = 1.28$ instead of 0.52). There must be a strong selection pressure to mature and breed early. What are the selective pressures working in the opposite direction? Cole's conclusions have been reexamined by Gadgil and Bossert (1970), Bryant (1971), and Charnov and Schaffer (1973) to which reference should be made by the critical reader.

Looking at reproduction in this way it becomes clear that a human female that breeds at 20 years contributes much more to the population growth than one that breeds at 30 years. This should be taken into account when formulating policy on family size. Also a female that produces females contributes more to subsequent population growth than does a female that produces males. We need only imagine two equal populations on different islands where on one there are 99 males and 1 female and on the other there are 99 females and 1 male. The difference between the growth rates of these populations should be obvious.

Lewontin (1965) considered selection for colonizing ability, or slight shifts within a general strategy, not radically different evolutionary strategies like iteroparity versus semelparity. Lewontin was interested in the age of first reproduction, the effect of timing of the peak of reproduction, and the population effect of the age at which the last offspring is produced. He was interested in small variation in these factors that could be selected for over a few generations because of changing conditions. He wanted to know also how the production of progeny by organisms that colonize unoccupied areas is likely to differ from progeny production in resident populations.

Lewontin asked what is a reasonable shape for the $l_x m_x$ curve, and found that a triangular shape was realistic (Fig. 7.12), just as Holling had

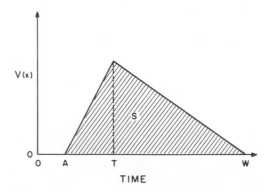

Fig. 7.12 A generalized triangular reproductive function $V(x)$ that represents the $l_x m_x$ curve of a cohort. $A =$ age at first reproduction, $T =$ peak reproduction, $W =$ age at last reproduction, $S =$ total number of offspring produced. From Lewontin 1965.

done (e.g., Fig. 5.10). Then by modifying the position of the reproductive function in time and changing its shape he could compute how these changes affected r. He could ask questions such as, "What is the relative advantage of increased fecundity of a certain amount as opposed to greater longevity? In order to increase r from 0.270 to 0.300 how much does fecundity have to be increased for different developmental rates?" These questions are actually asked in nature, not through rational means but because innumerable strategies in life history are attempted by genotypes and their phenotypes produced by a process with a random element in it. Only the best are selected for.

Only two examples are given. First, what is the effect of changing only the age of reproduction? (Fig. 7.13). What happens if natural selection reduces the time interval to first reproduction from 13 days to 10? If fecundity remains the same (at 600), the rate of increase changes from 0.270 to almost 0.330. To maintain the rate of increase at 0.270, a species with first reproduction at age 10 days would only have to produce 260 eggs instead of 600, a remarkable saving of energy as the result of a rather small adjustment in breeding time. The number of progeny that would have to be produced to increase r from 0.270 to 0.330 if reproduction started at day 13 is 2000. There is a considerable evolutionary choice in when to breed and how many progeny to produce.

The second example describes what happens when A and W remain constant and T changes (Fig. 7.14). How does the peak skewed to the left increase the rate of population increase? Here S is constant as the area of the reproductive function does not change. By moving T from day 28 to day 16 r increases from 0.270 to 0.330.

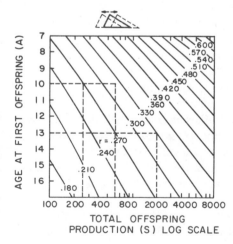

Fig. 7.13 The effect of changing age at first reproduction, A, on the intrinsic rate of increase, r. Solid lines give equal r values for changing A and S. The change in the reproductive function is given above the graph, thus with change in A, T and W also change. From Lewontin 1965.

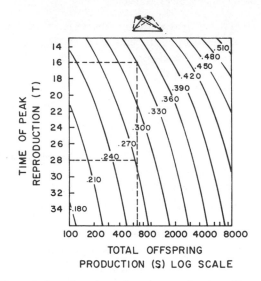

Fig. 7.14 The effect of changing time of peak reproduction, T, on the intrinsic rate of increase, r. Solid lines give equal r values for changing T. S does not change. The change in shape of the reproductive function is given above the graph; its position in time does not change; that is, T changes but A and W remain unchanged. From Lewontin 1965.

Another type of adjustment is related to differences between the sexes of the same species and differences between closely related species. For example, Blest (1963) found in saturniid moths that the postreproductive life of males and females differed from one species to another. He argued that selection should reduce the postreproductive life of cryptic and palatable species as old individuals may improve the speed of learning of the predator. Conversely selection should increase the postreproductive life of aposematic species as old individuals will play a role in the predator's learning process, without reducing the reproductive potential of the population, since neither males nor females feed. Kin selection must be involved here (see Chapter 16). Blest's reasoning is supported by data in Fig. 7.15 for males and Table 7.5 for females.

Landahl and Root (1969) found a similar situation with the aposematic milkweed bugs, *Oncopeltus fasciatus* and *O. unifasciatellus*, where males live longer than females. A high proportion of males in the population would reduce the probability of vertebrate predators taking females. Here males feed but "the cost of sustaining the 'surplus' males may be outweighed by their value as decoys."

Even adjustments in reproductive effort can be made by individuals according to availability of food. Murdoch (1966a, b) found in carabids

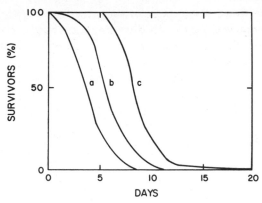

Fig. 7.15 Difference in post-reproductive survivorship curves of male saturniid moths (plotted as percent survivors) (*a*) for a cryptic leaf mimic which is palatable, (*b*) for a species with a forewing pattern that mimics a leaf, and the hind wings with eye-spots used in an intimidation display, but which is palatable, and (*c*) for an aposematic species. After Blest 1963.

Table 7.5   Post-reproductive survival of female saturniid moths.

Days after end of reproduction	Palatable females	Unpalatable females
1	10	0
2	3	13
3	0	6
4	0	12
5	0	7
6	0	4
7	0	1
8	0	0
9	0	2
Total	13	45

SOURCE.   From Blest 1963.

that at one time a female may breed early and thus reduce fecundity later, or another female of the same species at a different time may perform the reverse adjustment (see Chapter 8), rather like Lewontin's (1965) examples where T and W are manipulated.

Finally, as Frank (1968) points out, it may be tautological to say that long-lived species have lower population growth rates, and tend to live in stable environments. Many wood-feeding insects provide an example as seen in Chapter 6. But differences in r in stable and unstable environments are discussed again in this book.

For the last section of this chapter the subject of demography has merged with that of reproductive strategies of organisms, an area of ecology that is expanded on in the next chapter.

Chapter 8

STRATEGIES
IN REPRODUCTION

All species are bound to maximize progeny survival. The possibilities for achieving this end are enormous—from a mushroom producing a million progeny and disseminating them in the wind, to an elephant that produces four or five 200-lb calves in a lifetime and cares for each over a period of 4 years including the gestation and nursing periods. But this example oversimplifies the problem in understanding the diversity of reproductive strategies. Why is it that fairly closely related species (a) live for different lengths of time, (b) produce different numbers of progeny, or (c) produce several batches or a single batch of progeny? What are the factors that contribute to and detract from the fitness of an individual? Williams (1966a) says that fitness may be defined as "effective design for reproductive survival." Medawar (1960) says that fitness is in effect a system of pricing the endowments of organisms in the currency of off-spring. So what are the effective designs? How do organisms produce a solid currency? How can an individual contribute a more than average number of genes to future generations?

The answers to these questions are clearly a matter of dividing up the available energy as efficiently as possible, and utilizing the available time as efficiently as possible. Thus each strategic or tactical solution represents a partitioning of this time or energy. It should be stressed that the "choices" of strategies are made by the evolutionary process and not by the individuals themselves. To abbreviate explanations, organisms are frequently referred to as if they had choices, but it must be remembered that the process of natural selection makes the "decisions." Cody 1966 (following unpublished work by Levins and MacArthur) has called this partitioning to promote fitness the principle of allocation. He applied it to the variation of clutch size in birds. Until this paper was published, Lack's theory on the evolution of clutch size was the most widely accepted and this stated that "in most birds clutch-size has been evolved through natural selection to correspond with the largest number of young for which the parents can on the average find enough food" (Lack 1954). Cody agreed with Lack that in temperate regions, where periodic local catastrophes reduce populations and maintain populations below the carrying capacity, K, of the habitat, natural selection is proceeding to maximize r, the reproductive rate. In the tropics, however, with a more climatically stable environment, where catastrophes are rare, populations will be at saturation densities, and any adaptive variation that will increase the carrying capacity will usually be favored by natural selection (MacArthur 1962). Increasing K is equivalent to increasing the population density with the same resources. Here, by the principle of allocation, energy will be utilized in ways different from that in temperate regions. Selection will be for increased energy used in predator avoid-

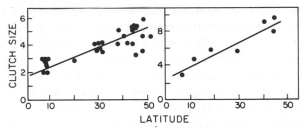

Fig. 8.1 Relationship between clutch size and latitude in birds. Left—for the family Icteridae (meadowlarks, blackbirds and orioles) in North and South America. Right—for the genus *Oxyura* (family Anatidae), world wide distribution. Both slightly modified from Cody 1966.

ance, intraspecific, and interspecific competition, and more energy expended per individual progeny reared (see also Cody 1971, Foster 1974). Thus Cody used Lack's theory, but also extended the theory to make it more generally valid.

The difference between *r* selection in temperate regions and *K* selection in tropical regions can be seen repeatedly by comparing clutch size within a family or genus of birds along a latitudinal gradient (Fig. 8.1). Examples of this trend are also seen in insects. Landahl and Root (1969) found that the temperate *Oncopeltus fasciatus* has a higher *r* than the tropical *O. unifasciatellus*. In this case higher *r* is not achieved by larger clutch size but by an earlier start of oviposition and a greater frequency of clutch production (Fig. 8.2). But Cody's basic tenet is supported. Lan-

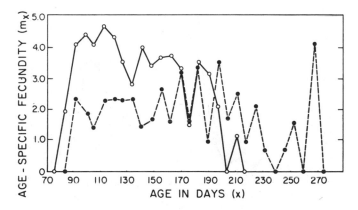

Fig. 8.2 The change in egg-production (female eggs only) with age for *Oncopeltus fasciatus* (solid line) and *O. unifasciatellus* (dashed line). Since clutch sizes were similar, the higher rate of the former species early in reproduction was achieved by more frequent clutch production. From Landahl and Root 1969.

dahl and Root remind us, however, that *O. fasciatus* is a migrant species so that even in stable environments we might expect a high *r*. In the chrysomelid beetle, *Chrysolina quadrigemina*, latitudinal differences within the species have been observed. After the beetle became established in California it was introduced into British Columbia, and now Peschken (1972) has been able to compare the two groups of populations. She found that the northern beetles lay more eggs than do the southern ones, and as we might predict, with selection working to increase *r*, these extra eggs are laid early in the beetle's life (see Fig. 8.3). In Lewontin's (1965) terminology (Fig. 7.12), both *A* and *T* have been shifted forward.

A third theory relating to the clutch size of birds is Ricklefs' (1970a) "counteradaptation hypothesis" in which he invokes the importance of differential coevolutionary rates of predator and prey as a regulator of food intake, and consequent energetic allocation to egg production. Therefore, Ricklefs slightly modifies Lack's theory but also incorporates some of Cody's general theory. Since evolutionary rates of predator and prey must be estimated, considerable difficulties exist in testing this hypothesis. A fourth hypothesis on determination of clutch size has been called the balanced mortality hypothesis (e.g., Price 1974a) and is discussed later in this chapter.

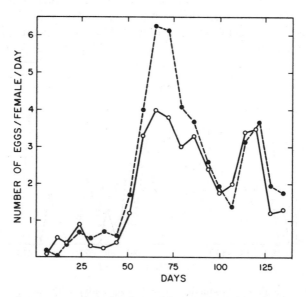

Fig. 8.3 The change in egg-production with age for *Chrysolina quadrigemina* in California (solid line) and British Columbia (dashed line), from day 1 to day 135 of their oviposition periods. From Peschken 1972.

Plants show a tremendous diversity in the strategies for producing seed (see Harper, Lovell, and Moore 1970). The double coconut palm, *Lodoicea maldivica*, produces seeds weighing up to 27,000 g and the orchid *Goodyera repens* produces seeds weighing about 2×10^{-6} g. What is the point of this contrast? In the former example, large seed size is often associated with a maritime habitat. Even in relatively small seeded species, maritime ecotypes tend to have larger seeds than their inland counterparts. The dense dispersing medium, the water, permits a species to produce a large seed and yet retain dispersability. In the case of the orchid, this characteristic of minute seeds is shared with other saprophytes and totally parasitic plants where the microhabitats in which the seeds will germinate are small and widely dispersed. The chances of a few seeds reaching these specialized locations are increased by production of masses of seeds. A contributing factor in orchids is the certainty of pollination and subsequent fertilization of large numbers of seeds because pollen transfer is in pollinia (coherent masses of pollen in a stalked sac that are carried intact by pollinators, e.g., Fig. 20.4). Perhaps an extreme example of microhabitat requirements is in *Orobanche* species (Broomrapes), which are obligate parasites, and germination occurs only when stimulated by a host-root exudate. Within a superfamily of green plants that also produce parasitic attachments to other plants (hemiparasites), the Rhinanthoideae which includes yellow-rattle, *Rhinanthus minor*, there is a sequence of decreasing host dependence associated with increasing seed size. That is, if the seed germination site occurs more frequently, it is better to put energy into strong germination from a larger seed than massive production of minute seeds. Very similar types of adaptation and energy allocation will be seen in insects.

Seed size may also be influenced by predators, as seeds form the principle source of food of many animals, for example, pea and bean weevils (Bruchidae) and seed wasps (Megastigmidae). There are two natural groups of woody legumes in Central America that differ in mean seed weight. The mean seed weight of 23 species that have toxic seeds (not eaten by bruchids) is 3.00 g. The mean seed weight of 13 species without toxic components is 0.26 g. Janzen (1969a) suggests that the smaller seed size of vulnerable species results in the greater subdivision of the reproductive effort, which increases the probability of escape from predation by dispersion. The number of seeds produced per cubic meter of canopy is very much greater in the vulnerable (1020) than in the unattacked species (14), although the total weight of seed produced is of the same order of magnitude. Smith (1970) has also found that species of conifers that produce large seeds have better protected seeds than in small seeded species. [Similarly, Labine (1968) shows that the chemically protected butterfly, *Heliconius erato*, lays large but few eggs compared to related species]. A third strategy is to produce very small seeds so that they are hard to find or too small to support the seed insects in the region, in this case bruchids. A single species of woody legume, *Indigophora suffruticosa*, seems to have adopted this line of defense. It is not attacked and its seeds weigh 0.003 g. This strategy is common in herbaceous legumes.

Plants also must spend energy in assuring that dispersal of seed and numbers, size, and dispersal potential are closely linked. Where plant succession is concerned, any species that is not in the climax community is doomed to local extinction and is a fugitive species to a greater or lesser degree. Two strategies are open to such a species. It can become less of a fugitive by digging in and adapting to tolerating the increasing competition as the conditions deteriorate. Here large seed size would increase progeny survival and a strong commitment to vegetative growth would promote competitive ability. The alternative strategy is to escape from succession by colonizing patches of ground that are at an earlier successional stage. Those individual plants whose seeds are lighter than average for the species and are more readily dispersed will be likely to leave more progeny in a new habitat. The two solutions to living in a changing environment are either to adapt to live with it or to adapt to escape from it, and again we see the contrasting strategies of a K species that allocates more energy per individual progeny than the r species that bets its survival on numbers.

Indeed these two strategies may be evolved by the same species under different environmental conditions (see Linhart 1974). In vernal pools the central part provides a relatively predictable environment but competition is intense. *Veronica peregrina*, an annual growing in these locations, produces fewer but heavier seeds which germinate rapidly. In contrast, plants of the same species at the periphery of the pools live in a less predictable environment and produced more and lighter seeds. These seeds have greater dispersability for escaping from poor sites; larger numbers increase chances of reaching favorable sites; and the greater variety of offspring increases the probability of producing a genotype adapted to conditions prevailing during the next generation. Differences in reproductive effort (see p. 158) were also found by Abrahamson and Gadgil (1973) among and within species of goldenrod (*Solidago*), with relatively high effort in early harsh stages of plant succession and low effort in mature communities. Many other aspects of seed quality and production are discussed by Harper, Lovell, and Moore (1970). Reproductive strategies of plants are likely to influence profoundly the life histories and the reproductive and dispersal strategies of the insects that feed on these plants. More attention is needed on the correlation between dispersal of plants and their insect herbivores.

   In insects many examples of the principle of allocation may be observed. There is a group of species of parasitic wasps (Ichneumonidae) that attack a single host (see Price 1970c, 1972c, 1973b,c, 1974a,b). Therefore, each species has roughly the same amount of food to utilize and to allocate to its different functions. Considerable differences in the allocation of building materials for body construction are evident. For example, a female parasitoid that attacks host larvae in the tree must have large wings for prolonged flight and they may be as large as 9 mm² per forewing. The large wings, the huge flight muscles, and the strong and large thorax to contain them are very expensive to produce, but essential to finding hosts and leaving progeny. The other extreme is seen in species that hunt for hosts on the ground. All these species have smaller wings than those searching in the tree canopy, but some are either brachypterous (short winged, flightless) or apterous (no wings) (Figs. 8.4 and 8.5). The thorax is much reduced and flight muscles hardly exist and the energy is reallocated to building a very robust body for searching through

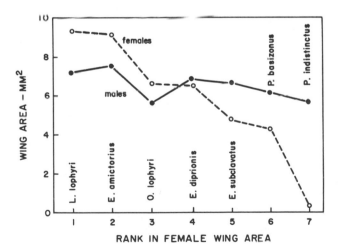

Fig. 8.4   Differences in area of one forewing of males and females of parasitoid wasps that attack the Swaine jack pine sawfly, *Neodiprion swainei*. The first four species attack larvae in the tree while the last three species attack cocooned larvae, pupae, and adults in the litter of the forest floor. *L=Lamachus, E* at rank 2 and 4 = *Exenterus, O=Olesicampe, E* at rank 5=*Endasys, P=Pleolophus*. From Price 1974b.

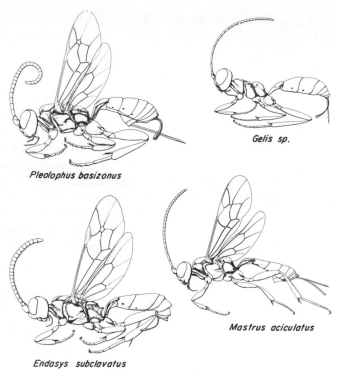

Fig. 8.5 Females of four species of parasitoid that attack cocoons of the Swaine jack pine sawfly, *Neodiprion swainei*. Note that the ultimate in the trend to reduce energy allocated to flying is reached in *Gelis* which completely lacks wings and consequently has a relatively small thorax and thus conserves much energy. From Townes 1969.

the loose leaf litter for hosts. Structure of the reproductive organs also differs radically from the large winged species to the smaller winged species (Price 1972c). The males of these ichneumonids perform a different function. They have to find females rather than hosts; thus males of all the species should be equipped in a similar way. The variation in size of the wing between species was small in the males (Fig. 8.4). Mean size was 6.56 mm², the largest species had a wing area of 7.55 mm², and the smallest 5.68 mm² out of seven species. In the females the mean size was 5.86 mm² and the range was from 9.32 mm² to 0.32 mm², discounting the apterous species.

In contrast to plants, moving organisms can adapt to placing their progeny in suitable situations for survival. In an interesting series of papers, Chandler (1967, 1968a, b, c) describes how adults of several species

of Syrphidae—flower or hover flies in which the larvae of some are predaceous on aphids and other small arthropods—are sensitive to the density of the aphids on a plant and lay eggs preferentially at certain
densities. The species illustrate differing strategies in the placement of
eggs. The obvious strategy is to lay most eggs where food for larvae is
most abundant, a behavior shown by *Syrphus balteatus* (Fig. 8.6). This,
however, may not always prove to be the best strategy as aphid populations frequently increase rapidly and then decline just as rapidly. If a
dense population happens to be on the decline, then laying many eggs at
that density is a wasteful activity. Another species, *Platycheirus manicatus*,
shows the alternative behavior of laying eggs almost independently of density and if host populations change rapidly, new ones may become available to progeny laid in the absence of hosts. Several other oviposition
patterns are seen in these Syrphidae.

Clustering of eggs may also increase progeny survival if grouped larvae
are more effective in defense than individuals. Among butterflies the
subfamily Nymphalidae has a disproportionately large number of members that cluster their eggs (Labine 1968). The larvae may have branched
spines, synchronous head jerking, or a deterrent odor, all defenses that
are enhanced by grouping (Ford 1957).

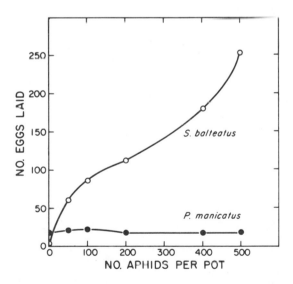

Fig. 8.6 Differences in egg-deposition strategies between two syrphid flies, *Syrphus balteatus* and *Platycheirus manicatus*, on field beans in pots with various population sizes of *Aphis fabae*. Data from Chandler 1968b.

It would be valuable to be able to quantify the amount of energy a plant or animal puts into reproduction. Here just the energy contained in progeny or propagules is not enough; the proportion of the total energy in the organism that is put into propagules must be known. Such a value would enable direct comparison between the reproductive effort of plants or animals in different populations or species, or even plants and animals. Harper and Ogden (1970) have proposed that the net reproductive effort is a reasonable estimate if defined as

$$\frac{\text{total energy as propagules (seeds)}}{\text{total energy as starting capital (original seed) plus net production}}$$

This would provide some insight into reproductive strategies. For example, when an organism comes under stress does it reduce or increase its commitment to reproduction? Has man been able to breed organisms, especially plants, with a high reproductive effort so that more energy is channeled into the crop we are interested in than into vegetative parts?

Harper and Ogden (1970) found that common groundsel, *Senecio vulgaris*, does respond to stress, in the form of limited rooting medium, by putting less into reproductive effort, although the decline is only slight over a large range of stresses (Fig. 8.7). The reproductive effort for this species was similar to other annual Compositae. An interesting point is that annual composites that have been cultivated as crop plants are

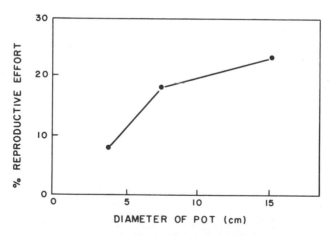

Fig. 8.7   The response of *Senecio vulgaris* plants to three stress treatments expressed as the percent of the total calorific value of the parts above ground put into reproductive effort. One plant was grown in each pot. Equivalent soil volumes for each pot diameter were 3.75 cm = 20 ml, 7.5 cm = 300 ml, 15 cm = 1700 ml, and these volumes show a ratio of 1–15–85. Therefore reproductive effort was relatively resistant to stress over a large range of soil volumes. Data from Harper and Ogden 1970.

apparently no more efficient as seed producers than are weed species in the same family. This is rather surprising when sunflowers (*Helianthus*) are compared with groundsel (*Senecio*). Additional studies have been completed on *Ranunculus* spp. (Sarukhán and Harper 1973, Sarukhán 1974) and on *Tussilago farfara* (Ogden 1974). It would be valuable to obtain for insects the sort of data that Harper and his students have, to help unravel the reasons for the array of reproductive strategies, even between closely related species.

Each reproductive strategy carries with it a cost of reproduction that influences the probability of survival of the parent. Williams (1966a) points out that it is convenient to recognize two categories of adaptation: (1) those that relate to the continued existence of the individual, provided it retains its reproductive ability; and (2) those that relate to reproduction itself. The two are intimately related. Williams says, "Heart failure and mammary failure have exactly equivalent effects on the fitness of a female mammal (except in the one bottle-manufacturing species)." Anyway, continued existence of the individual and reproductive effort must be balanced. Williams asks, "What determines how much effort an organism should expend, and to how much danger it should expose itself, in its efforts to reproduce?" Parental sacrifices are sometimes enormous and sometimes slight. Williams (1966a) says "In dealing with this problem, I will take it as a basic axiom that selection will adjust the amount of immediate reproductive effort in such a way that the cost in physiological stress and personal hazard will be justified by the probability of success." Tinkle (1969) was stimulated by this focus of Williams (1966a, b) to look at the reproductive patterns in lizards. A large clutch size is a more risky proposition for a female lizard than for a small one, and several clutches per year are riskier than a single one: (1) more energy must be channeled into eggs over a short period of time, (2) the female is loaded down with the heavy eggs and therefore is less able to escape predators, and (3) the female is exposed in an egg laying position for a longer time per season. Therefore it seems reasonable to anticipate that the species that have a larger fecundity per season will have a lower survivorship. This is the relationship Tinkle found in 13 species of lizard (Fig. 8.8).

Murdoch (1966a, b), working with ground beetles (Carabidae), found a similar relationship: "The survival of adult female Carabidae, from near the end of one breeding to the start of the next, is inversely proportional to the amount of reproduction done in that first breeding season."

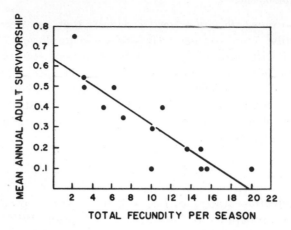

Fig. 8.8   The total fecundity per reproductive season in relation to the probability of surviving to a subsequent reproductive year for 14 populations of lizards representing 13 species. From D. W. Tinkle. The concept of reproductive effort and its relation to the evolution of life histories of lizards. *Amer. Natur.* **103**:501–516, published by the University of Chicago Press. © 1969 by the University of Chicago. All rights reserved.

He also suggested that this is one of the compensatory mechanisms leading to population stability in Carabidae, which may be widespread also in other insects. Apparently egg production was directly related to food supply (Murdoch 1966a) so that when food supply was poor in the fall, reproduction was low, survival to the following spring was increased, and in fact the major effort in reproduction was delayed until more favorable conditions prevailed. Survival of the reproducing individual is subject to evolutionary change, and even adaptive change within a generation in the case of carabid beetles.

What about survival of the progeny? In arthropods, just as in plants, the number of progeny produced is subject to considerable variation between species and two examples from very different organisms may help to understand the types of strategy involved. Mitchell's (1970) work on the analysis of dispersal in mites is revealing. In all except the soil mites, habitats for mites are discontinuous and transient. Many are predators and parasites and their minute size prevents them from actively seeking new habitats with fresh food resources. The number of progeny that actually find a resource must be maximized and is dependent on the number of progeny produced by a female, the probability of progeny finding food, and this in turn depends on the accuracy in the aim of the dispersal mechanism. Thus there exists a simple relationship:

$$F = NP_d$$

where F is the number of founders, N the number of dispersants, and P_d the probability of discovery of a new resource. A founder must be a female, and it must have mated or be parthenogenetic. If the sexes disperse independently and unmated, the number of actual founders is greatly reduced because a male and a female must arrive independently at the same place, thus reducing the probability of founding a colony. Actually where mites disperse before mating, they tend to disperse in groups rather than as single individuals. There seem to be three patterns in mites identified so far:

1. Tetranychid mites. *Eotetranychus sexmaculatus*, the prey species that Huffaker used in his orange-prey-predator experiments, is a member of this family. These tetranychids climb up stems, drop on a silken thread, and disperse in the wind. Dispersal as aerial plankton is potentially very wasteful of progeny and this waste may be compensated for in three ways according to Mitchell (1970). When resources begin to deteriorate, reproduction of females may be greatly increased so that there can be a significant increment to the standing crop of adult females within a week. Then, the males may be smaller and less abundant than females so that most of the standing crop biomass is females. Finally, mating usually occurs immediately after emergence of the female; thus almost all active females are mated and capable of founding a colony. Each of these ways seems to have been adopted by tetranychids. For example, one species, *Panonychus ulmi*, has males that weigh 2.8×10^{-6} g and make up 26% of the population. Females weigh 11.1×10^{-6} g and make up 74% of population. Thus the proportion of biomass of the population going into dispersants is $(0.74 \times 11.1)/(0.26 \times 2.8) + (0.74 \times 11.1) = 0.92$, or 92% of biomass! Similar and additional adaptations relative to dispersal have been described by Mitchell (1973) for *Tetranychus urticae*.

2. Mesostigmatid mites. One species that Springett (1968) studied is a predator of muscid fly eggs which are laid on carrion. For dispersal they are phoretic, and climb aboard carrion beetles (Silphidae) that have matured on the carrion; the beetles fly to fresh carrion and the mites reach new sources of fly eggs. This accounts for the large numbers of mites commonly seen on carrion beetles such as *Necrophorus* and *Necrodes* spp. In fact the relationship between the mites and the beetles is rather a beautiful one. If the beetles arrive at new car-

rion without mites their progeny die in competition with fly larvae. If mites are transported to the carrion, they eradicate this competition, and the beetles on which the mites depend survive: a good example of mutualism. Apparently, because of this reliable dispersal method there seems to be no budgeting of resources for increasing the numbers of dispersants. Males are only slightly smaller than females and there is a 50:50 sex ratio.

3. A scolytid egg parasite. This sort of mite is commonly found on the elytral declivity of scolytid beetles (which is often hollowed) and on the thorax. Scolytid beetles burrow into bark and lay an egg in each egg niche along a gallery in the bark. The fertilized female mites ride a beetle to a new breeding site and drop off as the beetle lays an egg. The egg is immediately walled off by the parent so a mite remains with a single egg. The mite matures and lays 60 eggs which hatch, and the hatchlings mate. There are only about three males in a brood and these mate with the females produced from the same beetle egg. Up to three female mites can produce full broods on a single egg, the progeny do not feed on the egg, and males die without ever having fed. Females disperse on newly emerged adult beetles and do not feed until after they drop off on a freshly deposited egg. The mites retain a high N by reproducing so effectively on a single egg. Also, they maintain a high P_d as only few beetle eggs are parasitized out of a total brood, so many beetle progeny can mature and carry the mites to new breeding sites. The efficiency of resource utilization for dispersants is high. Since males and females are the same size, the numbers yielded by a single female are adequate for the calculation of the proportion of biomass going into dispersal. This is $57/3+57=0.95$ or 95%. Here again the principle of allocation is at work to promote the fitness of reproducing females.

An ichneumon wasp faces a different problem, although a closely allied one. The female adult is the dispersal phase and she must find hosts in which to lay an egg. One of the evolutionary problems is how should a female gear up for egg production? Should she produce masses of eggs or few eggs? A large egg production would seem to be the better strategy and yet parasitoid species that all attack the same host may range in fecundity from 1000 to 30 eggs in a lifetime (Price 1973a, 1974a). A good index of this production is the number of ovarioles a female has in each ovary. This ranges from 50 in the species that produces 1000 eggs to three or four ovarioles in species that produce 30 eggs. It turns out

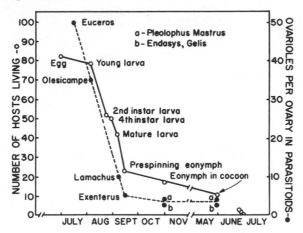

Fig. 8.9 The survivorship curve of the host, the Swaine jack pine sawfly, in a typical generation, ◯ and solid line (from McLeod 1972), and the number of ovarioles per ovary in parasitoids, ● and dashed line, plotted in synchrony with the time at which each species most commonly attacks the host. From Price 1974a.

that the highly fecund species attack the host early in its life cycle and the less fecund species later (Fig. 8.9). Fecundity in these species is adjusted to the ease in finding hosts, or food for progeny, and thus supports Lack's hypothesis. Early stages are the most abundant and can be readily discovered in the tree canopy. After considerable host mortality hosts become less abundant and are concealed in the forest litter so they are difficult to discover. In this case, there is no advantage to production of many eggs as a female probably could not find enough hosts to leave them in.

Another factor is that those parasitoids that attack early stages are also subject to more mortality in the form of predation and hyperparasitism, as they do not emerge until the following year. Those that attack later are exposed to less mortality simply because the host is harder to find and better protected from all mortality factors. Here is another example of how the number of progeny a female produces is a balance between several factors interacting in the environment.

This brings us to the fourth hypothesis relating to the clutch size debate and evolutionary strategies for egg production—the balanced mortality hypothesis (e.g., Price 1974a). Many people have expressed the view that egg production is adapted to counter the relative hostility of the environment in which the organism lives (e.g., Rensch 1938, Skutch 1949, 1967, and Smith 1954). Cole (1954b) states that the high fecundity frequently seen in parasites and marine organisms is an adaptation to ensure population survival when probability of death is high. Lack (1947a, 1949, 1954, 1966) has argued against this view but it has gained support from many (e.g., Dobzhansky 1950, Fretwell 1969, Pianka 1970, and Willson 1971). I think the supporters would argue that the adjustment of egg production through the action of natural selection during evolutionary time results in a degree of balance between fecundity and mortality in the long term, but cannot result in seasonal adjustment to mortality factors.

If the parasitoid example given earlier is examined, the validity of the hypothesis can be tested. The relative egg-production capacity of females is known and the probability of survival of progeny can be estimated from the survivorship curve of the host (from McLeod 1972), since immature parasitoids must suffer the same mortality as the host (see Fig. 8.9). Thus we know the actual probability of survival, derived from the host survivorship curve, and the predicted probability, derived from the balanced mortality hypothesis; that is, that the probability of survival is the reciprocal of fecundity (or in this case relative fecundity estimated by ovariole number). The predicted and actual values are closely correlated, the regression line accounting for 93% of the variance (Fig. 8.10). Since the number of eggs laid is also dependent on the supply of larval food (hosts) available to the searching female, both Lack's hypothesis and the balanced mortality hypothesis are supported by this analysis.

Williams (1966a) would argue that the hypothesis is back to front and that actually mortality balances fecundity. Since populations over long periods of time have a zero growth rate, an increase in fecundity automatically increases the number of individuals that die. Also a female with limited resources has two basic strategies available. She can put much energy into few progeny or little energy into many, with correspondingly predestined low and high mortality rates, respectively. However, the forces that cause increased fecundity must be understood. Another look at the parasitoid complex on *N. swainei*, and the family Ichneumonidae as a whole, may throw light on the debate. If the phylogeny of the Ichneumonidae is examined both the Tryphoninae and the Ephialtinae are considered to be primitive, and they have relatively low fecundities. An evolutionary trend of changing hosts or time of attack in this primitive stock would thus start from a female with low fecundity. If a female attacked an early and thus a vulnerable stage of a host in which mortality was high, she may well be unsuccessful in leaving viable progeny. Such a host could be exploited only with increased fecundity. Thus natural selection for increased fecundity results through the force of mortality. Mortality is the proximate selective factor that results, ulti-

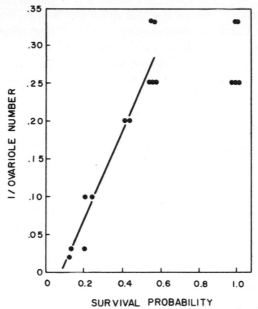

Fig. 8.10   The reciprocal of ovariole number, which predicts the probability of survival to maturity of progeny, in relation to the actual probability of survival estimated from the host survivorship curve. The regression line accounts for 93% of the variance. The five points at a survival probability of 1.0 were not included in the regression, since egg production must be geared for the more stringent conditions represented by a survival probability of 0.6. At both probabilities the same five species were involved (c.f., Fig. 8.9). From Price 1974a.

mately, in change in fecundity. Mortality is balanced by fecundity, in this case. Under other evolutionary conditions Williams may be correct. Willson (1971) also discusses conditions under which fecundity is balanced.

Reproductive strategies on rich food sources and in harsh conditions may lead to convergent strategies. Wilson (1971a) considered that pre-social behavior in insects has evolved repeatedly and frequently in very different situations. Where physical conditions are harsh it is frequently necessary for the mother to protect her progeny, as does a ground-dwelling cricket, *Anurogryllus muticus*, from excessive moisture and fungal growth. Conversely where rich food sources are exploited, competition is fierce and a parent may need to protect resources for her young. Such a case is seen in the *Necrophorous* beetles (e.g., *N. vespillio*) that build a nest and feed their young in a manner similar to birds.

Another strategy relating to rich resources is seen in some flesh flies, Sarcophagidae, where the females deposit third instar larvae on the food. These are relatively large, good competitors, and soon pupate, so that temporal exposure to a highly competitive, rapidly changing medium is brief.

In dung flies, Scatophagidae, the food source may be so localized, and competition so intense that many behavioral adaptations to cope with the situation have been observed. These have been described in a fascinating series of papers by Parker (1971, 1974, and references therein). One such behavioral adaptation is that males locate females on fresh cattle dung and then the pair may leave the dung and copulate away from it. This seems to be maladaptive, since copulation is more rapid on the warm dung surface than distant from it (Fig. 8.11). However on closer examination it appears that males gain an advantage by reducing the chances of being dislodged *in copulo* by another male, an observation reinforced by the density-dependent manner of the emigration (Fig. 8.12). And it is the males that control movements of the pair *in copulo*. The strategy here is to leave the site of severest competition and return to it later for oviposition.

Insects provide a wealth of closely related species and a diversity of reproductive strategies that should make their further study highly profitable and enlightening, and should help us to see patterns in the almost bewildering numbers of species available for study.

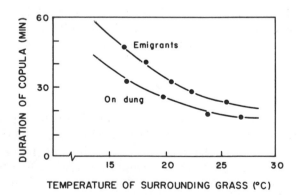

Fig. 8.11 The duration of copulation of the dung flies, *Scatophaga stercoraria* (Scatophagidae) on dung compared to those that emigrate to the surrounding grass, in relation to the temperature of the surrounding grass. After Parker 1971. Reproduced from *Journal of Animal Ecology* by permission of Blackwell Scientific Publications.

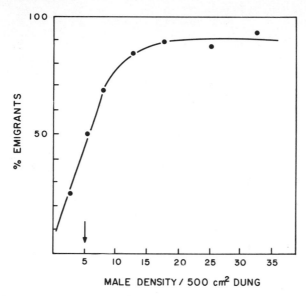

Fig. 8.12 The percentage of dung fly pairs that emigrate to the surrounding grass after meeting on dung, in relation to the density of searching males present on the dung surface. Arrow indicates a possible threshold density. From Parker 1971. Reproduced from *Journal of Animal Ecology* by permission of Blackwell Scientific Publications.

Chapter 9

POPULATION
DYNAMICS

Because population dynamics is a vast subject, any relatively short treatment of it must be highly selective. Rather than dealing principally with insect population dynamics the theories of the subject and the factors involved are emphasized here. This is because, although studies on insects have contributed significantly to the understanding of population dynamics, too many populations have been investigated and conclusions made without sufficient awareness or acknowledgement of other possible influential factors. Dispersal as a factor involved in population change is also emphasized here. Again entomologists have tended to underestimate the importance of colonization through dispersal, or ignore it because of difficulties in quantifying insect movement. The examples discussed in the last section of this chapter show how vital an understanding of dispersal is.

First of all some terms to work with are needed. A density-dependent factor is any factor in which its adverse effect increases, or its beneficial influence decreases, as a percentage of the population as the population increases in density (Fig. 9.1). Conversely any factor that shows no relationship in its influence on the population to the density of that population is a density-independent factor. Some confusion in the literature on the meaning of the key factor must also be clarified. Solomon (1949) defined it as the main controlling factor affecting a population. Morris (1959) defined it as the factor that causes a mortality closely related to the observed changes in the total population from generation to generation. Therefore these factors may be useful in predicting trends in the total population. In Morris' (1959) words, "A key factor was defined as any mortality factor that has useful predictive value and no attempt has been made to establish cause and effect, because single-factor data are

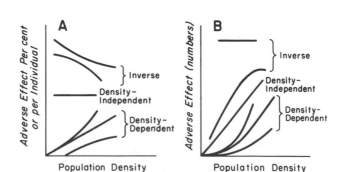

Fig. 9.1   Types of response to changes in density (*a*) expressed as a percentage response to increasing populations, (*b*) expressed as the numbers of individuals affected with increasing populations. From Solomon 1969 and reprint 1973.

scarcely suitable for this purpose." Note how different this is from Solomon's definition!

This difficulty of establishing cause and effect is a major one in population studies, and it is far safer to use Morris's definition than Solomon's when dealing with natural situations. Even when Varley and Gradwell's (1960, 1968) "key factor analysis" is used Morris' definition should be born in mind. Varley and Gradwell (1968) plotted population changes on a logarithmic scale, and they compared the killing power, or k-value, of each mortality factor by calculating the difference between the logarithm of population density before and after its action. Close correlation between population change and a k-value lead to the conclusion that this factor was the key factor in causing change. However correlation does not necessarily imply causation (e.g., see Eberhardt 1970) and the identified key factor may actually respond to changes caused by other factors. For example, predators of lemmings in the arctic respond to lemming cycles but they do not cause them.

A brief survey of theories on population regulation follows. The conceptual framework used in the chapter is summarized in Table 9.1, which also provides additional references. There are two basic concepts in population regulation: (1) that there are factors external to the population that influence population numbers (Table 9.1, Part A); and (2) that factors change within the population that affect numbers and produce regulation (Table 9.1, Part B). Within the first category there is the classic argument between proponents of regulation being caused by density-dependent factors: the Nicholson-Bailey school (Table 9.1, Section 1), and proponents that maintain that these factors are not important or the Davidson, Andrewartha, and Birch school (Table 9.1, Section 2). However, Andrewartha and Birch (1954) found little use for the terms density-dependent and density-independent. They concluded that there is no component of the environment such that its influence is independent of population density, but there is no need to regard density-dependent factors as having any special importance. Since the concepts are much in use at present they are used here, and as a corollary to their acceptance as legitimate terms, Andrewartha and Birch become proponents of density-independent regulation of populations (see p. 179).

The three factors that are most likely to operate in a density-dependent way are: (1) predation or parasitism will increase, (2) suitable food will become more and more scarce and increased mortality or decreased reproduction will result, and (3) space for living or breeding will also become more and more limiting.

Table 9.1   Theories on population regulation.

A.   Exogenous (extrinsic) population processes
1.   Density-dependent factors.
   (*a*)   Predation.

      Hosts and parasitoids (Nicholson 1933, 1954a,b, 1957, 1958, Nicholson and Bailey 1935).

      On microtine populations (Pearson 1964, Pitelka, Tomich and Treichel 1955).

      On plants (Harper 1968).

      On Kaibab deer herd (Allee et al. 1949).

      Herbivores in general (Hairston, Smith and Slobodkin 1960).

   (*b*)   Food.

      Nicholson and Bailey model assumes that predator is food limited.

      Decomposers, producers, and predators in general—"The Etude" (Hairston, Smith and Slobodkin 1960, see also Murdoch 1966c, Ehrlich and Birch 1967, Slobodkin, Smith and Hairston 1967, for debate).

      Birds (Lack 1954).

      Predator populations (Elton 1942).

      Ungulate populations (Caughley 1970, n.b. comments on Kaibab deer).

      Nutrient recovery hypothesis in microtine cycles. (Pitelka 1959, 1964, Schultz 1964, Batzli and Pitelka 1970).

      Supplemental food (Fordham 1971).

   (*c*)   Combination of predation and food (Readshaw 1965).

   (*d*)   Space, that is, favorable habitats: usually pressure to leave favorable habitat has social interaction as proximate factor and so could be classified under B3 below.

      Muskrat populations (*Ondatra zibethica*) (Errington 1946, 1967, see also Chapter 5).

      Chaffinch (*Fringilla coelebs*) in Holland (Glas 1960).

      Ground-dwelling Ichneumonidae (Price 1970c,d, 1971a).

      Emigration (e.g., Lidicker 1962), but may be caused by food shortage etc.

2.   Density-independent factors.
   (*a*)   Weather

      Weather influence on *Thrips imaginis* (Davidson and Andrewartha 1948a,b, see also Smith 1961, Reddingius 1971).

      Weather and the time available to reproduce (Andrewartha and Birch 1954).

      Release of the spruce budworm, *Choristoneura fumiferana*, (Greenbank 1956), lodgepole needle miner, *Recurvaria starki* (Stark 1959).

   (*b*)   Random changes in population due to random influences (Cole 1951, 1954a, Leslie 1959).

3.   Intermediate between 1 and 2.

      Imperfect density-dependence (Milne 1957a,b, 1962, Thompson 1939).

      Urceolaria mitra and *Enchytraeus albidus* (Reynoldson 1957).

Red squirrel, *Tamiasciurus hudsonicus* (Kemp and Keith 1970, cf. Lack 1954, on spruce cone crop and crossbill populations).

B. Endogenous (intrinsic) population processes (All are probably density-dependent)

1. Pathological effects in response to crowding (see Emlen 1973 for discussion).
   (a) Shock disease (e.g., Frank 1957).
   (b) Adreno-pituitary exhaustion (Christian 1950, 1959, Christian and Davis 1964).
2. Processes with a genetic component.
   (a) Density-dependent increase in
       (1) Proportion of congenitally less viable individuals (Chitty 1957, 1960).
       (2) Aggressive behavior (Chitty 1957, 1967, Krebs 1970).
   (b) Genetic breakdown of population during flush phase (Carson 1968, see also Ford 1957, 1964, Ford and Ford 1930, Ayala 1968).
   (c) Polymorphic behavior for dispersal and such in
       (1) *Malacosoma pluviale* (Wellington 1957, 1960, 1964).
       (2) *Microtus* spp. in Indiana (Myers and Krebs 1971).
   (d) Changes in development times, dispersal rates, and such, in *Porthetria dispar.* (Leonard 1970a,b).
   (e) Genetic feedback (Pimentel 1961b, 1968).
3. Social interaction.
   (a) Evolution of social checks on population (Wynne-Edwards 1962, 1964b, 1965, see also Hamilton 1964a,b).
   (b) Intraspecific competition for space (see A-d above).
   (c) Aggressive behavior (see 2(a)(2) above, Calhoun 1952).
4. Dispersal (see Johnson 1966, 1969).
   (a) The adaptive nature of dispersal (Johnson 1966, 1969, Gadgil 1971).
   (b) Evidence for density-regulated dispersal in insects (see also A-d above).
       (1) Broom insects (Dempster 1968, Waloff 1968a,b).
       (2) *Hyphantria cunea* (Morris 1971b).
       (3) *Ascia monuste phileta* (Chermock 1946, Nielsen 1961, Johnson 1969).
       (4) *Phryganidia californica* (Harville 1955).
       (5) Pierid butterflies (Shapiro 1970).

Supporting evidence for predation as a regulating factor comes from various sources. The models of predation (Lotka-Volterra and Nicholson-Bailey, see Chapter 5) suggest that prey populations can be regulated completely by predators or parasitoids. There are also field data that show extremely heavy predation such as that on a *Microtus* population in California by the predators: feral cats, gray foxes, raccoons, and skunks (Fig. 9.2) (Pearson 1964). Such heavy mortality may also be caused by parasitoids in insect populations (e.g., Baltensweiler 1968, Waloff 1968a,

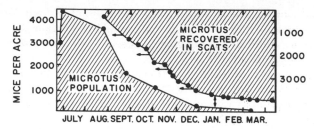

Fig. 9.2 Number of *Microtus* per acre during the year and the cumulative number recovered in predators' scats. Arrows indicate that the line should be moved to the left to compensate for the delay between the death of the mouse and its recovery in a scat. The vertical distance between the shaded areas (as shown for January) indicates the mortality not accounted for by predation. However the influence of predation may be overestimated, since predators may have taken diseased or even dead individuals. From Pearson 1964.

Price and Tripp 1972). As far as plants are concerned Harper (1968) says that there is abundant evidence that grazing animals act as selective predators in grassland, for example, sheep, reducing the numbers of grass plants, and enabling dicotyledonous species to gain a hold in the grassland community.

A well known example of the effect of predation (but see p. 176) on the prey population is that involving the mule deer (*Odocoileus hemionus*) on the Kaibab Plateau in Arizona, on the north rim of the Grand Canyon (see Allee et al. 1949 for account). In 1905 the deer population was about 4000 and this level seems to have been maintained by puma and wolf predation so that winter forage was never a limiting factor on the plateau. The carrying capacity was never reached (Fig. 9.3). Starting

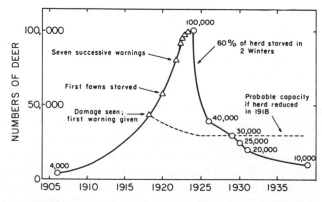

Fig. 9.3 Leopold's (1943) interpretation of population trends of the Kaibab deer herd 1906–1939 (see also Caughley 1970).

in 1907 hundreds of puma, wolves, and coyotes were killed, and the deer population began to increase. Excessive winter grazing depleted the range and in two winters 60% of the herd starved. The population leveled off at about 10,000 deer whereas the carrying capacity of the range was considered to be 30,000 deer before the range was depleted. Predators were strongly implicated in population regulation, although Caughley (1970) suggests other factors are important (p. 176).

Hairston, Smith, and Slobodkin (1960) argue for predation being the prime controlling influence on herbivores from a completely different standpoint (see also pp. 100 and below). In their study, which is fondly named "the étude," they argue as follows. The accumulation of fossil fuels is negligible. All energy fixed by photosynthesis must therefore flow through the biosphere. Therefore all organisms taken together must be food limited. Any population that is not resource limited must be limited to a level below that set by its resources. The obvious lack of depletion of green plants by herbivores are exceptions to the general picture. Therefore producers are neither herbivore nor catastrophe-limited; they must be limited by their own exhaustion of resources. Since we have seen that herbivores can deplete their food supply when numerous enough, that is in the absence of predators, and since there usually is little evidence of this in general, herbivores must be controlled by predation (but see below). So predation has been repeatedly implicated as an important population regulating agent.

How important is food? In the predator–prey models where there is a mutual interaction, clearly food for the predator is important. Thus the Lotka-Volterra and Nicholson-Bailey models support the idea of food being a critical factor. Hairston, Smith, and Slobodkin (1960) also cite food as the limiting factor for decomposers, producers, and predators in general, but papers debating the validity of this argument should be consulted (e.g., Murdoch 1966c, Erhlich and Birch 1967, Slobodkin, Smith, and Hairston 1967). For example, although the authors claim that only herbivores are predator-limited they may be limited by the amount of suitable food in tolerable microclimates (see Chapter 3). Based on indirect evidence Lack (1954) argues with the following points that food limits bird populations: (1) few adults appear to die from predation or disease, leaving food shortage as the likeliest cause of density-dependent loss; (2) birds are usually more numerous where their food is more abundant; (3) each species in the same region depends primarily on different foods and segregation of feeding habits is observed;

and (4) fighting for food is a regular feature of the winter behavior of several bird species. Cycles of arctic herbivores (for example, see Keith 1963) and their predators show how the latter are food limited. Whatever the actual causes of death in the predator population it is clear that food shortage is the single critical factor that precipitates the crash.

Caughley (1970) points out that data on the mule deer of the Kaibab Plateau are speculative and inadequate, and the eruption is also well correlated with other factors besides destruction of predators. Notably, sheep grazing was reduced drastically from 200,000 sheep in 1889 to 5000 by 1908. Essentially, an important competitor for food declined in population leaving much more food available to the mule deer herds, so that perhaps food was actually limiting the Kaibab deer. This would agree with data from other large herbivore populations where food has been found to be limiting. Caughley's conclusions on the population regulation of the thar, a goat-like ungulate from the Himalayas, liberated in New Zealand in 1904, should be consulted.

Pitelka (1964) and Schultz (1964) have come to the conclusion that cycles of the lemming, *Lemmus trimucronatus*, at Point Barrow, Alaska, result from an interaction between herbivore and vegetation mediated by factors of nutrient recovery and availability in the soil (Fig. 9.4). Thus population regulation depends on food quantity and quality. Food quality was also important in the population dynamics of the mirid bug, *Leptoterna dolabrata* (McNeill 1973).

In some population studies a combination of predation and food has been found to play a major role. For example, Readshaw (1965) studied the stick insect *Didymuria violescens* (Phasmatidae) in New South Wales and Victoria in Australia. He presents a theory based on his data that the stick insect exists under two systems of control: one at low density when increase is limited largely by egg parasitoids or birds or both; another at high density when increase is ultimately prevented by intraspecific competition for food. Birds are ineffective during peak years because of their limited total response to increase in numbers of the prey (supports discussion in Chapter 5, cf., *ES* in Fig. 5.10*b*).

Space as a limiting factor has been discussed already in relation to predation. Errington's studies (1946, 1967) on muskrats indicate that early colonizers choose the most suitable sites that provide plenty of food and very good cover. As the population increases young muskrats are forced to establish territories beyond the limits of the most suitable habitat as the older males will defend their territories against invasion. Beyond the

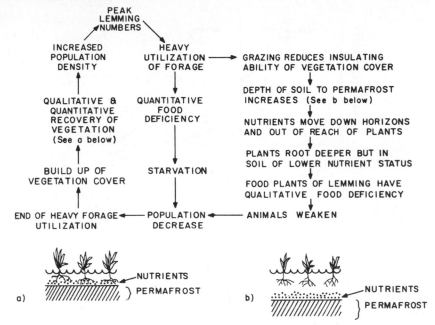

Fig. 9.4 Summary of the nutrient recovery hypothesis of Pitelka (1964) and Schultz (1964) for the lemming, *Lemmus trimucronatus*, at Point Barrow, Alaska (derived in part from Krebs 1964). Nutrients may be leached from the rooting medium as shown in *b*, or they may be diluted by being dispersed through a larger volume of soil. As grazing is reduced vegetation cover increases, the depth of permafrost decreases, nutrients are concentrated in the rooting zone, and a qualitative recovery of vegetation results.

best territories muskrats are subject to heavy predation, shortage of food, and a harsher climate. But ultimately shortage of suitable space that provides food and protection is the determining factor (Fig. 9.5).

Glas (1960) presents a clear example where space is limiting for the chaffinch (*Fringilla coelebs*). Glas studied a population in a small mixed wood and the adjacent pine wood in Holland. The birds showed preference for the mixed wood community: first, the mixed wood filled up with territorial males, and the available space limited the number that could remain resident. Then the colonizers overflowed into the pine wood, being forced out of the mixed wood by the territorial defenses of the resident males (Fig. 9.6). However, size of territory is frequently influenced by food supply (see Chapter 16).

Price (1970c,d, 1971a) has observed ichneumonid parasitoids that search for sawfly cocoons buried in the forest litter. The females are able to detect the presence of others by an odor left on the litter, and

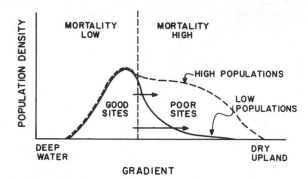

Fig 9.5 Summary of Errington's view of population regulation in muskrats and other organisms. Solid line indicates distribution of individuals during low populations. As populations increase more individuals move to harsher sites where mortality is high, so that the distribution indicated by the dashed line during high populations is only temporary.

they avoid this odor as it seems to be repellent. Therefore the maximum density of females that can exist in an area is not closely related to the host density. Rather, each female needs an amount of space so that contacts with the odors of others is not so frequent as to drive her from the area. Host density is ultimately limiting as cocooned larvae are the food

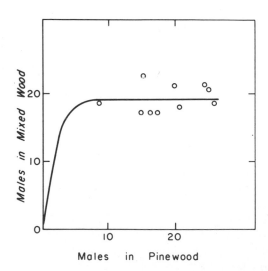

Fig. 9.6 The establishment of territories by male chaffinches between 1946 and 1955 in a small mixed wood and a neighboring pine wood. Note that the mixed wood regularly filled to capacity before the pine wood was utilized extensively. Slightly modified from Glas 1960.

source; thus higher host densities do permit higher parasitoid densities, but the females become sensitive to crowding long before the highest host populations are reached. In favorable sites where hosts are abundant, populations of parasitoids will therefore increase rapidly but many females will leave the site due to their avoidance behavior. The result is that at high population levels many unfavorable sites are colonized by these parasitoids, whereas at low population levels only the most favorable sites are occupied (Fig. 9.7, cf. Fig. 9.5 on muskrat populations).

The proponents of regulation by density-independent factors, such as mortality caused by weather or insecticide, have much evidence to draw on for support. Davidson, Andrewartha, and Birch have been the strongest proponents for population control by means of weather. Since weather may kill off numbers of individuals that are not correlated with population density, it is a density-independent factor. Andrewartha and Birch's (1954) book, *The distribution and abundance of animals,* is a treatise supporting their hypothesis that organisms are primarily limited by a shortage of time when weather conditions are so favorable that the population can increase. Therefore the population never has enough time to reproduce up to the carrying capacity, competition for food does not result, and density-dependent factors are unimportant in population regulation. (Does this mean that most species are *r* selected?). This is in direct opposition to Nicholson's arguments.

The data that inspired Davidson, Andrewartha, and Birch were col-

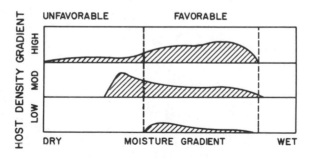

Fig. 9.7 Distribution of the ichneumonid parasitoid, *Pleolophus basizonus* in space defined by a moisture gradient and a host density gradient. As host density increases so parasitoid numbers increase and the dry marginal habitats become occupied only under this population pressure. The height of the distribution curves indicates the proportion of all species represented by *P. basizonus* and not actual abundance. After Price 1971a.

lected over 14 years, 1932–1946. The subject species was the apple blossom thrips, *Thrips imaginis,* and it was sampled on rose blossoms in the garden of the Waite Agricultural Research Institute, University of Adelaide, Australia. Davidson and Andrewartha (1948a,b) found that the yearly abundance curve of thrips typically showed a rapid rise to peak abundance and then a rapid decline (Fig. 9.8). They concluded that competition plays little or no part in determining the maximum density reached in late November or early December (Spring). Rapid reproduction was possible only for a limited period during spring and early summer. Insects increased rapidly but so did the flowers available to them, and the favorable period normally ended long before *Thrips* reached the carrying capacity of the flowers. In fact they found that a combination of four weather factors explained 78% of the total variance in the annual maximum density attained by the thrips population. These four factors combined must have been far more important than any

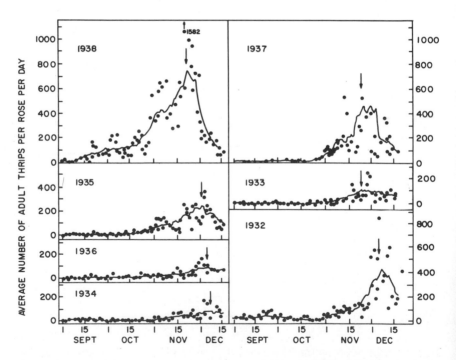

Fig. 9.8 The numbers of *Thrips imaginis* per rose per day during the spring of each year 1932–1938. The line is a 15-point moving average, and the arrow indicates the maximum abundance in each year. From H. G. Andrewartha and L. C. Birch. The distribution and abundance of animals, published by The University of Chicago Press. Copyright 1954 by the University of Chicago Press. All rights reserved.

others. The most important factor was winter temperatures which affected the earliness of appearance of blossoms, especially affecting the length of time for reproduction. The second most important factor was rainfall during September and October which promoted development of host plants and reduced mortality of pupal thrips in the soil. The third factor was winter temperatures of the previous year. Presumably they promoted survival of thrips just as factor 1. Finally, spring temperatures (during September and October) were important. These increased the rate of development of thrips and host plant. But these temperatures were usually sufficient during this period so that it was the least influential of the four factors.

However, there are some difficulties in the interpretation that weather has controlling influence (see also Smith 1961, Reddingius 1971). The carrying capacity of the environment is hard to determine. The roses did not actually serve as a breeding site for the thrips but acted as a trap, which indicated the density of the population in the area. We do not know how crowded the flowers were that supported breeding populations! Perhaps breeding sites were limiting the population. Also, the most important factor influencing thrips populations was winter temperature. This also influenced host plant growth and flower production. Therefore, it was influencing the carrying capacity and therefore population levels indirectly. Nicholson called such an influence a density-legislative factor. Thus weather can influence the food supply and so influence density-dependent processes. The third most important factor was the winter temperature of the previous year. Since winter temperature is most closely correlated with maximum population, Davidson and Andrewartha really found that the population in the current year is dependent on the population the year before, probably a density-dependent effect! Finally, Adelaide is practically speaking on the edge of the Great Victoria Desert and *Thrips imaginis* is at the end of its range in Adelaide. Therefore climatic stress is most likely to be seen in this population, although in the case of *Thrips* density-dependent factors cannot be ruled out.

Probably density-independent factors are more important at the edge of the range of a species, and density-dependent factors at the center (Fig. 9.9). Support for this statement was provided by Whittaker (1971) who studied the population dynamics of the cercopid, *Neophilaenus lineatus*, near the edge of its range and in more southerly sites in England. In the northern populations he found no evidence of density-dependent factors whereas in the south the generation mortality was density-dependent, and a dipteran parasitoid acted in a density-dependent manner.

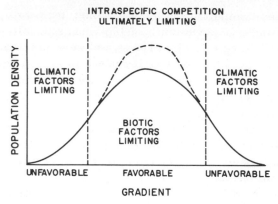

Fig. 9.9 Hypothetical relationship between the major regulating factors on a species throughout the geographic range of the species.

Another case where weather seems to exert a controlling influence is on the spruce budworm, *Choristoneura fumiferana*, in New Brunswick. Greenbank (1956) has suggested that a series of dry and sunny summers is beneficial to survival of the budworm and leads to a population release. The main reasons are that staminate flower production is higher, and these flowers act as a better food source for larvae, development is quicker, and fecundity is higher. Stark (1959) concluded that climatic release resulted in outbreaks of the lodgepole needle miner in the Canadian Rocky Mountains and reviews the literature on the subject. Wellington (1954a,b) has proposed a comprehensive theory of climatic release.

In between the density-dependent control camp and the density-independent control camp sit some people who wish to make peace and combine the two theories. Without doubt both types of control are important. Milne (1957a,b) has been the main proponent of a joint theory. Reynoldson (1957) showed that weather can be critical to one species and competition to another in the very same sewage tank. LeRoux et al. (1963) and Watt (1963a) concluded that the major factors influencing populations of five agricultural crop pests in Quebec were, for three species, migration of adults, parasitism, and bird predation, all likely to be density-dependent factors, and for the other two, frost and other weather conditions, which are density-independent factors. Among the many species of insect herbivores on broom, both density-dependent and

independent factors were important (Waloff 1968b). Intra- and interspecific competition, egg sterility at high densities, predation, parasitism,
and dispersal were significant influences on some species, and in the
same community other species were most affected by density-independent
factors: plant aging that affected nutrition, difficulty in establishment of
first instar larvae, and frosts.

Other examples show that weather controls the amount of food where
food is limiting, so that these factors interact to influence the herbivore
population, as suggested for *Thrips imaginis*. Kemp and Keith's (1970)
study on red squirrel population dynamics shows this relationship (Fig.
9.10). Lack (1954) gives a similar example where the population of cross-

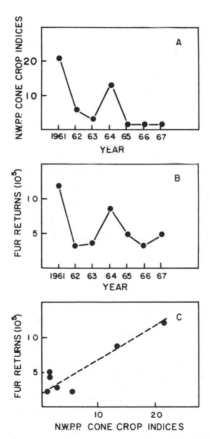

Fig. 9.10 The relationship between cone crop size (*a*) estimated from the North
Western Pulp and Power (N.W.P.P.) cone-crop indices, which is influenced by the
weather, and red squirrel abundance, (*b*) estimated by fur returns in Alberta, and the
correlation between the two (*c*). From Kemp and Keith 1970.

bills in Finland is related to the spruce cone crop. Release of the spruce budworm could be used as another case.

Finally, in relation to density-independent processes, Cole's papers (1951, 1954a) should be consulted as he suggests that population fluctuation (in particular population cycles) may be most appropriately described by assuming that there are so many influences on a population that the outcome is a random fluctuation. However, Moran (1954) takes exception to Cole's analysis as only the mean distance between peak populations was considered. Moran concluded that lynx and snowshoe hare populations oscillate in a nonrandom manner. A symposium on cycles in animal populations (Hewitt 1954) may be consulted for further details.

Now the possibility must be investigated that endogenous population processes are important in population regulation. Density-dependent pathological effects have been assumed to be important. Here the pathological effects of stress on animals is involved. Pathogenic organisms such as bacteria or viruses are not included as these would fit into the exogenous population processes, since the effects of a pathogen are likely to increase with density just as predation does. At high population densities animals are subjected to increased stresses in finding food and cover, and escaping predators. They may be forced to fight with other animals more frequently to obtain sufficient food or a mate. The body adapts physiologically to these stresses in vertebrates under the stimulus of increased hormone secretion from the adrenal and pituitary glands. These glands can compensate for stress only within certain limits, and when the stresses become very great, Christian (1950, 1959, Christian and Davis 1964) has postulated that death occurs through exhaustion of the adreno-pituitary system, and not through the action of food shortage, predators, or disease organisms. "Shock disease" is apparently also a manifestation of the same syndrome or perhaps a pathological condition that impairs the animal's ability to store glycogen. This disease has been observed in Minnesota in snowshoe hare cycles (Green and Larson 1938, Green and Evans 1940) and in meadow vole populations in Germany (Frank 1957). For further discussion see Emlen (1973).

Chitty (1957, 1960) who studied the vole, *Microtus agrestis*, at Lake Vyrnwy in Wales found that in a natural population of field voles that was declining, individuals were intrinsically less viable than their predecessors, and that changes in external mortality factors, such as weather and predators, were insufficient to account for the increased probability of death. Chitty (1960) proposed the hypothesis that all species are capable of regulating their own population densities without destroying the renewable resources of their environment, or without requiring enemies or bad weather to keep them from doing so. Under appropriate circumstances, indefinite increase in population density is prevented through a deterioration in the quality of the population. Chitty also pointed out that it is unsafe to assume that population density has no effect on the physiology of the individual or the genetics of the population. Therefore, contrary to the assumption that weather acts in a density-independent way, it is most improbable that the action of physical factors is independent of population density, as Andrewartha and Birch have stated. He therefore postulated that the effects of "independent" events, such as weather, become more severe as numbers rise and quality falls.

This hypothesis overcomes the difficulties in the density-dependent versus the density-independent control argument. The hypothesis is based on a set of known facts on population cycles: (1) declines in population can take place in a favorable environment; (2) high population density is not sufficient to start an immediate decline; (3) a low population is not sufficient to halt a decline; (4) the vast majority of animals die from unknown causes, males more rapidly than females; (5) the death rate can be greatly reduced by placing animals in captivity; and (6) the adult death rate is not abnormally high during the years of maximum abundance. These facts are consistent with the idea that susceptibility to natural hazards increases among generations descended from animals affected by adverse environmental conditions. In 1960 Chitty wrote that the mechanism of this process had yet to be discovered.

In 1967 Chitty published an exceptionally stimulating paper. He stated that mechanisms for the self-regulation of animal numbers are thought to be a consequence of selection under conditions of mutual interference, in favor of genotypes that have a worse effect on their neighbors than vice versa. The most puzzling aspect of small mammal populations during their periodic declines in numbers is the severity of mortality at relatively low densities after peak abundance. Now he suggested that there was no evidence that the animals are less viable than normal, although a decrease in some components of fitness may be expected. Aggressive behavior is the most likely characteristic to improve survival under conditions where mutual interference is inevitable. Chitty pointed out that individuals that have not been selected under conditions of intraspecific strife are likely to be mutually tolerant, and populations composed of such individuals should reach abnormal abundance before such selection takes place. Such populations may occur when new areas are invaded, when an existing source of heavy mortality is removed, or when populations have been seriously reduced by natural or artificial catastrophes.

At high populations aggressive individuals will be relatively more fit, and will be selected for, but as populations decline this trait will become maladaptive as energy is wasted. Thus populations may decline more than expected before aggressiveness is selected out of the population. Thus Chitty's theory depends on behavioral, physiological, and genetic changes in the population.

Carson (1968) has described the likely changes in genetic material in a population during a population increase, or flush, and the population crash. Small changes in the gene pool of a population may actually initiate a flush. Carson maintained a laboratory population of *Drosophila melanogaster* which was inbred and contained recessive mutant markers. About 160 *Drosophila* per generation could be maintained on a unit of food. He altered the genetic content of the population by adding a single male fly whose mother was from the population and whose father was from an unrelated wild-type laboratory strain. Without any change in food or space a population flush resulted and in nine generations the population had increased to three times its size (477 individuals). Even though food was unchanged, population growth was exponential. This change must have been due initially to higher Darwinian fitness of some of the genotypes following hybridization. After the peak the population fell abruptly and oscillated around a lower level.

In general there seem to be four stages to the flush and crash according to Carson. Stage 1—Initially new genetic material is injected into the gene pool, or environmental influences change so that mortality in the population is reduced or fecundity is increased. Stage 2—A flush in population results during the period of reduced natural selection and is accompanied by a breakdown in the genetic basis of fitness in the population. Stage 3—More stringent environmental conditions imposed on the population cause a crash in numbers because of severely lowered fitness in the population. Stage 4—As the crash reduces the population size toward the original level, it may carry the population to a size even smaller than at the inception of the cycle. This may be because of the lag between the appearance of stringent conditions and the multiplication by selection of individuals carrying genotypes with greater Darwinian fitness relative to these new conditions. This supports Chitty's point that low populations are not sufficient to halt a decline. Could this be a third possible explanation of the Kaibab deer decline below the original carrying capacity?

There may result considerable differences between the genotypes at stage 1 and the end of stage 4. The classic case of a natural population showing evolution in a similar way to that postulated by Carson was observed by H. D. and E. B. Ford and reported in 1930. They studied an isolated population of the marsh fritillary butterfly, *Melitaea* (*Euphy-dryas*) *aurinia*, in Cumberland, England, where changes in wing pattern could be relatively easily observed. They studied the population for 19 years in all (Ford 1964) and records of the population condition had been left by collectors during the previous 36 years; preserved specimens covering a period of 55 years were available for study! Collectors of butterflies look for unusual forms. Therefore the record was good for checking variability in the population. Also, the marsh fritillary has a particularly intricate pattern that reflects changes in genotype very sensitively. The general trends in population change in numbers and variability are given in Ford and Ford (1930), Ford (1957, 1964) and are summarized in Fig. 9.11.

It is remarkable that in 4–5 generations, 1920–1924, a visible evolution in wing pattern took place, and this was probably accompanied by pleiotropic gene effects that shifted the adaptive core of the population in response to the new environmental conditions prevailing in 1924. This shift was the result of the incredible diversity of genotypes that were subject to the selection in 1923 and 1924 when the population flush ended and the population stabilized, so that mortality increased to about 99% (assuming that a female lays 200 fertile eggs on average). During the flush phase, as described by Ford (1964), "an extraordinary outburst of

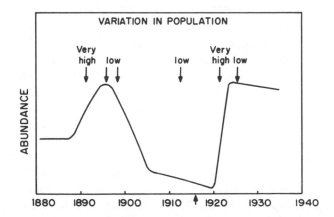

Fig. 9.11 Diagrammatic representation of population size of the marsh fritillary butterfly studied by Ford and Ford (1930), based on accounts by these authors, Ford (1957) and Ford (1964). Note that when selective pressure is released and populations are increasing rapidly, very high variation is seen in the population. In the period 1924 to 1935 the uniform type was recognizably distinct from that which prevailed during the period previous to 1920 showing that evolution had occurred in a span of 4 years. The arrow on the abscissa indicates the time at which the Fords began their own studies.

variability took place. Hardly two specimens were alike, while marked departures from the normal form of the species in color pattern, size and shape were common. A considerable proportion of these were deformed in various ways; the amount of deformity being closely correlated with the degree of variation, so that the more extreme departures from normality were clumsy upon the wing or even unable to fly." Little evolution occurred between 1896 and 1920 although the environment probably changed considerably during this time. A sudden flush permitted an increase in genetic diversity and rapid adaptation to the environment to take place so that a higher population could be maintained because of the greater fitness of individuals after stringent selection. The slow decline in abundance after 1924 may reflect a change in environment without a corresponding change in the butterfly gene pool. Tetley (1947) also found increased variability in an increasing population of the nymphalid butterfly, *Argynnis selene*. This type of evolution is harder to observe in organisms other than butterflies, but there is little doubt that in insects that undergo large and rapid population fluctuations there is an opportunity for populations to evolve very rapidly.

Polymorphic behavior for activity and dispersal may also be important in population dynamics. Wellington's (1957, 1960, 1964) studies on the western tent caterpillar, *Malacosoma pluviale*, demonstrate how influential qualitative aspects of populations can be. Wellington studied populations of the caterpillars and adults near Victoria, British Columbia, on Vancouver Island. He found the population was polymorphic in behavior. Some individuals were inactive; they oviposited near their birth place, produced mostly inactive offspring, exploited favorable habitats (Fig. 9.12a,b), and were killed by harsh climatic conditions (Fig. 9.12c). Other individuals were more active; they oviposited much further from their place of origin; they always produced a higher proportion of vigorous individuals among their progeny. These active migrants tended to colonize more severe habitats (Fig. 9.12a,b), or replenish the vigor of other populations (Fig. 9.12b). During harsh climatic conditions individuals in marginal habitats were killed and those in favorable habitats survived (Fig. 9.12c) to recolonize all the vacant areas as conditions permitted.

The spatial dynamics of this species are extremely important. Wellington has emphasized the qualitative variables in a population and how they are necessary in understanding the change in population numbers in any one site. What has been emphasized in Fig. 9.12 is the spatial rela-

A. During moderately favorable regional climatic conditions.

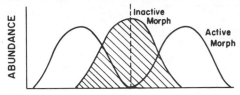

B. Changes when very favorable climatic conditions prevail.

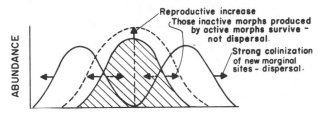

C. Changes when regional climatic conditions become harsh.

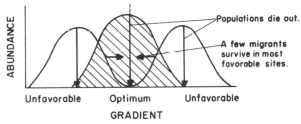

Fig. 9.12 Diagrams of population trends in western tent caterpillar populations under three sets of conditions. Inactive morph distribution shaded, active morph distribution unshaded.

tionships of a species in an area and how important it is to sample an extensive area to obtain a clear picture of what is happening in the population. Populations do move from place to place, and expand and contract; they do not just go up and down. Thus setting up a single sample plot in an area can produce some rather bewildering results and, probably in some cases, spurious conclusions (see also Morris 1971b, Price 1971b).

Leonard (1970a,b) has reported qualitative changes in populations of gypsy moth, *Porthetria dispar*. He has evidence that moth populations are numerically self-regulating because of a shift in the quality of individuals induced by changes in nutrition. This shift is rapid and does not depend on natural selection, but rather on a switch in the behavior of the first instar larvae (Fig. 9.13). In generation 1 larval food is plentiful

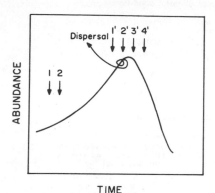

Fig. 9.13 Diagrammatic representation of trends in the gypsy moth showing when dispersal occurs. Generation 1 and 2 feed in uncrowded conditions, generations 1' to 4' exist in a food shortage.

and the resulting females produce eggs with large food reserves. In generation 2, large first instar larvae hatch from eggs; they rapidly settle and feed after eclosion; they moult four times in males and five times in females; and they produce females of high nutritional status. In contrast, in generation 1', larval food starts to be in short supply, and females result that produce smaller eggs with reduced food reserves. In generation 2', larvae are small and active and do not readily settle to feed. First instar development time is much longer with a longer prefeeding phase. The larvae are more sensitive to interference and readily drop and hang on a silken thread and thus became more readily dispersed by wind. Female adults are winged but cannot fly so that larvae on silk is the only possible dispersal phase. The same larval behavior is produced by crowded situations or starvation. At the end of their development these larvae usually have molted five times for males and six times for females. This was the most readily observed factor that led to detailed studies by Leonard that provided this understanding of the population dynamics. Thus in generations 3' and 4', those larvae that do not disperse eat the remains of the food and a population crash results. But high dispersal has already occurred and new sites with ample food have been colonized through this high dispersal at high densities. Food plays a critical role in the fluctuation but the important point is that there is a built-in mechanism that permits the population to respond to crowding or food shortage early enough so that many disperse before death by starvation becomes a critical factor.

Dispersal is adaptive. It permits a population to spread as the population increases, and it enables the colonization of new sites. New food sources can be exploited by dispersed individuals. It permits exchange of gene material between populations which, in the long run at least, is advantageous as a diverse gene pool promotes better population adjustment to the environment than a restricted one, and thus promotes the welfare of individuals in that population. However, dispersal is not an unmittigated benefit to the individual, although it probably is for the population. Since an individual insect that disperses from one food source usually has a small chance of discovering a distant food source in tolerable environmental conditions, under most conditions it will be maladaptive to disperse more than very locally. It helps to consider the fitness of individuals that have a choice of dispersing. Those that are fittest leave many progeny, or many of their genes in the gene pool. When food and other environmental factors are favorable it is best to exploit this situation. Favorable conditions promote survival and the leaving of progeny. As conditions worsen, either through food shortage or other factors, and the chances of leaving viable progeny *in situ* decrease, dispersal becomes a profitable undertaking. Ultimately when conditions are so severe that no progeny can survive, although dispersal is very costly, the probability of leaving viable progeny is increased by dispersal, and dispersing individuals will be, on the average, infinitely fitter than the residents. Thus any adaptation that permits an individual to respond to worsening conditions before they become intolerable will be strongly selected for. Dispersal by the gypsy moth's first instar larvae is a good example.

Dempster (1968) gives dispersal figures for adults of the herbivore psyllid, *Arytaina spartii*, which feeds on broom, *Sarothamnus scoparius*. He also provides data on the mean fecundity of females that did not disperse (Table 9.2). Note the strongly density-dependent response in dispersal and reproduction. The 1961 population was twice that in 1960 but the number dispersing was about 13 times greater. The dispersing females did not have much to lose by leaving, since those that remained only produced an average of 6.4 eggs per female. Of these eggs, which amounted to a mean of 49,992 eggs per bush, only 223 adults or 0.4% survived for the next generation. In fact those females that dispersed and discovered other broom bushes had a tremendous advantage over those that remained. There is an inflexion in the dispersal curve with increasing numbers suggesting that dispersal rate increased particularly rapidly near the peak abundance levels.

This example raises the interesting question of how selection is likely to modify dispersal time, dispersal rate, and amplitude of dispersal in a population (see also Dingle 1972, and Johnson 1969 for an extensive treatment of migration and dispersal). Gadgil (1971) presented a theory

Table 9.2 **Population dynamics of the psyllid** Arytaina spartii **on broom at the Imperial College Field Station, Silwood Park, England.**

Year	Number of adults per bush	Number dispersing, caught in suction trap	Mean fecundity of remaining females
1959	316	118	—
1960	3880	850	146.3
1961	7792	10,572	6.4
1962	223	131	267.5
1963	74	26	—

SOURCE. From Dempster 1968.

of dispersal based on a set of models he created. By considering such parameters as population density, carrying capacity, the fraction of the population dispersing, and any sensitivity to density in the fraction dispersing, he has been able to make some general statements about adaptive dispersal in relation to variability of the carrying capacity (K) in time and space.

Consider variability of K with time while keeping the spatial relationships of K constant. Such a situation would be a pattern of bodies of water in an area, each body representing a separate K, and each altering in K with time out of phase with other bodies of water. Some bodies of water would dry up sooner than others; rain and run-off water would replenish some and not others. So how are aquatic insects likely to adapt a dispersal pattern that is best equipped to exploit this variation in food resources with time? Note that carrying capacity is the ability of the environment to support a population, so while water availability is used in this example it must be assumed that plenty of water carries with it plenty of food.

In any given pool or puddle, therefore, K may suddenly change from low to high after rainfall and the population would move from a crowded to an uncrowded situation. During the crowded situation it would seem to be adaptive to disperse as the chances of finding a pool with a lower exploitation relative to the carrying capacity would be good. However this newly discovered site in an uncrowded state may rapidly dry up so that the fitness of the individual could be lower than if it had stayed put. In this situation it is probably just as adaptive for an individual to leave an uncrowded situation as a crowded one, as the condition of the newly colonized site is so unpredictable. Leaving an uncrowded site and arriving in a crowded one may actually improve the fitness of an individual if quite rapidly the conditions in the two ponds is reversed. Therefore the best strategy in this situation is for the population to maintain a relatively high magnitude of dispersal at all density levels. This strategy is seen in corixids studied by Brown (1951) where those in ephemeral situations had high dispersal rates and those in permanent bodies of water had low dispersal rates. This also seems to be the strategy of *Malacosoma pluviale*. Note that the western tent caterpillar is not only a forest dwelling species, but colonizes isolated trees that may be dispersed patchily.

In contrast it is possible to conceive of a condition where variability in K with time is synchronized throughout a fairly large area. Here the conditions of crowding are likely to be similar in each situation, so that frequent dispersal cannot be adaptive as a dispersing insect is likely to settle in another crowded area. The best strategy is to keep dispersal to a minimum so long as food is available, but to have a very sensitive dispersal-triggering mechanism so that dispersal is initiated just before the population is doomed through starvation. A good dispersal mechanism is also needed. Such a situation is likely to occur where climate has an effect on a food source, and the feeding population, over a wide area. For example, cone crop production and seed production would vary over wide areas, as would male cone production in relation to spruce budworm, and even vegetative production on trees that are host to the gypsy moth.

Perhaps it is because of the relatively static spatial relationship of forest and shade trees and the synchronous nature of the fluctuation of insect populations that feed on these trees that the most clear-cut density-dependent dispersal has been observed in these herbivores, forest insects, and insects in similar situations. Some examples include the gypsy moth, *Porthetria dispar* (Leonard 1970a,b), the California oak moth, *Phryganidia californica* (Harville 1955), the fall webworm, *Hyphantria cunea* (Morris 1971b), the broom psyllid, *Arytaina spartii* (Dempster 1968, Waloff 1968a,b), and perhaps the spruce budworm, *Choristoneura fumiferana* (Morris 1963).

Morris (1971b) provides interesting data on the fall webworm. He conducted very extensive road censuses of the conspicuous webs in areas of New Brunswick and Nova Scotia, and plotted the number of nests per 100 road miles against the percentage of agricultural land in the census route (Fig. 9.14). Fall webworm feed on deciduous trees and survive best on open grown trees, that is in agricultural sites. But in coastal areas, where densities are highest, forested areas sustain almost as high a population as the agricultural sites. This is not so in other regions. Morris offers these possible explanations: (1) There may be an interaction be-

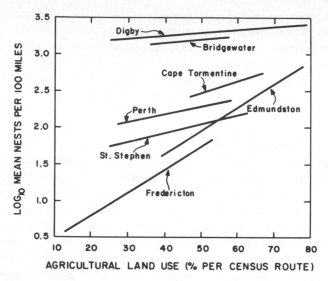

Fig. 9.14 Relation of mean population density of the fall webworm to land use in seven census areas for the years 1957–1968. As the percent of agricultural land increased, so the population density increased. Note that in the moist coastal areas around Digby and Bridgewater in Nova Scotia populations were almost as high in more forested areas as in more agricultural areas, and these were the two areas that showed very high populations in general. These areas contrast in particular with the inland sites of Fredericton and Edmundston, New Brunswick. For location of sites see Morris (1971a). From Morris 1971b.

tween vegetation and climate. Populations reach higher levels in humid coastal areas with longer developmental seasons. Under these favorable conditions the webworm may be less sensitive to land use and vegetation pattern than in drier continental areas. (2) As high populations develop on the favorable routes within an area, there may be a tendency for more nests to appear on unfavorable routes as a result of moth dispersal so that the population density is evened out. Morris stated: "In 1961, density exceeded 100 nests per mile on some of the best coastal routes but remained below 10 nests per mile inland. Relatively high nest populations were observed in the Bridgewater area in that year along the sides of very narrow woods roads through pure stands of oak. In view of the poor exposure, as well as the unfavorable nutritional quality of oak, it is probable that the moths responsible for the nests came from agricultural land outside the oak stands." Thus there exists evidence for density-dependent dispersal. (3) Other possibilities exist such as changes in genetic quality associated with high density, but it is not yet known whether they influence the dispersal habits of the moths. Certainly dispersal is playing an important part in the population dynamics of the fall webworm. Morris has found in his studies that climate, land use, tree species, tree density, population density, and genetic change all influence the dynamics of the fall webworm, not to mention parasitoids, predators, and disease (see Morris 1971a,b, Morris and Fulton 1970a, b, and references therein).

Is it possible to create a general theory for population dynamics? Statements on which regulating factor is likely to be most important in natural populations have been avoided, since each is likely to be significant for certain populations at certain times. Probably for each population there is a unique combination of factors regulating populations, if for no other reason because each population probably has a unique gene pool.

Because greater concern has been devoted to general theories on population regulation than to insect population studies in particular this chapter concludes with a short list of references that will provide ready access to the literature on insect population dynamics. These include symposium volumes on population dynamics and regulation (Duffey and Watt 1971, den Boer and Gradwell 1970, Watson 1970), books on biological control (de Bach 1964a, Huffaker 1971, van den Bosch and Messenger 1973), pest management (Rabb and Guthrie 1970, Geier, Clark, Anderson, and Nix 1973), insect migration and dispersal (Johnson 1969), and books, symposia, and reviews specifically on insect population studies (Clark, Geier, Hughes, and Morris 1967, Richards 1961, Southwood 1966, 1968, Solomon 1964, van Emden 1972a,b, LeRoux 1963) and monographs on the population dynamics of particular insect species (e.g., Morris 1963, Pottinger and LeRoux 1971).

The long-term studies, particularly on forest insects, are worthy of special attention, and include Baltensweiler's (e.g., 1958, 1964, 1968) and Auer's (1961, 1968) work on the grey larch tortrix, *Zeiraphera griseana*, Dixon's (e.g., 1970a,b, 1972, Dixon and Logan 1972) studies on the sycamore aphid, *Drepanosiphum platanoides*, Klomp's (e.g., 1966, 1968) work in Holland on the pine looper, *Bupalus piniarius*, Morris' studies on the spruce budworm, *Choristoneura fumiferana* (e.g., Morris 1963) and the fall webworm, *Hyphantria cunea* (e.g., Morris 1971a,b, 1972, Morris and Bennett 1967, Morris and Fulton 1970a,b), and Varley and Gradwell's (e.g., 1968, 1970, 1971, Varley 1970) investigation of the winter moth, *Operophtera brumata*. References to other important studies may be found in those cited above.

Chapter 10

ECOLOGICAL GENETICS

The process of natural selection depends on existence of genetic variation in populations. One of Darwin's nagging problems was to discover where this variation originated, since the then current concept of
heredity through pangenesis implied a blending process. Each generation
apparently became less variable than the one previous to it. With the
discovery of particulate inheritance through the pioneering work of
Mendel, and the genetic process of mutation and recombination, the
genetic sources of variation were identified, its maintenance was understood, and Darwin's dilemma was solved. Variation in natural populations must also be influenced by environmental factors, since these act as
forces in natural selection. Thus ecological genetics is the study of environmental influences on the genetics of populations: genetic aspects of
how populations are adapted to their environment.

Given Darwin's dilemma and the subsequent realization that variation
is not lost during reproduction, a natural step was to ask: (1) How much
genetic variation exists in populations? (2) How is it maintained? (3) Is
this variation indeed adaptive? Variation in populations was most easily
observed in species that showed polymorphism in the phenotype externally, and much ecological genetics has concentrated on these multi-
patterned and multishaped species (see examples in Ford 1964, Creed
1971a). When differences in relative abundance of morphs were observed
between populations, an attempt was made to interpret them in terms of
selective factors acting in different ways on each interbreeding group.
These qualitative differences in populations are useful in interpreting
the population dynamics of the species and genetic strategies for survival
in individuals and populations. Also in Chapter 21 on biogeography it
will be seen that species that disperse extensively become subject to
speciation, either by accumulating genetic differences as populations disperse as in the bees, *Hoplitis* sp., or by crossing areas that later become
barriers to gene flow as in the stoneflies, *Allocapnia* spp. For this to
happen, there must be intraspecific differences between populations, and
the study of population differences within a species is an important part
of biogeography, particularly if the factors that cause and maintain these
differences can be discovered.

Polymorphisms manifested as external morph differences are relatively easy to study but the number of species with two or more readily
observed morphs is limited. However, polymorphisms in chromosome
structure (chromosomal polymorphism) and in the migration rates of
enzymes (gene polymorphisms) when subjected to an electric potential
(electrophoresis) are also observable. The latter type of polymorphism
can be studied in practically all organisms and results derived from use
of this method are now providing a major thrust into the ecological

genetics of organisms. Examples of each type of polymorphism will be given after genetic polymorphism has been defined. After the study of some cases of polymorphism, the basic evolutionary questions mentioned above can be addressed.

Genetic polymorphism is the occurrence together in the same population of two or more discrete forms of a species in proportions greater than can be maintained by recurrent mutation alone (cf., Ford 1940, 1964). This polymorphism may be stable or balanced, or it may be transient. Balanced polymorphism may be defined in general terms as genetic polymorphism maintained by contending selective forces, so that the frequency of each morph reflects the relative strength of these forces (cf., Ford 1964). A more restrictive definition that describes the genetic mechanism for maintenance of polymorphism is given by Ford (1964) and Mayr (1963): genetic polymorphism in which there is a balance of opposed advantage and disadvantage where the heterozygote is favored compared with both homozygotes. Therefore, in balanced polymorphism, so long as the opposing selective pressures remain, polymorphism is maintained. In contrast, transient polymorphism is a temporary state in a population in which a rare gene with an unopposed advantage spreads until its former normal allele is reduced to the status of a mutant (Ford 1964).

By studying one of the most externally polymorphic insects, the swallowtail butterfly, *Popilio dardanus*, two of the basic questions in ecological genetics can be answered: how is polymorphism maintained and is it adaptive. However, the answers are specific to this case. Also possible pathways in the evolution of this polymorphism can be suggested. *Papilio dardanus*, the caterpillars of which feed on citrus plants, is restricted to the Ethiopian biogeographic realm (see Chapter 21). Within this range, eight races are recognizable (Fig. 10.1) and are distinguished by differences in the black markings on the wings of males and the morphology of the male genital armature (a race is defined as a class of individuals with common characteristics). The color pattern of males is always black and yellow and differs only in detail from race to race. They have tails on the hind wings characteristic of the genus *Papilio* (Fig. 10.2). Interbreeding occurs between races at the edges of their distributions indicated by shading in Fig. 10.1. In the races *meriones* on Madagascar and

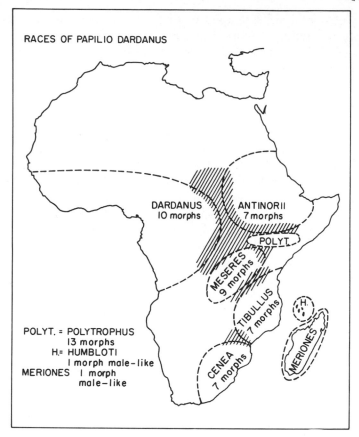

RACES OF PAPILIO DARDANUS

DARDANUS
10 morphs

ANTINORII
7 morphs

POLYT.

MESERES
9 morphs

TIBULLUS
7 morphs

H.

POLYT. = POLYTROPHUS
        13 morphs
H.= HUMBLOTI
        1 morph male-like
MERIONES   1 morph
        male-like

MERIONES

CENEA
7 morphs

Fig. 10.1 Distribution of the eight races of *Papilio dardanus* in Africa with the number of female morphs in each race indicated. Shaded areas indicate zones of interbreeding between races. After Sheppard 1962.

humbloti on the Comoro Islands, the females are male-like. In contrast, continental races have highly polymorphic females; for example, race *polytrophus* has 13 morphs alone. In fact, according to Sheppard (1962) there are 31 morphs, several of which are shared by four or five races. Most of the studies, and particularly the genetics of morphs, have been executed by Clarke and Sheppard (1960a,b, 1963) and Sheppard (1961, 1962).

How has natural selection produced this large variety of morphs in a single species? Ecological factors and particularly sympatric species must be examined. *Papilio dardanus* adults fly during the day; they are palatable, and therefore, subject to heavy predation by birds in particular. As

Fig. 10.2   Three specimens of *Papilio dardanus* and a model *Amauris niavius*. Non-mimetic males (*a*) from the mainland of Africa (race *dardanus*) and (*b*) from Mada-gascar (race *meriones*) showing that males of different races differ only in detail. Non-mimetic females appear very similar to the males but have a dark patch about one third up the costal margin of the forewing. (*c*) A model, *Amauris niavius niavius*; (*d*) a female *Papilio dardanus dardanus* (morph *hippocoon*), which mimics the *Amauris* sp. in coloration, pattern and shape. Photograph courtesy of James G. Sternburg.

seen in Chapter 4, one antipredation strategy available to palatable prey is Batesian mimicry, and this is the strategy involved in *P. dardanus* females. Since several models exist sympatrically, an equal number of mimics could evolve. Throughout the geographic range of *P. dardanus*, different species of models have been exploited, or geographic variation of a broadly distributed model has been mimicked, and thus many morphs have evolved. Each mimetic pattern is found only where the model is also present. There are a few exceptions where mimicry is poor, apparently because models became rare as a result of past unfavorable environmental conditions. The similarity between model and mimic is usually carried to a remarkable degree (e.g., Fig. 10.2). One distasteful

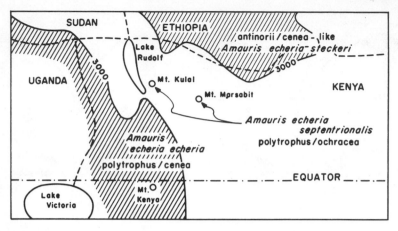

Fig. 10.3 Map of the higher plateau of East Africa showing local distribution of the distasteful model *Amauris echeria* and the mimic *Papilio dardanus*. Contour is 3000 ft. By each subspecies of *Amauris* the mimetic form is designated as race/morph. Thus for each subspecies of *Amauris* there is a distinct morph of the mimetic species. Constructed from information in Sheppard (1962).

model, *Amauris echeria,* is widely distributed on the higher plateau areas of Africa, and in Kenya it shows a local distribution as in Fig. 10.3. For each subspecies of the model there is a different morph that mimics it: race *polytrophus,* morph *cenea* mimics *A. echeria echeria;* race *polytrophus,* morph *ochracea* mimics *A. echeria septentrionalis;* and race *antenorii,* morph *cenea*-like mimics *A. echeria steckeri.*

Repeated examples like this provide almost certain proof that predators are the agents in natural selection, producing in many cases precise mimetic patterns of distasteful models. Protection of mimics from predation has been thoroughly documented for the North American nymphalid butterflies in the genus *Limenitis* (e.g., Brower 1958a,b, Platt and Brower 1968, Platt et al. 1971). But how do the selection pressures work and how does the variation arise that lends itself to selection for mimicry? There is a big difference between the primitive pattern and shape, and that of the mimicking morph, and it is inconceivable that such perfect mimics could be produced by a single chance mutation. It is equally inconceivable that it could occur by the gradual change of the primitive pattern. There is no way in which intermediate forms could be selected for because the predators would not confuse them with any models and the adaptive nature of the primitive pattern, whatever that might be, would also be forfeited. Sheppard's (1962) reasoning is followed here. Assume that there is a range of color patterns numbered from 0 to 5 on an arbitrary scale (Fig. 10.4). Then the relative fitness of each color pattern can

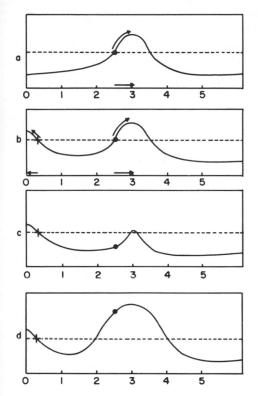

Fig. 10.4 The relationship between color patterns of palatable morphs (abscissa) and their relative fitness (ordinate) when the model has a color pattern designated as 3. Color patterns are assumed to be similar on contiguous parts of the pattern range and more and more different as distance on the arbitrary scale increases. If a morph has a color pattern of 3, it is a perfect mimic. Color patterns at 2.5 and 2.0 and so on and 3.5 and 4.0 and so on show decreasing mimetic resemblances to the model. Therefore as shown in (a) the morph with a pattern at 2.5 can increase fitness by approaching 3 but below 2.5 or above 3.5 fitness declines steadily as the resemblance fades. The following relationships are figured: (a) when a model has a color pattern at 3; (b) when a model has a color pattern at 3, but there is also a selective advantage of a cryptic pattern at 0; (c) when the model is at a relatively low population density, or is not very unpalatable, (d) when the model is at a high population density, or very unpalatable. Arrows indicate direction of selection. The dashed line indicates the relative fitness of the mimetic morph in a and b, and the cryptic pattern in b, c, and d. The solid circle represents the position of the mimetic morph and a cross the cryptic morph. From Sheppard 1962.

be plotted on the ordinate. If a distasteful model is assumed to have a color pattern at 3 then maximum fitness of a mimetic morph will be achieved by evolving an exact copy of the model, or acquisition of a color pattern 3. A mimetic morph with a pattern at 2.5 (Fig. 10.4a) will have less than maximal fitness but one that is greater than any other morph with a pattern from 2.5 to 0 or 3.5 to 5, since in these cases the mimetic resemblance fades. Any pattern more like the model than the mimic at 2.5 will be selected for, since such an insect will be less often distinguished from the model by a predator. As the color pattern becomes less like the model the selective advantage declines until it is completely unlike the model and therefore no further change will produce a disadvantage relative to the mimic at 2.5.

If the pattern happens to become more cryptic as it diverges from that of the model at 3, then the disadvantage of being a poor mimic or a nonmimic may be converted into an advantage as predation will once again be avoided, say at 0.3 (Fig. 10.4b). Thus two morphs may exist that will be selected for simultaneously, one cryptic and one mimetic. Therefore a highly cryptic morph at 0.3 is unlikely to become mimetic unless a single mutation moves the pattern from 0.3 to between 2.5 and 3.5, because all patterns between and beyond these values have a lower selective advantage, as they will be protected neither by crypsis nor mimicry. As seen in Chapters 4 and 5 on predation, if the model is not very abundant and becomes rarer than the mimic, the selective advantage for the mimic will be much reduced because the predators will be less able to learn that the model is distasteful (Fig. 10.4c). Conversely, if the model is very abundant, the mimic will gain a large selective advantage (Fig. 10.3d), and less exact fits to the model will still have a selective advantage so that the evolution of mimicry is more likely under these conditions. The same contrasting results will be seen where the model is only moderately unpalatable and where the model is highly unpalatable.

Suppose the two patterns at 0.3 and 2.5 were controlled by a single pair of alleles. In Fig. 10.4d where the model is very abundant the allele producing the cryptic pattern at 0.3 would be at a disadvantage and would tend to be eliminated by natural selection. However, as the mimic becomes commoner, its advantage will decrease and may be converted to a disadvantage before the cryptic pattern is lost, in which case both morphs will be maintained in the population, in a state of balance; balanced or stable polymorphism. If the model is very abundant, the selective advantage to the mimetic morph will continue until all cryptic morphs are selected out of the population and the species becomes monomorphic and mimetic. In the case shown in Fig. 10.4c the opposite trends would be seen. The advantage of the pattern at 0.3 might also be assumed to be due to another model with this pattern. Then the population would have two morphs both mimetic, and the situation in *Papilio dardanus* can be envisaged where there are many morphs equivalent to the many models present within the range of a race.

To establish a new mimetic form, supposing the species is monomorphic at 0.3, a new mutant must produce a color pattern of at least 2.5 in case b, at least 3 in case c, and at least 2 in case d (Fig. 10.4) to ensure that it is not immediately selected out of the population. That is, the chance of a mutant producing a new morph increases with increasing model population density and increasing unpalatability. In fact for a new morph to be selected for, as opposed to the cryptic morph, it must have a selective advantage slightly higher than that of the cryptic morph. Once a mutant produces a morph that is selected for, then selection will improve the fit of the mimic to the model by accumulation of small genetic changes that all together confer great similarity of the mimic to the model. Thus selection will gradually move the pattern in the direction of the arrows in examples a and b (Fig. 10.4).

This line of reasoning led Sheppard to make certain theoretical conclusions, which are actually supported by the genetic data he and Clarke secured. Sheppard (1962) states that: (1) A model must be common, easily recognized, and well protected against predators. (2) The evolution of a mimetic form usually requires a large initial phenotypic change, because a small change is not likely to be advantageous. Consequently most mimetic patterns are largely controlled by a single gene. (3) If the model is not very abundant compared with the mimetic species, or if it is not well protected, a stable polymorphism is likely to result. (4) The abundance of a mimetic form in a polymorphic species will depend on (a) the abundance of the model, (b) its degree of distastefulness, (c) the number of mimics of other species occupying the same model, and (d) the strength of the selective force imposed by visually hunting predators (in the absence of predation mimicry, or cryptic coloration can have no advantage). (5) The likelihood of mimicry evolving will depend not only on the availability of suitable models and the occurrence of suitable mutations, but also on how many other mimics of the available models are present. Thus when there are no other mimics, quite a poor copy of a model might be advantageous and become established. (For support of this contention see Brower, Alcock, and Brower 1971). But when another species already copies the model in the area, the mimicry might have to be initially very good to be advantageous, or it might never be advantageous if as many mimics were already present as could be "accommodated" by the model in terms of relative abundance of all mimics and the model. (6) Once the mimicry is established, the rest of the genetic constitution can change to produce a more perfect resemblance: supergenes are involved. A supergene is formed when mutually advantageous genes become closely associated on the same chromosome, by selection for this beneficial union, so that separation of the genes becomes so rare that they act together as if they were a single gene (see Ford 1964). (7) If dominance were initially absent it would tend to evolve, the new mimetic form being dominant.

   Polymorphism can also evolve independently of the presence of distasteful models, and still under the influence of predation, by having
different morphs suited, by crypsis, to different habitats. An example of
this situation is seen in the wood snail, *Cepaea nemoralis*, and the garden
snail, *Cepaea hortensis*, which occur in Britain and much of Europe.
From these detailed studies many inferences can be made about the
maintenance of polymorphism in insects. Both species are highly polymorphic for shell color and banding on the shell, and they have many
morphs in common. Cain and Sheppard (1950, 1954a) found that in
beechwoods there was usually a high proportion of brown unbanded and
pink unbanded shells, which approximately match the background of
uniform brown leaf litter. In hedgerows and rough herbage there was
often a greater proportion of yellow banded forms, which more nearly
matched the greenish background with linear shapes. Figure 10.5 on
Cepaea nemoralis morph distribution shows this distinction between
habitats clearly. These differences seem to be due to thrush predation in
particular, where the thrush takes proportionately more of those individuals whose shells stand out visibly against their background. *Cepaea
hortensis* shows similar distributions, although the camouflage in the
wooded areas is achieved in a different way.
   How is the balance between morphs maintained? Why are there not
all brown and pink morphs in woodlands, and yellow and banded
morphs in hedgerows and rough herbage? *Cepaea* shells that showed
polymorphism have been found from the Neolithic. Thus many morphs
have been in existence a very long time, and almost certainly represent
a stable polymorphism. The morphs can also be seen over a wide area
in England and Europe suggesting strongly that it is not of the transient
type of polymorphism. One remarkable thing about *Cepaea* polymorphism is that very few of the morphs are truly cryptic. In every situation
some morphs are less visible than others but rarely is the crypsis very
convincing, as it can be for many organisms. For example, the bands are
very distinct, but they would serve as camouflage far better if they were
less so. The single banded morphs often have a white strip below the
band that actually accentuates the band. In fact, it might be that crypsis
is not so important as a selective advantage of having the morphs looking
very different from each other. Because there are no models for *Cepaea*
to mimic, one wonders how predators can maintain a nonmimetic polymorphism. Clarke (1962a) brings together considerable evidence that if a
predator is faced with a polymorphic prey it will always tend to select
one morph over another. This is the same type of selection that Tinbergen (1960) explained by his search image hypothesis. In this sort of
situation the selective advantage of a phenotype would vary inversely

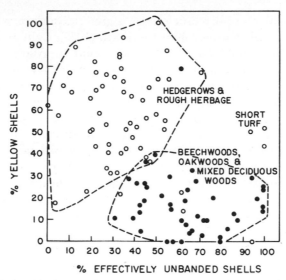

Fig 10.5   Relationship between percent yellow shells and percent effectively unbanded shells and the habitat in *Cepaea nemoralis* colonies. The dashed lines encircle the majority of points for each habitat group. Note that in wooded areas yellow shells are less abundant and unbanded shells are more abundant than in hedgerows and rough herbage. Slightly modified from Cain and Sheppard 1954a.

with its frequency, and the polymorphism would be maintained. Therefore, if the morphs do not depend on crypsis then mutations producing new morphs will have a great advantage because they will be so rare and they will increase, and thus a population with two morphs is likely to increase in the number and diversity of morphs as is found in *Cepaea*. The upper limit to this diversity is presumably defined by the number of patterns that can be sufficiently different so the predator does not confuse patterns. An intermediate morph mutant that shared the characters of two established morphs would have a disadvantage because it would stand a good chance of being selected as food either when the predator was searching for one or other of the established morphs. Clarke called this type of nonmimetic polymorphism that is maintained by predators apostatic polymorphism, because the selective advantage is conferred on those morphs that stand out visibly from the norm, the apostates; apostasy being defined as the abandonment of one's religion, political party, or color pattern. It is a form of frequency-dependent selection where advantage is gained by being relatively rare (see Paulson 1973 for discussion, support, and an extension of the hypothesis to include apostatic selection on predators).

If this form of polymorphism carries a great advantage why are not all palatable animals polymorphic? Kettlewell (1955), Cain and Sheppard (see Clarke 1962a), and Clarke (1962a) all found in aviary experiments that bird predators become less selective as they became more familiar with their prey. Therefore, predators cannot be expected to maintain apostatic polymorphisms in prey species that are common and highly palatable. Conversely if a potential prey species is rarely seen by a predator, it is unlikely that the predator will recognize, or form a search image, for even the commonest morph. Thus a new rare morph will have little or no selective advantage in being apostatic. Very distasteful species will gain most protection by having homogeneous form so that all members of the species can be recognized as belonging to this distasteful prey. There will be strong selection against polymorphism, especially if the species is common. One might think of this as Müllerian mimicry within a species. It is also unlikely that apostatic selection will work on a cryptically colored species, because there is probably only one good fit to the background against which the cryptic species must be concealed. Only if several different backgrounds are used as resting places will polymorphism be selected for. Here the most obvious examples are color varieties that blend with the soil in the area or the color of the pond bottom. But then this is not polymorphism as the morphs must be sympatric by definition. Thus the most favorable situations for apostatic polymorphism seem to be where the prey is eaten only occasionally by its major predators, either because it is fairly uncommon, or because it is slightly distasteful. In the case of *Cepaea* it has been found that thrushes kill snails in large numbers only when other food is scarce. Another point of interest is that it is mainly climbing snails that are polymorphic. This climbing habit will make the snail more obvious and it will make a cryptic pattern much less effective, as the background will change considerably as it climbs off the brown leaves, onto the grey trunk, and from there onto the green background of herbaceous plants for example. Since crypsis would therefore be a poor strategy the next best thing may be apostatic polymorphism.

There is one more point that illustrates the importance of the ecological setting in the evolution of polymorphism. This relates to Sheppard's (1962) statements that the abundance of a mimetic form, or an apostatically selected morph, and the likelihood of mimicry or apostatic morphs evolving at all, will depend in part on the number of similar morphs of other species that are already present. Clearly, if a morph is very abundant, then the selective advantage for the same morph to arise in another species is practically nil (compared to other morphs in the same species) and can only gain selective advantage in the absence of the same morph of the other species. In other words, the greatest advantage is gained when the same morphs of different species are allopatric, at least locally. This pattern was observed in the two species of *Cepaea* with similar morphs, *nemoralis* and *hortensis* (Fig. 10.6). As expected the yellow morphs were more common in grassland and rough herbage and the other morphs were more common in woodland areas. In fact, when *nemoralis* yellows were plotted against *hortensis* yellow unbanded there was a strong negative correlation between the presence of the morphs in hedgerows and rough herbage. When *nemoralis* was high in abundance, *hortensis* was low and vice versa. This was to be expected if visual selection by predators is the controlling force in this polymorphism. However, in fairness to another school of thought that proposes climatic influence on the maitenance of polymorphism in snails, Jones (1973) should be consulted.

So far, examples of polymorphism have been of the balanced form. However, under some environmental conditions one morph may become

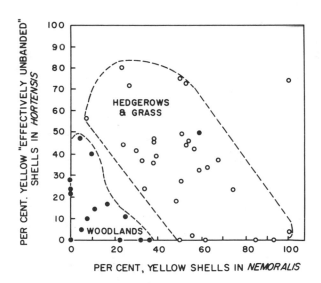

Fig. 10.6 Relationship between percent "effectively unbanded" shells in *Cepaea hortensis* and the percent yellow shells in *C. nemoralis* where colonies coexist. Note the negative relationship between abundance of similar morphs in the two species in the two major types of habitat. The dashed lines encircle the majority of points for each habitat group. Slightly modified from Clarke 1962b.

more abundant at the expense of another morph until the transition is complete. This transient polymorphism has been witnessed many times where industrial melanism has been involved. Cases in the Lepidoptera have been reviewed by Kettlewell (1961) who has also established convincingly that bird predation acts as the selective force for melanic forms in polluted areas and nonmelanic forms in pristeen environments (Kettlewell 1956, 1959). The fact that polymorphism is transient does not mean that it is irreversible. Now that industrial pollution in the British Isles is abating, some species show an increasing trend toward the nonmelanic morph, for example, in the coccinellid beetle, *Adalia bipunctata* (Creed 1971b).

In the foregoing examples of external polymorphism, there is ample evidence to show that more than one morph can be maintained in a population by the selective pressure from visually hunting predators. An adaptive advantage for each morph exists under slightly different environmental conditions. By contrast many internal polymorphisms may be maintained by influences other than predators. The study of chromosomal and gene polymorphisms has broadened the scope of ecological genetics tremendously and has led to important discoveries on one of the original basic questions: how much genetic variation exists in populations. These studies have also enabled insight into the genetic strategies in response to differing environmental conditions.

Chromosomal or inversion polymorphisms have been found to be extremely common in some species of *Drosophila* and other flies. Crossing-over may be suppressed within an inversion and thus favorable combinations of genes can be maintained indefinitely. Therefore, in predictable environments inversion polymorphisms are likely to be common, and in unpredictable environments they should be rare, since genetic plasticity is most adaptive in harsh environments (see Parsons and McKenzie 1972). For example, populations in the center of the range of *Drosophila robusta* have seven to nine inversions whereas peripheral populations have only one to six inversions (Carson 1958a,b). Inversion polymorphism in *Drosophila willistoni* is greatest at the center of its range and decreases rapidly toward the margins (Dobzhansky et al. 1950, Da Cunha and Dobzhansky 1954, Da Cunha et al. 1959). It is also significant that a cosmopolitan species like *Drosophila melanogaster* has low levels of polymorphism or none (Parsons and McKenzie 1972), when the genetic system for an opportunistic way of life is best kept in a form that ensures high variability in the population. However, not all species show these patterns suggesting that other forms of genetic adaptation exist (e.g., Crumpacker and Williams 1974).

The adaptive significance of many inversion morphs is not understood but some show changes in frequency that are related to change in temperature and other factors. Dobzhansky (1948) found that there were consistant changes in the frequency of chromosomal morphs in *Drosophila pseudoobscura* (Fig. 10.7). The seasonal and altitudinal changes in frequency of morphs are produced by natural selection. The carriers of the different gene arrangements have different adaptive values and are subject to very high selective pressures (see Wright and Dobzhansky 1946, Dobzhansky 1947). For example, at 25°C, experiments were started with 50% of each chromosome type, Chiricahua (CH) and Standard (ST), and there was a highly significant increase in frequency of ST at the expense of CH. The relative selective values were estimated at 0.70:1.00:0.30 for ST/ST, ST/CH, and CH/CH, respectively, so that equilibrium was reached at 70% Standard and 30% Chiricahua, indicating the strong selective advantage of the Standard chromosome type at this temperature. Dobzhansky noted that the morphs may be regarded as equivalent to the ecotypes of plants (Turesson 1922), with the Standard chromosome morph conferring an advantage in warm situations and the Arrowhead morph conferring an advantage in cooler situations. Clines in relative frequency of inversion morphs have also been observed by Brncic (1962, 1968), Mayhew et al. (1966), and Tonzctich and Ward (1973a,b). The last authors showed that one inversion morph conferred greater pupal survival in hot, dry conditions, while individuals with a different morph survived better in cooler, moister conditions. Nickerson and

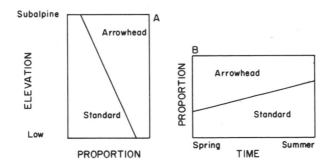

Fig. 10.7 General trends in frequency of the chromosomal inversion morphs Standard and Arrowhead in *Drosophila pseudoobscura,* (a) with elevation in the Yosemite region of the Sierra Nevada, California, and (b) with time from Spring to Summer at Aspen and Mather close to the west boundary of Yosemite National Park, during 1947. Presumably the trend is reversed during the Fall and Winter.

Druger (1973) showed that inversion polymorphisms also affect the fecundity, longevity, and competitive fitness in *Drosophila*. These polymorphisms permit a population to adapt to a variable environment by efficiently accommodating environmental variation (Parsons and McKenzie 1972). This is possible and adaptive only if the generation time is relatively short compared to the rate of change in the environment. But by using *Drosophila* species with a short generation time, much progress has been made in understanding the adaptive nature of variability and the genetic systems that can influence the amount of this variability in response to environmental factors.

The basic question of how much genetic variation exists in a population might never have been answered without the fundamentally different approach initiated by Lewontin and Hubby (1966). These authors demonstrated that differential migration rates of proteins during gel electrophoresis can be used to study enzyme or gene polymorphism at a single locus. Thus by sampling many randomly selected loci an estimate of the total gene polymorphism in individuals and populations could be estimated. Since genes are the basic substance of variation this new approach offered great promise and has indeed provided tremendous impetus to the field of ecological genetics. Even now the potential of the method has not been fully realized.

The early results were remarkable. Lewontin and Hubby (1966) found that an average population of *Drosophila pseudoobscura* was polymorphic for 30% of all loci and an average individual was heterozygous for 12% of its loci. Even these high values that document the existence of extreme variation in populations were considered to be low estimates. Lewontin (1974) postulates that only 25% of gene morphs may be identified by electrophoresis (see Harris 1970 for explanations). The high levels of enzyme polymorphism have been found repeatedly for many taxa: for example, *Drosophila* spp. (Ayala et al. 1972a,b, Ayala et al. 1974, Kojima et al. 1970, Prakash 1969, Prakash et al. 1969, Richmond 1972, Yang et al. 1972); the marine arthropod *Limulus* (Selander et al. 1970); the mollusc *Tridacna* (Ayala et al. 1973); birds (Ohno et al. 1969); mice (Berry and Murphy 1970, Petras et al. 1969); and man (Harris 1971, Harris and Hopkinson 1972, Lewis 1971). However, some species show little or no enzyme polymorphism. The reason for this and its significance are not understood for *Drosophila simulans* (Berger 1970), but in northern elephant seals lack of polymorphism may be due to fixation of alleles in small populations resulting from heavy mortality inflicted by sealers in the nineteenth century (Bonnell and Selander 1974).

With the discovery of high genic polymorphism came a new dilemma. Could such high levels of variation be maintained by natural selection or was much of it adaptively neutral? (See Johnson 1973, Lewontin 1974 for discussion). Johnson (1973) concluded after reviewing the literature that this polymorphism is maintained by selection and the high levels of enzyme polymorphism may provide "metabolic flexibility in a changeable environment." Bryant (1974) examined eight sets of data (five on invertebrates, three on vertebrates) for geographic variation in polymorphisms in relation to temporal variation in climate. He found that approximately 70% of the variation could be accounted for by variations in climate and concluded that shifts in morph frequency were therefore adaptive. It was interesting that Bryant found the frequency of morphs in poikilotherms slightly better correlated with environmental factors than in homeotherms, perhaps because the latter are buffered physiologically better against climatic change.

The solution of one scientific problem usually leads to the creation of another. Although the debate on selective neutrality has not been resolved, there is considerable evidence that many enzyme polymorphisms show frequency shifts that are correlated with observed environmental changes. The inference is that the shift is caused by different selective regimes. If so, what adaptive functions do the enzymes perform? What is their biochemical role? Gillespie and Kojima (1968) suggested that since substrates for enzyme action are likely to differ over a range of habitats, enzyme polymorphism is adapted to a variety of substrates. Johnson (1971, 1974) hypothesized that the enzymes are associated with regulatory reactions in metabolism. Since environmental factors ultimately influence the cellular environment, polymorphism for enzymes enables cellular homeostasis in spite of these changes. A judgement on the validity of these two hypotheses would be premature although both may be correct (see Johnson 1974). If Gillespie and Kojima are correct then enzymes that work on external substrates, particularly those derived from food, should be more polymorphic than enzymes for substrates that are produced metabolically within the organisms. This was indeed the pattern found in 13 species of *Drosophila*, but much work is necessary before a general pattern can be established for enzyme polymorphism in relation to biochemical activity.

There is no longer any doubt that a large amount of genetic variability exists in natural populations, that at least some of it is maintained under the influence of differing selective regimes, and that it is adaptive. The full significance of such great variability has yet to be understood. As seen in Chapter 3, biochemistry and ecology must play mutually supportive roles in this important area. The building blocks of the community, the gene, the cell, the organism, and the population, can be integrated into a unified population biology by the study of ecological genetics. Indeed it would now seem unreasonable to ignore ecological genetics in any study on population dynamics, competition, and biogeography, and many other aspects of ecology could be enlightened by this approach.

For further reading, excellent reviews are available on ecological genetics of *Drosophila* (Parsons and McKenzie 1972), and enzyme polymorphism in general (Johnson 1973, 1974, Selander and Johnson 1973, LeCam et al. 1972). Many examples of studies in ecological genetics are given by Ford (1964) and Creed (1971a). Dobzhansky (1970), Lewontin (1974), Wright (1968, 1969), Kimura and Ohta (1971), and Crow and Kimura (1970) provide comprehensive treatments of population genetics. Ricklefs (1973) and Wilson and Bossert (1971) give a good introduction to the subject.

Chapter II

POPULATIONS
UNDER
INSECTICIDE
STRESS

The use of insecticides has mushroomed since World War II so that now every ecosystem in the world contains persistent man-made toxic substances (e.g., see Tatton and Ruzicka 1967). Certainly these are a new stress on natural populations, but the environment is full of natural stresses that populations live through. Is one more going to make much difference when a species has already adapted to many other environmental mortality factors? Pesticides have some features peculiar to themselves: they are often toxic to a broad spectrum of organisms, and the more persistent of them may have a "half-life" of 10 years or more. These two particular characteristics of pesticides are special problems for humans for obvious and important reasons. But regarding other organisms, are pesticides sufficiently different from other mortality factors to justify setting them aside as exceptional in any way? This should be done only after it has been established that these toxicants have unique influences in population ecology. It is safer, as far as population dynamics is concerned, to treat pesticides as just another factor of environmental resistance and so expect the same sorts of response by organisms to them as to any other mortality factor, until some fundamental differences are observed. My thesis is that we should think of pesticides as one more factor in environmental resistance along with all the rest, and then qualify this statement only for certain types of organisms and only when pesticides have a unique impact on certain species.

One example enables study of one aspect of the ecological role of insecticide. During the deep contemplation and introspection typical of those ensconced on a privy, the local folk of Chatham County, Georgia, found themselves repeatedly distracted by masses of soldier flies (*Hermetia illucens*). The affairs of state would suffer if the quietude of the privy continued to be disrupted by buzzing flies, so eradication was necessary. DDT was carefully applied down each hole, and the community settled down for the uninterrupted bliss of day-dreaming. But soon privies were infested with swarms of flies again, and they were found to be house flies, *Musca domestica*, dangerous germ carriers as compared to the pristeen record for the soldier flies. By the application of an insecticide a relatively innocuous species had been replaced by a serious pest. Kilpatrick and Schoof (1959) found that *Hermetia* larvae survived well in the semi-aquatic medium in the privy before DDT application. The activity of the larvae and the activity of micro-organisms continually liquefied the medium. Under these circumstances house fly larvae could not mature as they normally require a more solid substrate. The DDT was very effective in killing *Hermetia* larvae as they had not been exposed to much insecticide. Thus the substrate remained in its original state without being broken down into a liquefied medium. Under these conditions house fly larvae survived, particularly since populations had been previously exposed to DDT and had already adapted to this environmental stress. Thus the situation had been worsened by the blind application of an insecticide.

As far as the two fly species were concerned, for the soldier fly the former microenvironment was highly favorable and it became unfavorable. For the house fly the situation was unfavorable and it became favorable. The competitive balance between the two species was tilted toward *M. domestica* by the change in conditions. It does not necessarily help to say that the house fly population was resistant to insecticide because this immediately takes insecticide application out of its ecological context. It is more helpful to state that the house fly population was more tolerant of this environmental stress than was the soldier fly population, just as the house fly is probably more tolerant of desiccating conditions in buildings, and the larvae of the soldier fly are more tolerant than the house fly of extremely wet conditions.

There is little doubt that an insecticide application has a catastrophic impact on an insect population. But is it justified to consider insecticides in the environment as just another stress factor, along with all the other factors that constitute environmental resistance? Reference to previous studies is necessary to see if the response to natural catastrophes, or applied catastrophes other than insecticide, bears any relationship to population crashes produced by insecticide application. One difficulty is that good data on the population response to natural catastrophes are hard to find. Somebody must be studying a population before the happening and must have the drive to continue after the population has been practically wiped out. Very interesting observations have been made by Coulson and Deans (1970) who studied shags, sea birds on the Farne Islands on the east coast of northern England. The study was initiated several years before the disaster and continued for several seasons afterwards. An 80% kill resulted from very heavy seas that washed away many of the nests. In every season since then breeding success has improved in all age classes, over that observed before the disaster, so the population is rapidly increasing to its original size. This rapid return is due largely to a considerable increase in survival of the nestlings, and this is particularly so when young are reared by inexperienced parents. This response can be explained by two main factors: (1) In territorial animals there is frequently a reservoir of nonbreeding individuals at high population levels, so that at low density they have an opportunity to breed and act as a buffer against disaster. (2) When the population is low, young birds can utilize good nest sites, whereas at high densities they are forced to breed in poorer sites and therefore breed less successfully. This is another buffer against disaster.

Most other populations seem to be buffered in one way or another to create a rapid response after a catastrophe. Wynne-Edwards (1962) remarks on the spectacular recovery in numbers of several species of commercial fish during the 4 years of the first world war, when the fishing vessels were otherwise engaged and the Dogger Bank was covered by minefields. These populations were hardly subjected to a "natural catastrophe" but they were part of a very natural experiment by man. Sheppard (1956) observed a huge population flush in the moth, *Panaxia dominula*, after a fire swept through an area in March 1953. As far as other manipulated populations go, Davis (1953) reduced rat populations 50–90% and the recovery rates were higher than for populations that were only slightly reduced. Emlen, Stokes, and Windsor (1948) obtained similar results and concluded that population growth of brown rats in Baltimore was logistic: if high mortality occurred the response was initially exponential, whereas if low mortality occurred the recovery rate was slow. Lindsdale (1946) provides similar results for the California ground squirrel.

In experimental populations of the sheep blowfly, *Lucilia cuprina*, Nicholson (1954a,b) found that the destruction of 50% of the total adult population every other day produced no significant change in the mean adult population, compared with a similar culture in which there was no imposed mortality. Silliman and Gutsell (1958) conducted an experiment on guppies that lasted over 3 years. They showed that when stable populations of guppies were cropped by removal of a proportion of the fish at regular intervals, the remainder responded by producing more young that survived, so that losses were compensated for. Frank (1952) found that after sudden release from crowding there was a response in natality in *Daphnia* populations.

There seems to be considerable evidence that populations do respond to severe mortality by rapidly increased birth and survival rates, so that the mortality is rapidly compensated for. Does the same thing happen in insect populations after insecticide application? The available evidence suggests that it certainly does, and a bounce back of a population should be expected. Already in 1956, Ripper recognized that resurgence of insect numbers was a common feature of post-spray populations. He provided a table of over 50 phytophagous arthropod species in which there was a tremendous increase of the target organism after spraying, or of a non-target organism that had been insignificant before spraying. Some of the reasons for this resurgence are listed below:

1. Reduction of natural enemies.

    (a) Poisoned insects are more readily available to predators than unpoisoned and therefore predators eat large dosages of insecticide.
    (b) Predators are more mobile than their prey and are thus exposed to more insecticide.
    (c) Predators eat many prey and concentrate poison.
    (d) Any predator–prey population model (see Chapter 5) would predict prey release, since predators are exposed to greater hazards and population response is therefore reduced.

2. Reduction of competition for food stimulates both natality and survival.
3. With reduced pest pressure on host, plant growth improves, thus improving food source of herbivore.

A classic example of a "man-made pest" is the fruit tree red spider mite, *Metatetranychus ulmi*, in orchards in Britain (see Moreton 1969). This mite infests mostly apple and plum trees, and sprays against it are a regular part of the annual spray program. Yet before 1923 it was an unknown pest. Its pest status arose due to the use of new and more powerful insecticides in the 1920s. In an unsprayed orchard, the fruit tree red spider mite is subject to predation by numerous mirid and other bugs, several lacewings, ladybirds, a rove beetle, and typhlodromid mites. By the spring the proportion of viable winter eggs might have been reduced by 40%, and during the summer predation was heavy; these factors kept the mite population at a very low level. In a sprayed orchard winter washes of tar oil and others to kill eggs of pests such as aphids, killed lichens on the bark, and the overwintering predators in the lichen mats. The predators were provided with less cover during the year so that they in turn were subjected to higher predation. When spider mites hatched there were few predators to eat them. With the wide-spread adoption of tar-oil winter washes in the 1920s the spider-mite began to occur as a pest. In the sprayed orchards there were fewer species of predatory insect.

although numbers of individuals of certain species could be very high at intervals. Populations of these predators fluctuated violently just as expected in a very simple environment, so that acaricides had to be used frequently to reduce a large infestation of the spider mite, which further disrupted the stability that had existed.

The first dilemma posed by insecticide use may be impossible to overcome. Rarely can permanent control be achieved by a single application of spray, and yet multiple application, to keep the resurging population down, merely results in a more rapid adaptation on the part of the insect population to a higher threshold of tolerance to this additional environmental factor. For insect populations insecticides seem to act just as any other mortality factor. Since insects have been preeminently successful at adapting to heavy mortality, it is hopeless on the long term to try to control them with chemicals in an effort to beat them at the coevolutionary race for the food we grow, without severe toxic effects on the environment. Rather than merely adding another environmental factor with which they are preadapted to cope, we are faced with the necessity of restoring low equilibrium population levels by modifying biotic environmental factors, or radically disrupting the ecology of the pest to control them. This is why the most promising methods of insect control that are being developed today are depending heavily on sophisticated application of knowledge on the genetics, mating behavior, sex attraction, and hormonal balance of insects (see Chapter 12 on biological control).

There may be only one possible situation where insecticides prove to have a lasting effect, without need for repeated application. McLeod (1972) provides interesting data on this point. In Quebec the Swaine jack pine sawfly, *Neodiprion swainei*, has been studied since 1956, and population estimates have been made each year on several different stages in development. Thus a continuous record was available for 10 years before spray application in August 1965 and for 5 years afterwards. As so often happens in large scale aerial spray operations one control plot was contaminated with insecticide, but the results are revealing nevertheless. In the one unsprayed plot populations remained high and had the potential for killing trees (Fig. 11.1), so that the spray application was economically and aesthetically justified. In the properly sprayed plots, control was very effective, and populations have not recovered to the point where they cause significant defoliation. In the hypothetical control plot that received spray drift the population had recovered almost to its original

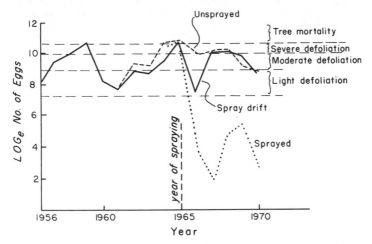

Fig. 11.1   Population trends ($\log_e$ number per 1000 ft)^2 of the egg stage of Swaine jack pine sawfly in Quebec from 1956 to 1970 in an unsprayed plot, a plot sprayed with Phosphamidon in 1965, and a plot that received spray drift. After McLeod 1972.

level by 1967. This was because of what is now expected—a tremendous increase in survival (Fig. 11.2). Spray was applied after the egg census in 1965, so that all numbers after this were affected by the spray. But notice how small the mortality was in the year after spraying, 1966, as compared to all the other years.

Why was there so much difference between the area that was accidentally sprayed and that which was sprayed purposely? In spray plots that received the correct spray dosage mortality between the second and fourth instar larvae was 99.67 and 99.42%. For a species that lays about 60–80 eggs per female this is an extremely effective control, and unusually effective. The plot that received spray drift had a second to fourth instar interval mortality of 65%, a level of control that is nearer the normal success for a typical spray program on other species. The control plot that remained uncontaminated showed an interval mortality of 3%. The most likely explanation, for the long-term control in the sprayed plots, with no appreciable population developing, is that for once the insecticide did radically change the ecology of the insect. The population of sawflies probably became so sparse the males could not cue in on the females and mating success was extremely low. Unless this level of control is achieved we must expect the population to bounce back to its former level very rapidly so that repeated spraying is necessary.

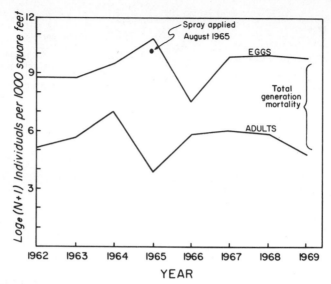

Fig. 11.2 Population trends of the egg stage and adult stage of the Swaine jack pine sawfly in Quebec from 1962 to 1969 expressed as $\log_e$ (number + 1) of individuals per 1000 ft² of ground surface area. Note that mortality was very high in 1965, the year spray was applied, but in 1966 mortality was abnormally low. This resulted in a bounce back in egg numbers in 1967. After McLeod 1972.

In New Brunswick government and industry concerted their efforts to control the spruce budworm. They started spraying in 1952 to save large tracts of spruce and fir forest from defoliation and death. About 200,000 acres were sprayed that year (Webb et al. 1961). In the following years typical mortalities achieved were (from internal reports): 1960, 29–92%; 1961, 53–86%; 1963, 38–88%. With these mortalities, and remembering that a female budworm lays 150–180 eggs on average in good conditions (Miller 1957), there is always a good population to replenish the numbers, and this has resulted in more and more land being sprayed. Almost every year up to the present, that is for more than 20 years, insecticides have been applied. Now the area sprayed is usually around 2 million acres, at about a dollar per acre. Once spraying was started government and industry were locked into a cycle of events that merely increased their commitment to spraying, and increased the potential destruction of the forest if they did not spray. The forest was spared from destruction but what were the real environmental costs involved?

Watt (1963b) and MacDonald and Webb (1963) remark on the characteristic increased survival in post-spray generations of budworm (Fig. 11.3) (except the first instar larvae of the first generation after spraying

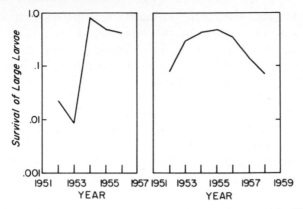

Fig. 11.3 Survival of large larvae of the spruce budworm after spray in 1953 (left) and after starvation in 1952 and 1953. From Watt 1963b.

that feed on sprayed foliage before the toxins have weathered during the winter after spraying). This resurgence is also paralleled by the response to natural mortality caused by starvation, although not so dramatic.

If insect populations respond to insecticide stress so effectively, just as another environmental factor, how do they differ from other organisms, such as the osprey, which is known to be severely affected by DDT poisoning? Populations have declined dramatically. To ospreys insecticides are a threat of a new and different kind. The peregrine falcon is also suffering from the same stress. In 1970 eyries were examined by Cade and his associates (Cade and Fyfe 1970). In southern parts of its breeding range, that is, nearest human habitation and agricultural practices, 4 eyries were occupied out of 82, a 5% occupation. In the taiga of Canada and Alaska 34 eyries were occupied out of 64 (52%), and in the arctic tundra, 31 eyries were occupied out of 53 (60%). In both tundra and taiga, populations have declined locally since 1966. Reproductive success of falcons has diminished in association with egg shells that are 15–20% thinner than they were in these populations before 1947 (when DDT was first used) (Cade et al. 1971). Thin eggshells lead to crushing of eggs during incubation. There is a highly significant negative correlation between chlorinated hydrocarbon residue levels in the egg contents (or the adult tissues) and the thickness of eggshells. High DDT concentration in eggs also leads to mortality of embryos. Cade and Fyfe (1970) predict that the peregrine may become extinct in the 1970s if the current rate of decline continues.

Insecticide gets to the top predators in a food chain, even though pesticides are not applied in the ecosystem to which some of these species belong. Movement of pesticides from one ecosystem to another is affected by wind and water transport. Insecticide is leached out of agricultural soils and appears in runoff that contaminates rivers, lakes, estuaries, and coastal waters. In water the concentration of DDT may be undetectable, but small aquatic organisms take in large amounts of water, and selectively retain chlorinated hydrocarbons in fatty tissues. This occurs at each level of the food chain; thus the toxins are more and more concentrated (Fig. 11.4). This process is termed biological concentration. The process can occur only with insecticides that are not easily

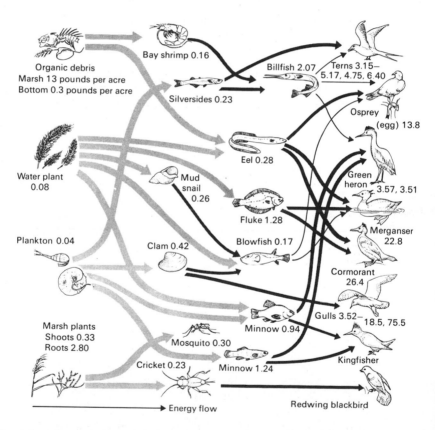

Fig. 11.4   The movement of DDT in part of the food web in a Long Island estuary, New York. Energy and DDT flows in direction of arrows and DDT concentrations are expressed in parts per million (see also Woodwell et al. 1967). Adapted from Toxic substances and ecological cycles by G. M. Woodwell. Copyright © 1967 by Scientific American, Inc. All rights reserved.

biodegradeable, such as the chlorinated hydrocarbons, DDT, and dieldrin. Other commonly used insecticides are the organophosphates and carbamates that are more readily degraded.

The big differences between the effects of insecticide on insects and the top predators that are so seriously affected are basically threefold: (1) Insects usually occupy the second and third trophic levels in the food chain, and therefore their foods have not accumulated large concentrations of insecticide. Top predators eat concentrated DDT. (2) Insects are very short-lived so that there is less chance for the selective absorption of DDT and its residues to result in a large accumulation of toxins in the body. Their production/assimilation efficiency is high so less material per gram biomass passes along metabolic pathways after passing in through the gut wall. Therefore, there is a correspondingly smaller degree of retention of pesticide residues. (3) Because of the small size, short life, high populations, and static feeding habits of many insect herbivores, not all individuals in a population will be exposed to an insecticide during their lifetime. However top carnivores, such as birds of prey, live a long time; they eat a diverse array of foods, all of which have had a good chance of being contaminated, with the result that every individual in a population is likely to be exposed to insecticide residues. These characteristics also influence profoundly the rate of adaptation to insecticide stress (see Moore 1967). Insect herbivores have relatively high populations, a diverse gene pool, high and immediate mortality following insecticide application, and therefore rapid selection for behavioral and physiological resistance (see also Hunt and Bischoff 1960). In contrast, predators have relatively low populations, a less diverse gene pool, less direct and less immediate mortality, a relatively long life cycle, and thus a relatively slow or negligible adaptation to pesticide stress.

Here is the second dilemma posed by insecticide use. Insecticides are not a serious threat to insect pests; they are a serious threat to most organisms higher in the food web that can act as effective regulating influences on the pest insects, and particularly to the top carnivores. There is little chance for these top predators to adapt to a world contaminated by insecticides, where the processes in the food web aim the toxicants directly at them, although the chemicals are applied on plants.

The two major problems with insecticide use mentioned in this chapter have led to a great increase in research on ways in which to reduce or abandon its application. A resurgence of interest on biological control (see Chapter 12) has returned this line of research to the limelight it enjoyed in the 1920s and 1930s before DDT was used commercially. The scope of this research has broadened greatly. The concept of pest control by use of insecticide has yielded to the more recent approach of pest management using an integration of cultural, biological, and chemical control. An introductory treatment of the latter area has been presented by Metcalf and Luckmann (1975).

Chapter 12

BIOLOGICAL CONTROL

B iological control can be broadly defined as any method of pest control that utilizes living organisms or their natural (nontoxic) products. This means that there exists a wide variety of approaches even if our attention is restricted to the control of insects. The term control is generally applied where pests are maintained at a level below that at which crop or other damage is too severe, that is below the economic threshold. Since there are several good books that consider biological control (e.g., DeBach 1964a, 1974, Huffaker 1971, Rabb and Guthrie 1970, National Academy of Sciences (NAS) 1969, 1972, Franz and Krieg 1972, Van den Bosch and Messenger 1973) each approach is not considered but some are listed with a pertinent reference for easy entry into the literature:

1. Introduction of exotic species (DeBach 1964a, Huffaker 1971).
2. Mass release of parasitoids and predators (Schuster et al. 1971, Parker 1971).
3. Supplemental food or habitat for natural populations of predators and parasitoids (e.g., Doutt and Nakata 1973).
4. Insect pathogens (Burges and Hussey 1971, Falcon 1971, DeBach 1964a, Heimpel 1972).
5. Pheromone trapping (e.g., Roelofs et al. 1970, Beroza 1972).
6. Hormonal control (Robbins 1972).
7. Sterilization techniques (Knipling 1972, NAS 1969).
8. Genetic manipulation (e.g., Whitten 1970, NAS 1969).
9. Plant resistance (Pathak 1970, Day 1972).

However, others (e.g., Stehr 1975) prefer to restrict the term biological control to the management of predators, parasitoids, pathogens, and phytophagous species attacking weeds.

Biological control has been used in many parts of the world, and some regional references in biological control may help the reader to appreciate the amount of effort and the massive numbers of organisms that have been shipped around the world for this purpose. The five most informative references are Clausen (1956) on biological control in the United States, McLeod et al. (1962) and Anonymous (1971) on Canada, Franz (1961) on Europe, and Wilson (1960a) on Australia. Hagen and Franz (1973) provide a survey of many geographic regions.

The need for biological control is almost self-evident. Natural imbalances in communities occur and others are commonly induced by man, either by gross simplification of an environment or by the accidental transport of pests without their natural enemies. A restoration of balance may be achieved by reuniting the pest and its natural enemies by importing the latter as in the examples given below. Biological control uses the most natural ways of treating problems and circumvents problems of toxicity of chemicals, persistence of toxins in the environment, and the short-term control that is achieved with chemicals. Because of the problems with pesticides already mentioned in Chapter 11, there have been concerted efforts to reduce pesticide application by using strategies that make best possible use of biological control in conjunction with cultural control and pesticides, now called pest management. The literature on this subject is growing rapidly (see Metcalf and Luckmann 1975, Geier et al. 1973, Huffaker 1971, NAS 1969, 1972, Rabb and Guthrie 1970) and this area of applied research is one in which the insect ecologist can play an important role by bringing ecological principles to bear on management problems (e.g., see Price and Waldbauer 1975).

With so much readily available literature on biological control this chapter is spent on three classic cases of successful biological control, the interesting debates that emphasize ecological factors, and finally the functioning of predators and parasitoids as control agents. That is the original and classic method of biological control is examined, where control agents are introduced into pest populations. Since about 75% of these biological control attempts have not resulted in adequate control (DeBach 1974), the possible reasons for this should be examined carefully.

Three outstanding examples of successful biological control are described below.

1. Cottony-cushion scale, *Icerya purchasi* (Homoptera), controlled by the vedalia beetle, *Rodolia cardinalis*, in California, 1888 (see Doutt 1958, 1964 for details).

In 1887 the young citrus industry in California was threatened with destruction because of a massive infestation of cottony-cushion scale. Riley, Chief of the Division of Entomology in the Federal Government, gave a talk to the Convention of Fruit Growers meeting in Riverside, California, in April 1887 and stated that the original location of cottony-cushion scale was Australia, no records of parasitism had been cited in California, the scale was probably introduced around 1868 (only 20 years before it was destroying an industry), and that it would be advisable to send a man to Australia to study the parasites there and to find those best for introduction into the United States. He estimated that the cost of this project would be $1500–$2000.

Albert Koebele, who was a well-known entomologist in California at that time, sailed for Australia on August 25, 1888; a sailing date that, for biological control, may be likened to the impact of Darwin's setting sail on the Beagle on the development of evolutionary theory. By October 1888 Koebele had found one very numerous fly parasite, *Cryptochaetum*, a lacewing predator, *Chrysopa*, and an unprepossessing number of a coccinellid predator, *Rodolia*. More attention was paid to the abundant cryptochaetid fly parasite than to the lady beetle.

In November 1888 Coquillet, who had been hired to manage the shipments of insects from Koebele, received 28 specimens of *Rodolia*. In December he received 44 specimens, and in January 1889, 57 specimens, making 129 beetles in all. All were placed on a tree infested with the scale under a tent, and by April practically all the scale had been consumed. The tent was then removed and adults spread to other trees, and colonies were distributed to various parts of the state. By June 10,000 lady beetles had been shipped to other areas. In the original area, practically all the scale had been destroyed by June and whole valleys were free of the scale by the end of 1889. Shipments of oranges from Los Angeles County alone jumped in one year from 700–2000 car loads, and the cost of the project was $1500.

In 1891 the California State legislature appropriated $5000 to send an entomologist on another expedition to Australia to search for other predators and parasitoids of scale insects. Koebele was skyrocketed to fame in California and received a gold watch for his troubles, and Mrs. Koebele was presented with diamond earrings! And so was launched biological control as a means of regulating pests.

2. Prickly pear cactus, principally *Opuntia stricta*, controlled by the moth *Cactoblastis cactorum* in Australia, 1926 (see Dodd 1940 for details).

All insects and associated problems and answers did not flow in one direction and here the reverse movements developed into a problem. Cacti (i.e., the family Cactaceae) are native to the western hemisphere, and *Opuntia* species were transported to Australia very early in its colonial history, for use as ornamentals. Even in 1787 the Governor of Australia was importing insects that feed on *Opuntia*; not for its control, but for dye production as cochineal insects; for example *Dactylopius* sp., feed on cacti.

By 1900 *Opuntia stricta* was becoming a serious problem and occupied an estimated 10 million acres of range land. By 1925 an estimated 60 million acres had been infested, and the value of the land varied from 5–30 shillings per acre, that is, about 60 cents to $4.00 per acre. Most of the infestation was in Queensland (N.E. Australia) and in places the cacti formed an impenetrable mass so that cattle could not reach what little grass remained. Since chemical or mechanical control cost £10/acre, that is, about $30, this was absolutely unfeasible.

In 1920 areas of the United States, Mexico, and Argentina were searched for *Opuntia* insects. Many were found and a few were released. In 1925 a shipment of 2750 eggs of the moth *Cactoblastis cactorum* was received from Argentina and the reared larvae fed readily on *Opuntia stricta*. By 1926, 2.5 million eggs had been produced and 2.25 million were released in the field. By 1927 the insect was so common that no more releases were necessary. By 1930–1932 mass destruction of *Opuntia* was evident. Mass starvation of *Cactoblastis* larvae occurred; some resurgence of *Opuntia* was seen but *Cactoblastis* has really been effective ever since. Now there is a game of hide and seek between the plant and the herbivore.

3.   Klamath weed, *Hypericum perforatum*, controlled by the chrysomelid beetle *Chrysolina quadrigemina* in California, 1946 (see Huffaker 1967, Huffaker and Kennett 1969 for details).

The European weed, *Hypericum perforatum*, was called Klamath weed in the United States because it was first reported in California in 1900 on the Klamath River. By 1944 it occupied more than 2 million acres of useful rangeland. Useful food plants were suppressed and the introduced weed was toxic to cattle and sheep. Prices of land went down to about one-third of that in uninfested areas. Again the areas might have been treated with weed killers, but the cost and inaccessibility of the land made large scale operations impracticable, but a little was done.

In Australia encouraging control of Klamath weed had been achieved by the introduction of a chrysomelid beetle, *Chrysolina quadrigemina*. California gained permission to introduce this beetle provided feeding tests were made to ensure that the beetle would not become a pest on the following crops, sugar-beet, flax, hemp, sweet potato, tobacco, and cotton. Shipments from Australia were begun in 1944. Actually the beetle was a native of Europe but it could not be collected there during the Second World War. The beetles had to be acclimated phenologically to the northern summer and, since the beetles did not feed on any of the crops tested, the first releases were made in 1946. After three generations it was possible to collect thousands of beetles for redistribution where only

5000 adults had been introduced. By 1950 millions of beetles had been collected at the release site.

The beetle larvae feed on the basal growth of the Klamath weed just before the dry summers start, they prevent flowering and seed production, and, after 3 years, all the root reserves have been used up and the plants die. Within 10 years after release of the beetle Klamath weed was reduced from an extremely important pest to merely a roadside weed, and land prices had been restored in infested areas of California. Between the years 1953–1959 savings from the increase in land values in California plus the stop of herbicidal treatment amounted to almost $9 million. Since 1953, the feeding of cattle on the reclaimed land has netted $2 million annually. The total cost was only a few hundred thousand dollars.

Some generalities common to these examples help to identify the essential features of a problem that permits success in biological control. (1) All pests were having a drastic impact on the vegetation and the economy, so that the impetus to control was strong and the rewards potentially large. (2) All pests provided a completely unexploited food source because they were introduced, without natural enemies, and no native enemies adapted to them. (3) All pests were extremely abundant, providing almost solid stands of food for any carnivore on scale insects and any herbivore on the weeds, and providing very simple habitats in which to exploit food. (4) All pests were practically immobile and defenseless. The scale insect is sedentary, the spines on prickly pear are no defense against insects, and the toxin in *Hypericum*, hypericin, acts as the feeding cue for *Chrysolina* (Rees 1969). (5) All pests occupied exposed situations, so that they could be easily discovered. (6) All pests occurred in quite mild climates; mediterranean to warm temperate. (7) All cases occurred on continents and not islands. However, because of geographical and climatic barriers the examples may be considered to have occurred on ecological islands.

These sorts of observations and the quest for guiding principles in biological control have led to a series of debates on the conditions most likely to permit success and on the strategies in biological control. All the debates involve ecological principles, and they should sharpen our awareness of the need for more careful study of the alternatives available (see also Van den Bosch 1971).

Debate 1.   Oceanic and ecological islands.   Workers have not agreed on whether successes in biological control are more frequent on islands than on continents. Sweetman (1936) reviewed 26 cases of successful biological control: 21 cases were on islands (mainly New Zealand, Japan, Mauritius, Hawaiian Islands, Fiji Islands, and Cuba), and the remainder occurred in California (2), Italy (1), British Columbia (1), and Manitoba (1). Sweetman classified California and Italy as ecological islands because of the geographical barriers that surround them. Wilson (1960b) has pointed out, however, that control on a continent over an area equivalent to the size of an island is usually not sufficient. Because of the heterogeneity of conditions on continents several species of control agent, each adapted to slightly different conditions, are probably necessary to do the job where one would suffice on an island. Thus it is probably more difficult to achieve success on any large area, independently of its isolation. DeBach (1964b) analyzed 113 cases of biological control attempts, which had been at least partially successful, and found that the idea that islands are more conducive to success in biological control is no longer supported. He found 55% of the successes occurred on continents and that the number of successes was proportional to the number of importations of biological control agents.

So far Askew (1971) has had the last word; he says, "The very successful application of biological control on oceanic islands merits further consideration. Whilst the method has often been successful in continental regions, California being a case in point, the record for islands probably still remains superior." Askew cites three main reasons for this. (1) Islands such as Hawaii and Fiji have long been centers of activity in the field of biological control. Hawaiian sugar planters in particular have promoted this method. (2) On islands the main crops are very often sugar or copra (coconut meat) and in both cases the commercial product is extracted from the plant. Therefore minor pest damage is invisible in the product whereas, if the commercial product is a fruit or vegetable, its external appearance is vital in marketing. (3) Climate of oceanic islands is usually equable. This permits continuous development of insects so that populations consist of all stages simultaneously; thus unsynchronized parasitoids and predators always have a food supply. Equable climatic conditions also promote general stability in the community where density-dependent regulation by parasitoids and predators is likely to be effective.

Debate 2. Are successes more frequent in tropical than in temperate climates? If one subscribes to the idea of more successes on islands one must subscribe to the notion that more successes have occurred in tropical than in temperate climates. But because DeBach argues against this point, we will let it rest. Clearly another good review of the literature on biological control is needed to clear up these points. A review that examines location, area, and heterogeneity of islands and the mainland in the light of modern biogeographic theory (see Chapters 18 and 21), and considers probability of success treated in the other debates on biological control, would be most valuable.

Debate 3. Are sedentary pests more easily controled than are active pests? Sweetman (1936) pointed out that of the 26 successful cases of biological control 14 pests were in the order Homoptera and were either scale insects such as *Icerya purchasi*, mealy bugs, aphids, or leafhoppers. Apart from the last family they are all relatively sedentary, slow in active dispersal, gregarious, and attack a limited number of hosts. Therefore, they are especially susceptible to attack by parasites and predators. DeBach (1964b) makes some additional points about scale insects or coccids: "1. Coccids are easily transported and are among the most common of accidentally introduced pests, thus they have presented more problems to be solved; 2. They have often occurred on expensive crops and have defied easy chemical control; thus there has been considerable economic pressure and backing for biological control attempts; 3. The early success with the cottony-cushion scale led to continued emphasis on biological control of coccids, especially on citrus (crops); 4. Coccids have certain biological attributes which make them more susceptible than the average pest to control by natural enemies." The one factor that has not been already mentioned specifically is that they usually feed on woody perennial host plants so that there is a chronological host-population stability that is advantageous to parasitoids and predators. Thus it is not clear whether Homoptera are relatively easily controlled because many species, particularly coccids, are sedentary or because of other features common to the taxon. Most students of biological control would agree that many factors are involved, as listed in the generalities common to the three case histories given earlier in this chapter.

Debate 4. Which are usually more successful, parasitoids or predators? DeBach (1964b) says that parasitoids have produced control about four times as frequently as predators, but we do not know what proportion of imported control agents were parasitoids; thus it is hard to judge which has the more potential. Probably the most significant difference between the two is that parasitoids are more host-specific than are predators. Parasitoids will be most effective in preventing population increase at low host densities because they cannot switch to another food source. But at very low host populations they may become locally extinct so that the host can increase without the controlling influence of the parasitoid. Both parasitoids and predators have valuable properties and no doubt it is better to establish both than to concentrate on one.

Debate 5. Is biological control more likely to be successful in agri-

cultural or forest and orchard crops? Varley (1959) summarized the effectiveness of biological control projects in the United States up to 1950 and showed that 33% of attempts on orchard, forest, and ornamental tree pests had resulted in effective control, compared to only 5% of attempts in field and garden crops. This difference is no doubt due to the relative permanency of orchards, plantations, and forests, and also to the frequency of ecologically disturbing cultural routines that are applied to field and garden crops. Even within orchards biological and natural control usually improve as the diversity of weed species in the orchard increases (e.g., Askew 1971, Leius 1967). Another factor is that the economic threshold for adequate control in agricultural crops, such as fruits, vegetables, and flowers, is artificially low because of demand for unblemished produce. Cosmetic damage occurs at low pest population levels. The best solution here is to reduce the standards for perfect produce to a realistic level based on an understanding that low pest populations are less deleterious than high rates of insecticide application. Then perhaps more biological control attempts on agricultural crops may be rated as successful.

Debate 6. Should control agents be released one at a time or should multiple introductions be used? Turnbull and Chant (1961) have argued for the introduction of one controlling organism on any given pest as opposed to the introduction of many. They give two reasons: (1) In the past many organisms have been introduced and it has been impossible to find out why some species have failed and why some have been effective. Therefore biological control has remained on an empirical, trial and error basis, with no means of it progressing into a predictive science. If one control organism were introduced at a time, then its impact could be studied and the outcome of the introduction determined. (2) If two or more organisms are introduced they are almost certain to enter into competition. Turnbull and Chant state: "The more species of agents that attack the pest, the sooner competition will start and the more severe will be its effects. We should, therefore, be wary of introducing large numbers of different organisms to attack a single host. A single efficient organism introduced without competitors would appear to serve our purposes best. Assuming that it possessed an adequate reproductive potential, and adequate searching efficiency, was synchronized with its intended host, and was suited to the physical environment of the new area, such an organism could multiply without restraint to the limit of its food supply. In such a situation, population oscillations will almost inevitably be set up, but if the biotic agent possesses characteristics as defined, the peaks of pest numbers should not be excessive." There are some reasons to question the validity of Turnbull and Chant's argument.

An ideal parasitoid or predator such as described should be effective, but how frequently can one be found, especially when we consider the inherent limitations of parasitoids covered later in this chapter? Also Quednau (1970) has shown that, although two species of parasitoid compete for larch case bearer hosts, the net result in some seasons is increased total parasitism. Finally, it is possible to determine why some parasitoids and predators are effective. We know the conditions under which control agents are most influential and by competition studies and niche analysis the role of each species in a community can be determined (e.g., Price 1970c, 1971a, 1972a).

Doutt and DeBach (1964) have discussed the single versus multiple introduction debate. They mention that Pemberton and Willard in 1918 had argued that multiple parasitism was detrimental to the potentially more influential species. Already in 1929 Smith had refuted their claims and Doutt and DeBach present a good deal of evidence in support of Smith's view. They say, "In the light of all available evidence, we must concur with Smith (1929) who stated that 'On theoretical grounds as well as on the data so far available, the policy of entomologists in introducing all available primary parasites of an injurious species is justified, and . . . this policy should be continued.' "

Debate 7. Are exotic pests more easily controlled than indigenous pests? Turnbull (1967) has argued that the chance of competitive displacement of one species of parasitoid by another increases with increased saturation of the community: "The kind of species that can colonize a given site depends to large extent upon what species are already there, and the more species that are present, the more difficult it becomes for an immigrant species to invade." Turnbull goes on to say that most communities into which we introduce entomophagous species are near species saturation and thus there is a remote chance of finding species that can successfully colonize. He thus explains the large number of failures in biological control and implies the futility of further efforts.

Turnbull's paper raises the important question of how saturated are the parasitoid and predator complexes on pest species, and emphasizes the need for introducing species into vacant niches, if the vacancies or the species to fill them can be discovered (see also Price 1972a). Van den Bosch (1968) has argued that "exotic pests characteristically are not attacked by effective natural enemies in the invaded environments and therefore competition from such species is rarely a factor where exotic entomophages are colonized." He points out that successes in biological control with exotic pests have been reasonably frequent, the main cause for failure being the introduction of species that are maladapted for various reasons. Concerning indigenous pests Van den Bosch agrees that

Turnbull's arguments are valid. A careful literature survey would help us gain insight into the merits of these points of view and the worth of attempting biological control on indigenous pests.

Debate 8.   Should r or K selected parasitoids be used?   Force (1972) states that since biological control is frequently attempted in disturbed environments (e.g., agricultural sites) r selected species should be released as they are much better colonizers than are K strategists (see Chapter 8 for discussion of r and K selection). For annual crops this view is probably justified. However, when conditions become ameliorated with time, r selected species may be outcompeted by K strategists and the latter may exert an important controlling influence on the host population. This was true for the parasitoid complex on the Swaine jack pine sawfly (Price 1973b). Thus it is probably best to attempt introduction of both r and K strategists, but care must be taken that each type is liberated at the correct stage in the development of the community.

The last section of this chapter is devoted to the functioning of predators and parasitoids in natural communities. In particular biological attributes that limit their potential as efficient control agents are emphasized, an approach that is not prevalent in the literature, but one that should help in understanding the need for detailed studies on each species used in control. In contrast to the analyses on successful biological control attempts, there is a dearth of critical appraisal of why the greater proportion of attempts have failed. Because usually a failure is not well recorded, it is impossible to go back to find reasons. But in general because there has been a lack of concern for understanding the natural checks on the controlling ability of parasitoids and predators, many studying biological control take it for granted that parasitoids and predators should always be able to regulate pest populations. By examining some of the limitations on parasitoid and predator success a more realistic impression may be obtained.

In the coevolutionary race the organism on the lower trophic level always has the advantage, and is usually able to stay ahead, by evolution of new methods of avoiding being fed upon. If it does not the parasitoid species will also go extinct. Thus frequently we see stages of insects, particularly eggs and pupae, neatly concealed by being buried in plant material or dead organic matter. Larvae often feed in concealed situations and all this hiding probably results from the advantage acquired in these relatively equable microclimates, but very likely predation pressure was a strong selective force in reinforcing any cryptic behavior. Sawfly larvae drop from trees and spin cocoons in the forest litter and become available to many predators and parasitoids. The deeper they burrow into the litter the less likely they are to be found. In the spring when an average of 60% of cocoons were lost through parasitism, none of those that were buried deeply and were in prolonged diapause were parasitized or preyed upon (Price and Tripp 1972). In fact 10% of the population was immune from predation and emerged the following year. In other years up to 40% of the cocoon population may be in prolonged diapause so that it is impossible for parasitoids to be very effective under these circumstances.

Parasitoids may attack a nonrandom sample of the available prey, and therefore they have a qualitative influence on the prey population. If attack is nonrandom then there is the strong probability that reduced mortality will result by adaptation resulting from this selective factor. In the case of the cocoon parasitoids, they seem to be selecting those cocoons that are nearest the surface, and since the adults from these cocoons emerge earliest, parasitism is actually selecting against early emergers and selecting for deep burriers (Fig. 12.1). Thus the parasitoids can survive only by evolving more robust build for burrowing into the forest litter more deeply. But the host is always ahead in this coevolution. As the host goes deeper host finding becomes more difficult and time consuming, fewer parasitoid eggs can be laid, and the parasitoid becomes less effective. There is also selective action of another type for early emergence of the sawfly. Particularly cold weather in the fall will select against larvae that have been laid by a late emerging female. Thus the spectrum

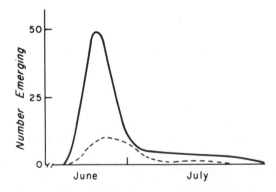

Fig. 12.1   The qualitative effect of cocoon parasitoid activity on sawfly emergence. The solid line represents emergence when attack by parasitoids is prevented and the dashed line emergence after parasitoid attack. Note how most attacks occurred on the would be early emergers. After Price and Tripp 1972.

of individuals in populations is likely to show an adaptive balance between these two selective forces.

There is also a limitation on parasitoid reproduction imposed by the time available per season. Since parasitoids do not kill the host when they deposit an egg, the adults must be highly specialized for planting an egg safely and securely on or in the host. The specialization is often sufficient to prevent a parasitoid from attacking a wide range of host stages, so that only one of the stages, young larvae, old larvae, final instar larvae, or cocooned stages, may usually be attacked by a single species. Quite apart from the problem of temporal synchronization of the parasitoid with host development, there is actually very little time for a parasitoid population to exploit the particular stage of the host to which it is adapted. An extreme case is that of *Exenterus* species that attack only the last nonfeeding instar of sawflies before they spin a cocoon and become unavailable to *Exenterus*. In fact an individual eonymph may be available for parasitization for only 6 hours from ecdysis to spinning of the cocoon. In a very real sense there is shortage of time in which conditions are favorable for reproduction, supporting Andrewartha and Birch's (1954) theory of population regulation.

For the cocoon parasitoids time is also an important limiting factor. Once spring conditions become favorable for activity, cocoon parasitoids emerge and attack other cocoons, but the sawfly host is developing and starts to emerge in late June. There is a selective pressure for parasitoids to emerge early and attack the host before it emerges. The difference in success between an early emerging parasitoid and a later one are obvious (Fig. 12.2). Parasitoid 1 emerges before the sawfly host and can attack a high population of hosts. Parasitoid 2 emerges closer to sawfly emergence

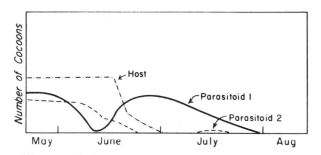

Fig. 12.2 The effect of time for reproduction on the success of parasitoids. Parasitoid 1, *Pleolophus basizonus*, emerges early and produces a large second generation whereas parasitoid 2, *Endasys subclavatus*, emerges later and produces a very small second generation. See Fig. 8.5 for illustrations of these two species. After Price and Tripp 1972.

and attacks a population that is rapidly depleted by host emergence, and consequently produces a much smaller generation. The more time there is available the bigger the population can become.

Environmental heterogeneity also plays an important role in limiting the effectiveness of natural control agents. From Huffaker's (1958) experiments on the six-spotted mite and its predator we know that the more complex the environment the greater the chance of coexistence of predator and prey. Most natural environments are exceedingly complex. Thus there is a good chance that the prey species has refuges from predation or that the prey becomes too sparse to be efficiently exploited. For example, Dixon (1970b) found that sycamore aphids had to be at a certain minimum density on a leaf before they could be successfully exploited by the lady beetle, *Adalia bipunctata*. The first instar larvae of the beetle could not survive in the field unless the population density of young aphids exceeded $2/100$ cm^2. From the point of view of the lady beetle larva the habitat becomes too heterogeneous below this density to permit it to survive.

There are ways of filtering out the tremendous complexity of any given habitat. Townes (1962) has pointed out that parasitoids do not search for hosts at random but usually restrict their search to microhabitats that have a particular common characteristic. This characteristic is usually a purely physical one rather than a taxonomic one. For example, the ichneumonid *Apistephialtes nucicola* (i.e., nut loving) will attack a variety of hosts in diverse taxa, Lepidoptera, sawflies, and cynipid wasps. However all these hosts are found either in walnuts, hazel nuts, acorns, oak galls, or willow galls. There is no relationship between these sites except their general shape and texture, and clearly the parasitoid is searching out round objects in the complex environment. Other parasitoids will concentrate their search on the bark of trees, on the shoots and cones of conifers, or on rolled leaves that may contain all sorts of potential hosts. In the case of *Apistephialtes* all environmental cues are filtered out except the stimulus of a round object, presumably of a reasonably large size.

Chemical cues can be important also in finding hosts to parasitize, and, since odors are quite specific, cueing in on an odor is an efficient way of filtering out extraneous information from the environment. Read et al. (1970) studied parasitoid host selection in relation to aphids on *Brassica* (crucifer crop varieties such as collards, cabbage, and cauliflower). The cabbage aphid, *Brevicoryne brassicae*, is thought to select its host because of the mustard oils contained in the leaves of its host plant. *Myzus persicae*, the peach aphid, also feeds on cabbage and many other plants that do not contain mustard oils. When these hosts are on cabbage, both are attacked by the braconid parasitoid females of *Diaeretiella rapae*, but neither host is commonly attacked when on members of other plant families that do not contain mustard oils. By olfactometer experiments they found that *Diaeretiella* females were attracted to the cabbage plant odor and in this way they could locate their hosts, the aphids. The parasitoids were using chemical cues contained in the host plant of their host (*B. brassicae*) for finding their food (Fig. 12.3). A third link in the food chain, a hyperparasitoid of *Diaeretiella*, the cynipid wasp, *Charips brassicae*, was shown to be attracted to the odor of the *Diaeretiella* individuals. This microcommunity is held together by chemical cues that permit these minute insects to operate in a complex environment as if the complexity did not exist at all.

Other parasitoids also use host odor as a cue in their search. Vinson

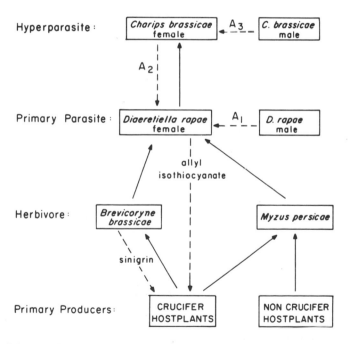

Fig. 12.3   The cohesive nature of a food web on collards showing trophic relationships (solid lines) and chemical cues (dashed lines) that bind the species of this microcommunity. A_1 and A_3 are suspected sex pheromones of *D. rapae* and *C. brassicae* respectively, and A_2 is the suspected attractant used by *C. brassicae* females to locate *D. rapae* females. From Read et al. 1970.

(1968) found that the braconid parasitoid *Cardiochiles nigriceps* responds to the mandibular gland secretion of *Heliothis virescens* which is secreted while feeding, and is stimulated to begin directed searching movements. Similar responses may be found perhaps in species that are known to actively search among damaged foliage for hosts. Another parasitoid, the braconid *Microplitis croceipes*, has its host-seeking response elicited by a substance in the frass of its hosts, *Heliothis zea*, *H. virescens*, *H. subflexa*, and others (Lewis and Jones 1971). Lewis et al. (1971) also found that adult moth odor left on the substrate by the Indian meal moth, *Plodia interpunctella*, significantly increased parasitism of eggs by *Trichogramma evanescens*. It seems that parasitoids are able to cue in on various chemicals and thereby reduce environmental complexity dramatically.

Another way in which host discovery may be improved is through searching behavior. As soon as a food item is found search behavior is intensified. Croze (1970) called this area restricted search (see Chapter 4). This was observed in the carrion crows that Croze studied and it has been seen in the chalcid parasitoid, *Trichogramma evanescens* (Laing 1937). Searching ichneumonids avoid areas they have already searched and so improve their efficiency (Price 1970d, 1972b), although Fleschner (1950) claimed that the larvae of three predators of the citrus red mite, *Stethorus*, *Chrysopa*, and *Conwentzia*, search for hosts at random.

Reproductive strategies and the limits on fecundity also influence the efficiency of natural control agents. From Chapter 8 we know that some parasitoids have a small egg production, so that at high host densities a female is likely to lay all her eggs, but still leave many hosts unattacked. The functional response will level off, not because of handling time, but because of egg-production time.

Social interactions also limit the effect of parasitoids as regulating agents. Intraspecific recognition and dispersal are especially important. In the 1930s Salt wrote a classic series of papers on the searching behavior of a small chalcid wasp, *Trichogramma evanescens*, which is a parasitoid of many insect eggs (Salt 1934a,b, 1935, 1936, 1937). He found that once a female *Trichogramma* had even so much as walked over an egg host, this egg was rejected as a host by another female. The second female discriminated against that host. Salt (1937) showed conclusively that the former female had actually left a chemical trace on the egg that was recognizable by another female. This type of discrimination has been shown to be characteristic of many parasitoids. Several authors have suggested that this is adaptive because if the first female laid an egg on the host, the second female may waste an egg by laying it on the same host, as usually only one parasitoid can survive per host. This discrimination has usually been thought of as an adaptive avoidance of parasitized hosts, which therefore saves the wastage of eggs and improves the efficiency of the parasitoid individual, and the population as a whole.

But is this a valid interpretation? What most people have ignored in Salt's work is that in Salt's (1937) words, "The chemical trace left on the surface of the host is not the general body odour of the parasite but a more specific smell probably produced by glands on the tarsi. It is left not only on hosts but also on the substratum on which the parasite walks." Vinson and Guillot (1972) have found that the odor used to mark hosts is secreted by the alkaline (Dufour's) gland in two braconid parasitoids, *Cardiochiles nigriceps* and *Microplitis croceipes*. If a second female avoids the odor left on the host she will also avoid the odor on the substrate and therefore not search areas that have been searched by a previous female. If the previous female did not find all the hosts in that area they are essentially immune from attack until the odor of a searching female has evaporated. The effect on a population is important. Avoidance of trails leads to the spreading out of a parasitoid population and thus prevents an effective increase in density of parasitoids in response to host density. In confined conditions females will spend more time avoiding others and trying to escape than in ovipositing, and this results in reduced number of hosts attacked with increased parasitoid density. This is what prompted Hassell and Varley (1969) to propose their new host-parasitoid population model (see also Chapter 5, Hassell and Rogers 1972, Hassell and May 1973, and Rogers and Hassell 1974).

This recognition of a trail odor is also seen in ichneumonids, and as shown in Fig. 9.7, as parasitoid density increases, the population covers a correspondingly larger area. Therefore, by increasing a female's own efficiency in finding hosts because she avoids her own odor, this recognition actually decreases the efficiency of the population in controlling the host, as parasitoids leave the site with abundant hosts and parasitoids because it is too contaminated with trail odors. This odor is also recognized interspecifically (Price 1970d), and this raises a problem. What is the point of one species discriminating against a host that contains the egg of another parasitoid? Even a female of a species whose larvae will normally kill the larva of another species if they are about the same age will avoid the trail of the female parent that produces the inferior larva (cf., *Pleolophus indistinctus* and *P. basizonus* in Price 1970c, 1971a, 1972b). This is a really maladaptive trait and it can only be explained satisfactorily by looking at the situation from the point of view of the fitness of a female parasitoid. A female lays a helpless egg on a host, or in a host, and this host remains available to all other parasitoids of the same species, or other species that attack that host. An obvious way of improving its fitness is to mark the host with a deterrent defensive secretion so that all other parasitoids are repelled by the host. Salt (1937) also used the term deterrent. Thus discrimination is the wrong word. The odor is a repellant and the second parasitoid avoids this stimulus. We might regard this as a peculiar type of territoriality (see Chapter 16), but certainly it is an allelochemical defense (see Chapter 3).

Finally, host-parasitoid interactions, including host resistance, are much more complex than has been thought. As far as internal parasitoids are concerned they are vulnerable to the internal defense mechanisms of the host, particularly through phagocytosis and encapsulation by many hemocytes (for additional information see Salt 1963, 1968, 1970). Mechanisms for avoiding this host resistance may include (1) suppression of encapsulation by reducing blood cells responsible for encapsulation and (2) avoidance of recognition as aliens by their hosts (see Vinson 1971). It appears that the parent female may significantly disrupt internal defense of the host by injecting substances during oviposition, and also increase survival of progeny considerably (Guillot and Vinson 1972, Vinson 1972). Guillot and Vinson (1972) found that a combination of poison gland contents and calyx fluid in very low dosage caused this result, both reducing growth of the host and increasing survival. The poison gland is closely associated with the ovipositor and the calyx is an expanded section of the lateral oviduct (see Vinson 1969).

Again we see the effect of attack and counterattack between members of adjacent trophic levels and the resultant coevolved systems with intricacies that require much more study before we fully understand them. In spite of all these limitations on the efficacy of natural control agents the value and further use of biological control is assured. Public demand for conservation of environmental quality, if sustained, will exert considerable pressure for use of more biological control methods. With the increase in understanding of entomophagous insects and the interactions with their hosts we should expect to see the ratio of successes to failures increase. The further use of empirical methods in biological control is completely unjustified, although further careful analysis of the existing records would help to clarify situations in which the approach has its greatest potential. There is a continuing need for good experimental work on the processes involved in biological control.

Part III

COEXISTENCE

AND

COMPETITION

S pecies adapt to exploit a certain set of necessary resources (Chapter 13). Those with similar requirements compete for these (Chapter 14), and with evolutionary time there tends to be a divergence of exploitation patterns and subdivision of resources. Refuges from competition develop so that coexistence is possible (Chapter 13). Thus a certain number of species become packed into the same community depending on the resources available and how they are subdivided by organisms present (Chapter 15). Although competitive elements remain within social groups, overt competition is suppressed, and cooperation results in a few to many individuals coexisting in an area with each group adequately spaced from other such groups in terms of breeding space and resources required for breeding (Chapter 16).

The extent to which species compete or coexist influences the number of species in each community and the succession of species through time spans of several years to a hundred or more. The patterns of species presence and abundance are therefore molded by competition and these may be seen also on a much larger scale in geological time and in geographic distribution (Part IV).

Chapter 13

THE NICHE CONCEPT AND DIVISION OF RESOURCES

To the practiced eye and to those who are familiar with organisms in the field, even very similar species can be differentiated. And the differences between species have really been the focus of taxonomists and ecologists alike. The obvious corollary to differences in shape and size is that organisms differ in what they do. The larger the differences there are between species, or the more the differences in what animals do in a given area, the greater the number of species that can live together in the same area. Darwin (1859b) called this the principle of divergence.

Just as the obvious differences between species demanded that they be given different names, so there was a necessity for an ecological classification of the roles of these organisms in the environment, and Grinnell in 1917 was the first to coin the word "niche" to describe the place of an organism in the environment. Grinnell pointed out that the California thrasher was dependent on a certain set of physical factors and biotic factors in the environment and that these factors together defined the niche of the species. Elton (1927), however, placed emphasis on the function of an organism in relation to other organisms; an animal's "place in the biotic environment, its relation to food and enemies." He was not so concerned with the physiological adaptation of a species to a particular set of environmental conditions. The difficulties with this classical concept of the niche are that often species have more than one role in the environment, for example, larvae and adults of many holometabolous insects, or species that show sexual dimorphism in shape or behavior. To be useful the niche should be defined in terms of the species, rather than subdivision within a species. Also the species' niche may be modified by the presence and absence of other species, so that it is necessary to differentiate between the actual niche and the potential niche of a species (i.e., the niche occupied when in the presence of competing species and the niche occupied in their absence). The role of a species probably changes little when other species are present but its success and abundance may be greatly modified by other species. The role of a species also presents problems when we wish to quantify it. How does one measure the role of a species?

The more modern niche concept, developed independently by Pitelka (1941), Macfadyen (1957), and Hutchinson (1957), attempts to circumvent these problems by making the niche a quality of the environment rather than a quality of a species. Pitelka (1941) wrote, "The niche of a particular species is obviously difficult to define and entails an extensive study of environmental relations. However, one refers to the niche most conveniently in terms of the place within the environment characteristically frequented by the species." Macfadyen's (1957) concept of the niche was "that set of ecological conditions under which a species can exploit a

source of energy effectively enough to be able to reproduce and colonize
further such sets of conditions." Hutchinson has formalized the definition so that it becomes clear how to determine the niche requirements
of a species. If the temperature requirements of a species are considered
it is possible to determine the tolerance range of a species in relation to
this resource, or on this dimension of the niche: a one-dimensional niche
(see Fig. 13.1). If the species eats seed then it can eat a certain range of
seed sizes within those available in the habitat, and combined with temperature, we have a two-dimensional niche, an area. Assume this same
species lays its eggs in plant stems. A third dimension might be the width
of the stem of the host plant required by an ovipositing insect and a
three-dimensional niche is described, a volume. By adding more essential
resources to this niche volume, the niche can be defined as an n-dimen-
sional hypervolume in the environment, the perimeter of which circum-
scribes the area in which a species can reproduce indefinitely.

Conceptualizing the niche as a quality of the environment also helps in
the realization that a species must constantly adapt better ways of exploiting that environment, and modifications of the niche exploitation pat-

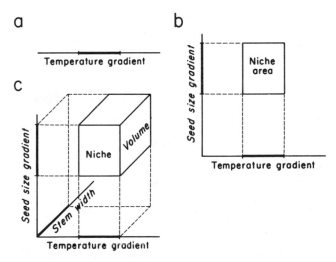

Fig. 13.1 Diagrammatic representation of the niche, with the range over which a
species can utilize each resource marked with a heavier line. (*a*) A niche defined by one
dimension, (*b*) a niche defined by two dimensions, and (*c*) a niche defined by three
dimensions. The niche volume represents the space in which a species can survive and
reproduce indefinitely.

tern, a phrase first used by Root in 1967, are required as the environment changes. Root (1967) studied this pattern in the blue-gray gnatcatcher, *Polioptila caerulea*, in California to see how the species copes with a constantly changing environment. Interestingly, the gnatcatcher seemed to be primarily adapted to those features of the environment that changed least through the season, and these adaptations differed considerably from the other coexisting species. Root found that the blue-gray gnatcatcher differed most from other coexisting insectivorous birds in its foot length, and chord of wing (Fig. 13.2). Associated with its smaller size was its utilization of smaller foraging perches, meaning that gnatcatchers forage in the periphery of the canopy in woody plants, irrespective of species or vegetation type. Its smaller wings enable high maneuverability for catching most prey encountered in the foraging zone defined by perch

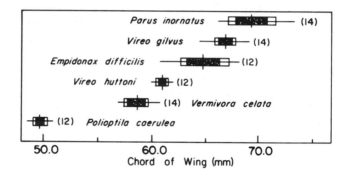

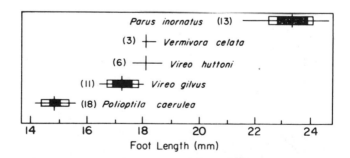

Fig. 13.2 Length of wing and foot in the foliage-gleaning guild of which the blue-gray gnatchatcher, *Polioptila caerulea*, is a member. Note how much this species differs from other guild members. The horizontal lines represent the observed ranges; the rectangles mark one standard deviation on either side of the mean, with the solid portion indicating the 95% confidence limit for the mean. Numbers in parentheses are sample sizes. From Root 1967.

size. At the beginning of the breeding season insects were most abundant in the chapparal vegetation and territories were established in bushes. Later in the season the insects became more abundant in nearby oak woods. As the insect abundance moved, so the foraging of the gnatcatchers moved, and thus they essentially remained in a niche with sufficient food by making this shift. The niche was therefore not defined in terms of plant species, but rather by the perch size and abundance of insects, and any plant that sustained a good insect population and provided adequate small perches was included in the niche exploitation pattern.

Of necessity, though, this pattern was pliable, especially to cope with the extra stress of feeding young in the nest. When individuals were feeding to maintain themselves a large majority of time was spent feeding on insects on foliage, the mode of feeding to which they are clearly adapted. However, when they needed extra food for young, food-catching routines that were energetically more expensive were seen more and more frequently, for example, catching insects in the air and gleaning on herbs (Table 13.1). In fact the species became much more of a

Table 13.1 Feeding pattern of the blue gray gnatcatcher in March, late June, and July, expressed as the percent of each type of feeding in the total feeding time. In March foliage was only partially developed and much time was spent feeding on twigs. In June and July during self maintenance most time was spent feeding on insects on foliage, but while feeding young a shift was made to more feeding in the air and on herbs.

Feeding location	Self-maintenance (%)		Feeding young (%)
	March	June and July	June and July
Foliage	14.5	78.5	57.2
Air	21.0	11.9	26.1
Twigs	64.5	7.7	6.9
Herbs	0.0	1.9	9.8

SOURCE. From Root 1967.

generalist in its feeding behavior to obtain sufficient food. The niche exploitation pattern was very pliable to meet the changing environmental demands imposed by the presence of young and changes in food supply. It is interesting to wonder just how this pliability is related to the mental capacity of an organism, and how pliability, intelligence, and longevity interact. The longer a species lives, presumably the more pliable it must be, and perhaps more intelligent. And perhaps insects, by living briefly, have circumvented the need for a plastic behavioral system. However, whatever the species mental capacity is the niche exploitation pattern is likely to change with changing density as seen in Chapter 9 on population dynamics.

Two important points emerge from Root's study. The niche exploitation pattern not only describes the limits on the species breeding ability that would be described by the Hutchinsonian niche concept, but also describes the distribution of abundance of a species within these limits. A population response to a range of qualities in any resource is superimposed on the Hutchinsonian niche, which greatly increases the value and precision of niche description. This population response is incorporated into the definition of the niche by Whittaker, Levin, and Root (1973) (see Chapter 15 on species packing, p. 314). The second point is that a species distribution may be defined by parameters of a very different scale. On the one hand perch size determines distribution within a community, but food availability determines distribution between habitats. Whittaker et al. reserve the term niche for within community responses; they recognize the habitat as another scale to which species respond, and that these combined responses constitute the "ecotope" of a species (see p. 314 for further description).

Once the species population response to a gradient of conditions is known, the niche of a species can be calculated using simple formulae. Resources that the organism needs to survive and reproduce must be selected and its distribution on each resource sampled in turn. Each resource can be considered as a composite of many smaller resources so that this set makes up one dimension of the niche. A simple case would be to consider the available temperature range of a species as the resource set from $-10°C$ to $+40°C$, and this set can be divided up into units of $10°C$ each, and the abundance of the species can be sampled in each temperature class (cf., Fig. 13.3). The niche breadth of the species on this resource set can be quantified by Levins' (1968) formula:

$$\text{niche breadth } B = \frac{1}{\sum_{i=1}^{s} p_i{}^2(S)}$$

where p_i = proportion of a species found in the ith unit of a resource set, S = total units on each resource set, $B_{max} = 1.0$, and $B_{min} = 1/S$. B can easily be scaled to vary between 1 and 0, so that it can be used to compare species distributions on resource sets with different numbers of units. This

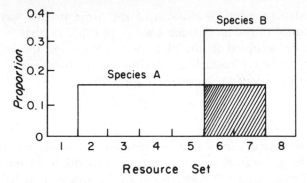

Fig. 13.3 Hypothetical distributions of a species (a) with a broad niche and a species (b) with a narrower niche, on a resource set subdivided into eight resource units. The species have the same proportional similarity which measures the shaded zone, but species a overlaps b more than b overlaps a.

formula, or slight modifications of it, have been used frequently in niche analysis studies (e.g., Levins 1968, Pianka 1969, Price 1971).

The similarity between species distributions on a resource set can be quantified simply by the formula:

$$\text{proportional similarity } PS = \sum_{i=1}^{n} p_{mi} \qquad \text{or} \qquad PS = 1 - \frac{1}{2}\sum_{j=1}^{n} |p_{ij} - p_{hj}|$$

where p_{mi} = the proportion of the less abundant species of a pair in the ith unit of a resource set with n units, and p_{ij} and p_{hj} are the proportions of species i and h, respectively, in resource unit j.

Finally the niche overlap of one species with another can be quantified by the formula from Levins (1968):

$$\text{niche overlap } \alpha_{ij} = \sum_{h=1}^{n} p_{ih} p_{jh}(B_i)$$

where α_{ij} = niche overlap of species i over species j, p_{ih} and p_{jh} = proportion of each species in the hth unit of a resource set, and B_i = niche breadth of species i. These formulae adequately quantify the differences between species A and B in Fig. 13.3. Species A has a larger niche breadth than species B, species A and B have the same proportional similarity, and A will have a greater niche overlap on B than B will on A.

These formulae, or similar formulae, are at present those used commonly in niche analysis studies of communities or guilds. While each formula has conceptual difficulties attached to it, they are still extremely useful in quantifying the niche of species, and interactions between species. By studying several dimensions of the niche in this way a picture may be obtained of the fundamental niche of a species, that is, that niche that would be occupied in the absence of competing species, how this niche is modified by coexisting species, the realized niche, and how resources are partitioned between guild members.

Two species with very similar environmental needs are unlikely to coexist for long, because, sooner or later, competition for food will lead to the local extinction or displacement of the species that has a slightly inferior competitive ability. This has been expressed in varying ways, probably starting with Grinnell in 1904 although Darwin obviously understood the principle. A sampling of attitudes on competitive displacement, or competitive exclusion, is presented below (see also Brown 1958b, Cole 1960). Grinnell (1904) stated, "Every animal tends to increase at a geometric ratio, and is checked only by limit of food supply. It is only by adaptations to different sorts of food, or modes of food getting that more than one species can occupy the same locality." Later Grinnell (1917) wrote, "It is, of course, axiomatic that no two species regularly established in a single fauna have precisely the same niche relationships." Gause (1934) found that competition for common food in protozoa led to a complete displacement of one species by another. Hutchinson and Deevey (1949) stated it another way: "Two species with the same niche requirements cannot form steady-state populations in the same region." More recently MacArthur (1958) wrote, "To permit coexistence it seems necessary that each species, when very abundant, should inhibit its own further increase more than it inhibits the others." DeBach's (1966) review of the subject should also be consulted.

Two examples of competitive exclusion follow; the first case was studied by DeBach and Sundby (1963) and the second by Connell (1961). The California red scale, *Aonidiella aurantii*, is a common pest of citrus trees in southern California, around Santa Barbara, Los Angeles, Long Beach, and San Diego. Around 1900, purely by chance, a parasitoid *Aphytis chrysomphali* was introduced from the Mediterranean region. This species spread and became an effective parasitoid on the scale, but it was certainly more effective in the milder climates of the coastal areas (Fig. 13.4). In 1948 a new species of *Aphytis, lingnanensis*, was obtained from South China and was reared and colonized in all areas where *Aphytis chrysomphali* occurred. The *A. lingnanensis* became more abundant than *A. chrysomphali* and by 1958 *A. chrysomphali* was almost completely displaced from the whole area, and by 1961 *A. chrysomphali* could be

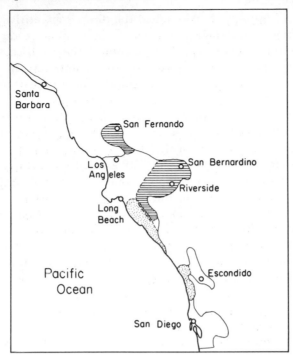

Fig. 13.4 Citrus-growing areas of southern California and the distribution of *Aphytis* species from 1948–1961. In 1948 *A. chrysomphali* occurred in all citrus areas. By 1959 this species had been largely displaced in all areas by *A. lingnanensis*, but populations remained in the dotted zones. In 1961 *A. chrysomphali* was very rare in dotted zones, and *A. melinus* had displaced *A. lingnanensis* from many areas in the interior (hatched). After DeBach and Sundby 1963.

found in only three areas where it represented 32, 6, and 14% of the total *Aphytis* population.

In 1956 and 1957 another species of *Aphytis*, *melinus*, was imported from India and West Pakistan, areas with relatively large annual climatic fluctuations resembling those of the interior citrus areas of Southern California. This was done in the hope that biological control would be improved in the interior where *A. lingnanensis* was not really effective, although it had displaced *A. chrysomphali*. *Aphytis melinus* was liberated in all the citrus areas in Southern California and it was soon clear that this species was displacing *A. lingnanensis* in the interior. At the original release sites competitive displacement of *A. lingnanensis* by *A. melinus* occurred within about 1 year, or eight or nine generations. By 1961 *A. melinus* accounted for 94–99% of the total *Aphytis* population in large areas in the interior.

DeBach and Sundby (1963) studied the direct competitive interactions of these species, and their paper makes interesting reading. But this example should be remembered when competition is discussed (Chapter 14). Lack of competition permitted broad exploitation, in this case by the first parasitoid species, *A. chrysomphali*, and competition forced the species back into a more specialized exploitation pattern. This is a clear-cut example of species with very similar niches being unable to coexist, resulting in competitive exclusion of one by the other. DeBach and Sundby (1963) make the claim that food was never a limiting factor for these parasitoids and yet the competitive exclusion principle obviously implies competition for a common resource in limited supply. Perhaps all hosts were not available to the parasitoids for various reasons or, as Huffaker and Laing (1972) point out in an interesting discussion on DeBach and Sundby's studies, interference competition may have been important. Pheromone interactions and response of parasitoids to increasing density may indicate that space was limiting rather than hosts, as suggested for parasitoids of sawfly cocoons in Chapter 12. Huffaker and Laing conclude that competition must be involved for displacement to occur. Bess and Haramoto (1958) describe a similar case of competitive exclusion in parasitoids of the oriental fruit fly.

Competitive exclusion has also been demonstrated for two species of barnacle that occur together on the intertidal rocky shore at Millport, Isle of Cumbrae, Scotland. Connell (1961) noticed that the adults of the two species occupied two separate horizontal zones on rocks, with a small area of overlap, although the young barnacles of the upper species occupied much of the lower zone (Fig. 13.5). The upper species, *Chthamalus stel-*

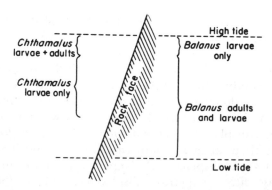

Fig. 13.5 Distribution of adults and larvae of *Chthamalus stellatus* and *Balanus balanoides* on a rock face in the intertidal zone. Relationships to tides are more complex than indicated here. After Connell 1961.

latus, was apparently able to settle in the lower zone but was unable to survive there. In the lower zone *Balanus balanoides* adults and larvae were the most abundant. Connell argued that, since space for attachment and growth is often extremely limited in the rocky intertidal region, *Balanus* may eliminate *Chthamalus* larvae from the lower zone by competition for this common resource that was in limited supply. Both barnacles are prevented from colonizing higher parts of rocks because desiccation is too severe; however, because *Chthamalus* larvae are more resistant to desiccation than *Balanus*, they can exist near the high tide mark whereas *Balanus* cannot. The lower limit of both species may be due to interspecific competition from other organisms but this is not well understood.

When Connell cleared a rock face and allowed *Chthamalus* larvae to settle in the *Balanus* zone, they survived well so long as *Balanus* was prevented from settling in the cleared area. Without *Balanus*, mortality of *Chthamalus* over one year was 9% in one experiment, and with *Balanus*, mortality was 98%. *Balanus* settled more densely than *Chthamalus*, grew faster and actually lifted up, crushed, or smothered *Chthamalus*. *Balanus* clearly out-competed the *Chthamalus* for space (Fig. 13.6). The outcome is the zonation in distribution where *Balanus* competitively displaces *Chthamalus* into a refuge; a refuge from competition because *Balanus* are unable to survive the harsh conditions near the high tide mark. The common demand for space on a rock within the intertidal zone makes the ecology of these two species too similar to permit coexistence. This is probably the best documented case of competitive exclusion.

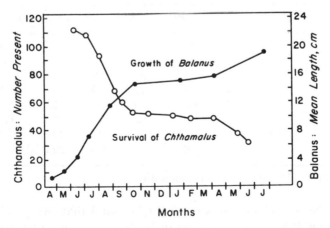

Fig. 13.6 Survival of *Chthamalus* with time in relation to the growth of *Balanus*. From Connell 1961.

There are at least two cases, however, where it appears (or used to appear) that species can exploit the same niche and coexist. Ross (1957) found that six species in the leafhopper genus *Erythroneura* lived together on sycamore leaves in Illinois. In spite of Savage's (1958, see also response by Ross 1958) early criticism of Ross's interpretation, many authors have used Ross's example in support of their own arguments (e.g., Hairston, Smith, and Slobodkin 1960, Hutchinson 1965, Ayala 1970, Edington and Edington 1972). McClure (1974) has taken the first steps in a reanalysis of this situation and should provide the necessary information to determine the validity of this apparent exception to the competitive exclusion principle. More recent data (McClure personal communication) suggest that the eight species of *Erythroneura* now found on sycamore leaves segregate the available food resources in several ways, for example, by feeding on different parts of the leaf blade and in different parts of the geographical range of sycamore (Table 13.2). These and other differences result in very little overlap between the species.

Table 13.2   Latitudinal distribution of sycamore leafhoppers (Erythroneura spp.) expressed as the proportion of each species found in each zone, based on at least 2000 total specimens collected at four or five sites in each zone. Note that the majority of species are most abundant (italic) in a zone where no other species shows peak abundance. The gradient ran from northern Illinois to southern Tennessee.

Species	Zone (°N)							
	North							South
	43–42	42–41	41–40	40–39	39–38	38–37	37–36	36–35
E. arta	*21.9*	6.0	0.5	4.4	8.0	15.7	19.7	*23.8*
E. bella	0	0	0	0	10.3	16.4	29.7	*43.6*
E. hymettana	0	0	0	0	0	0	29.3	*70.7*
E. ingrata	0	0	0	8.3	0	*66.7*	25.0	0
E. lawsoni	8.3	24.5	*33.0*	22.1	5.5	3.5	2.9	0.2
E. morgani	0	2.0	2.1	*35.2*	28.3	24.1	6.9	1.4
E. torella	1.1	*50.0*	16.7	13.2	1.8	13.8	3.4	0
E. usitata	0	0	0	12.4	*47.1*	22.2	13.2	5.1

SOURCE.   From McClure, personal communication.

In northern England Broadhead (1958) found that two psocid species in the genus *Mesopsocus* coexisted in larch plantations. The species were similar in size, body form, phenology, and food preferences. They oc-

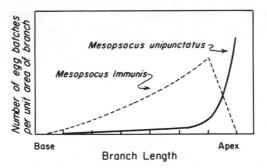

Fig. 13.7   Abundance of egg batches of *Mesopsocus immunis* and *M. unipunctatus* along the length of a larch branch. After Broadhead and Wapshere 1966.

curred on the same twigs and often at high density in almost equal numbers. There was no apparent difference between the ecologies of these species. By 1966, however, Broadhead and Wapshere had found that there was a significant difference between the species and their paper illustrates the detailed work that enabled them to find this difference. When they checked the density of egg batches along a branch of a larch tree they found that the species distributions differed (Fig. 13.7). In fact the species were ovipositing in rather different sets of microhabitats. *Mesopsocus immunis* laid most eggs in axils of dwarf side shoots and *M. unipunctatus* laid most eggs on girdle scars and leaf scars (Fig. 13.8). It appears that the population of each species of *Mesopsocus* was limited

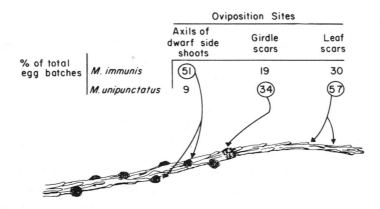

Fig. 13.8   The difference in oviposition sites between *Mesopsocus immunis* and *M. unipunctatus* on a larch branch. The partial refuges from competition are indicated by the circled numbers and arrows indicating the sites. Leaves are not shown. Data from Broadhead and Wapshere 1966.

by the number of oviposition sites that it could utilize on a larch twig. When populations became too high, density-dependent emigration took place, caused by intraspecific competition, and there was no evidence of interspecific competition. Thus these species have attained a stable co-existence by diverging in their oviposition sites, which are in shorter supply than food.

If species have very similar niche exploitation, what modifications or adaptations enable them to coexist? These differences can clearly be very subtle as in the case of the psocids on larch, and actually there are many evolutionary answers for the avoidance of competitive displacement. These include character displacement, habitat selection, microhabitat differences, temporal differences, and diet. Examples of each follow.

Brown and Wilson (1956) have suggested that where two species overlap in their distributions, the differences between them are accentuated in the zone of overlap and are weakened or lost entirely in the parts of the range outside this zone. Morphological, behavioral, and ecological or physiological characters may diverge in this fashion and Brown and Wilson have proposed the term character displacement for divergence in the overlap zone.

The classic case of character displacement in beak lengths of the rock nuthatches, *Sitta neumayer* and *Sitta tephronota*, in Asia, was described by Vaurie (1951). He showed that the two species are nearly identical in areas outside the zone of overlap and can be distinguished only by an experienced taxonomist. These two species differ from other nuthatches in habitat as they frequent rocky hill slopes and find their food on the rocks and the ground. Where sympatric, they both occupy the same rocky habitats. But where these species do occur in more or less equal numbers *Sitta neumayer* shows a marked reduction in bill length and overall bill size, and in the width, size, and distinctness of the facial stripe. *Sitta tephronota*, however, shows an increase in all these characters, having a larger bill and a darker facial stripe (see Fig. 13.9). Apparently the differences in size and shape of the bill permit sufficiently different feeding habits that allow the species to coexist. Differences in facial markings reinforce any other ecological isolating mechanisms and promote intraspecific recognition. In fact by coevolution in the contact zone an apparently single feeding niche has been subdivided so that two species can utilize the same resources where there was originally room for one. Wilson (1955) has shown that where the ants *Lasius flavus* and *L. nearc-*

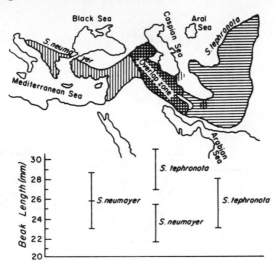

Fig. 13.9   Ranges (above) and beak-length (below) of the western rock nuthatch, *Sitta neumayer*, and the eastern rock nuthatch, *S. tephronota*. After Vaurie 1951, and Lack 1971.

ticus coexist in the eastern United States, they differ by eight characters. Where *L. nearcticus* is rare or absent in the west, *L. flavus* is so variable that species differences are almost nonexistent.

A well-known example of the subdivision of a habitat is that of the five warblers (*Dendroica* sp.) that feed in spruce trees together during the breeding season. MacArthur (1958) studied the species in Maine and Vermont in different plots containing either white, red, or black spruce, or balsam fir. The five species are congeneric, have about the same size and shape, and all are mainly insectivorous. How do they manage to coexist? Why is not one species slightly superior in competitive ability so that it displaces all other species? MacArthur studied the time budget of each species and found that each spent most time in a fairly discrete part of the spruce tree canopy (Fig. 13.10). The Cape May warbler foraged in the top of the tree at the branch tips. The Myrtle warbler foraged near the ground and on the inside of the branch canopy. The black-throated green warbler spent most of its time half way down the canopy between the other two. So here there is a neat subdivision of what may have been thought of as one niche, by behavioral differences in foraging, so that each species has a part of its food source not utilized by the others. This example is of particular interest to an understanding of insect population dynamics. It indicates that a bird may not search all potential niches for food (cf., Royama 1970 and Chapter 4) and that

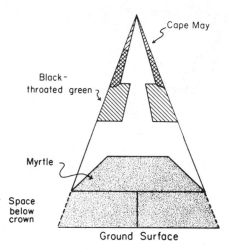

Cape May

Black-
throated green

Myrtle

Space
below
crown

Ground Surface

Fig. 13.10 Cross section of a spruce tree showing zones of most concentrated foraging activity of warblers in the genus *Dendroica*. The original study should be consulted for details on the blackburnian and baybreasted warblers. After MacArthur 1958.

a bird population census without knowing details of niche characteristics may grossly overestimate the intensity of predation on insect populations.

Price (1971a) has shown that three species of ichneumonid are able to survive together because of different responses to habitats defined by moisture content in the litter and host density (Fig. 13.11). A similar response was found by Turnbull (1966) in which the lycosid spiders *Pardosa milvina* and *P. sexatilus* showed niche segregation on a moisture gradient.

As seen in the *Mesopsocus* species, microhabitat differences may be sufficient to permit coexistence. In Chapter 15 on species packing it is seen that species of *Megarhyssa* (Ichneumonidae) also divide up the available resources at the microhabitat level. O'Neill (1967) found that seven species of diplopod coexist in decaying material in maple-oak

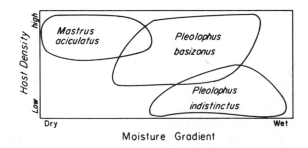

Fig. 13.11 Zones of dominance occupied by three species of ichneumonid in a space defined by moisture and host density gradients. After Price 1971a.

forests in central Illinois. However each was found to be dominant in only one of seven microhabitats: heartwood at center of logs, superficial wood of logs, outer surface of logs beneath bark, under log but on log surface, under log but on ground surface, within leaves of litter, beneath litter on ground surface. Two parasitic mites on the damselfly, *Cercion hieroglyphicum*, colonize different parts of the host's body, one on the thorax and another on the abdomen (Mitchell 1968). Two congeneric flea beetles on crucifers, *Phyllotreta cruciferae* and *P. striolata*, occupy different surfaces of leaves of *Brassica oleracea* (Tahvanainen 1972) (Fig. 13.12). The preference for shady microhabitats in open sites shown by *P. striolata* correlates nicely with the greater abundance of this species on shaded wild crucifers in meadows and woods. Finally, Fitzgerald (1973) found three species of bark-mining moth in the genus *Marmara* (Gracillariidae) on green ash subdividing the bark resources into three. One species attacked the main stem at the base of the tree and the root collar. The upper parts of the tree were divided by one species feeding in the periderm, and the other feeding in the cortex of the bark. Many more examples could be added.

Another way of subdividing resources is by utilizing these resources at different times. Linsley, MacSwain, and Raven (1963b) found that some bees do this in the Great Basin when collecting nectar and pollen from the evening primrose, *Oenothera clavaeformis* (Fig. 13.13). The figure shows that *Andrena rozeni* forages only when the flower is new and *Andrena chylismiae* forages only when the flower is old, and thus they segregate time completely, but *Andrena raveni* forages at both times and thus competes directly with both species.

Time may also be divided between species on a seasonal basis, not only on a daily basis. Clench (1967) found that coexisting hesperiine butterflies tend to fly at different periods of the year, each species being associated in time with the flowering of a different plant species so that competition

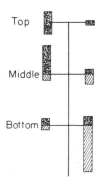

Fig. 13.12 Percentage distribution of *Phyllotreta cruciferae* (left) and *P. striolata* (right) between top leaves, upper surface (solid bars), and lower surface (hatched bars) of middle and bottom leaves of *Brassica oleracea*. Note the strong dominance of *P. cruciferae* in sunny locations and of *P. striolata* in shaded locations. From Tahvanainen 1972.

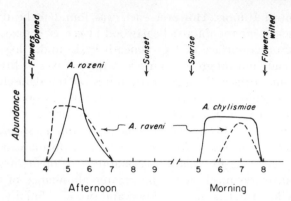

Fig. 13.13 The pollen gathering activity of three species of *Andrena* on *Oenothera clavaeformis*, a white evening primrose which opens in the late afternoon. Data from Linsley, MacSwain, and Raven 1963b.

for nectar was effectively eliminated. Istock (1973) has also collected data that suggests that population peaks of the two dominant waterboatman species (Corixidae) in ponds of northern Michigan are segregated in time. Thus coexistence is permitted at least in part by one species breeding early in the season and one late (Fig. 13.14).

All these ecological differences between closely related species result in reduced competition for food. But another obvious way for species to coexist is to eat different foods. Such dietary differences have been observed by Paine (1962) in the conchs of the genus *Busycon* in Alligator Harbor, Florida. Two species, *B. contrarium* and *B. spiratum*, are both predacious, feeding primarily on pelecypods. The pelecypods differ in that some can shut their valves completely, and others cannot. The former predator is larger and has a thicker shell and feeds principally on

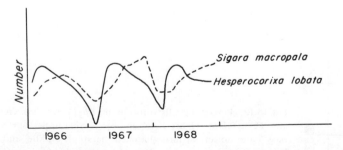

Fig 13.14 Population size of two corixid species over 3 years showing tendency for population increase of each species to occur at a different time of the year. After Istock 1973.

those pelecypods that can shut their valves completely. The latter species of predator feeds on those that cannot and on a considerable amount of carrion. Thus these two coexisting species show less than 10% overlap in their diets. Differences in the size and form of the chelicerae of soil dwelling mites result in use of different particle sizes of food and other factors associated with their diet (Wallwork 1958).

Aquatic insects show a similar partitioning of resources. MacKay and Kalff (1973) have provided one example observed in caddisfly larvae (Trichoptera) in Quebec, Canada. Ninety percent of *Pycnopsyche gentilis* larvae occurred in fallen leaves and 10% in detritus. *Pycnopsyche luculenta* occurred in detritus (50%) or in leaves close to detritus (50%) and fed less on leaves if twigs were available. Thus competition is almost completely eliminated.

Fellows and Heed (1972) found extreme host specificity in larvae of *Drosophila* species inhabiting fermenting cactus stems in the Sonoran Desert. For each cactus species there seemed to be one resident species of *Drosophila* that frequently represented over 90% of the specimens reared from a sample. This specificity is accomplished by well-developed host plant discrimination by feeding and presumably ovipositing adults, and competitive dominance of the resident species' larvae over larvae of other species. Thus competitive exclusion of invading species may still operate in these situations and selection for increased specificity of the invading species may be underway. However there are clearly other strategies available to *Drosophila* species on rotting cacti, although narrow niche exploitation seems to be the predominant one.

In spiders the foraging strategy may be different between coexisting species and thus result in different diets. Such a case is described by Kiritani et al. (1972), in rice paddies in Japan. *Lycosa pseudoannulata* is a hunting spider, *Oedothorax insecticeps* and *Enoplognatha japonica* are web spinners that occasionally hunt, and *Tetragnatha* sp. is a typical web spinning spider. In the period 1968–1970 each species utilized a different percentage of each food type available to it (Table 13.3). Calculating the proportional similarities between all pairs of species shows that diets were from 48 to 77% similar, and that there is not a clear cut segregation of foods between species, although the observed differences are probably an important factor in coexistence. These sorts of results would cause the observer to look more closely at dietary constituents, or to start looking at other dimensions of the niche to find other differences. For example, Kiritani et al. found that *Oedothorax* was most active around noon and thus would catch insects active at this time whereas the other species were more crepuscular in activity. Also, webs may be placed in different microhabitats, so that although the same food is

Table 13.3   Percent composition of various foods in the diet of four species of spider. The proportional similarity (PS) in diets of species pairs are given below.

Food type		Lycosa (%)	Oedo-thorax (%)	Enoplog-natha (%)	Tetrag-natha (%)
			Spider genus		
Green rice leafhopper	Adult	26	4	12	16
	Nymph	27	35	28	10
Brown planthopper	Adult	10	5	12	12
	Nymph	15	19	12	6
Spiders		9	16	3	2
Miscellaneous arthropods		13	21	33	54
		100	100	100	100

$$PS = 0.73 \quad PS = 0.75 \quad PS = 0.75$$
$$PS = 0.77$$
$$PS = 0.57$$
$$PS = 0.48$$

SOURCE.   From Kiritani et al. 1972.

utilized, different segments of it are exploited. For example, Enders (1974) has shown that the orb-web spiders *Argiope aurantia* and *A. trifasciata* place their webs at different heights.

The opposite of niche segregation due to coevolved exploitation patterns is where a species has colonized an area where a diversity of niches remain vacant. If such an area provides adequate geographical barriers that result in restricted gene flow, divergence of characters ensues and speciation is the end result. Resumed sympatry reinforces the differences and we see a group of closely related species occupying an area with an otherwise depauperate fauna of competing species. The extent of this adaptive radiation depends on the number of isolated habitats that are vacant, the number of competitors already present, if any, the distance between such habitats, and the time available for speciation since colonization. These factors are considered in Chapter 21 on biogeography.

The most likely geographical locations in which we will observe adaptive radiation are archipelagos. In the Galapagos Islands the great diversity of Darwin's finches has evolved from a common ancestor (Lack 1947b). On the Hawaiian Islands 22 species of honey creepers have probably derived from one or two colonizing species (Amadon 1950). Here the speciation of insects has been almost incredible (Zimmerman 1948, Mayr 1963) with some species arising in a matter of 1000 years (Zimmerman 1960). Mayr (1963) points out that on average every immigrant beetle species to the Hawaiian Islands has given rise to about 32 descendent species. However it appears that *Drosophila* speciation has been even more extensive than this (see Carson et al. 1970), and in some cases niche specialization is extreme. For example, two sibling species of *Drosophila* utilize the slime flux of a single tree, but one occupies the flux while it is on the tree, while the other is found only in caked soil moistened by flux that has dripped from above (Kaneshiro et al. 1973).

In spite of the frequently observed differences between species exploitation patterns, competition is a reality for many organisms. The strongest argument for this is that we do see division of resources so frequently between coexisting closely related species, signifying that competition has been prolonged and intense enough to produce evolutionary divergence of niche exploitation (see Schoener 1974 for many examples not cited in this chapter). Thus the study of competition is taken up in more detail in the next chapter.

Chapter 14

INTRASPECIFIC AND INTERSPECIFIC COMPETITION

I f the probability is accepted that many populations increase until they reach the carrying capacity of the environment, the inevitable result is that the resource in shortest supply becomes the limiting factor. Liebig in 1840 expressed this in what is now called Liebig's law of the minimum, and expressed in modern terms (Odum 1971), "Under 'steady-state' conditions the essential material available in amounts most closely approaching the critical minimum needed, will tend to be the limiting one. This law is less applicable under 'transient-state' conditions when the amounts, and hence the effects, of many constituents are rapidly changing." Actually, excesses may also become limiting, such as excessive moisture for terrestrial organisms or excessive lead or copper in the soil for plants, and it is the tolerance of organisms to a range of concentrations of a resource that is critical. In 1913 Shelford expressed this in what is now called Shelford's law of tolerance, which states, "Absence or failure of an organism can be controlled by the qualitative or quantitative deficiency or excess with respect to any one of several factors which may approach the limits of tolerance for that organism" (Odum 1971).

These two laws actually relate to individual organisms, and the survival of an individual in a given set of conditions, independent of others in the same niche. They relate to physiological limits to existence. Clearly limiting factors that operate because they are in excess will not be influenced by the number of organisms present. But limiting factors such as food and shelter that are minimal will become more and more limiting for survival, the more individuals there are making an active demand on this resource. Of course physiological limits such as temperature cannot be influenced directly by competition. That resource that is most limiting will be competed for by organisms in a given habitat and this competition will be most severe between organisms that have the most similar demands—individuals within the same species that are involved in intraspecific competition. The difference between the exponential growth curve and the logistic curve may be due solely to intraspecific competition for the resource that determines the carrying capacity (the exceptions are in microbial cultures where the growth rate falls off because of intolerance to accumulating metabolites, such as alcohol or other toxins).

Density-dependent factors often involve intraspecific competition for food as seen in Chapter 9 so that any adaptation that will reduce this competition will be strongly selected for. Individuals that are most different from the majority of the population will suffer least from competition because their requirements will be slightly different and not sought after by so many individuals. Therefore intraspecific competition will select for as diverse an array of qualities as possible within a population to minimize competition. Phenotypic diversity will be held at a maximum so that there will be a broadbased exploitation pattern on the part of the population (Fig. 14.1*a*). An obvious evolutionary solution to reduce intraspecific competition by broadening the exploitation pattern is to develop a polymorphic population. An example is the sexual dimorphism, both morphological and behavioral, seen in a good many birds and insects (Fig. 14.1*b*). Here polymorphism results in two or more adaptive modes in a population.

Selander (1966) makes a strong case for believing that sexual dimorphism has ecological significance in adapting the sexes to different subniches in the case of woodpeckers. For example, the only species of woodpecker on Haiti and the Dominican Republic is the Hispaniolan

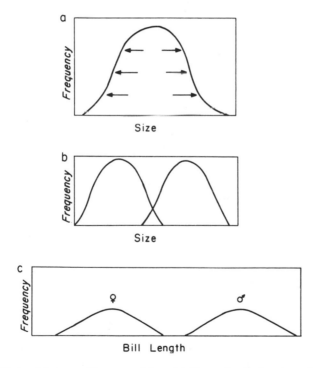

Fig. 14.1   Effects of intraspecific competition. (*a*) Natural selection to reduce competition tends to broaden the frequency distribution of any character involved in the competitive interaction. (*b*) Dimorphism in characters that results in a broader exploitation pattern in the species. (*c*) Sexual dimorphism in the Hispaniolan woodpecker. Part *c* after Selander 1966.

woodpecker, *Centurus striatus*, and the bill lengths of males and females do not overlap at all (Fig. 14.1*c*). This sexual divergence must reduce the intersexual competition for food considerably and must be of high adaptive value. We would see similar distributions of size in mouthparts or rostra of sexually dimorphic insects, but I am not aware of any detailed studies (e.g., many Brentidae and Curculionidae show gross sexual dimorphism in size of rostrum and position of antennae, see Fig. 14.2). Certainly it is a wide open ecological field for an entomologist and a review of the literature would make an interesting, but probably frustrating study, because of shortage of data.

Schoener (1967) found that in the lizard, *Anolis conspersus*, adult males captured prey of larger size, and occupied perches of significantly greater diameter and height than did adult females. This food size and microhabitat dimorphism clearly reduced competition considerably. In bird studies it is becoming common to find that the sexes of a given species forage in different microhabitats. For example, Williamson (1971) found a considerable difference between foraging height in male and female red-eyed vireos (*Vireo olivaceus*) (Fig. 14.3). All these aspects of sexual dimorphism would be so easy to study in insects, because they are generally so much more abundant than vertebrates; thus analysis can be more rigorous and convincing. But there are not enough entomologists interested in this sort of study.

Perhaps the ultimate strategy in avoiding intraspecific competition has been achieved in the developmental polymorphism in holometabolous insects (those insects that have a radically different morphology and ecology in the larval and adult stages). Since there are about 750,000 species of named insects and 85% of these are holometabolous, there are many examples to choose from. A larval flea feeds in the debris of the host nest and the adult feeds on the host itself. A larval fly may mine the mesophyll tissue of a leaf and the adult feeds on sugary solutions such as honeydew or nectar. In hemimetabolous insects (those in which the morphology and the ecology of the nymphs are very similar to those of the adult) the immature stages are very vulnerable. They usually feed in exposed situations just as the adults, and yet they do not have wings that permit them rapid escape. They are also constrained from evolving into forms that would permit better concealment, because they must remain very similar to the adult. This is perhaps the reason for the commonness of hopping in hemimetabolous species, as this is the best escape method for exposed wingless nymphs, and for the overwhelming diversity of defensive secretions produced by members of these orders.

As soon as the larval morphology and ecology can diverge from that of the adult, because of holometabolous development, the obvious evolu-

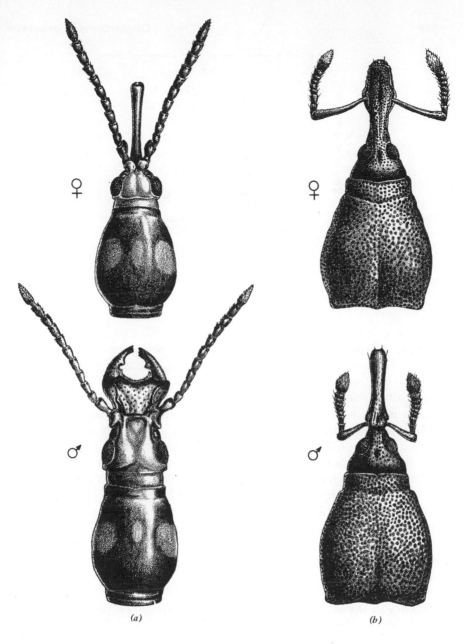

(a)   (b)

Fig. 14.2 Head and prothorax of female and male *Arrhenodes minutus* (Brentidae) (*a*) and *Mesites tardii* (Curculionidae) (*b*) showing sexual dimorphism in rostrum and mouth parts. In the latter case the position of the antennae differ also. In both species larvae are wood boring but the adaptive significance of sexual dimorphism is not understood.

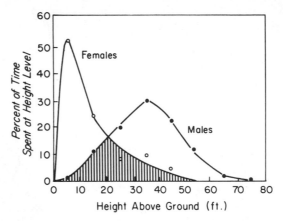

Fig. 14.3 Differences in foraging height of males and females of the red-eyed vireo. Shaded portion shows zone of overlap. After Williamson 1971.

tionary strategy is to diverge as far as possible away from the adult, into concealed, equable, lucrative subniches. Intraspecific competition is completely subdued between parent and offspring, and automatically higher population levels can be maintained on a given resource. Also, the adult must adapt to provisioning its progeny with food, so that the larva adapts into a very efficient eating machine—an energy transformer. This is Darwin's principle of divergence operating again, only within species, so that more individuals per species can coexist per unit area because of this divergence (see also Chapter 2). The success of the aculeate Hymenoptera really hinges on this provisioning ability, which varies from laying an egg on or in a host in the parasitic Hymenoptera and the digger wasps, right up to the highly developed provisioning in the social insects, wasps, bees, and ants, where food is brought into a central nursery. The larva is a sedentary metabolic factory and energy store while the adult is a highly mobile and sensitive transport system, both maintaining the present factory and setting up new ones. Thus both forms can be exquisitely adapted to their individual functions and achieve a tremendous efficiency in the utilization of resources (see Wilson 1971a for an account of division of labor in social insects).

Basically there are two types of intraspecific competition. Nicholson (1954b) made a clear distinction between them and fully realized their population consequences. He gave the name contest competition to those situations where the winner in the competition "obtains as much of the governing requisite as it needs for survival and reproduction" and the loser "relinquishes the requisite to its successful competitors." Nicholson used the example of plants competing for sunlit space, where, as the plants grow, fewer and fewer survive, and the surviving plants get all the sunlight they need. But now that more is known about plant competition, this is not really a clear-cut contest. A much better example is that of territoriality of any sort, where so long as the defender is successful it has an exclusive resource on which to feed. Territories of birds, at least, are usually adjusted in size according to food abundance, so that each territory owner has enough food for maintenance and reproduction. Where breeding sites are limited, as with cliff nesting birds, a young bird must contest the right to maintain that breeding site either by direct aggression or by intimidation displays. But there is no doubt that contest is involved. In fact in any breeding population the most favorable sites are often limited, so that contest ability becomes an important part of the social structure of the population (see Chapter 16 for discussion of territoriality in insects).

In nonterritorial animals such as the gallinaceous birds and the large ungulates, a social hierarchy or peck order is present and this also is a manifestation of contest competition, where the dominant individuals get all they need and the subordinates take what is left, if there is any. In *Polistes* wasps a dominance hierarchy of a truncated form appears to exist among the foundress females on a single nest, where the queen gains her state by dominating other reproductives, and, should she be killed or die, a subordinate female may gain this dominance (Evans and Eberhard 1970).

The population result of contest competition is that the population increases in an area until the carrying capacity is reached and because each organism has enough to live on the population can maintain this level indefinitely (Fig. 14.4a). The term interference competition is more

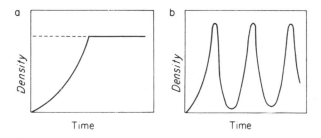

Fig. 14.4 Population trends in (a) contest competition, (b) scramble competition.

commonly used now than is contest competition and is applied to both intraspecific and interspecific competition. It is defined by Miller (1967) as "any activity which either directly or indirectly limits a competitor's access to a necessary resource or requirement." Interference competition is discussed in experiments with *Drosophila* species, for example, in which although food is abundant one species is outcompeted by "conditioning" of the meduim, presumably by waste products released into the medium (see Gilpin 1974, Budnik and Brncic 1974). Pheromone trails of parasitoids would be another example, as would many other examples of allelopathy. Strictly speaking, however, we should retain the term contest competition because interference does not ensure that the winner gains a sufficient supply of food; it merely increases its chance of getting sufficient food. Thus contest competition is a refined type of interference competition that does not cover the range ,of possibilities in interference competition.

   While on the subject of contest competition perhaps a short digression to discuss proximate and ultimate factors in natural selection is in order. Birds do face a problem in setting up territories. They must select a site that will supply abundant food for feeding nestlings, long before that food is abundant, particularly in the case of an insectivorous bird. It is adaptive to synchronize feeding of nestlings with peak abundance of insects, and yet the environmental trigger for the sequence territorial behavior, courtship, nest building, egg laying, and feeding young must be divorced from insect abundance because insects are not abundant when breeding motivation is initiated. If insects were abundant at this time then they probably would not be still abundant when they were most essential for feeding young. Thus although birds must adapt to rearing young when food abundance is greatest, they must also adapt to utilizing a completely different environmental cue for initiating breeding activity. For temperate birds this cue is frequently photoperiod, and when day length reaches a certain value, breeding activity is initiated through the triggering of the hormonal systems involved with reproduction.
   Adaptation to a certain photoperiodic trigger could never be understood unless it is seen in the context of the ultimate limiting factor— food. Selection works toward synchronization with abundance of this ultimate factor during progeny feeding by synchronizing physiologically with a certain photoperiod—a proximate factor in natural selection. Thus it is often important to distinguish between proximate and ulti-

mate factors in trying to understand the evolutionary significance of a particular trait. Physiologists in particular should realize the importance of ultimate factors, which are usually associated with limiting conditions such as food, space, or inclement weather, quite dissociated from the physiological triggers to which organisms respond.

The other sort of intraspecific competition that Nicholson (1954b) distinguished is scramble competition. Here all members of a population have equal access to the limited resource, and a free-for-all results. This is the most common form of competition in insects, because territoriality and other social interactions that would tend toward contest competition are not well developed in the class (but see Chapter 16). However, this statement may stem from ignorance rather than from reality, since there is still a great deal to learn about insect competition.

Nicholson pointed out that the characteristic of scramble competition is that success is commonly incomplete, so that some, and at times all, of the requisite secured by the competing animals takes no part in sustaining the population. The energy available is dissipated by individuals that obtain insufficient for survival. Nicholson studied the effect of scramble competition on laboratory populations of the sheep blowfly, *Lucilia cuprina*, because these were a serious threat to the sheep industry in Australia. When few larvae fed on 1 g of homogenized bullock's brain production of adults was high, and the highest number of adults (16.5) was produced when 30 larvae were placed on the bullock's brain (Fig. 14.5). Above this density, production of adults fell off rapidly until none were produced if 200 or more larvae were placed on the medium. At around the 180 larvae level, very few adults were produced; these would lay few eggs on the 1 g of medium, and the progeny would be successful and produce a large brood of adults again. If this interaction is viewed in time, with the amount of food kept constant in time, a series of peak populations will result from this scramble-type of competition, in contrast to the population pattern resulting from contest competition (Fig. 14.4b). Thus the best way to control sheep blowfly on sheep carcasses is to let nature take its course and allow females to lay enough eggs to overpopulate the carcass so that few or none survive. Then there are fewer adults to lay eggs on sores on living sheep, where the larvae do the real damage. But this scrambling for food can be adaptive, and in some circumstances an advantage over territorial partitioning of available resources. This is so when resources are locally superabundant, relative to the requirements of a breeding pair, just as a carcass is to breeding blowflies.

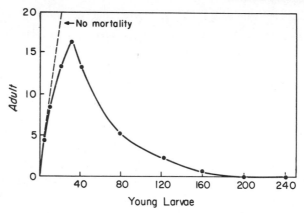

Fig. 14.5 Effect of competition for food among larvae of *Lucilia cuprina* upon the number of adults produced. Numbers are expressed per 1 g of homogenized bullock's brain. After Nicholson 1954b.

The term more commonly used now for scramble competition is exploitation competition or competition for a resource once access to it has been achieved and maintained. In the case of competing *Drosophila* populations both exploitation competition and interference competition seem to be involved (Gilpin 1974, Budnik and Brncic 1974). When species compete the same forms of competition are apparent. Gill (1974) has argued that the results of pure exploitation competition between species can be predicted from knowledge of the population parameters r and K of the species in monoculture. However when interference competition is evident, a third parameter, α, which is an estimate of the amount by which the species impairs the reproductive rate of a competitor, must be involved. Thus natural selection may work to promote fitness in any of three ways, through selection for increased r, increased K, or increased α.

The study of interspecific competition has a longer history than that of intraspecific competition. Gause's (1934) classic studies on interspecific competition between *Paramecium caudatum* and *Paramecium aurelia* are worth examination. Both species feed on the same food; in Gause's experiments this was the pathogenic bacterium *Bacillus pyocyaneus*. Since *P. aurelia* was much smaller than *P. caudatum*, to make a direct comparison between the species Gause expressed the populations as "volumes." The "volume" was actually the number of *P. caudatum* unaltered,

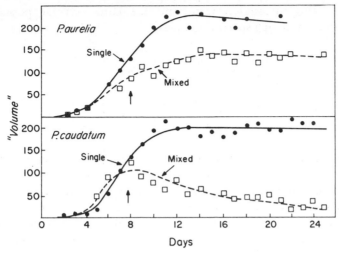

Fig. 14.6 The growth of single and mixed populations of *Paramecium aurelia* and *P. caudatum* in the competition experiments conducted by Gause. "Volume" refers to the actual numbers of *P. caudatum* and the numbers of *P. aurelia* multiplied by a factor of 0.39. After Gause 1934.

and the number of *P. aurelia* multiplied by a factor of 0.39. He placed 20 individuals of a species in a 10-ml tube, with a constant bacterial food source, and monitored the population growth. He also placed 20 of each species in a single microcosm to see how the populations interacted. It is clear from Fig. 14.6 that *P. aurelia* had a much stronger population depressing effect on *P. caudatum* than *P. caudatum* had on *P. aurelia*. Thus *P. caudatum* was pushed to extinction.

This difference in the power of interaction had already been incorporated into the population growth formula by Lotka (1925), Volterra (1926), and Gause (1934) on theoretical grounds. The equations do not permit any steady state to develop except in the remotely likely case where the population depressing effects of one species on the other is the same for both species, or more realistically where a density-dependent intraspecific competition halts growth before the competitor is eliminated. The rate of growth of the first species in a mixed population, dN_1/dt, is equal to the potential increase of the population (r_1N_1) multiplied by the degree to which the carrying capacity is already filled, or the number of still vacant places $(K_1-(N_1+N_2)/K_1$. But perhaps N_2 consumes more food than N_1 so that N_2 will actually reduce the growth of N_1 more strongly than mere numbers can indicate. A factor must be introduced to represent this interaction term and the equations for population growth of two competing species become:

$$\frac{dN_1}{dt} = r_1 N_1 \left[\frac{K_1 - (N_1 + \alpha N_2)}{K_1} \right]$$

$$\frac{dN_2}{dt} = r_2 N_2 \left[\frac{K_2 - (N_2 + \beta N_1)}{K_2} \right]$$

where α and β are coefficients of competition and are proportional to the population-depressing effect of one species on the other. Gause and Witt (1935) point out that if an individual of species N_2 eats twice as much food as does an individual of species N_1 per unit time, it will restrict the growth of species 1 twice more than species 1 will depress its own growth. Then α will be 2. But the reverse action of the first species on the second will be twice feebler than the action of the second species on itself ($\beta = 1/2$). If $\alpha = 2$ then the carrying capacity (i.e., number of individuals that can survive on a given amount of food) of K_2 must be less than K_1 because species 2 needs more food per individual than species 1. Therefore the species with the greater carrying capacity, species 1, will survive, while species 2 will go to extinction, independently of the initial concentrations of the species. Thus if populations of species 1 are plotted against populations of species 2 the outcome can be predicted if K, α, and β are known (Fig. 14.7a). When these conditions hold, as populations increase to beyond the carrying capacity, K_2, species 2 will always be pushed toward extinction. Of course, the opposite set of conditions leads to extinction of species 1, and where α and β are large either species can win depending on the initial combination of species (Fig. 14.7b). A stable equilibrium between the two species can exist if population growth is reduced by density-dependent intraspecific competition that halts growth before the competitor is eliminated (i.e., results of competition are frequency-dependent) (Fig. 14.7c). In general species 1 wins when $\alpha < K_1/K_2$ and $\beta > K_2/K_1$, and species 2 wins when $\alpha > K_1/K_2$ and $\beta < K_2/K_1$.

Philip (1955) provides a good example of the essential difference between the successful and unsuccessful competitor (Fig. 14.8). Here although species 2 has a higher fecundity than species 1, it is insufficient to offset the only slightly greater tolerance of species 1 to low levels of food supply. Philip's example looks very similar to the actual population changes in Gause's *Paramecium caudatum-P. aurelia* experiments. Since the larger *P. caudatum* is likely to suffer from food shortage earlier than *P. aurelia*, the Lotka, Volterra, and Gause competition model may

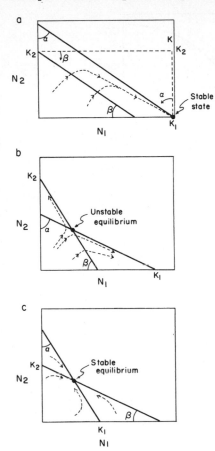

Fig. 14.7 Some types of competitive interaction between two species (a) when $K_1 > K_2$, (b) where α and β are both large, (c) where density-dependent intraspecific competition prevents growth of each species beyond the equilibrium point, so that stability is reached.

well describe this interaction quite accurately. As might be expected, Andrewartha and Birch (1953, 1954) have criticized the Lotka-Volterra equations, but the reader should also consult Philip (1955) who has defended them.

Even in the *Paramecium caudatum-aurelia* situation, where *P. aurelia* always wins there are complex interactions that are not directly related to competition for food. Gause's (1934) book, *The Struggle for existence*, should be consulted for details. Some of the complicating factors in interspecific competition can be seen by looking at Park's work on the flour

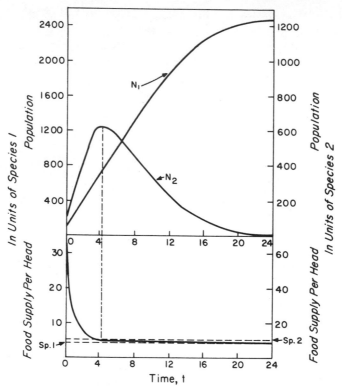

Fig. 14.8 Trends in population growth when two species compete, species 2 with a higher fecundity but species 1 with a slightly lower food requirement cf. sp. 1 → and sp. 2 ←. After Philip 1955.

beetles, *Tribolium confusum* and *Tribolium castaneum*. Chapman had only introduced *Tribolium* as a laboratory animal in 1928 (Chapman 1928) and Park at the University of Chicago was already publishing papers on *Tribolium* in 1932. As his students are still studying competitive interactions in *Tribolium*, they obviously have not got all the answers yet, but they have probably gone further than anybody else in understanding competitive relationships, in invertebrates at least. However, perhaps the *Tribolium* system is more complex than others, and actually less applicable to general concepts of competition. The fact that we have no natural populations to work with should make us cautious about extrapolating *Tribolium* results beyond the confines of flour bins.

Park (1948) showed that in *Tribolium* there is rarely a clear-cut winner in competition. Given a certain set of conditions, if many replicates are run, a certain probability in the outcome can be expressed, but for any single replicate predictability of the result is low. Park kept all populations in dark incubators at a constant temperature of 29.5°C and at a relative humidity of 60–75%. As long as the flour medium in which beetles lived was changed frequently, populations of individual species would last indefinitely at a fairly stable density, *T. confusum* being more dense at equilibrium than *T. castaneum* (Fig. 14.9*a*).

When both species were reared together, both species never survived. Out of 74 trials *T. confusum* became extinct 8 times and *T. castaneum* became extinct 66 times. It appears that the species with the higher carry-

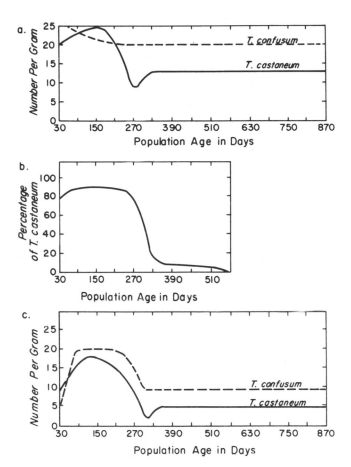

Fig. 14.9 Diagrammatic representation of populations of flour beetles (*a*) total number of individuals per gram of medium in individual cultures, with *T. confusum* maintaining a higher population than *T. castaneum*, (*b*) extinction curve of *T. castaneum* in the presence of *T. confusum*, (*c*) total number of adults per gram of medium in individual cultures in the presence of *Adelina tribolii*. After Park 1948.

ing capacity is most likely to win in competition. But this victory is achieved because of the interaction of another organism. The extinction curve of *T. castaneum* typically shows a dramatic drop in numbers around the 300th day (Fig. 14.9*b*). Even in single culture *T. castaneum* suffers a large mortality around the 300th day. This is actually caused by a pathogenic coccidian parasite *Adelina tribolii*. In single culture *T. castaneum* recovers, but in the presence of *T. confusum*, *T. castaneum* is unable to recover and goes extinct soon after the 300th day. On those occasions when *Adelina* does not cause a severe drop in numbers then *T. castaneum* causes *T. confusum* to go extinct, that is in 8 times out of 74. And, indeed, in *Adelina*-free cultures *T. castaneum* won in competition 12 out of 18 times.

This is not a trivial finding. Here, a third party, an endemic pathogen in this case, alters the competitive balance between two organisms because of its differential impact. There are probably abundant cases where a similar situation exists, but it has not been demonstrated in many. There is a great need for the study of such interactions. For example, how much influence do herbivores have on the competitive balances in plant communities? Really the whole process of succession of plants and animals, at least after the first stage of colonization, depends on an independent organism creating a situation that favors one species over another. Also, when a plant evolves to reduce herbivore pressure, how does this alter the competitive balance between two herbivores exploiting this plant? We would do well to consider the third-party effect on competition more often, and in much more detail than we have to date.

When we realize that *Adelina* is an endemic disease, and that *T. confusum* wins 89% of the competitive encounters when this is present, it seems that *T. castaneum* has a poor chance of surviving as a species if this is a general phenomenon. Perhaps *T. castaneum* is a fugitive species, constantly colonizing food that has not been discovered by *T. confusum*. Before accepting this view we should, as Park did, examine their relative competitive prowess under different conditions to see if the balance is changed. Perhaps in the 1948 experiments conditions were optimal for *T. confusum,* and marginal for *T. castaneum*. Park (1954a, b) set up a factorial design experiment of *Adelina*-free cultures with three temperatures, 24, 29, and 34°C and two humidities, 30 and 70% relative humidity, with replicates in the six treatments. He obtained the results given in Table 14.1. There are indeed situations in which *T. castaneum* wins quite regularly. These are in moist conditions at temperate and high temperatures, and thus *T. castaneum* does have a refuge from the superior competitive ability of *T. confusum* found in the 1948 experiments. Their niches defined by two resources differ (Fig. 14.10). *Tribolium confusum*

Table 14.1 Conditions and results of experiments conducted by Park (1954a,b) on competition between Tribolium confusum and T. castaneum. The prediction column indicates those results that could be predicted from a comparison of the carrying capacities of the two species in single species cultures—see text to follow.

Treatment	Conditions	Temper- ature (°C)	Relative Humidity (%)	Result: Percent of replicates won	Prediction
I	Hot and moist	34	70	*T. castaneum* wins 100	X
II	Hot and dry	34	30	*T. confusum* wins 90	√
III	Temperate and moist	29	70	*T. castaneum* wins 86	√
IV	Temperate and dry	29	30	*T. confusum* wins 87	√
V	Cold and moist	24	70	*T. confusum* wins 69	X
VI	Cold and dry	24	30	*T. confusum* wins 100	√

is dominant in one part of the available resources and *T. castaneum* in another. If conditions change in time, for example, from temperate and moist to cold and dry, and if this change is reversed frequently enough so that there is not enough time for one species to be driven to extinction, the two species may coexist indefinitely. And this may be the case for many pairs of species as Hutchinson (1953) pointed out, particularly for fairly short generation species such as many insects.

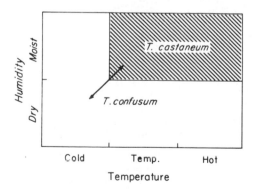

Fig. 14.10 The ecological niches to *Tribolium confusum* and *T. castaneum* defined by two gradients, temperature and humidity. Note that as these physical parameters fluctuate first one species may be favored and then another, as indicated by the arrows.

It would certainly be gratifying if we could predict the outcome of competition between these species by looking at individual characteristics. Understanding of the process of competition would be advanced if characteristics that resulted in competitive superiority could be identified. Some population characteristics of the species grown in pure culture, with the same factorial design as before, provide some clues (Fig. 14.11). If the hypothesis is adopted that the species that has the higher population at carrying capacity is most likely to win in competition, we see that *T. confusum* should always win at 30% R.H. but only at 70% R.H. when at 34°C. In fact the predicted result comes close to the actual result, but all of the six results cannot be predicted. But being able to predict two thirds of the results is encouraging. That still leaves two perplexing exceptions, and this really illustrates how elusive the quality of competitive ability is. Many questions remain: (1) What is the physiological explanation for changes in the carrying capacity of the medium at different temperatures and humidities? (2) Why is the carrying capacity of equivalent habitats different for species as similar as *T. confusum* and *T. castaneum?* (3) What is this intangible element that prevents us from a perfect prediction in competition? (4) What makes a species dominant? (5) Why are animals such as murine rodents, the old world rats and mice, so successful? Frank, a student of Thomas Park's, used an aquatic system

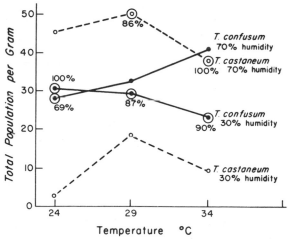

Fig. 14.11   Analysis to test the hypothesis that the species which can exist at the higher carrying capacity in pure culture will win in competition. Equilibrium numbers in total population per gram for each species grown in pure culture are plotted for each humidity on a temperature gradient. For each treatment the outcome of competition in other experiments is shown by a circle around the winning species with the percentage of replicates that it won. We see that we can predict four of the six results correctly. Data from Park 1954b.

for studying competition so that interaction was more easily observed and availability of food was a more easily monitored quality in the system. Thus his papers (1952, 1957) make interesting reading and should be consulted for more information on laboratory studies on competition. More recently it has been possible to explain the outcome of competition between two species on the basis of monoculture characteristics (Goudrian and deWit 1973), an encouraging result. Also Gill (1974) claims that where this prediction is not possible, as in the *Tribolium* studies, interference competition was probably involved.

An important field study of interspecific competition contrasts nicely with those laboratory studies already described in approach and execution. Reynoldson and his students have been studying triclads (planarians) in North Wales since 1948 (see Reynoldson 1966). Just as Andrewartha and Birch were interested in the determinants of animal distribution and abundance, Reynoldson has been primarily concerned with the regulating factors in distribution and abundance of triclads. The exceptional quality of Reynoldson's study is that he studied in detail all five of the possible determinants and has not assumed that any factor is unimportant. However, qualitative changes in populations were not studied. His studies also show how the scientific approach can solve field problems by using direct observation, and field and laboratory experiments. The five factors studied were, as in Andrewartha and Birch (1954), (1) weather; (2) a place to live; (3) food; (4) organisms of the same species which may be involved in cooperation, cannibalism, or intraspecific competition; and (5) organisms of different species, which include predators and parasites, and competitors. Reynoldson concentrated his studies on four species of triclad: *Polycelis nigra, Polycelis tenuis, Dugesia polychroa* (= *lugubris*), and *Dendrocoelum lacteum*.

All species are predators on the littoral fauna in fresh-water lakes, and the best habitats are sheltered lake edges up to 1 ft under water, with small stones and pebbles. The four species show many similarities in their ecology, such as habitat, feeding mechanism, and life cycle. The five determining factors will be examined in turn:

1. Weather. Reynoldson studied weather in detail and found the tolerances, especially to temperature, of each species. Temperature is the most important factor in an aquatic system, especially as the littoral zone is likely to have an abundant oxygen supply. He con-

cluded that weather has no direct bearing on the characteristic pattern of distribution and abundance of the four triclad species.

2. A place to live. All populations were sampled on rocky, sheltered shores, so that the differences between places were canceled out. The chemistry of the water changed from lake to lake but this did not affect the longevity or reproduction of triclads directly. However the nutritional status of the water did affect the amount of food that was available to the triclads, but this is a secondary effect.

3. Food. As food increased with the calcium content of the water, so the total population of triclads increased (Fig. 14.12), and also

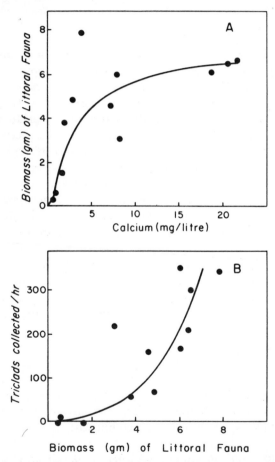

Fig. 14.12 (a) The increase of biomass (g) of littoral fauna (potential food) collected per hour, excluding triclads, with increase in calcium content of water, in Scottish lakes. (b) Increase in number of triclads collected per hour with the increase of biomass (g) of littoral fauna. Data from Reynoldson 1966.

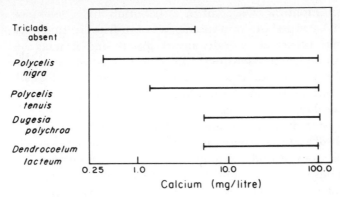

Fig. 14.13 The species of triclad present in lakes of differing calcium content. After Reynoldson 1966.

the number of species coexisting increased (Fig. 14.13). It is clear that food is limiting to all species of triclad and it has a strong influence on the distribution of the species. But is this an intraspecific effect or an interspecific one? The fourth and fifth determinants of distribution and abundance must be examined in some detail.

4. Organisms of the same species. Reynoldson states that cooperation has never been observed, and cannibalism is rare, which leaves only intraspecific competition in need of close examination. Reynoldson found that feeding is restricted to damaged prey (cf., Chapter 5 on predation), so that triclads cannot overexploit their food source, and they actually suffer an absolute shortage of food. In nature they show a high degree of population homeostasis and, with supplemental food, populations increase dramatically (Table 14.2). Reynoldson

Table 14.2 Effect of increasing food supply upon total recruitment, and proportion of adults in single species populations.

Triclad species	Total recruitment		Percentage adults	
	Normal (%)	Increased food (%)	Normal	Increased food
Polycelis tenuis	50	350	4.3	55.2
Dugesia polychroa	38	137	2.2	32.9
Polycelis nigra	90	500	—	—

SOURCE. From Reynoldson 1964.

states: "From the viewpoint of distribution and abundance, the important feature of intra-specific relationships is that serious food shortage occurs periodically in all species and it is against such a background that inter-specific relationships must be considered." If there is an absolute food shortage, the species must be eating different foods, or all but one would go extinct because the remainder of their ecology is too similar.

5. Organisms of different species. Predators and parasites. Predation was insufficient to reduce populations below the level at which intra-specific competition for food regulated the population. Davies and Reynoldson (1971) should be consulted to see how much work was needed to establish this fact. Competitors may compete for living space, which was found not to be critical, or food, for which there was strong competition. For example, the size of *Polycelis nigra* populations in the absence and presence of *Polycelis tenuis* are very different under natural conditions (Table 14.3). *Polycelis tenuis* has

Table 14.3   The size of Polycelis nigra populations in the absence and presence of P. tenuis in natural conditions. Size of populations was estimated by the number collected per hour.

	Ca mg/l				
	<5.0	5.1–10.0	10.1–20.0	20.1–40.0	>40.0
P. nigra alone	17	—	140	173	179
P. nigra in presence of *P. tenuis*	42	49	76	40	38
P. nigra + *P. tenuis*	53	136	226	209	222

SOURCE.   From Reynoldson 1966.

a marked depressive effect on size of *P. nigra* populations, showing that they compete for food. But it is clear that they do not overlap completely as the carrying capacity of a lake for triclads is always increased by the presence of *P. tenuis*. This can be inferred as the species are the same size, and therefore eat the same amount of food, so that numbers of each species can be compared directly.

How then are the species able to coexist in nature? Reynoldson and Davies (1970) studied the diet of each triclad species with a serological technique (see Chapter 2). This permitted identification of the prey animals, which were represented as juices in the gut of field collected triclads. Triclads ingest mainly semi-liquid food by pumping action of a muscular pharynx. The differences in the food dimension of the niches in nature are well-defined (Tables 14.4 and 14.5). Therefore the distribu-

Table 14.4 The proportion of meals on each prey item expressed as a percentage of total meals per 500 triclads per day. Food refuges are circled.

	Asellus	Gammarus	Oligochaeta	Gastropoda
Polycelis tenuis	25	8	(57)	10
Polycelis nigra	8	7	(68)	17
Dugesia polychroa	16	4	22	(57)
Dendrocoelum lacteum	(63)	23	14	0

SOURCE. From Reynoldson and Davies 1970. Reproduced from *Journal of Animal Ecology* by permission of Blackwell Scientific Publications.

Table 14.5 Comparison of feeding of Polycelis nigra and P. tenuis on different families of Oligochaeta. Food refuges are circled.

	Percent triclads feeding on			
	Naididae	Tubificidae	Lumbriculidae	Lumbricidae
Polycelis nigra	(46)	8	42	4
Polycelis tenuis	9	(45)	42	4

SOURCE. From Reynoldson and Davies 1970. Reproduced from *Journal of Animal Ecology* by permission of Blackwell Scientific Publications.

tion and abundance of these four triclads is controlled by food availability, and the diversity of species depends on the diversity of foods in any lake.

Reynoldson is not satisfied with this hypothesis until he has actually tested it in the field and has proved that he can predict the species and their abundance by the types of food that are present. It will be interesting to follow this work right through to completion.

Further insight into competitive interactions may be gained by looking at what seem to be at present special cases in competition. Although now that we are aware of them they may be found to be more common than it now seems. In 1958 MacArthur stated, "To permit coexistence it seems necessary that each species, when very abundant, should inhibit its own further increase more than it inhibits the other's." This is what we saw in one of the competition models derived from the Gause, Lotka, and Volterra equations. In other words competition between species is frequency-dependent. When frequencies of the potentially dominant species are low, it is a good competitor; when frequencies are high, it is a poor competitor. This frequency-dependence has been observed in animals and plants.

Ayala (1971) set up competition experiments between larvae of *Drosophila pseudoobscura* and *D. willistoni*, starting each experiment with different ratios of each species. He compared the input ratios with the output ratios, or the results of the competitive reaction. Without frequency-dependence we should expect a one to one relationship between the input and output ratios, but Ayala found that there was a significant and inverse relationship between the initial frequency of a species and its competitive fitness (Fig. 14.14). Stable equilibrium would result at the intersection of the regression lines and the predicted line where fitness is 1 for each species. This equilibrium is quite different for different strains of *D. willistoni* just as different strains of *Tribolium* have very different competitive abilities (e.g., Park, Leslie, and Mertz 1964).

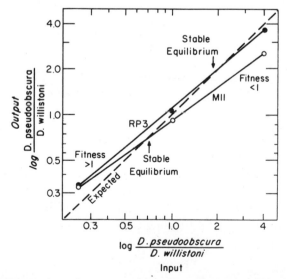

Fig. 14.14 Frequency-dependent competition in *Drosophila* species. Line RP3 represents the outcome of competition (output) at various initial ratios (input) between strain 211 of *D. pseudoobscura* and strain RP3 of *D. willistoni*. Line M11 is for the same strain of the former species and strain M11 of *D. willistoni*. The expected line indicates a slope of 1 with an input:output ratio of 1, or a fitness of 1. After Ayala 1971.

DeWit (1960, 1961) had conducted similar experiments on plants much earlier and in one case found a similar result (DeWit 1961). He tested competition between ryegrass, *Lolium perenne*, and clover, *Trifolium repens*, and plotted the input ratios of length of stolon of clover and the number of tillers of ryegrass at the start and end of the growing season (Fig. 14.15). Presumably as clover becomes more abundant in the mixture than 50 times the ryegrass it becomes less fit relative to ryegrass. Marshall and Jain (1969) have found similar results at certain densities of competing species of wild oats (*Avena*). Intraspecific competition during mate selection also has been found to be frequency-dependent in species of *Drosophila* and *Mormoniella* (e.g., Grant et al. 1974 and references therein).

These examples show that competing species can maintain a stable equilibrium and therefore they can coexist indefinitely. But it is also possible for competing species to coexist without developing a stable equilibrium. Hutchinson (1953) gives two situations where this may occur. First, where catastrophes frequently create new empty habitats for

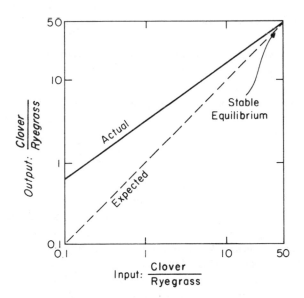

Fig. 14.15 Frequency-dependent competition between clover and ryegrass. Note that clover competes much more successfully at low input ratios than at high, and a stable equilibrium is reached when clover is 50 times more abundant than ryegrass. After deWit 1961.

colonization, two very similar species may arrive at the same time, and one will tend to outcompete the other. Before competition goes to completion a new habitat becomes available; it is colonized by both species and a catastrophe destroys the former habitat and this process may continue. It will appear that the two species coexist. Hutchinson points out, however, that probably "the tendency of the weaker species to disappear by competition must be balanced by a tendency for it to spread a little more easily than the stronger; it must in fact be a fugitive species." In a similar vein, Skellam (1951) concluded from theoretical considerations that competitors with different dispersal rates could continue to coexist if the species with the faster dispersal rate had a lower reproductive rate.

A second nonequilibrium type of coexistence of very similar species may be seen where several generations occur in a year and thus each generation may be exposed to rather different environmental conditions. One species may be favored in one generation and the other in another, and competition will never run to completion. This situation can be visualized for *Tribolium castaneum* and *T. confusum* during temperature fluctuations as described earlier in this chapter. Thus coexistence may result in these species, whereas Hutchinson points out that species with long generation times, such as a year or more, should demonstrate the competitive exclusion principle, as should very short-lived species such as bacteria where competition will be so rapid as to be completed before the environment changes.

An interesting case of coexistence has been described by Istock (1967) concerning two whirligig beetles, *Dineutes nigrior* and *D. horni*. The former species has a more northerly distribution; it occurs more commonly on ponds than on lakes and appears to be adapted to boreal conditions in the absence of competition. *Dineutes horni* is more temperate; it coexists with other species throughout its range, and therefore must be a successful competitor, and it is most commonly found in lakes. During high spring waters adults of *D. horni* swam into ponds along channels from the lakes and oviposited. Their larvae were more successful than were the resident *D. nigrior* larvae, and competitive displacement was evident. However, before *D. nigrior* was completely displaced, the larvae of both species pupated, and the adults emerged and dispersed by flight in the late summer. This flight erased the advance in competition made by *D. horni* during larval growth in the pond, since a late summer census showed *D. nigrior* to be more abundant. Presumably in the region as a whole more *D. nigrior* were produced than were *D. horni*. Thus competitive displacement was only transient because the competitive edge was lost by the adults of this holometabolous insect. Might this not be a common phenomenon in such organisms?

As described in Chapter 19 coexistence may also be permitted by a predator that prevents the potentially dominant species or both species from becoming abundant (see also Slatkin 1974).

Before completing this discussion on competition it should be pointed out that islands offer situations of reduced competition because of their relatively depauperate fauna, and the study of island populations in comparison to those on the mainland should be valuable. The adaptive radiation in archipelagos, and the very broad niche of the Hispaniolan woodpecker, have been discussed. Much of the work of this nature has been on birds (e.g., Crowell 1962, Grant 1966a,b, Ricklefs 1970b, Ricklefs and Cox 1972, Greenslade 1968), and Lack (1971) has summarized much of the literature, and he provides a ready source of additional examples. Finding similar examples in insects is difficult although Wilson (1961), Greenslade (1969), and Ricklefs (1973) provide access to the literature. Since we will be in a better situation to consider competition on islands after discovering more about island biotas themselves, I delay treating this aspect until the chapter on biogeography. Meanwhile another angle on competition as an organizing factor in communities is investigated in the next chapter.

Chapter 15

SPECIES PACKING

I n Chapter 13 on the niche concept and division of resources it was seen that two species with the same niche requirements could not form steady-state populations in the same region. At any given time one species would be increasing at the expense of the other, and unless the environment changed the competitive balance, one species would be competitively displaced. For species to coexist they must be different, and it becomes an interesting problem to define how different species must be to permit coexistence. This is an important question in relation to understanding how communities of animals or plants are arranged, particularly in relation to organization on the same trophic level.

For example, there is a large insect fauna of nectar feeders in any given area, and the nectar is available at different depths according to the flower form of the species of plant that secretes the nectar. Nectar at the base of long-trumpeted flowers will be normally available only to insects with long extendable mouthparts like bees, butterflies, and moths. Brian (1957) discussed proboscis length of four species of bumblebee, *Bombus*, in relation to corolla tube length of flowers visited and found a strong positive correlation between the two. Even within a species such as *Bombus agrorum* those with longer mouthparts will visit flowers in which nectar is deeper than other flowers, and the individuals with shorter mouthparts are restricted to shallower flowers (Cumber 1949). Nectar in shallow flowers such as buttercups and roses will be available to many more species, but in general species with short mouthparts will be better adapted to tapping this food source.

Thus if the range of flower depths in a given area is known, that is, if we know in detail the range of sizes of one structural feature of the environment, perhaps the number of species that utilize this resource and still coexist can be predicted (Fig. 15.1). As Brian found, there is bound to be some sort of relationship like that indicated by the line XY, except that any given size of mouthpart can probably exploit a range of depths more efficiently than species with larger or smaller mouthparts, and thus outcompete other species. This range can be represented on the graph as species a, b, and c. Here each species exploits a range of the resource that is not exploited by any other species, and coexistence is possible, even though species b is only 50% larger than species a—or the ratio of the larger to the smaller is 1.5 (the ratio $c:b$ is 1.33).

Now the question arises, given the range of depths at which nectar is secreted in an area, and given the three species a, b, and c, exploiting this nectar, is there an unfilled niche here? Is there room for another species to fit in between a and b, or b and c, a' and b', so that the ratio of the larger to the smaller is only $a':a=1.25$, $b:a'=1.20$, $b':b=1.17$, $c:b'=1.14$. This has to be tested by observing how similar coexisting species are in

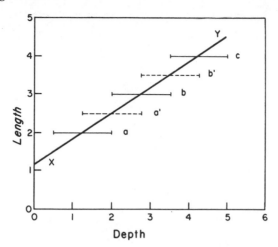

Fig. 15.1 The anticipated relationship between the length of the mouthparts of an insect and the depth at which the nectar is secreted in the flower. The general trend of the relationship is indicated by the line XY. Each mouthpart length will be able to exploit a range of flower depths and these ranges are indicated for species a, b, and c. The possibility that new species a' and b' could fit into this community and coexist is examined in the text.

nature, and the results of the very few studies made so far are quite surprising. It is much easier to measure differences in size of coexisting species than to measure the differences in the range of a given food source that species exploit. In most studies so far the analysis has concentrated on morphological differences of species and the supposition has been made that differences in size of mouth parts for example reflect different modes of food exploitation.

If it is assumed, along with Hutchinson (1968), that all characters are adaptive, or closely related to adaptations through pleiotropy, then differences in size of mouthparts must reflect different adaptive strategies for obtaining food. And the adaptive peak, or adaptive mode, of a species' trophic apparatus dimensions will reflect an equivalent set of values of an environmental variable (Fig. 15.2). Data are really needed on how species utilize the latter, but lacking this information in the practical application of these ideas we must be content to study morphological differences.

The Ashmoles (1967) have explained how specialization at the adaptive peak or mode will be maintained. Unless each species is more efficient than the other in utilizing the food that it chooses, there will be no selective pressure favoring the maintenance of behavioral differences.

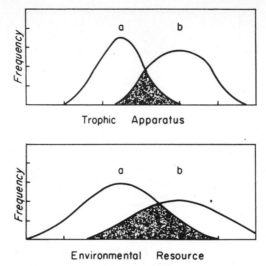

Fig. 15.2 The relationships between the size distribution of trophic apparatus of species *A* and *B* and the distribution of the measurable resource utilized during exploitation.

Behavioral differences in feeding will be accompanied by structural adaptations to the species' own feeding niche. The extent of this specialization must be sufficient to ensure that when circumstances are critical [e.g., when density-dependent factors operate (definition in Chapter 9)] each species can occupy its own feeding niche more efficiently than any of the other sympatric species.

Thus a species can specialize in one way, by becoming larger or smaller than the other sympatric species in its trophic apparatus, and there are pros and cons for each strategy (Miller 1967). A smaller species can feed in, and utilize smaller microhabitats than can a larger one, and thus escape competition from larger species that presumably have greater competitive ability (see Van Valen 1973 for additional discussion). Thus a small species of bark beetle may be able to burrow in a wide range of bark thicknesses, but a large bark beetle may be very limited in the barks it can exploit, and perhaps it will be restricted to the main trunk of the tree (Figs. 15.3, and 15.4). In fact, Klopfer (1962) found that in pairs of species of birds that occupied very similar niches, for example, the downy and hairy woodpecker, there was generally an inverse relation between body size and niche size, suggesting that, as Miller (1967) comments (1) larger body size may confer competitive advantage, but (2) animals with smaller body size are adapted to a wider range of ecological conditions and are better able to survive outside preferred habitats, often

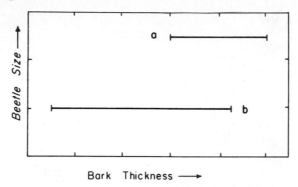

Fig. 15.3   The probable relationship between the size of a species (e.g., a bark beetle) and the range of an environmental resource which it can exploit (cf., Fig. 15.4). Exceptions may be seen in seed eaters and species with similar types of exploitation where brute force may enable a wider range of resources to be utilized.

on smaller food particles. Smaller size is also associated with a higher population growth rate and thus a more rapid response to increasing resources in spite of the possibility of reduced competitive ability. Perhaps this is why Holling (1959b) found that the very small masked shrew, *Sorex cinereus*, showed a strong numerical response to prey density while the larger deer mouse, *Peromyscus maniculatus*, and the shorttail shrew, *Blarina brevicauda*, showed a weak response (Fig. 15.5).

Schoener (1969) explored in detail the strategies of small and large size. One avenue of thought involved a series of prey items distributed log normally in size (a normal distribution on a log scale), an assumption supported by available data. Therefore large prey are less abundant than are meduim sized prey. Large predators are able to extract more energy per unit feeding time from relatively rare and large items than from small common ones. Therefore a large predator will feed on large rare items first and then progress toward smaller items as the larger ones are used up. Small predators will feed on the smaller but more common items first and as those become overexploited they will feed on the rarer species. Thus large predators should have curves of energy gained per unit time like those of specialists, and small predators more like those of generalists (Fig. 15.6). This conclusion agrees with our considerations on bark beetle and woodpecker niche size.

The specialist versus generalist energy time curves differ. A specialist will be very efficient in gaining energy from a few abundant types of food after which rate of energy acquisition will fall off rapidly. The generalist is less efficient on all food items but it loses efficiency over a spectrum of prey items less rapidly than the specialist. Thus at point *P*

Fig. 15.4 The relationship between size of bark beetles and the area and thickness of bark they attack, on white pine, *Pinus strobus*, in the Northeastern United States of America and Eastern Canada. The relative sizes of the beetles are shown. The red terpentine beetle, *Dendroctonus valens*, is restricted to the base of trees. The pine engraver, *Ips pini*, attacks the upper trunk and large branches and is usually much more abundant than *D. valens*. *Pityogenes hopkinsi* enters thin bark on smaller branches, which provide a very large area for attack, and this species is considered to be one of the most abundant bark beetles of the northeast.

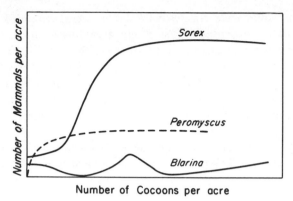

Fig. 15.5 Numerical responses of the small mammals *Sorex, Peromyscus,* and *Blarina* to sawfly cocoon density. After Holling 1959b.

both strategies are equally matched. But at high food abundances or low metabolic rates specialists are favored over generalists, and at low food abundances or high metabolic rates generalists are favored.

In a well-known paper, "Homage to Santa Rosalia or why are there so many kinds of animals?" Hutchinson (1959) looked at the size differ-

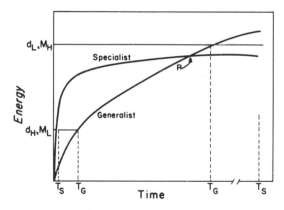

Fig. 15.6 Energy capture with time for a generalist (e.g., a small predator) and a specialist (e.g., a large predator). At high food abundances or low metabolic rates (d_H, M_L) specialists are favored over generalists $(T_S < T_G$, or up to P a specialist can gain more energy per unit time than a generalist), but at low food abundances or high metabolic rates (d_L, M_H) generalists are favored $(T_G < T_S)$. P is the point at which the two do equally well. From Schoener 1969.

ences between congeneric species when they were sympatric and allo-patric. This paper provides a first attempt at answering the question, "How similar can organisms be and still coexist?" More data are needed and no doubt conclusions will be modified for different types of organisms as different taxa are carefully examined. Comparisons were made be-tween measurements that reflected differences in feeding apparatus (Table 15.1). The mean ratio of all the species pairs he examined was 1.28 and

Table 15.1   Size relationships, the ratio of the larger to the smaller dimension, between congeneric species when sympatric and allopatric.

Animals and character measured	Species	Measure-ment when sympatric (mm)	Measure-ment when allopatric (mm)	Ratio when sympatric	Ratio when allopatric
Weasels (skull)	*Mustela nivalis* *Mustela erminea*	Male 39.3 } Male 50.4 }	42.9 } 46.0 }	1.28	1.07
Mice (skull)	*Apodemus sylvaticus* *Apodemus flavicollis*	24.8 } 27.0 }		1.09	
Nuthatches (culmen)	*Sitta tephronota* *Sitta neumayer*	29.0 } 23.5 }	25.5 } 26.0 }	1.24	1.02
Darwin's finches (culmen)	*Geospiza fortis* *Geospiza fuliginosa*	12.0 } 8.4 }	10.5 } 9.3 }	1.43	1.13

SOURCE.   From Hutchinson, 1959, from various sources.

the range for coexisting species was 1.1 to 1.43. Hutchinson concluded that the mean value of 1.28 may be used tentatively as an indication of the kind of difference necessary to permit two species to co-occur in dif-ferent niches, but at the same trophic level. In the areas of allopatry the sizes are much more similar, suggesting that character displacement has taken place in contact zones and this has permitted coexistence. On the basis of these data, using 1.28 as the minimum size ratio that permits coexistence, we would predict that in our original example (Fig. 15.1) species a' and b' could not fit into the complex as there was insufficient room between species a and b, and b and c, although species a' might just be able to squeeze in. But at least this approach permits us to pre-dict roughly how many species can fit into a given set of resources, and by defining the number of resources in a community and the dimensions of these resources we can start building toward a predictive analysis of the structure of the community.

However Heatwole and Davis (1965) have provided some interesting data on ichneumonid ovipositor lengths that show that prediction of species numbers on a given resource may be difficult. The ovipositor of a parasitoid can be regarded as a food-finding or provisioning apparatus for the larva, so that differences in ovipositor length are as important in segregating species niches as bill lengths in birds. Ovipositor length probably offers a purer measure of niche segregation than bill length (Price 1972c). Heatwole and Davis observed three species of *Megarhyssa*: *greenei, macrurus,* and *atrata,* all of which attack the same host, a wood boring siricid larva, the pigeon tremex, *Tremex columba.* Each species has a long ovipositor with which it bores into the wood and oviposits on the host larva, but they are of radically different lengths: *greenei* 40 mm, *macrurus* 80 mm, and *atrata* 120 mm. The authors also found that each female inserted her ovipositor fully before laying an egg, so that essentially the females were attacking hosts at different depths in the logs and were therefore not competing. As the log began to decay the *Tremex* larvae would tunnel in the outer rotting areas and would be available to *greenei,* and *greenei* was always the first to appear on the logs. Later *Tremex* larvae would burrow more deeply, *greenei* could not reach these larvae, but *macrurus* would be next in succession, followed by *atrata* when the hosts were very deep. This resource was neatly divided into three, permitting three species to coexist.

But are these three species exploiting the resource fully, or is there room for other species in the community (Fig. 15.7)? According to Hutchinson's predictions there is plenty of room between species *atrata* (*a*), *macrurus* (*m*), and *greenei* (*g*) (*a*:*m* = 1.5, *m*:*g* = 2.0). What would happen

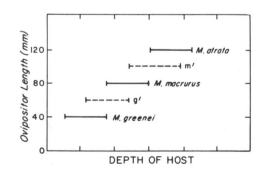

Fig. 15.7 Species packing in the genus *Megarhyssa*, and the possibility of a new species *m'* fitting between *M. atrata* and *M. macrurus* in the community and species *g'* fitting between *M. macrurus* and *M. greenei.* The packing is based on the ovipositor length in relation to the depth of the host that is being exploited. Data of the real species from Heatwole and Davis 1965.

to another species that colonizes the area with an exactly intermediate sized ovipositor? It looks as if there is room for another species in this community ($a:m' = 1.2$, $m':m = 1.25$, $m:g' = 1.3$, $g':g = 1.5$), and we would have predicted four species instead of three. The problem for a new colonizer is that it must be preadapted to the niche it must fill; that is, it must have almost precisely the correct size ovipositor before trying to colonize the community, because any divergence from this midposition will bring it into strong competition with an already established species.

Therefore, the potential colonizing ability of a species depends to a large extent on which species are already present, and how it is preadapted to fitting between existing species. The problem in predicting numbers of species lies in the fact that if three species of widely divergent size colonize an area first, then they define rather precisely the sizes of organisms for which niches remain. In fact species of such a size may not exist, and the selective advantage to evolving and adapting into the existing niche may not be sufficiently strong for the nearest species to undergo modification in this direction. As a result unfilled niches remain.

Use of Hutchinsonian distances do not provide us with all the answers in predicting species numbers from knowledge of available resources. However they may have helped in predicting the results of the introduction of a new parasitoid into a guild of four indigenous species that attack the same host in the cocoon stage (see Price 1970c, 1972c). In the primeval forests of Canada only four species coexisted, with ovipositor length ratios as follows (see Fig. 8.5 for illustrations of three species):

Mastrus aciculatus	}	
Pleolophus indistinctus	}	1.11
Endasys subclavatus	}	1.19
Gelis urbanus	}	1.41

The first three species were very closely packed, but at least the species had differences equivalent to the smallest differences between coexisting vertebrates that Hutchinson found. Then a fifth species was introduced in the late 1930s to help control the European spruce sawfly outbreak. Its ovipositor length was intermediate between *M. aciculatus* and *P. indistinctus*, so that the space between these was split in two, producing a difference of only 1.05 between the first two pairs of species. We see this reflected in the abundance of species during severe competition (Fig. 15.8).

Thus if the people responsible for importing the parasitoid had made measurements of all the species involved when they released *P. basizonus*, they might have predicted two eventualities. The first that *P. basizonus* would be a strong competitor and therefore displace *P. indistinctus* and *M. aciculatus* from the most favorable sites. Or conversely, that *P. basi-*

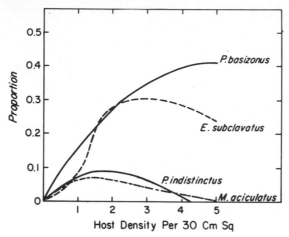

Fig. 15.8 The response of parasitoids to increasing host density illustrated by the change in the proportion of each species in the total parasitoid complex. As the host density increased, competition between parasitoids became more severe (see original reference for explanation). Note that as the introduced *P. basizonus* increases, the first species to be suppressed are those closest in ovipositor lengths. After Price 1970c.

zonus would be a poor competitor and therefore it would go extinct because its niche requirements were too similar to two existing species (given that the host selection pattern of each species was the same). We see in Chapter 21 on biogeography that they might have predicted the former (see Price 1971a) had they read Darlington's (1959) paper, published the same year as Hutchinson's, "Area, climate and evolution," since *P. basizonus* occurs at the center of abundance of species in the genus. But it is clear that this resource of host cocoons has a tightly packed set of species and the likelihood of another species coexisting with these is very small indeed.

In addition to the problems in predicting the number of species, for example of *Megarhyssa*, from the number of resources available, it is possible that species may converge in characteristics in zones of sympatry. Cody (1969) considered that this convergence affected only characters used for territorial defense, particularly color pattern and voice, and the improved competitor recognition and interspecific territoriality were adaptive. However, MacArthur and Levins (1967) have argued on theoretical grounds that convergence of exploitation patterns on a limiting resource may be adaptive under different conditions. If two coexisting

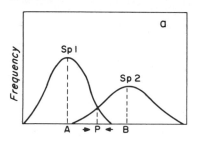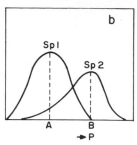

Range of Characters

Fig. 15.9 Phenotypic ranges ot characters for species 1 and 2, and the position of the adaptive mode (P) of a third species, (a) when Sp 1 and 2 have substantially different ranges, (b) when Sp 1 is competitively stronger than Sp 2 so the frequency distribution of Sp 2 is skewed. We assume that species are packed closely to the left of Sp 1 and to the right of Sp2. After MacArthur and Levins 1967.

species have substantially different ranges of phenotypic characters as in Fig. 15.9a, a third species that colonizes would gain advantage by diverging as far as possible from each of the two residents. The adaptive mode of the colonizing species (P) would diverge from the modes of Sp 1 (A) and Sp 2 (B) as far as possible and assume a position at P.

If on the other hand Sp 1 and Sp 2 are more similar, and Sp 1 is competitively stronger than Sp 2 such that the phenotypic frequency distribution of Sp 2 is skewed, an invading species with characters between A and B will face a strongly competitive situation and its fitness will be improved by converging towards Sp 2 (Fig. 15.9b). This advantage can be gained only where the third species has a higher carrying capacity than Sp 2 and thus convergence will be seen only in nonequilibrium conditions. We might predict then that this problem in prediction will be more serious in temperate than in tropical communities, since species packing can be tighter in predictable, more productive environments (see MacArthur and Levins 1967).

If species are really packed into a habitat quite tightly, so that it is unlikely that further species could colonize the area, an increase in resident species correlated with habitats of more complexity should be expected. A more complex habitat will have wider ranges of essential resources. To study this point it is important to view complexity as the animals view it and not as we are likely to view it—in taxonomic terms.

In the gnatcatcher study by Root (1967) we saw in Chapter 13 that structural features of the habitat provided the clue to understanding how a species adapts to exploiting a certain niche. MacArthur and MacArthur (1961) had also found that structural features in the environment were of more predictive value than were taxonomic features. These authors wanted to know how the number of bird species in a given habitat could be predicted, or what permitted a more diverse avian fauna in tropical forests as compared to temperate, or a mixed wood compared to a field. MacArthur and MacArthur measured the structure of many habitats by estimating the density of foliage (measured in square feet of leaf silhouette per cubic foot of space), at several heights in the canopy—so that foliage profiles could be drawn (Fig. 15.10). They observed the number of species of birds and their abundance in each habitat. They calculated the diversity of the birds in an area and the diversity of the foliage height using a formula given in Chapter 19. The deciduous forest clearly has a much more diverse foliage height structure than does grassland. The authors found that when bird species diversity was plotted against foliage height diversity, these two parameters were closely correlated, and thus a structural feature of the habitat has predictive value, while no added information is provided by knowing the species of plants in the area (Fig. 15.11). Tomoff (1974) suggests that a knowledge of physiognomic diversity also has predictive value.

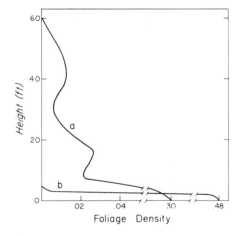

Fig. 15.10 The foliage profiles of (a) a Vermont woodland with a dense shrub layer, foliage height diversity (F.H.D.) = 1.009, bird species diversity (B.S.D.) = 2.739, and (b) a grassland in Vermont (F.H.D. = 0.043, B.S.D. = 0.639). After MacArthur and MacArthur 1961.

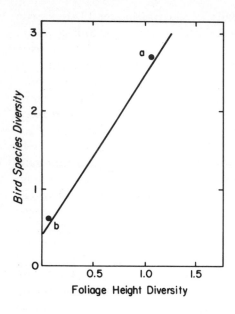

Fig. 15.11 The relationship between foliage height diversity and bird species diversity, (*a*) in the Vermont woodland, (*b*) in the Vermont grassland for which foliage profiles were given in Fig. 15.10. The regression line is based on data from 13 study areas. After MacArthur and MacArthur 1961.

It appears that as the diversity of a resource is increased more species can pack into an area, and therefore the habitat structure and diversity must be a very important organizing influence in community development. There is lots of room for similar work in insect community studies where it would be very valuable to be able to predict the abundance and diversity of insects from structural features of a given habitat. For example, Murdoch, Evans, and Peterson (1972) tested the influence of plant species and structure on insect herbivores in old fields in Michigan. Both factors become closely correlated when grasses and forbs are involved. These authors found that both plant species diversity and plant structural diversity were good predictors of insect herbivore diversity when factors were compared between fields of substantially different structure. However, within a field, herbivore diversity was not generally well predicted from characters in the plant community. This paper has pioneered investigations on insects derived from the MacArthurs' original work, but clearly more needs to be done. For example, we need to know what factors determine within-field diversity differences in insect herbivores. How does increased specificity in insects, compared to birds for example, affect the predictive value of plant structural diversity?

Not all resources can be arranged on gradients and not all species will exploit a part of a gradient. For example, host species are discrete and cannot be readily organized onto gradients. A seed wasp of the genus *Megastigmus*, will exploit the immature seeds in the cones of a single tree species, and the arrangement of the seeds in the cones may be sufficiently uniform to permit the conclusion that there is no appreciable gradient of depth at which the seeds are located. In this case only one species of *Megastigmus* can exploit this resource, that one which happens to be best adapted to exploiting seeds in this situation. Thus the species that exploits such a discrete and uniform resource will not be influenced by other species on the same trophic level and the abundance of this species will be determined by the density of the resource. Here there is no question of packing species and a prediction of species numbers will merely be the sum of discrete resources that can be visualized in a habitat.

The environment may be regarded as a mass of grains, each grain representing a food item, so that there are say three types of grain. Then a species that exploits only one of these types, such as the *Megastigmus* wasps, will relate to the habitat as if it contained a series of large grains of food on which it specializes. This has been called a coarse-grained species by MacArthur and Levins (1964), and it is typified by a species occupying an exclusive niche, without competition, and its abundance is determined by the abundance of the resource.

On the other hand a species that utilizes a particular proportion of a mixture of two or more resources will have to pick and choose among the grains and the species will relate to the habitat as if it were a series of small grains from which it must select certain proportions. This was called a fine-grained species by MacArthur and Levins. Many insects, such as bark beetles fit here, where each species must select a certain thickness of bark among a large range of thicknesses, and the occupation zone will also depend on other species present. Here the species will be found only where their favored proportion of foods is found, and they will be replaced by other species in other habitats where the proportion of the grains favors a new species that can therefore outcompete all others. This type of species will be regulated in abundance and evolutionary strategy very much by other species that are feeding on the same or similar sets of food grains, but in different proportions. These species are the ones concerned in species packing. Therefore when resources are examined a determination should be made on whether it represents a discrete, uniform food source, or one that is sufficiently variable to permit several species to utilize it as if it were several different resources.

Unless we understand precisely the habitat a species occupies, it may be impossible to understand why species are not packed in more tightly. Many discontinuities in available habitat occur. For example, in a boreal bog there are probably two or three very different sizes of body of water in which aquatic Diptera can breed: holes in the bog mat, free water uncolonized by bog species, and the water contained in pitcher plants, *Sarracenia* sp. Here the sizes of closely related aquatic species will probably show discontinuities that reflect discontinuities in the habitat. Hutchinson (1968) gives an example where he considers a species of rotifer found in the axils of leaves, which make an angle between 30 and 40° with the stem. And another related species lives on the free stem. The angle defining the shape of the habitat would be between 30 and 40° in the first case, and 180° in the other. If no projections from the stem provided angles of 60 or 90° for example, part of the niche space would be empty and uncolonizeable. Hutchinson states: "When, as in this case, the geometrical arrangement of habitats provides discontinuities, we might expect to find the organisms inhabiting them also showing discontinuities."

Another way of looking at species packing is to see how closely related species are distributed in relation to one another. If it is assumed that congeneric species will have the most similar resource requirements, then these species will compete most strongly with one another, and we can expect congeneric species to show differences in habitat selection because their requirements are too similar for them to coexist (e.g., the parasitoids studied earlier in the genus *Pleolophus*). Therefore, if small habitats are examined we should expect to find fewer congeneric species coexisting than are present in a large area representing many different communities. Unfortunately this approach has yet to provide unequivocal conclusions since the data available have not been ideally suited for such analyses, as explained later. However, data collected explicitly to test the prediction would be valuable.

Elton (1946) found evidence to support the prediction and in his extensive analysis he found that there was a fairly constant and high percentage of genera with only one species present in a habitat. The average was 86% for animals and 84% for plants and the average numbers of species per genus were 1.38 and 1.22 respectively. These figures differ considerably from those of a faunal list of any large region. For example, the percentage of genera with only one species present for 11 large British insect orders is 50%, and the average number of species per genus for all British insects is 4.23. Thus it looks as if congeneric species occupy different habitats, probably to reduce competitive interaction. Indeed, Jordan (1905) had reached the same conclusion long before and had stated it in a general law of distribution: "Given any species in any region, the nearest related species is not likely to be found in the same region nor in a remote region, but in a neighboring district separated from the first by a barrier of some sort."

Williams studied the same problem and has published on the subject (1947b, 1951, 1964). In each set of data he analyzed he found the opposite to Elton's findings; that there are more species per genus in a given habitat than would be expected. Thus Williams (1951) concludes: (1) "That biological competition between closely related species is probably on an average greater than that between those less closely related." (2) "That closely related species are probably more suited to similar physical environments, and to similar extra-generic competition." (3) "That the balance of these two major factors, physical and biological, which determine the survival of species in different habitats, as shown by actual proportional survival in Nature, appears to indicate that the advantages of close relationship are on average greater than the drawbacks." However no advantage need be involved; it could just be that once species have diverged sufficiently to permit coexistence there is no pressure for species to become adapted to different habitats. If two species are derived from a common ancestor they are most likely to have similar habitat requirements.

So the problem is not resolved, and until further data analysis is made we cannot use this sort of argument in the analysis of species packing. This approach also detracts from the use of the more ecologically meaningful guild as a unit for community studies. Bagenal (1951) found fault with both Elton's and Williams' arguments on the grounds that the data used were unsuitable for at least three reasons: (1) The so-called habitats used were extremely heterogeneous, including whole English counties in some instances, or massive areas of fenland in others. Thus species could live in very different communities and never compete and yet be included in the same "habitat." (2) Organisms were sampled by a variety of sampling devices and thus organisms that are never likely to compete were grouped. (3) Communities were also sampled over long periods of time and thus seasonal or yearly differences in abundance that would reduce competition were ignored. Andrewartha and Birch (1954) have added support to Bagenal's criticism.

Bagenal concluded that the confusion in the results obtained by Elton and Williams was based on differences in usage of the word habitat. These differences still exist, which prompted an incisive argument by Whittaker, Levin, and Root (1973) for the precise use of the terms niche, habitat, and ecotope in ecology. The original paper should be consulted as only some conclusions can be given here:

1. The term niche should be used only for a species resource utilization within a community.
2. The term biotope should be used for the environment in which a community exists.
3. The term habitat applies to the abiotic environment in which a species exist. (However in Chapter 13, p. 251, habitat also involved biotic characteristics, and particularly for animals these will probably have to be included in the definition of habitat.)
4. Thus a species existence and distribution is defined by factors on two variables, its niche and its habitat, and where the total resources utilized by a species are considered the term ecotope is suggested. "We suggest that henceforth it represent the species relation to the full range of environmental and biotic variables affecting it."

These terms allow a distinction to be made between rather different determinants of species distribution, and by further definition Hutchinson's definition of the niche can be improved upon, since population size in a series of resource units is taken into account; something that is done when using Levin's niche breadth formula (see Chapter 13) but which was not incorporated explicitly into the definition of the niche. Thus Whittaker, Levin, and Root suggest the following:

1. The variables of the physical and chemical environment that form spatial gradients in a landscape or area define as axes a habitat hyperspace. The part of this hyperspace a given species occupies is its habitat hypervolume. The species' population response to habitat variables within this hypervolume describes its habitat.
2. The variables by which species in a given community are adaptively related define as axes a niche hyperspace. The part of this hyperspace in which a species exists is its niche hypervolume. The species' population response within its niche hypervolume describes its niche.
3. The variables of habitats and niches may be combined to define as axes an ecotope hyperspace. The part of this hyperspace to which a given species is adapted is its ecotope hypervolume, and population responses in this hypervolume define the ecotope of the species.

Whittaker (1969) also makes the important point that time is involved in terms of a successional gradient, and he considers how species in a given area evolve in relation to this compound hyperspace defined by habitat, niche, and succession by using the following simile:

> One might think of the compound hyperspace as an n-dimensional dance floor on which occur, as a kind of evolutionary dance, those adaptive maneuvers with which we are concerned. The couples move on the dance floor in such ways that each has a dancing space of its own with minimum competition from other couples. They move to disperse themselves in the space available. In moving on the dance floor to avoid one another the dancers will move in both niche and habitat dimensions at the same time. A species can move by either combination of one and two steps in relation to niche and habitat gradients, or one and a half of each. Such possibilities are illustrated by Schoener's (1965) observation of wider niche difference on small islands, which restrict habitat difference, and Grant's (1966a) observation of three congeneric pairs of birds—one pair with strong habitat differentiation and small bill-length difference, one pair with little habitat differentiation but large bill-length difference, and a third pair with an intermediate degree of habitat overlap and bill-length difference. As additional dancers enter the floor, such maneuvers make space for them, with reduction of the dance areas of the remaining couples. There may come a time, however, when a part of the floor becomes so crowded that the rate at which new dancers enter is equaled by the rate of departure of couples discouraged or crowded off the floor.

Terborgh (1973) has argued that in this dynamic situation "dancers" are more likely to move in certain directions than others. He considers a species in a site rich in species that may increase in fitness either by evolving improved competitive ability, and thus increase in density with the consequent decline in other species, or by invading adjacent more impoverished communities where competition is reduced. Thus species packing in these communities tends to equalize over time, if species movement is not prevented or slowed by barriers. This equalization will occur mostly in large contiguous areas under stable conditions that are substantially mesic environments, with high numbers of species, and thus they represent core biotopes. Nonmesic sites frequently occur in patches or as margins of natural features; they are poorer in species and represent peripheral biotopes. Peripheral biotopes are relatively small, and patchy, suggesting that high extinction rates may, at least in part, account for the depauperate biota, caused by instability resulting from geological and biological succession (but see also discussion of the theory of island biogeography in Chapter 21). This environmental evolution thus "accounts for the relative rarity and instability of peripheral biotopes and for the commonness and comparative stability of mesic biotopes."

Thus it should be predicted that the flow of species, or the general trend of dancing couples, will be from core to peripheral biotopes with very little movement in the opposite direction. The latter case exists because of lack of selection for competitive prowess in peripheral biotopes, and since extinction is quite rapid, lack of time for acquisition of sufficient genetic change to enable reinvasion.

Perhaps it has been realized that consideration of species packing provides a natural link between the niche concept and competition and community organization, and for that matter biogeography. Before taking this natural step there is one more important aspect of coexistence and competition that must be covered, and that in the next chapter.

Chapter 16

SOCIAL SYSTEMS
AND BEHAVIOR

B ehavior and sociality are important aspects of the way in which organisms relate to the environment. They have been discussed several times in this book. In Chapter 5 optimization of yield by predator populations was related to Wynne-Edwards' hypothesis on group selection. In Chapter 8 on reproductive strategies the risks to parents during breeding and parental care was weighed against time and number of progeny produced. Chapter 9 on population dynamics discussed social interactions that influence the rate of change and size of populations. In Chapter 14 contest competition was discussed, and territoriality and social hierarchies were seen to be important in promoting population stability. Interactions between groups of social bees are discussed in Chapter 20 on pollination ecology. In turn, the environment influences the kinds of sociality and behavior that can be seen in any community.

Wilson (1971a) defined a society as "a group of individuals that belong to the same species and are organized in a cooperative manner." He said that "reciprocal communication of a cooperative nature is the essential intuitive criterion of a society." But he excluded a courting pair of animals, stating that "bird flocks, wolf packs, locust swarms, and groups of communally nesting bees are good examples of elementary societies. So are parents and young if they communicate reciprocally." Michener (1969, see also Wilson 1971a) provided a classification of the levels of insect sociality from subsocial organisms, where adults care for their progeny for a certain period of time, to the eusocial insects in which members of the same generation use the same nest and cooperate in brood care, and there is an overlap in generations so that offspring assist parents.

Lewontin (1968, 1970) has described three principles involved in the modern concept of evolution by natural selection: (1) Each individual in a population is different from others in morphology, physiology, and behavior (phenotypic variation). (2) Each phenotype has a different rate of survival and reproduction in different environments (differential fitness). (3) The contribution to future generations made by parents and offspring is correlated (fitness is heritable). As mutations constantly generate new variation populations will evolve. Lewontin emphasizes the generality of these principles by saying that any unit in nature that has variation, reproduction, and heritability will evolve. Thus, the word population can be substituted for individual in Lewontin's principles, and they will illustrate how a population may increase in size relative to others in the same species. In a similar way these principles can be applied to the persistence, increase, or decrease of types relative to others in the same category in prebiotic molecules and aggregations of these, genes, chromosomes, organisms, populations, species, communities, and ecosystems.

Brown (1966), Lewontin (1970), and Wilson (1973) among others have recognized that natural selection above the level of the individual takes two different forms. (1) Lineage groups such as a family group may form a unit of selection where the process was termed kin selection by Maynard Smith (1964). (2) All individuals in a breeding population may form the unit of selection when populations with different gene pools survive for different lengths of time at different levels of abundance. The process was termed interdemic selection by Wilson (1973). Brown (1966) suggested that the term group selection may be used to cover both these forms of selection, and now it seems that the phrase is generally accepted (cf., Wilson 1973).

The clarification of concepts on selection above the individual level was only possible after Haldane (1932, 1955) had envisioned the evolution of altruism in small groups, and Wynne-Edwards had focused much attention on group selection by the publication of his book, *Animal dispersion in relation to social behaviour* (1962) and several articles on the same subject (Wynne-Edwards 1959, 1963, 1964a,b, 1965). Wynne-Edwards' concept of group selection was different from that described above. He suggested that population stability was maintained by altruistic acts, or self-denial, through reduced fecundity or abstinence from breeding when high population density was sensed. The sensing was made possible by epideictic displays (meaning the presentation of a sample) which involved the mass activity of individuals in a population: the dancing of gnats and midges, the milling of whirligig beetles, the chorusing of insects, frogs, and birds. Through this activity each individual could sense the population level and adjust breeding activity accordingly. Thus optimal population levels could be maintained and food would not be overexploited. However, altruism, where a behavior reduces the fitness of the performing individual while enhancing the fitness of other unrelated individuals, cannot be selected for. Selfish genes will spread but altruistic genes will be selected out of the population because fitness is always lowered. Behaviors that may be misinterpreted as altruism at first sight, such as parental care, do not reduce the fitness of the individual but enhance it, since progeny survival is the measure of success. Lack (1966) explains that all the apparently group selected traits that Wynne-Edwards describes can be accounted for by invoking natural selection on individuals. Other critical appraisals have been made by Maynard Smith (1964), Perrins (1964), Hamilton (1964a,b), Williams (1966a) and Wiens (1966), which have led to the present concepts on group selection involving kin selection and interdemic selection. Williams (1971) has collected some of these papers and others into a book on group selection.

A commonly cited case of apparent altruism is the warning call made by an animal in a group when the approach of a hungry predator is first observed. This animal attracts attention to itself while warning the group and making early escape possible. The extent of reduction in fitness of this "altruistic" member of the group must be examined. Marler (1955) found that alarm calls of birds frequently have a nonlocatable quality, characterized by being narrow-band or pure tone signals (Konishi 1973). This sound quality is also characteristic of audible communication by many Orthoptera thus preventing predators from locating prey readily (Marler 1955). High frequency calls are also reflected by even small objects so that detection of the source is difficult. If warning calls are indeed nonlocatable the perpetrator of the call suffers no lowered fitness and may actually improve survival of its progeny if they are in the same foraging group.

Another case of apparent altruism is where sterile castes of ants and termites assist their mother, the queen, in producing more progeny. However, Hamilton (1964a,b, see also 1971, 1972) developed the lead given by Haldane (1932, 1955) into an important principle from his model of social behavior: "The social behaviour of a species evolves in such a way that in each distinct behaviour-evoking situation the individual will seem to value his neighbours' fitness against his own according to the coefficients of relationship appropriate to that situation." Therefore, in biparental siblings that have on the average 50% of their genes in common "altruistic" acts that lower their own fitness will be selected for provided that the benefit to a sib is more than twice as great (the ratio of cost to the acting sib to the benefit for the recipient sib is greater than $1/2$). Here the frequency of the gene that influences this behavior will increase, since the lowered fitness of the "altruist" will be more than compensated for by the improved fitness of sibs. Therefore Hamilton (1964a) suggests the term inclusive fitness as a measure of the success an individual has in leaving genes in a population the same as its own both through its own reproductive success and its effects on the reproductive success of its relatives. Evolution will tend to improve the inclusive fitness of individuals. The opportunity to increase inclusive fitness is greatest where relatives are closely related and numerous.

In the Hymenoptera, a peculiar type of sex determination (haplodiploidy) confers a particularly close relationship between sisters. This is probably the cause of evolution of eusocial behavior in the Hymenoptera more often than in other insects [at least 11 times in Hymenoptera versus once in all other insects, in the termites (Wilson 1971a)]. Males are haploid and produce sperm with a genotype identical to their own. Females are diploid and as usual produce two types of ovum, each with the maternal pairs of chromosomes represented once. (See Askew 1968 for consideration of the effect of haplodiploidy on speciation rates.) Therefore female progeny have 100% of genes from the father in common and 50% of the genes from the mother in common. Sisters have on average 75% of the same genes (Fig. 16.1). Therefore when a female matures her inclusive fitness may be improved more by helping her mother produce more sisters (75% related) than by rearing progeny of her own which share only 50% of her genes. It is significant that the highest form of social organization, eusociality, is observed in the Hymenoptera where many species of wasps, bees, and ants live in colonies with cooperative brood rearing (cf., Evans and Eberhard 1970). Also as should be predicted from the genetic relatedness of brothers and sisters, only females act as workers in helping the queen. Males can contribute to the next generation better by mating.

However, Trivers and Hare (1975) have suggested that haplodiploidy in itself does not confer an increased probability of eusociality, and this system evolves only if the sex ratio can be skewed towards females or if there are laying workers. In the first place, the degree of relatedness, $r°$, which is the probability that a gamete of a relative has a given gene (Hamilton 1972), is on average the same for $r°$'s of parents to progeny and between sibs for both male and female Hymenoptera. A male is related to his daughters by $r° = 1$ and to his mate's sons by $r° = 0$ (sons are produced by parthenogenesis), so his average $r°$ to progeny is $1/2$ if the sex ratio is $1:1$. Also a male has an $r° = 1/2$ to siblings. Similarly a female is related to sons and daughters by $r° = 1/2$, she has an $r° = 3/4$ to

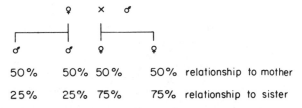

Fig. 16.1 Relationships within a group of social Hymenoptera. Note that the male progeny are produced parthenogenetically, they contain none of their father's genes, whereas female progeny contain all of their father's genes. Consult Hamilton (1964b) for details on calculation of relationships.

full sisters, but $r^\circ = 1/4$ to brothers, and thus on average $r^\circ = 1/2$ to siblings. Therefore, haplodiploidy does not favor the evolution of female workers rather than male workers. A female working caste will be favored only if workers can bias the sex ratio in their favor, for example, by killing males, or if female workers produce male eggs themselves. In the latter case, a worker will raise sisters ($r^\circ = 3/4$) and sons ($r^\circ = 1/2$) with an average r° of 5/8, which is superior to independent production of her own progeny. Therefore this practice will be selected for, and is a common phenomenon in the social Hymenoptera (Hamilton 1972). It is not universal, however, and Trivers and Hare have good evidence that the ratio of investment in reproductives (sex ratio and biomass) is commonly biased toward females, especially when there are no laying workers. This tension in the colony between a queen and worker puts the social system of Hymenoptera in a new light and brings to mind the highly competitive aspects of vertebrate societies.

In most other organisms, males are diploid and produce two types of sperm and therefore sibs are 50% related to each other. Thus in termites, which are also eusocial, brothers and sisters are 50% related and both males and females make up the worker caste. In this case it is just as adaptive to help a mother produce sisters and brothers as it is to set up a new colony. However, this 50% relationship would be reduced by multiple mating of a queen, and in termites usually only a single royal pair is tolerated. The reason for the evolution of highly developed social organization in termites is probably because anal feeding is essential after each molt. By this process, the voided gut is inoculated again with the protozoan symbionts that digest the large proportion of cellulose in the termite diet. Thus close and continued contact between individuals must be maintained. In addition, the inclusive fitness of progeny is probably increased by assisting the parents in an established colony rather than starting nest building and brood rearing independently (see Hamilton 1972).

Therefore, the apparent altruism of workers in eusocial systems can be explained on the basis of natural selection for cooperation. The important considerations that enable this conclusion are the concepts of degree of relatedness and inclusive fitness.

The evolution of social systems that function through the assertion of dominance without involving altruism is easier to explain than that for eusocial insects. An individual strives to dominate others in a certain area and if successful it maintains a territory: a territory being any defended area. Alternatively individuals within the same social group living in the same area may be dominated and a social hierarchy develops. Thus behaviors and intelligence that enable assertion of dominance are strongly selected for. It is also adaptive for less assertive individuals to recognize the prowess of a more dominant member of the species, to submit to this dominance, and to live a passive existence until greater ability in dominating others is acquired. Fitness can be improved by being temporarily submissive. Dominance hierarchies have been observed in three species of crickets in the laboratory (Kato and Hyasaka 1958, Alexander 1961), among foundresses of *Polistes* paper wasps living together (Evans and Eberhard 1970, Wilson 1971a), and between reproductives, or queens and worker bees (Wilson 1971a). Primitive social groups such as halictine bees, bumblebees, and polistine wasps tend to have queens that assert dominance by aggression (Wilson 1971a). With time, however, workers may learn to recognize the queen's odor and avoid her on this basis (Butler 1967). Social organization through dominance hierarchies is apparently rare in other insects (cf., Evans and Eberhard 1970). Territoriality, which involves dominance over all intruders, is much more common among insects.

Territoriality in insects takes many different forms and is represented in many orders (Table 16.1). The recurrent pattern is that territories are established for mating purposes. Males defend an area and mate with females that enter it. This is carried one step further in the Odonata where males apparently defend ovipositing females from other males (see also Moore 1957, 1960, Kormondy 1961). Territoriality, therefore, leads to stable densities of males and ovipositing females, but nymphal densities can be highly variable (Moore 1964). However the limitation through territoriality of the number of males and females that actually breed must lead to greater stability in populations of progeny than would be realized when all individuals breed, particularly at high population levels (cf., Chapter 9). At low population levels territorality may also improve breeding success by aiding discovery of mates. Alexander (1961) has suggested that territorality in crickets functions principally in low density populations where males defend an area and attract females from a considerable distance by chirping. Spieth (1968) described the behavior of some Hawaiian Drosophilidae where conspicuously patterned males gather together and each defends a small territory independent of food. This form of territoriality is termed a lek, where the combined advertisement by males presumably attracts more females per male than is possible by individual displays. In this case it seems that heavy predation at breeding sites has selected for dissociation of mating and ovipositing activities. Lek formation may also be observed in euglossine bees (Dodson et al. 1969, see also Chapter 20).

Table 16.1 Some examples of territoriality in insects. In some cases territoriality has been identified and in others it is probable.

Order	Common name	Scientific name for taxon	Sex	Type of territoriality	Reference
Odonata	Many dragon flies	Anisoptera	♂	Defend area	Moore 1964
	Many damsel flies	Zygoptera	♂	Guard females	Moore 1964
	Dragon fly	*Leucorrhinia rubicunda*	♂	Defend area	Pajunen 1966
	Dragon fly	*Perithemis tenera*	♂	Guard females	Jacobs 1955
	Dragon fly	*Plathemis lydia*	♂	Defend area	Jacobs 1955
			♂	Guard females	
Orthoptera	Field crickets	Gryllinae	♂	Mating territory	Alexander 1961
	Field cricket	*Acheta assimilis*	♂	Fighting	Snodgrass 1925
	Field cricket	*Gryllus campestris*	♂	Fighting	Darwin 1871
	Meadow grasshoppers	*Orchelimum* spp. *Conocephalus* sp.	♂	Mating territory	Morris 1971, 1972
Isoptera	Termites	Many species	○ and ○	Defend nest and foraging trails	For example, Wilson 1971a, Stuart 1972, Butler 1967
Hemiptera	Waterboatmen	*Cenocorixa* spp.	♂	Stridulation, fighting and spacing	Jansson 1973
Coleoptera	Burying beetles	*Necrophorus* spp.	♂ and ♀	*Defend carcass	Pukowski 1933
	Bark and ambrosia beetles	Scolytidae	♂ or ♀	Defends entrance to galleries	For example, Swaine 1918, Barr 1969, Schedl 1958
	Azuki bean weevil	*Callosobruchus chinensis*	♀	*†Chemical defense of larval feeding site	Oshima et al. 1973

Table 16.1 Continued.

Order	Common name	Scientific name for taxon	Sex	Type of territoriality	Reference
Lepidoptera	Pearly eye butterfly	*Lethe portlandica*	♂	Mating territory	Klots 1951
	Purple emperor butterfly	*Apatura iris*	♂	Mating territory	Joy, in Baker 1972
	Peacock butterfly	*Inachis io*	♂	Mating territory	Baker 1972
	Small tortoiseshell butterfly	*Aglais urticae*	♂	*Mating territory at oviposition site	Baker 1972
Diptera	Knapweed gall fly	*Urophora jaceana*	♂	Mating territory	Varley 1947
	Fruit fly	*Drosophila grimshawi*	♂	Lek	Spieth 1968
	Fruit fly	*Drosophila comatifemora*	♂	Lek	Spieth 1968
	Fruit fly	*Idiomyia planitibia*	♂	Lek	Spieth 1968
	Apple maggot	*Rhagoletis pomonella*	♀	*†Chemical defense of larval feeding site	Prokopy 1972
	Queensland fruit fly	*Dacus tryoni*	♀	*†Chemical defense of larval feeding site	Pritchard 1969
	Olive fruit fly	*Dacus oleae*	♀	*†Marks larval feeding site	Cirio, in Prokopy 1972
Hymenoptera	Ichneumon wasps	Ichneumonidae	♀	*†Chemical defense of larval feeding site	For example, Price 1970d, 1972b
	Braconid wasps	Braconidae	♀	*†Chemical defense of larval feeding site	For example, Vinson and Guillot 1972
	Chalicidoid wasps	Chalicidoidea	♀	*†Chemical defense of larval feeding site	For example, Salt 1937
	(a) Scelionid wasp	*Asolcus basalis*	♀	*†Physical defense of eggs in hosts	Wilson 1961

325

Table 16.1 Continued.

Order	Common name	Scientific name for taxon	Sex	Type of territoriality	Reference
(b) Scelionid wasp		*Asolcus basalis*	♂	Mating territory on egg mass with emerging females	Wilson 1961
	Pteromalid wasp	*Nasonia vitripennis*	♂	Mating territory on host puparium with emerging females	King et al. 1969
	Euglossine bees	Many species	♂	Mating territory, may involve lek	Dodson et al. 1969
	Euglossine bees	*Centris* and *Eulaema* spp.	♂	*Mating territory at food source	Dodson and Frymire 1961
	Megachilid bee	*Anthidium manicatum*	♂	*Mating territory? and food defense	Pechuman 1967
	Eusocial ants, wasps and bees	Formicidae, Vespidae and Apoidea	Sterile ♀	*Defense of nests and foraging sites	For example, Wilson 1971a

* Those forms of territoriality that are related to food protection.
† Those without any form of reciprocal response.

When territorities are established in relation to food supply for progeny increased population stability is likely to result. Although male insects such as bees may defend such territories, food for progeny is more commonly defended by the deposition of a chemical by the ovipositing female. We see convergent evolution for this type of territoriality when resources for larvae occur in relatively small units and the larvae are defenseless. Females of bean weevils, fruit flies, and parasitoid wasps (Table 16.1) mark the surface of the food source into which they oviposit with a chemical that deters oviposition by other females. This may deter any further oviposition on that morsel of food, as in parasitoids, or on an area related to the amount of food or space required by a larva to reach maturity, as in fruit flies (Prokopy 1972).

It is significant that territoriality in relation to food becomes increasingly common with evolutionary advancement in the insects, with the Hymenoptera providing by far the largest number of examples. Indeed, Alexander (1961) has focused on the relationship between the evolution of territoriality and the evolution of social behavior. Territoriality leads to an isolation of breeding pairs, attachment to a particular location, modification of this location to form a nest of some sort, chemical marking of the site, and close relationships between parents and offspring. For example, a mated pair of *Necrophorus* beetles cooperate to defend a corpse against all other beetles; they form a nest in which the young are reared, and young are fed from food regurgitated by the mother (Pukowski 1933, see also Wilson 1971a). In many respects this pattern may be similar to that of territorial birds. Where territoriality is related to food supply it is likely to have an important stabilizing influence on insect populations as in birds (cf., Nice 1941, Hinde 1956, Brown 1964, Schoener 1968, Watson and Moss 1970) and territory size may be related to the amount of food required as in some birds (Fig. 16.2). This has been noted by Prokopy (1972) in fruit flies, and Moore (1964) observed that the size of territory was positively correlated with size of dragonflies as Schoeher (1968) found for birds.

Without the development of dominance and consequent subordination between individuals of the same species overt competition results, the most extreme case of which is cannibalism, or intraspecific predation. Examples in predatory insects are too numerous to mention (see Fox 1975 for references) but cases also occur among insects otherwise considered to be herbivores (e.g., *Tribolium* beetles, Mertz and Davies 1968, Mertz and Robertson 1970; *Labidomera* beetles, Eickwort 1973; and

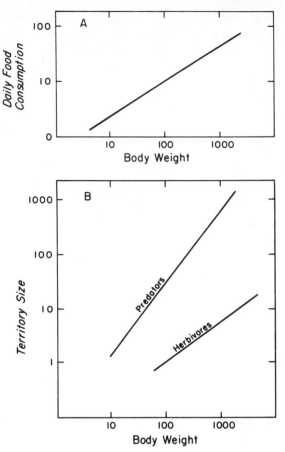

Fig. 16.2   Relationships between body weight (g), food requirements per day (g), and territory size (acres) for birds. After Shoener 1968.

Heliconius caterpillars, Gilbert 1975). Fox (1975) expressed the view that cannibalism is analagous in its effects to forms of dominance that space animals, and reduces densities below the carrying capacity, thereby ensuring that at least some individuals survive and reproduce. Wilson (1971b) also regarded cannibalism as a form of contest competition. Therefore, the subject is worthy of more attention than it has received to date. Particularly when food was in short supply cannibalism by the larger members of a population of backswimmers *Notonecta hoffmanni* was heavy on early instars. Thus breeding adult populations were maintained by immature stages which constituted up to 50% of the diet.

When the inclusive fitness of an individual is considered, cannibalism among siblings may be selected for (see Eickwort 1973), although it may seem maladaptive at first sight. Eickwort found that development of *Labidomera clivicollis* larvae which were cannibalistic was accelerated, particularly in the first instar. Thus the probability of survival of these individuals increased. Indeed even if development was accelerated by only 2 days, Eickwort calculated that the inclusive fitness of individuals expressing the gene that conferred the cannibalistic trait would be increased. This increased survival more than compensated for the death of siblings. The nutritional benefits of cannibalism in *Tribolium* have been documented by Ho and Dawson (1966) and Mertz and Robertson (1970).

Those males that, through asserting dominance, are able to establish a mating territory, gain exclusive access to females entering the area, and thereby increase chances of breeding. The commonness of this territoriality in insects (see Table 16.1) suggests the strength of competition for mates. The large amount of energy expended by males in maintaining a mating territory indicates that sexual selection ranks high in the energy budget. The importance of sexual selection among insects was documented by Darwin (1871), and the subject has continued to be an active field of inquiry (e.g., Richards 1927, Spieth 1968, Petit and Ehrman 1969, Campbell 1972, and Parker 1974). Darwin defined sexual selection as the advantage that certain individuals have over others of the same sex and species only with respect to reproduction. Since individuals select a mate, and since both the number of mates and their quality determine fitness, this selection is an important process.

The development of mating territories is only one solution to the competitive interaction for mates. Nonterritorial males must search for females, and the search strategy becomes an important aspect of sexual selection. Parker (1974 and references therein) has investigated in detail the searching by male dung flies, *Scatophaga stercoraria* (see also Chapter 8). Gravid females are attracted to freshly deposited cattle droppings. Females approach upwind to the dung and rest in grass for prolonged periods. They are most attracted to dung about 50–60 minutes after its deposition. On the dung females are outnumbered by males, intermale competition is intense, and the behavioral repertoire of males shows extensive adaptation for maximizing insemination. Males patrol dung and the surrounding grass and extend this search most in the direction

of approaching females. Thus many females are discovered and inseminated before the oviposition site is reached. Males copulate with a
female unmolested and away from the dung, and then fly with her to
the dung and defend her against other males that attempt to copulate
during oviposition. A male thus protects his investment in sperm, and
the degree to which he is successful in repeatedly finding mates and
preventing take-overs by other males reflects directly on his contribution
to the next generation. The male's prowess in selecting a mate and
guarding her until oviposition is complete is severely tested in each
generation.

Sexual selection may play an important role in the maintenance of
genetic polymorphism. For example, sexual vigor of fruit fly males is
greatest when they are heterozygous (Petit and Ehrman 1969, Ehrman
1972) as measured by the proportion of females they inseminate when
in competition with homozygous males. In addition frequency-dependent
sexual selection has been observed repeatedly. Here rare male phenotypes
have an advantage over common males and again polymorphism is maintained (see Petit and Ehrman 1969 for review). Mating success can be
estimated by use of the formula:

$$K = \frac{(A_i/a_i)}{(B_j/b_j)}$$

where K is the coefficient of mating success, A is the number of females
inseminated by type i males, and B is the number inseminated by type j
males, and a and b are the numbers of males of type i and j, respectively.
Thus with random mating $K = 1$, when type i males have an advantage
$K > 1$ and when type j males have an advantage $K < 1$. When white type
and wild type *Drosophila melanogaster* males were tested $K_{(white)}$ was
1.93 at a frequency of 6% white males but only 0.62 at a frequency of
69% (see Petit and Ehrman 1969). A stable polymorphism was established
at about 40% white males. More recent studies have been completed by
Nassar et al. (1973), and Grant et al. (1974).

Reproductive isolation between sympatric species can be maintained
principally by sexual selection. If the love song of a male fruit fly fails
to make a female receptive isolation is complete. These songs are species-
specific (Bennet-Clark and Ewing 1968, 1970, Ewing and Bennet-Clark
1968). *Drosophila melanogaster* males produce single sound pulses lasting about three thousandths of a second, with a tone of 330/CPS by
beating one wing and then the other. When positioned close to a female
she becomes receptive to the male if the song is accompanied also by
appropriate chemical cues. Since each species of a sympatric group has a
distinct song, hybridization is rare in nature.

The opportunities for further study on social systems and behavior in insects are immense. Many field entomologists realize that territoriality in insects is much more common than documentation of it would indicate. In the cases that are described the impact of territoriality on populations must be better understood (see Alexander 1961 and Moore 1964, for detailed discussions on this point). The role of cannibalism has hardly been treated in a conceptual manner, and further studies on sexual selection in insects should broaden from the sound base created by studies on Diptera to other taxa. The predictions derived from Hamilton's and Trivers' studies on social insects must be tested by detailed studies on sex ratios and queen and worker behavior. But the contributions toward an understanding of sociobiology that can be made by the study of insects are immense.

Part IV

COMMUNITIES

AND

DISTRIBUTIONS

Species colonize a location at different times and the competitive balance between them shifts with time, thereby creating a succession of species in a certain area (Chapter 17). There is a change of communities with time, since resources change. The resources available in each community in turn influence the number of species in the community and their relative abundance (Chapter 18). The number or range of resources tends to increase with time and on latitudinal gradients from the poles to the equator, resulting in the patterns seen in diversity and stability of communities (Chapter 19). The relationships between food, plant, and animal populations, competition, and coexistence as influences in the organization of communities are integrated in the study of pollination ecology (Chapter 20). All factors, both contemporary and historical, that influence the presence or absence of a species at a particular site, contribute to the determination of the geographic range and paleological record for the species (Chapter 21).

Chapter 17

NATURAL COMMUNITIES AND THE SUCCESSION OF PLANTS AND INSECTS

Plant and animal species change from one location to another and it has been a natural occupation of ecologists to investigate the reasons why this should be so. In fact, this type of study was one of the earliest undertaken by ecologists; therefore, this area of ecology has one of the most fascinating histories that reaches into the last century. It has created some of the fiercest discussions and rivalry, and it has provided a field in which many of the great men of ecology have established their reputations. Therefore this subject is worthy of a book rather than a single chapter. Unfortunately this hive of activity, enthusiasm, and discussion has all but left out insects completely. And while one sifts through the large literature relating to plant communities it is a rare occasion to discover a paper relating to insect communities and succession.

Species occupy a particular area because the conditions in that area—the physical factors, and food resources—match the requirements of the organism—their niche and habitat requirements. If the environment is stable, then a species can remain indefinitely. If this same environment is very extensive, then the species can occupy an equally extensive area. Conversely a changing environment produces an ephemeral occupation of a location and a very localized environment produces a very restricted range in a species. Thus the actual distribution of species depends primarily on what the sorts of resources are to which a species becomes adapted, and how much a species is forced into a specialized exploitation pattern by interspecific competition.

But it is evident that there is frequently an inevitable change in communities with time, and that this change is often of a predictable nature. It has been called succession. This change is caused by several factors, two of which are most important. First, the species that arrive at a certain site actually change that site and may make it more suitable for new species and less suitable for resident species. For example, a plant that colonizes a bare patch of soil will create more shade; it will contribute organic matter to the soil that changes soil texture and nutrient status, allelochemicals may be secreted that may be toxic to themselves or other plants; and it may attract animals, including insects, that further change factors in the environment by burrowing in soil, producing excrement, trampling the ground, and eating plants. Herbivores may play an important role in succession by altering the competitive balance between plant species, but we know very little about this interaction that offers a wide-open area for research. In general, then, some species may be actively involved with the dynamics of succession because they cause change, and others are passive, since they merely respond to the change. Second, species are bound to arrive at different times and thus succession will result in part from differences in the rate of dispersal of colonizers. An open patch of ground will be rapidly colonized by germination of resident seeds and small seeds dispersed by wind, the seeds of typical weedy species which are windborn. As time passes heavier seeds are likely to arrive which produce seedlings with greater competitive ability, and this process may continue for decades. The types of species that become established are defined by the resources available at the site and the intensity of competition.

The first people to realize that there was as succession of communities with time were Cowles (1899) who studied the vegetation of sand dunes bordering Lake Michigan, and Clements (1916) who built up a conceptual framework about communities and succession. One can understand why sand dunes provided an early recognized example of succession by walking from the edge of the sea over the dune land and into a wooded area, and watching to see how the plants and insects are distributed. Chevin (1966) made a study like this on the west coast of Northern France, and a cross section of a transect is given in Fig. 17.1. Since sand is constantly being added at the west end of the dune area, the whole chronology of dune succession is set out in space. Early stages of succession can be seen in the west and late stages in the east. Physical factors change with time and thus change the resident species, and the species themselves change the conditions that allow others to colonize.

For example, since these are sea coast dunes, salt concentration is high so that only halophytes can tolerate these early conditions. Salt is gradually leached from the sand so that other species can colonize. But also nutrients in the form of chemicals from sea shells and drying seaweed are high early in succession and species such as sand couch grass, *Agropyron junceum*, do well but as nutrients are leached out, the sand is lowered in nutrient status. The mobile sand offers a very difficult substrate to colonize but some species such as lyme grass, *Elymus arenarius*, and marram grass, *Ammophila arenaria*, are adapted to this condition and they colonize the dunes, slow down sand movement, and create a fixed dune environment that can be colonized by other less specialized plants. As conditions become more stable more species are able to colonize, organic matter in the soil increases, and with time a forest would develop; except in Chevin's study these areas are cultivated. Since stable sites are a result of succession, these sites become larger and larger until huge areas are occupied by very stable communities with long-lived species [cf., Terborgh (1973), discussed in Chapter 15 on species packing]. Thus we see in this transect a succession of rather clearly defined com-

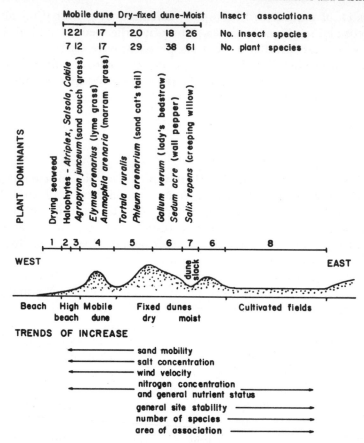

Fig. 17.1 Cross section of sand dunes on west coast of Cotentin, France (adapted from Chevin 1966). Note that with a prevailing westerly wind sand is piled against the mainland so the oldest sand occurs in the east and the newest in the west. Below the cross section, the many factors that change and so influence plant succession are listed, the arrows indicating the direction of increase in the factor. Above, the dominant plants in each association are given, and the number of plant and insect species per association. Note that as succession proceeds more and more plants colonize the increasingly equable biotopes.

munities or associations of plants (Numbers 2–8 where 8 would be woodland under natural conditions, Fig. 17.1). Each plant association represents a seral stage, each necessary for the conditioning of the site for the subsequent association, ultimately leading to a climax vegetation that is self-reproducing, and therefore perpetual, and defined according to Clements (1916) by the climate in the area.

Chevin also studied the insects on this transect and found them harder to classify into associations, merely because they were less specific to edaphic factors in their requirements. One species of chrysomelid, *Psylloides marcida*, was specific to *Cakile maritima*, but most were not so specific. Thus while seven fairly distinct plant associations could be identified only three associations of insects were recognized (Table 17.1).

Table 17.1   Some families of insects represented in the three insect associations recognized by Chevin (1966) in his study on sand dunes. See Fig. 17.1 for location of associations in relation to dune development.

Mobile dune association
   Scarabaeidae   — Scarab beetles
   Tenebrionidae — Darkling beetles
   Curculionidae — Weevils or snout beetles
   Pompilidae   — Spider wasps
   Pentatomidae — Stink bugs
Dry fixed dune association
   Acrididae   — Short-horned grasshoppers or locusts
   Lygaeidae   — Lygaeid bugs
   Chrysomelidae — Leaf beetles
   Carabidae   — Ground beetles
Moist fixed dune association
   Acrididae   — Short-horned grasshoppers or locusts
   Tettigoniidae — Long-horned grasshoppers
   Lepidoptera   — Butterflies and moths

This is no doubt partly due to the mobility of insects, and illustrates the difficulty of trying to identify animals that are associated in their distributions. Note that at least some of the insects are likely to have influenced succession considerably. Scarabaeid larvae feeding on roots of the mobile dune species may well prolong this stage of succession by reducing growth rates and binding power of root systems. Curculionids may also reduce plant vigor, while acridids that are less likely to be species-specific may have influenced the competitive balance in the fixed dune association. Impact studies of herbivores in succession are sorely needed!

Other studies on succession of insects and other arthropods include tiger beetle succession on dune land (Shelford 1907), and other species on dunes (Shelford 1913), pseudoscorpions on sand banks (Weygoldt 1969) (Fig. 17.2), insects on broom (Waloff 1968a,b), insects on rotting logs (Blackman and Stage 1924), insects in pine plantations (Martin 1966), insects in stored wheat (Coombs and Woodroffe 1973), parasitoids on the aphid, *Therioaphis trifolii* (van den Bosch et al. 1964), and carabids, diplopods, and isopods on spoil heaps of coal mines (Neumann 1971).

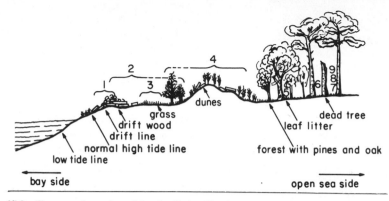

Fig. 17.2   Cross section of an island off the North Carolina mainland showing the distribution of nine different pseudoscorpion species in relation to the development of the vegetation. From Weygoldt 1969.

From the known biology of the species involved in these examples it is possible to infer that some are actively involved in the dynamics of succession, and some are passive, although for some species not enough is known to be able to classify them in this way. For example, insects in rotting logs radically change conditions in the log and are thus active and necessary for succession to occur. Insects on stored wheat act in a similar way by breaking down the grains and making them available to other species. Tiger beetles and pseudoscorpions are probably passive and merely respond to changes caused by other factors. Arthropods on spoil heaps of coal mines probably have considerable influence on succession but their actual roles are unknown. The examples provided by Waloff (1968a,b) and Martin (1966) show that succession of insects may occur as a single host plant ages, as nutritional status and canopy conditions change. Thus succession should not be regarded as a single trend in time. There are multiple successions at any one site all of which interact to generate the observed patterns.

The term association denotes a grouping of communities defined primarily by the presence of a common set of character species. That such associations exist, with species constantly occurring together, has been supported by several schools of thought (see Whittaker 1962 for details): the Zürich-Montpellier school led by Braun-Blanquet, the Swedish-Finnish school in which DuRietz was preeminent, the British school influenced profoundly by Tansley, and the early American school dominated by Clements. Much attention has been given to the definition of these associations of plants. Although it is clear that certain species usually exist together and are thus associated, the application of the concept to all vegetation runs into difficulties.

An extreme view of succession was taken by Clements (1916) who regarded the development of a climax community as if it were the growth of an individual. He argued that just as individuals reproduce so does the climax community: "The life-history of a formation is a complex but definite process, comparable in its chief features with the life-history of an individual plant." Each association in succession was a part of the growth toward the climax community. Objective study of plant communities, discussed later in this chapter, have invalidated this concept (see also Colinvaux 1973).

Further limitations of the association concept may be seen by studying data provided by Kontkanen (1950) who studied leafhoppers (Cicadellidae) in meadows in North Karelia, Finland. He made sweep-net collections in four main types of meadow: rich fens, poor fens, peaty meadows, and grass meadows. Thus all the samples could be placed on a gradient of soil moisture content from the very wet fens to the grass meadow on a well-drained moraine. But on this gradient there were actually many different sets of associated plant species, or associations, because within each major grouping, meadows showed different species composition.

When Kontkanen plotted the distribution of cicadellids on this moisture gradient, he found there were groups of species that showed similar distributions. It seemed as if they were truly associated species, which required a similar set of environmental factors for their reproduction and survival. But these groups were not spatially discrete, and could not be delimited spatially because many other species overlapped their distributions (Fig. 17.3). Therefore Kontkanen used Sørensen's similarity quotient (QS) to determine the degree of similarity between samples to define which samples belonged in the same association. The formula is

$$QS = \frac{2c \times 100}{a + b}$$

where a = number of species in sample A, b = number of species in sample B, and c = number of species common to both samples. Then he erected a trellis or matrix of similarity values to see if there were clusters of samples with close similarity that could be grouped into associations of cicadellid species. We can see from Fig. 17.3 that three associations would be identified by this method. But these associations are defined principally by the species with narrow tolerances, and not by those with wide tolerances. Also only three associations of cicadellids can be seen where

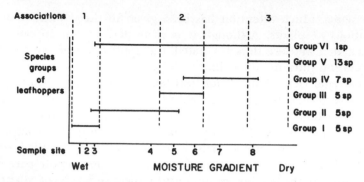

Fig. 17.3 Distribution of leafhopper species on a moisture gradient in meadows in North Karelia, Finland (data from Kontkanen 1950). See Table 17.2 for analysis of similarities between sample sites. These were selected to illustrate the difficulty in delimiting associations and were not those used by Kontkanen.

about nine plant associations could be identified, rather like the sand dune example. However, the definition of limits between associations is impossible (Table 17.2). There is an apparent boundary between sites

Table 17.2 Comparison of community similarity (QS) of cicadellids studied by Kontkanen. For each pair of sample sites located as in Fig. 17.3 on a moisture gradient the parameters, a, b, and c are given, from which the QS has been calculated. When communities have a QS of less than 50% they are arbitrarily considered to be distinct, but the margins of these communities cannot be identified (see text for further explanation).

Sample site		Parameters in QS formula			
A	B	c	a	b	QS
1	2	5	5	5	100
1	3	5	5	11	62
1	4	0	5	6	0
3	4	6	11	6	70
3	5	6	11	11	55
3	6	1	11	13	8
4	5	6	6	11	70
4	6	1	6	13	10
5	6	6	11	13	50
5	7	1	11	8	10
6	7	8	13	8	80
6	8	8	13	21	47

1 and 4, which have a $QS=0$ but there is none between 1 and 3 ($QS=62$) or 3 and 4 ($QS=70$). Similarly there is a boundary between sites 4 and 6 ($QS=10$) but none between 4 and 5 ($QS=70$) and 5 and 6 ($QS=50$). Thus although samples can be grouped according to their similarity of 50% or more, discrete associations cannot be defined.

The general attitude now is that the method that is used to analyze distributions of plants and animals should not presuppose that species groupings do exist, and yet the method must permit their identification should they happen to occur. Whittaker (1952) took this point of view when he studied the distribution of foliage insects in the Great Smoky Mountains. He set up sampling points on gradients of elevation, from the valley to the peaks, and humidity, from the deep coves to the well-drained peaks and ridges. On both these gradients he found that each species of insect was distributed independently of the others. Each species distribution was represented by a bell-shaped curve of abundance along the gradient, with the population density tapering off into unfavorable habitats (see Fig. 17.4). As Chevin and Kontkanen found, an insect population is not limited to one plant community, but may spread over many. The same sorts of pattern were evident on the moisture gradient. If an association of species is not presupposed in the sampling procedure it turns out, at least where gradients in sites are steep as in a mountain-

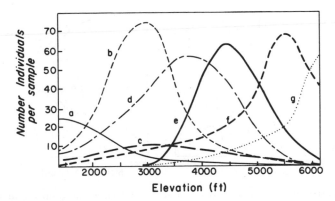

Fig. 17.4   Distribution of seven insect species along an elevation gradient in mesic sites. (a) *Graphocephala coccinea* (Cicadellidae), (b) *Caecilius* sp. (Psocidae), (c) *Agalliopsis novella* (Cicadellidae), (d) *Polypsocus corruptus* (Psocidae), (e) *Anaspis rufa* (Mordellidae), (f) *Cicadella flavoscuta* (Cicadellidae)×0.5, (g) *Oncopsis sp.* (Cicadellidae). From Whittaker 1952.

ous area, that species are distributed more or less independently of each other.

Whittaker (1956) also established this form of distribution for the trees and shrubs in the Great Smoky Mountains. By plotting the abundance of species on both the moisture and elevation gradients simultaneously he obtained distribution charts using contours of similar abundance (Fig. 17.5). To sum up in Whittaker's (1952) words: "Of the results of the attempt to sort [insect] species into associations it may be simply observed that no two distribution patterns are alike and that it is not possible objectively to define associations, formations, or zones with them. These results are in complete agreement with those obtained for plant populations, using more satisfactory data for organisms which do not migrate."

This method of gradient analysis has been extensively used in phyto-sociology and Whittaker has written an excellent review (1967). The approach has been applied to animal distributions although less frequently, and it should be used more often in insect studies. All sorts of gradients may be used; elevation, moisture, wind velocity, light intensity, and others. Essentially the distribution of individuals is studied, as opposed to groupings as in the association concept. That emphasis should be placed on the individual rather than the grouping was stressed by Ramensky (1926) in Russia and Gleason (1926) in the United States, among other

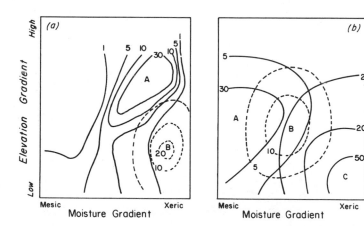

Fig. 17.5 Distribution of organisms on moisture and elevation gradients in the Great Smoky Mountains. (a) The lines of equal abundance for the oaks, A—*Quercus borealis* and B—*Quercus coccinea*; (b) Distribution of three insect species, A—*Polypsocus corruptus* (Psocidae), B—*Leptopeza compta* (Empididae), and C—*Kleidocerys resedae* (Lygaeidae). Note how each species has a distinct distribution in response to the two habitat parameters. After Whittaker 1952, 1956.

people. Their views were expressed in protest of the schools of phyto-sociology that were actively describing clearly defined plant associations, where the sets of associated species were duplicated over and over again in an extensive area, as mentioned earlier in this chapter.

Ramensky (1926) made the following points in support of his individ-ualistic, or continuum, concept of plant distribution: (1) vegetation is modified continuously in space; (2) the sharp boundary between com-munities is an individual instance in need of special explanation (either influence of discontinuous alteration of other factors, influence of culture, etc.); (3) each species reacts to the other unique factors and occurs as an independent member of the community; and (4) there are no two groups that end up with identical abundance in a community. Gleason (1939) argued that the grouping of plants in an area depends on the seeds that arrive there, and the survival of these seeds. Since each environment is likely to be different anyway, and changing at different rates, and since communities have no genetic or dynamic connection, a precisely logical classification of communities is not possible.

In addition to looking at major physical factors on gradients as plant ecologists do, animal ecologists must also take into account the influence of the vegetation on distribution. For example, Terborgh (1971) created three models in an effort to discover what actually defined the limits of a species' distribution on a gradient (Fig. 17.6). The first model predicted

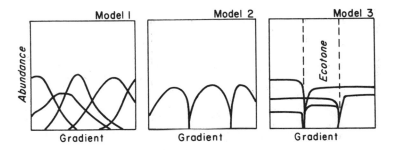

Fig. 17.6 The three models proposed by Terborgh: Model 1—Abundances of species along an environmental gradient are independent of one another. 2—Abundances are truncated where competitors meet. 3—Abundances are sharply truncated at ecotones. After Terborgh 1971.

that abundances and ecological amplitudes (i.e., distance taken upon the gradient) on the gradient are independent of one another. They are therefore defined by change of physical or biological conditions and the mode in which the animals' set of adaptations permits them to exist. The second predicted that competitive exclusion limits distribution and the third that environmental discontinuities (ecotones) limit distribution. Terborgh made a preliminary analysis of bird distributions on an elevation gradient in the Eastern Andes of Peru. He was able to estimate the relative importance of each of the three factors in determining the bird distribution. Ecotones accounted for about 18% of the distributional limits of species, competitive exclusion about 32%, and gradually changing conditions along the gradient for about 50% of the limits. Thus here again individual responses to the environment appear to be most important in defining the distribution of a species, but other factors are of considerable importance.

Even though it appears that organisms respond to environments independently, it is possible to see some general patterns in change of species with time, and these patterns are best understood for plants. Odum (1969) has defined in very broad strokes these trends in succession (Fig. 17.7, Table 17.3). If a plant community becomes established the young stages of succession must have a photosynthesis (P):respiration (R) ratio greater than 1, while in older stages this ratio approaches 1, since the climax community merely maintains itself. The energy fixed tends to be balanced by the energy cost of maintenance in the climax community, and therefore the $P:R$ ratio should be an excellent functional index of the relative

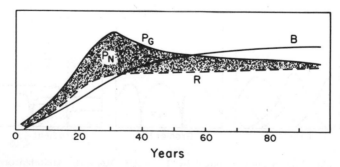

Fig. 17.7   Trends in succession leading to climax forest. R, total community respiration; B, total biomass; P_G, gross production due to photosynthesis; P_N, net production. From Odum 1969.

Table 17.3 Summary of trends in ecological succession.

	Ecosystem attributes	Developmental stages	Mature stages
	Community energetics		
1.	Gross production/community respiration (P/R ratio)	Greater or less than 1	Approaches 1
2.	Gross production/standing crop biomass (P/B ratio)	High	Low
3.	Biomass supported/unit energy flow (B/E ratio)	Low	High
4.	Net community production (yield)	High	Low
5.	Food chains	Linear, predominantly grazing	Weblike, predominantly detritus
	Community structure		
6.	Total organic matter	Small	Large
7.	Inorganic nutrients	Extrabiotic	Intrabiotic
8.	Species diversity—variety component	Low	High
9.	Species diversity—equitability component	Low	High
10.	Biochemical diversity	Low	High
11.	Stratification and spatial heterogeneity (pattern diversity)	Poorly organized	Well-organized
	Life history		
12.	Niche specialization	Broad	Narrow
13.	Size of organism	Small	Large
14.	Life cycles	Short, simple	Long, complex
	Nutrient cycling		
15.	Mineral cycles	Open	Closed
16.	Nutrient exchange rate, between organisms and environment	Rapid	Slow
17.	Role of detritus in nutrient regeneration	Unimportant	Important
	Selection pressure		
18.	Growth form	For rapid growth ("r-selection")	For feedback control ("K-selection")
19.	Production	Quantity	Quality
	Overall homeostasis		
20.	Internal symbiosis	Undeveloped	Developed
21.	Nutrient conservation	Poor	Good
22.	Stability (resistance to external perturbations)	Poor	Good
23.	Entropy	High	Low
24.	Information	Low	High

SOURCE. From Odum 1969.

maturity of the system. So long as P exceeds R, organic matter and biomass (B) will accumulate in the system and B/P will tend to increase and B/R and B/E (energy utilization) will increase. Theoretically, then, the amount of standing crop biomass supported by the available energy flow increases to a maximum in the mature or climax stages. As a consequence, the net community production in an annual cycle is large in young systems and small or zero in mature systems.

Some aspects listed in Table 17.3 have already been touched upon in this book. In Chapter 6 productivity was seen to increase as the woody component in the community increased (e.g., Table 6.4). Early stages in succession were composed of short-lived organisms whereas later stages contained long-lived species of plants and insects. Also detritivores were seen to be extremely important in mature deciduous forests. In Chapter 8 reproductive strategies involving differences in size of seeds were discussed. It was concluded that r selected species, which produced many small seeds, were good colonizers but poor competitors, and the large seeded K selected species were poor dispersers but good competitors that became dominant in later stages of succession. In the discussions on niche specialization (Chapter 13), competition (Chapter 14), and species packing (Chapter 15) we saw that in equilibrium communities competition would be severe and species packing tight with a necessity for narrow niche specialization, as expected in mature stages of succession. By contrast, where competition is relaxed and opportunists or fugitive species exist, species may show broad exploitation patterns. Aspects of diversity and stability in succession are treated in Chapter 19. Thus succession provides an important concept that links many areas of ecology.

Even now many new trends in succession are being discovered that support the generalizations listed in Table 17.3. For example Levin (1974) found that the oil content and weight of seeds was greater in species late in succession, indicating that there is a trend from r to K selection with succession as quality of progeny is improved. For 300 species of legumes the mean oil content in seeds of herbs was 5.6%; it was 7.8% for shrubs, 10.6% for shrubby trees, and 11.4% for trees. Mean seed weight was 0.012 g in herbs, 0.047 g in shrubs, 0.087 g in shrubby trees, and 0.186 g in trees.

Trends in defense against herbivores with successional stage may also be anticipated (Cates and Orians 1975). Since early species are short-lived and disperse well, they are available to herbivores for a short time and individuals may also escape herbivores by seed dispersal. Therefore little energy should be devoted to herbivore defense. Species later in succession are long-lived, with a long prereproductive period and poor dispersal of seed. Escape from herbivores is almost impossible for such species and strong selection for herbivore protection should result in considerable energy being channeled into defense. Weigert and Owen (1971) made a similar prediction in relation to their arguments on food chain length (Chapter 6). As stated in Table 17.3 biochemical diversity should be high in maturer stages of succession for reasons of chemical defense alone. Cates and Orians (1975) tested 100 plant species for palatability to two species of slugs and confirmed their prediction that early successional plants are more palatable than are late successional or climax community species. Indeed, even perennial plants in early succession were less palatable than were annuals in the same stage of succession.

Further studies on these and similar trends in succession are in progress and many more are possible. Together they will form an integrated body of knowledge with succession as a central theme, providing one of the important unifying concepts in ecology.

Chapter 18

COMMUNITY DEVELOPMENT, STRUCTURE, AND ORGANIZATION

In the last chapter it was argued that it is very hard, and maybe completely unrealistic, to identify natural groupings of animals that would qualify as associations of species. This view was based on the study of the distribution of populations of a species, and not on the whole species. Thus it is natural to look at the distribution of species to see if different species have similar distributions. This gets into the realm of biogeography (see Chapter 21), but it helps here in identifying a natural ecological classification of the environment. Merriam (1894, 1898) proposed that temperature was the main controlling factor in the distribution of plants and animals and that North America could therefore be divided into zones of similar temperature: Life Zones. Pitelka (1941) criticized this view as had Shelford and Kendeigh before him on the grounds that although this system worked in the west, in very mountainous terrain, the belts of similar temperature in the east contained several different assemblages of plants and animals, and therefore the system was inadequate. Pitelka saw that bird species showed fairly clearly defined distributions related to major structural changes in the habitat [which is supported incidentally by MacArthur and MacArthur's (1961) study discussed in Chapter 15]. The distributions extended up to a major ecotone, such as between deciduous forest, and grassland, or between coniferous forest and deciduous forest. It seemed to be these major structural features of the environment to which birds and other animals were responding. Any grouping of communities that has similar structure is called a Biome or Formation. Other examples besides grassland and deciduous and coniferous forest, are tundra, desert, and chapparal. It is generally agreed that biomes provide a natural classification of plant and animal distribution. However, we are left wondering if there is not a smaller unit than the biome than can be studied as an ecological unit, that is bigger than the population or the species.

In Chapter 1 the community was defined as a set of coexisting interdependent populations. If the populations of different species in a given area are truly interdependent, then this is the unit of classification that deserves careful study. Here concern is focused on the presence, and absence of species in a given area and not on total distribution of species. Study is concentrated on a woodlot, a field, a rotting log, a tree hole, or slime flux, or practically any unit that contains several species. Thus the community is perhaps the largest unit in an ecological classification in which relationships can be studied in fair detail. Once study of the biome is undertaken a systems analysis approach is usually necessary and the guild may be the smallest unit of study that can be realistically treated. Thus community ecology offers the last, but biggest chance of looking at the interrelations of organisms with each other, and their physical setting in detail.

After finding difficulty in applying the association concept to animal distributions, it is essential first to establish the reality of the community. MacArthur and MacArthur (1961) discovered that a given structural diversity of a biotope usually supports a certain diversity of bird species. That is the number of species and their relative abundance is dictated by the biotope. If this diversity of birds is so predictable from biotope characteristics it suggests that each biotope must be filled up with bird species, and no more could colonize the site. If the biotopes were not filled many points below the regression line between bird species diversity and foliage height diversity should have been observed. But the diversity index, H' (see definition in Chapter 19), has two important components, the number of species and the evenness of abundance of these species, so that it is difficult using this method to see what is actually limiting. Number of species per biotope is a simpler value to look at first.

A study on arthropod communities supports the view that biotopes have a certain limit for species. Wilson and Simberloff set out to test some of the theories of island biogeography proposed by MacArthur and Wilson in 1963 and 1967. In 1966 Wilson and Simberloff carefully found all the species of arthropods (insects and spiders) that existed on each of several islands of red mangrove (*Rhizophora mangle*), off the west coast of Florida, in Florida Bay. In late 1966 and early 1967 they then fumigated each island by putting tents over the island and pumping in methyl bromide. All arthropods were killed except a very few individual wood borers (Wilson and Simberloff 1969). Since then they have monitored the recolonization of the sites (Simberloff and Wilson 1969, 1970), and some of the colonization curves are given in Fig. 18.1. The shape of the colonization curve appears to be quite typical of all but the furthest islands from the mainland. Colonization is rapid at first, the number of species overshoots the equilibrium number before defaunation, and then drops rather rapidly to an equilibrium state. The more distant the island from the species pool of potential colonizers the slower is the process. The islands seem to have a definite limit for a certain number of species. This limit will impose a sorting action on the arrivals; only those that can exploit a discrete set of resources can survive, and those that cannot will be departures from the community, through extinction. Thus there must be a self-organizing quality in the community, which therefore justifies its study as a natural unit in the hierarchy of ecological assemblages of organisms.

Wilson (1969) postulates four stages in the organization of a community: noninteractive, interactive, assortative, and evolutionary (Fig. 18.2). Noninteractive conditions exist when the population densities and numbers of species are too low to cause competition for resources, and there is insufficient biomass for predators and parasites to exploit effec-

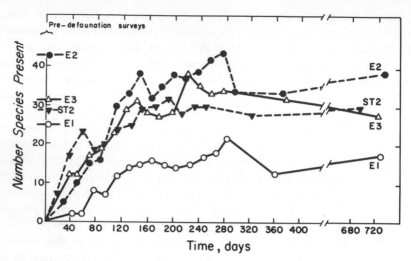

Fig. 18.1 Colonization curves for four small mangrove islands in the lower Florida Keys after fauna had been exterminated by fumigation with methyl bromide. Numbers of species present before defaunation are given for each island on the ordinate. The near island E2 had the most species, the furthest island E1 the fewest, and the intermediate islands ST2 and E3 intermediate numbers. From Simberloff and Wilson 1970.

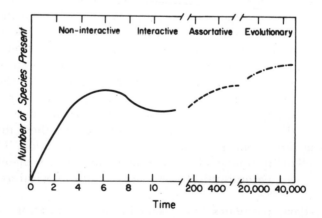

Fig. 18.2 A theoretical sequence of equilibrium number of species in a community with time. The time scale represents relative periods of time that it would take to reach the different equilibrial states. From Wilson 1969.

tively. The interactive equilibrium is due to competition, the extinction of some species and the establishment of predators and parasitoids. Many species will go extinct through this interaction but others will colonize the area, and during this assortative phase those species that can coexist and utilize the resources most efficiently will remain. The assortative phase sorts species for efficient coexistence, and this efficiency in the community permits more species to pack in. Finally coevolution of species makes their total exploitation more efficient still and there will be a further increase in coexisting species. This evolutionary aspect is shown by Southwood's (1961) data on the number of insect species on different tree species in Europe. For example, in Britain, the longer and more abundant a tree species has been in the islands, the more species exist on that tree (Fig. 18.3).

Studies by Heatwole and Levins support the findings of Wilson and Simberloff, the theory of island biogeography, and the contention that communities are organized in a predictable way (e.g., see Heatwole and Levins 1972a,b, 1973, Levins and Heatwole 1973). They found that equilibrium numbers of species were reached rapidly on small islands of the

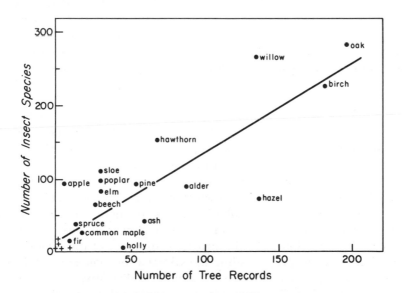

Fig. 18.3   The relationship between the abundance and length of time available (given by the number of records of Quarternary remains) for colonization by insects, and the number of herbivorous insect species present on trees in Britain. + indicates numbers of insects on introduced tree species. From Southwood 1961, by permission of Blackwell Scientific Publications.

Puerto Rican Bank and that species turnover rates were high. In spite of the high immigration and extinction rates trophic structure of the community remained remarkably stable, suggesting that only species that could interact effectively with other existing species were able to establish on these islands. The interactive phase in colonization is important in sorting species.

This approach to community study need not apply only to oceanic islands. Janzen (1968, 1973a) has emphasized that the host plants of insects can be regarded as islands in space and in time. Southwood's data support this view and Opler's (1974) study, "Oaks as evolutionary islands for leaf-mining insects," is particularly relevant. Many more studies on island biogeography of insects are needed. A plant crop is clearly an island and many natural areas form islands on continents. Vuilleumier (1970) has published a paper, "Insular biogeography in continental regions," dealing with the paramo islands in Ecuador, Colombia, and Venezuela in relation to bird communities. Brown (1971) also regarded mountain tops as islands in relation to mammal communities. Although not alluding to island biogeography specifically, Mani (1968) provides much information on insects at high altitudes, of interest to the continental island biogeographer. Culver et al. (1973) have studied the islands that are available to cave-dwelling organisms. Thus "island biogeography" is just as important to mainland situations, since many communities represent effective islands. For an application of island biogeography to agricultural crops and pest management see Price and Waldbauer (1975).

For any given community five major factors can be identified that determine the number of species it contains. First of all there is the historical factor: the time it has been available for colonization. Then two external factors are important: the number of potential colonizers; that is the size of the species pool from which colonization can occur, and the distance from the source of colonizers. Finally there are two internal factors that relate to the structural diversity of the biotope: the size of the biotope, which influences the structural diversity of the biotope, and interaction between species leading to extinction of some and survival of others, which depends in part on the structural diversity.

The factors within the community that regulate the number of species present are discussed here and external factors are discussed in Chapter 21. There is a fundamental need for species to exploit an unshared resource. Therefore the numbers of species depends on the diversity of resources within the biotope. Since this diversity within biotopes of similar structure is likely to be similar, the number of species they can support should be similar, just as MacArthur and MacArthur (1961) have shown for bird species and Patrick and Strawbridge (1963) for diatoms in waters of similar quality. In Chapter 15 it was seen that the range of quality in a resource was important in determining the number of species that could coexist on that type of resource. It might be argued, however, that the larger the quantity of the resource the more species it can sustain. This is not supported by Rozensweig's (1971) models, where increasing a resource (enrichment) decreased the stability of a two-species system, and therefore increased the chance of one of the species going extinct. Similar results were obtained by Riebesell (1974) when he considered enrichment in relation to competition models. Also Patrick and Strawbridge (1963) argue that dominant species are often characteristic of faunas and floras that have an excess of nutrients, or light, or water. For example, temperate forests have one or two dominant species and here the sites have reserve nutrients, whereas in the tropical forests many species are supported on lateritic soils of very low nutrient status. Woodwell's (1974) studies suggest that where nutrients are in short supply niche segregation of species is necessarily greater. Terborgh (1973) argues that the high numbers of species seen in deserts of North America is the result of the diversity of ways in which plants have evolved to partition the water which is in short supply. Stephensen (1973) has shown that increased fertilization of old field communities reduced species richness and evenness, and Yoda et al. (1963) found that less fertile soils supported a larger number of small plants than fertile soils. Pollution frequently has a similar effect since large amounts of one substance are deposited. For example, Harman (1972) found that pollutants reduced the number of benthic substrate types and therefore reduced the number of freshwater molluscs present.

Thus large quantities of a resource favor one or two species and not others, so that dominance develops and species diversity is reduced. This was seen in Chapter 15 on species packing where as host density increased, *Pleolophus basizonus* became dominant and several other species of cocoon parasitoid became extinct, or reduced in numbers. The diversity changed as in Fig. 18.4. There is close similarity between this trend and the colonization curve for an island community. Therefore within the community the quantity and quality ranges of resources have an organizing influence, and these will be influenced in turn by the size of the habitat, which is intimately connected with the structural diversity of the habitat. The quality range of resources influences the number of species supported while the quantity of the resource affects the population size of each species (Fig. 18.5 and 18.6). Therefore the internal factors

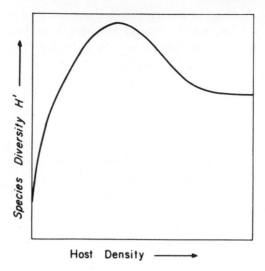

Fig. 18.4 The trend in species diversity in the parasitoid fauna as the food resources (host cocoons) become more abundant. The reason for the decline in diversity is the increased dominance of one species, *Pleolophus basizonus* (see Fig. 15.8 for details. See Chapter 19 for definition of H'). After Price 1970c.

influencing the number of species that can exist in a community can be redefined more accurately: (1) the number of resources available, (2) the quality range (or size range) in each resource, and (3) the quantity of a resource in each quality category.

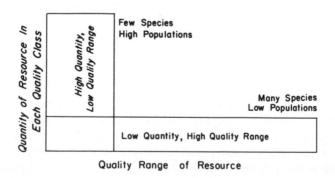

Fig. 18.5 Relationships between abundance of resources and range of resources in a community, and their effects on numbers of species present and population sizes. Quality ranges may include size ranges of seeds for granivores, nectar depths in flowers for pollinators, range of bark thicknesses available to bark beetles, and such. The two extremes in resource distribution have equal amounts of energy available.

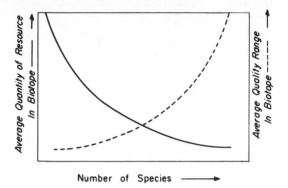

Fig. 18.6 Relationships between the quantity and quality of resources in a community and the number of species that will coexist in that community. Average quantity of resource relates to the average of amounts in each quality class.

Until many more data on the structure of habitats are obtained we are forced to leave this line of analysis, which is comparable to the component analysis approach that Holling used in studying predation. More general approaches to community organization must be used, and Hairston (1959) briefly reviews the different ways of using species abundance as an index to the type of organization in the community. For example, early plant ecologists such as Gleason (1922, 1925) and Cain (1938) saw a way of avoiding the association concept difficulties by plotting the number of species per unit area. If repeated samples are taken in the same community then the number of species collected, as the sample area increased, would increase to a plateau. This would be the limit of species for that community (Fig. 18.7). As the sample area

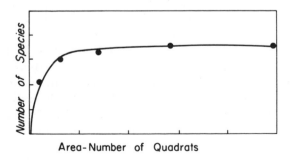

Fig. 18.7 Species-area curve in which the cumulative number of species recorded in successive samples increases as more quadrat samples are taken, up to a plateau at which all species have been discovered.

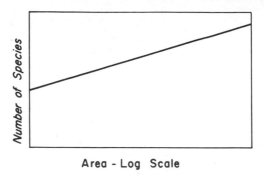

Fig. 18.8   The straight line relationship between number of species, plotted on an arithmetic scale and the area sampled, on a logarithmic scale.

increased, other communities would be sampled and the number of species would continue to increase, and Gleason (1922) found that the number of species increases linearly with the logarithm of the sample area (Fig. 18.8).

In fact species can be added indefinitely so long as new biotopes are added, and thus area is closely related to the number of species, but not directly. MacArthur and Wilson (1967) say in their book *The theory of Island Biogeography*: "Theories, like islands, are often reached by stepping stones. The 'species-area' curves are such stepping stones. Our ultimate theory of species diversity may not mention area, because area seldom exerts a direct effect on a species presence. More often area allows a large enough sample of habitats, which in turn control species occurrence. However, in the absence of good information on diversity of habitats, we first turn to island areas." They give an example from Darlington's (1957) study on the number of species of amphibians and reptiles in relation to the area of the West Indian Islands (Fig. 18.9). As a general rule of thumb it seems that if area is increased by a factor of 10 the number of species found is doubled: 10 miles^2 gives 7 species; 100 miles^2 gives 14 species; and 100,000 miles^2 gives 112 species. It does look as if the idea of a limit to species per biotope can be extrapolated into extensive areas containing many communities, and from community ecology we merge imperceptibly into biogeography. This is exemplified by the title of MacArthur's (1972) last book, *Geographical Ecology*.

But it was concluded earlier that there are three important components of the biotope: number, quantity, and quality of resources; these influence not only the number of species but also the abundance of each species. Thus any analysis of community organization should include the number of species and their relative abundance. Such an analysis has

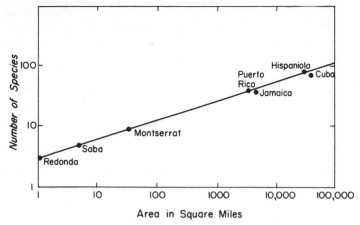

Fig 18.9   Species-area relationship for the amphibians and reptiles of the West Indian Islands. From MacArthur and Wilson 1967, data from Darlington 1957.

been made by Fisher, Corbet, and Williams (1943) and Williams (1944, 1947a). Williams used a so-called random sample of Macrolepidoptera caught in a light-trap at Rothamsted Experimental Station. He identified 15,609 moths to species of which there were 240. The frequency distribution of numbers of individuals per species is given in Fig. 18.10. For

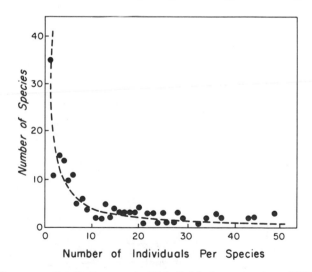

Fig. 18.10   Frequency distribution, up to 50 individuals per species, of Williams' light-trap catches of moths at Rothamsted Experimental Station. The distribution is approximated by the dotted line which resembles a hyperbola. After Williams, in Fisher, Corbet, and Williams 1943.

example, 35 species were represented by a single individual each, 115 species by 10 or fewer individuals, 205 species by 100 or fewer, 35 species had over 100 individuals, and 1 species contained 2349 individuals. This distribution looks as if it might be represented by a hyperbola, with n_1 representing the number of species with 1 individual, and the series would be

$$n_1, \frac{n_1}{2}, \frac{n_1}{3}, \frac{n_1}{4}, \ldots$$

But a hyperbola never reaches the axis, which means that there have to be an infinite number of species in the sample and the number of individuals per species must reach below one. These requirements clearly are not met and a more realistic series was proposed by Fisher which fitted the data well (Fig. 18.11), that is the logarithmic series:

$$n_1, \frac{n_1 x}{2}, \frac{n_1 x^2}{3}, \frac{n_1 x^3}{4}, \ldots$$

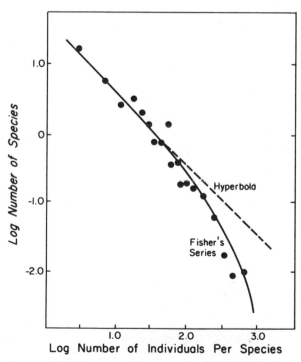

Fig. 18.11 Logarithmic frequency distribution of means of observed values of Williams' light-trap catches of moths showing how the hyperbolic series overestimates the number of species with many individuals. After Williams, in Fisher, Corbet, and Williams 1943 from *Journal of Animal Ecology* by permission of Blackwell Scientific Publications.

where n_1 is the number of species with 1 individual and x is a number less than 1. In later papers and his book (1964), Williams has applied the logarithmic series to all sorts of situations. But unfortunately it is an empirical mathematical description with no apparent biological explanation.

In 1948 Preston proposed a different method of representing the same data because he objected to the fact that the logarithmic series requires more individuals of very low abundance than any other category. Preston argued that there appear to be no more very rare species than very abundant species, and that most species seem to have an intermediate position. In 1962 Preston extended his theory to discuss the species-area curves from archepelagoes. Preston (1948) pointed out that commonness is a relative measure, and we talk of a species being twice as common as another. Therefore a natural series of groups representing commonness would run:

Species group	A	B	C	D	E	F	G	H	etc.
Number of specimens per species	1	2	4	8	16	32	64	128	etc.

This is a geometric or logarithmic series, and Preston shows that the abundance of species appears to be a simple normal distribution on this series, that is a "lognormal" distribution. To permit grouping of species that are similarly common or rare it is convenient to make the numbers of the logarithmic series the limits of the groups as follows:

Species group	A	B	C	D	E	F	G	
Limits of abundance groups	1	2	4	8	16	32	64	128

so that all species with 9 to 15 specimens fall into group D. The intervals delimiting groups can be called octaves, since they bear a $1:2$ relationship, just as the wavelengths of C and C' on a musical scale. To plot Williams' moth data, for example, we find the number of individuals per species, assign the species to its appropriate octave, count the number of species in each octave, and plot the total species per octave on the ordinate, using the scale of octaves of increasing commonness as the abscissa (Fig. 18.12).

Now if species abundances are distributed in a lognormal way we have a very useful method of determining the universe from which this sample was taken. The curve obtained for Williams' data is typical of insect data in that the veil line is close to the mode of the lognormal distribution. But more easily sampled animals such as birds are represented by much more of the lognormal curve; the veil line is moved back (Fig. 18.13). This suggests that increasing the sampling effort will reveal more rare species, and we can predict how many species are missing in the sample. For example, by doubling the sampling effort, twice as many

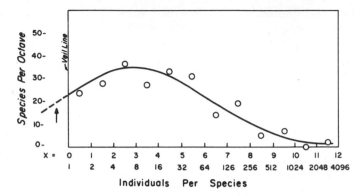

Fig 18.12   Preston's lognormal plot of Williams data on moths showing the frequency distribution per octave. The limits of each octave are defined by $x = \log_2 i$, where i is the number of individuals per species. Presumably, by doubling the sampling effort the veil line will be moved one octave to the left. From Preston 1948.

individuals per species will be collected and all species will move to the next octave, and some more very rare species will appear from under the veil line as a single specimen per species. The veil line merely represents an artificial limit to the distribution imposed by being able to sample only whole individuals. If one could sample 1/2, 1/4, 1/8 individuals then the veil line would presumably be unnecessary.

As entomologists, where we can collect vast numbers of individuals and large numbers of species in certain taxa, it is worth studying this distribution more with new data to see whether it is a realistic description of commonness and rarity in a community, and to try to understand why this distribution should exist. This is an important point to study because the ways in which species divide up the available energy in the

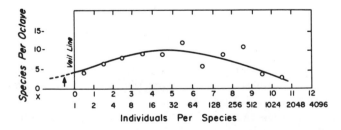

Fig. 18.13   Preston's lognormal plot of Saunder's breeding birds in Quaker Run Valley in western New York State. Note the more complete normal distribution on the log plot than in Fig. 18.12 illustrated by these animals that are easier to sample and therefore more completely sampled than insects. From Preston 1948.

community can be observed. It is important also to remember that a line can be fitted to any distribution data, and it does not mean that it is a good model, nor that the explanation for the fit is necessarily the only explanation. Pielou (1969) and Poole (1974) should be consulted for critical analyses of the models discussed in this chapter.

MacArthur (1957) argued that it is more fruitful to predict the relative abundance of species on the basis of simple biological hypotheses and to compare the predictions with what is observed in the field. For opportunistic species it is hard to obtain any biologically meaningful model, because their abundance depends very much on rapidly changing nonstable situations. As a new resource becomes available they will colonize it briefly and then leave as competition increases, or as the new resource is exhausted. Thus no steady state is achieved as the populations are not residents, and the abundance of an opportunistic species is not related to the presence of other species in the habitat. Therefore we must turn to equilibrium species to find ways of predicting their abundance. These are species that live together in a community and therefore they share a set of resources, at least one of which is limiting. MacArthur suggests that there are two possible ways in which this limiting resource can be divided up among the species. In the first case he assumes that the total number of individuals of all species together is constant. Thus an increase in one species will decrease the numbers of another species. That is, niches cannot overlap. Thus the resource can be conceived as a stick and the boundaries of niches are marked on the stick at random. Thus each segment represents niche size. If this stick is then broken at each boundary some long segments and some short result. Then the segments can be arranged in order from the longest to the shortest. The lengths of the segments, or the abundance of the species concerned, should be distributed according to the following series, which gives the expected proportion of the jth species from the rarest to the most abundant (see Poole 1974):

$$\frac{N_j}{N} = \frac{1}{S}\sum_{i=1}^{j}\frac{1}{S+1-i}$$

where N is the total number of individuals, N_j the number in the jth species, and S the total number of species present. Thus if 20 species are present the series is:

$$\frac{N_j}{N} = \frac{1}{20}\left[\frac{1}{20+1-1} + \frac{1}{20+1-2} + \frac{1}{20+1-3}\cdots + \frac{1}{20+1-j}\right]$$

Thus the proportion per species in the total number of individuals increases as the series is extended, but the increase is not rapid. Plotting the abundance of species according to the rank of their importance a distribution is obtained as in Fig. 18.14. This has been called MacArthur's broken stick model or the random niche boundary hypothesis (Whittaker 1965, 1970b). The alternative hypothesis is to assume that the abundance of different species is truly independent and that niches can overlap, and the amount of overlap does not affect the species concerned. Since Mac-Arthur found no data to fit this model and since all evidence points to an interdependence of species in the community there is no point in developing it here.

One other hypothesis is worth examining—what Whittaker (1970b, 1972) calls the niche preemption hypothesis. Here successful species preempt part of the niche space, whereas less successful species occupy what is left. If the dominant species occupies 50% of the niche space, the second-ranked species 50% of what remains, and the third species 50% of what is left from the first two species, a geometric series of abundances results. This plots as a straight line on a semilog plot (Fig. 18.14). Finally if these models are compared with the distribution that Preston predicts, the lognormal distribution, we can see how these predict actual situations. The lognormal distribution predicts a very few very important spe-

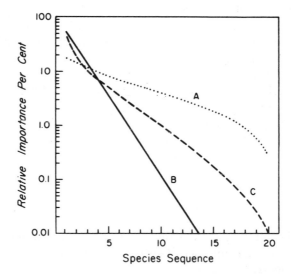

Fig. 18.14 Dominance-diversity curves derived from three different distributions. (*a*) The broken stick or random niche boundary model of MacArthur. (*b*) The niche preemption model of Motomura (1932) named by Whittaker (1970b). (*c*) The lognormal model of Preston (1948). Importance values may be numbers of individuals, biomass or energy content. These are plotted on a log scale against the rank of importance from the most important species to the least important. From Whittaker 1965, 1970b.

cies, many species of moderate importance, and very few very rare species (Fig. 18.14). Whittaker (1970b, 1972) points out that there are data available now, where some fit (*A*), some fit (*B*), and some fit (*C*). So it is not a question of one being correct and the others being false, and it becomes important to understand when a particular model is likely to be applicable.

Model *A*, the random niche boundary hypothesis, or the broken stick model appears to fit small samples of taxonomically related animals from homogeneous communities; for example, the nesting birds of a limited area of forest. It seems to apply to higher animals, with stable populations and relatively long life cycles, with contest competition having an important organizing influence. Numerical dominance is not strongly developed, since the abundance of the most abundant species is not much greater than that of the last ranked species.

In Model *B*, as expected, some plant communities can be fitted to the series derived from the niche preemption hypothesis. In severe environments with a small number of species involved dominance is strongly developed, for example, in subalpine fir forest in the Great Smoky Mountains, Tennessee. This therefore represents the other extreme to Model *A* where dominance was not strongly developed, for here each species is much more abundant than the next in rank.

Model *C* seems to fit communities that are very rich in species such as the cove forest in the Great Smoky Mountains, or tropical rain forest communities, when taken from a homogeneous area, or samples of insect communities. We have also seen that the sample of moths in a light trap, obviously a sample from a range of environments and communities, fits the lognormal distribution too. Thus the lognormal distribution may be a composite of the other two models that may exist in single communities represented in the sample.

One word of caution is needed in the light of Griffiths' (1973) experience with selection of units to be used for calculation of importance values. When he expressed importance values in terms of numbers they fitted the geometric series. When expressed as biomass they fitted the lognormal series, although the slope was hardly steeper than that of the broken stick model. The selection of parameters for use in these dominance-diversity relations must be made carefully.

It may be concluded that (1) the models that fit the data available reinforce the view that basically species divide up the niche space relative to each other and thereby reduce competition. (2) The way in which this space is divided varies according to the organisms involved and the habitats they exist in. (3) The relative abundance of species in a community and the expression of dominance in the communities seems to range from a geometric distribution (B) through lognormal (C) to the random boundary model (A), with the expression of dominance highest in (B).

As Whittaker (1972) points out these models have not been as useful as we would have liked since interpretation of the processes that result in these distributions is "a tactic of weak inference." Thus it is necessary to look at simpler communities to gain more directly an understanding of the forces working in community organization. The value of studying the relatively simple insect faunae on families of poisonous plants was mentioned in Chapter 3. For example Root (1973 and references therein) and his associates have studied the community organization on collards, members of the family Cruciferae, which contain mustard oils. Even simpler communities may be found in hot springs, and several workers have analyzed organization here (e.g., Brock 1967, 1970, Brock and Brock 1966, 1968, 1971, Brock, Wiegert, and Brock 1969, Stockner 1971, Wiegert and Mitchell 1973, Zeikus and Brock 1972). These examples, and further developments in studies on these simpler communities should be followed carefully. The relative abundance of species is discussed further in the next chapter.

Progress in understanding community organization will be ensured best by detailed studies of individuals as they interact with other individuals of the same and other species (e.g., Colwell 1973, Gilbert 1975). Gilbert (1975) provides an impressive example of the incisive nature of this approach. The brief account given here must make many short cuts and will create a rather crude picture of the interactions involved. From detailed studies on the biology of the butterflies in the genus *Heliconius*, their larval food plants, *Passiflora*, and their adult food plants, *Anguria*, which provide pollen and nectar, Gilbert was able to determine how these coevolving species interacted to produce organization at the individual, population and community levels (Fig. 18.15). *Heliconius* butterflies are long lived, since they are able to digest pollen rich in amino acids (Gilbert 1972). They have a highly developed visual system, and learning ability. They roost gregariously and trap-line for the widely dispersed *Anguria* plants in flower. Young butterflies learn routes by following older members of the roost and regular roosting at the same site enables the first plants on the trap-line to be found in the early morning when pollen and nectar supplies are high but when light conditions are very poor. Thus there is strong selection for male *Anguria* individuals that produce large inflorescences that provide open flowers over a prolonged period,

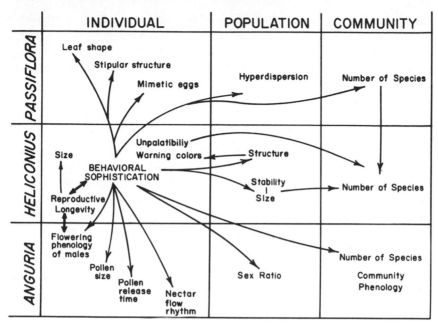

Fig. 18.15 A summary of interactions between *Heliconius* butterflies, species of *Passiflora* (Passifloraceae) which are hosts to larvae, and the dioecious species of *Anguria* (Cucurbitaceae) which provide pollen and nectar to the butterflies. From Gilbert 1975.

large amounts of pollen, and large pollen grains that can be utilized easily by *Heliconius* adults. Female flowering may be short, inflorescences small, and much energy is channeled into fruit and seed production. Because of heavy herbivore pressure plants are widely dispersed and few species are found in the same community. In addition, in coexisting *Anguria* species temporal differences in anther dehiscence and nectar flow are apparent so only few species can segregate adequately within a day. These factors and the inconspicuous nature of the flowers makes flowers of this species a poor food source unless visual acuity and learning ability for trap lining are highly developed as in *Heliconius* butterflies. Since female flowers of *Anguria* are visited mainly "by mistake" by female *Heliconius,* a high proportion of females in the population would enable the highly intelligent pollinators to discriminate against them. The sex ratio (about 10:1) is actually heavily skewed toward males allowing the mimetic female flowers to receive sufficient visits to ensure pollination. Thus Gilbert explains factors involving the evolution of individual, population, and community characteristics of *Anguria* species as shown in Fig. 18.15.

In a similar fashion *Heliconius* spp. influence evolutionary trends in the *Passiflora* hosts of the larvae. A highly visual parent searching for food for its larvae may cue in on leaf shape of the host plant. Gilbert documented the remarkable diversity of leaf shapes present among sympatric species of *Passiflora*, presumably resulting from heavy selection for divergent patterns under the influence of a visually searching herbivore. Species diversity of *Passiflora* in a community may be limited to the number of shapes that are sufficiently different not to be confused by hunting *Heliconius* females. Since *Heliconius* species are quite host specific, this in turn limits the number of *Heliconius* species in a community. A remarkable adaptation that reduces herbivore attack in some species of *Passiflora* is the development of stipule tips that mimic eggs of *Heliconius* and give the impression that the host has been preempted. *Heliconius* larvae are cannibalistic and females search potential host plants carefully before ovipositing and avoid plants with an egg present. In addition extrafloral nectaries on many species of *Passiflora* attract ants, wasps, and egg parasitoids of *Heliconius*, all effective defenders of the plant. Heavy herbivore pressure and the effectiveness of searching for hosts has resulted in the hyperdispersion of *Passiflora* populations.

Other results of interaction between *Heliconius, Anguria* and *Passiflora* are given in Fig. 18.15. The study highlights the importance of a detailed understanding of individuals in ecological research (cf., Chapter 1 and 9). The success of Gilbert's study in leading to an understanding of community interactions should encourage the initiation of many similar projects in many different community types.

Chapter 19

DIVERSITY
AND STABILITY

$\mathbf{D}$iversity is most easily defined by use of a formula. Many indices of diversity have been proposed (see Pielou 1969, Poole 1974), but the one most commonly used is the Shannon-Weaver diversity index H', where

$$H' = -\Sigma p_i \log_e p_i$$

and p_i is the proportion of the ith species in the total sample. If two species are unevenly abundant their diversity is lower than when they are equally abundant (Table 19.1). Also adding species increases the

Table 19.1 Examples of how diversity measured by H′ changes with the evenness of distribution of species and the number of species present (or species richness).

	Sp 1	Sp 2	Sp 3	H'
2 species	90	10		0.33
2 species	50	50		0.69
3 species	80	10	10	0.70
3 species	33.3	33.3	33.3	1.10

diversity so that a community with three species is likely to have a diversity higher than a community with only two species, even though the latter may be evenly distributed. Thus number of species (species richness) in the community and their evenness in abundance are the two parameters that define H'. As species are added, diversity increases, and as species become evenly distributed in abundance, diversity increases. In a diverse situation species cannot be very dominant, and in a low diversity community one or two species will be much more abundant than others. These trends may be seen by comparing Figs. 15.8 and 18.4 which relate to the same study by Price (1970c). Species diversity was highest where four species were most evenly abundant at about two to three hosts per 30 cm², and then diversity declined rapidly when two species went extinct and one species increased through its competitive dominance at high host density. This index is commonly used because it is easily calculated, it includes the two components of diversity that are intuitively important, and these components can be readily separated since the number of species can be counted, and their evenness, J', can be estimated from the formula

$$J' = \frac{H'}{H'_{max}} = \frac{H'}{\log_e S}$$

where S is the number of species present. H'_{max} may be calculated also by assuming that all p_i's are equal in the calculation of H' (see Lloyd and Ghelardi 1964, Lloyd, Zar, and Karr 1968). A frequently used alternative to H' is to simply use the number of species present when abundance data are lacking.

How does diversity change from one community to another? Whittaker (1969) gives a good summary of the way in which plant species diversity changes in response to many different gradients in time and space. As far as plant succession is concerned he says that diversity increases during succession, but may in many cases decrease from some stage before the climax into the climax itself. He gives ten references to this trend. In a plant succession from bare ground caused by fire to a mature oak forest on Long Island, New York, Whittaker and Woodwell (1968, 1969) found the trends shown in Fig. 19.1. That is, the more extreme early stages of succession have fewer plants adapted to such extreme environmental conditions, species diversity, production, and biomass are low, but these rise to a plateau (cf., Fig. 17.7). Species diversity reaches a maximum at about 50 years in the early forest stage when some of the grasses and forbs of earlier successional stages are still present. These eventually fail in the community and the diversity declines slightly.

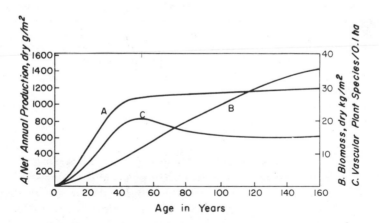

Fig. 19.1 Trends in production (*a*), biomass (*b*), and plant species diversity (richness) (*c*) in forest succession after fire on Long Island, New York. Data from Whittaker and Woodwell 1968, 1969. Reprinted with permission of Macmillan Publishing Co., Inc. from Communities and Ecosystems by R. H. Whittaker. Copyright © 1970 by Robert H. Whittaker.

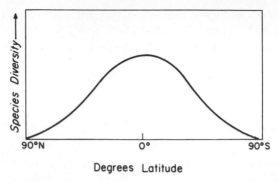

Fig. 19 2   Trend in species diversity from the north pole (90°N), across the equator (0°), to the south pole (90°S).

A similar trend to that of the first 50 years in the forest studied by Whittaker and Woodwell can be seen in species diversity on a latitudinal gradient from the high harsh latitudes to low latitudes with an equable climate (Fig. 19.2). This trend is shown by insects, molluscs, vertebrates, plants, and many other taxa (e.g., Table 19.2), although fresh water inver-

Table 19.2   Latitudinal trends in numbers of species (richness) in insect taxa showing an increase with decreasing latitude.

Beetles*		Ants†		Dragonflies††	
Labrador	169 sp	Alaska	7 sp	Nearctic	59 sp
Massachusetts	2000 sp	Iowa	73 sp	Neotropical	135 sp
Florida	4000 sp	Trinidad	134 sp		

* From Clarke (1954).
† From Fischer (1960).
†† From Williams (1964).

tebrates and phytoplankton seem to be exceptions. These sorts of trends have for a long time fascinated biogeographers and ecologists. Why is there such a diversity of species in the tropics? What are the critical factors that promote, or permit, this diversity? How is natural selection affecting community organization? Connell and Orias (1964) and Pianka (1966) have summarized some of the theories that have been proposed to explain this diversity gradient, and here Pianka's explanations are followed. Wilson (1974) also considers some of the theories.

1. **The time theory.** Proponents of this theory assume that all com-communities tend to diversify with time, and therefore the older communities have more species than do newer ones. For example, temperate regions have much younger communities than do tropical regions because of recent glaciations. Thus temperate faunas and floras are impoverished (*a*) because species that could live in temperate regions have not migrated back from unglaciated areas; and (*b*) because species have not had time to evolve to enable exploitation of temperate areas. Southwood's (1961) data on insects in trees in Britain support this theory (see Chapter 18 and Fig. 18.3). The longer the time available, the more species adapt to the resource. Also Wilson's (1969) hypothesis on the four stages in community development, the noninteractive, interactive, assortative, and evolutionary, subscribes to the same view. Simpson (1964b) has argued against this theory on the grounds that warm temperate regions have had a long undisturbed history, from the Eocene to the present, and yet they contain fewer species than the tropics. Also if the time theory were correct, the steepest gradient in species diversity should occur in recently glaciated temperate zones. In North American mammals at least, the gradient is not steep, so that the theory is not supported by data on mammals. More data are needed, but Wilson (1974) should be consulted for a reanalysis.

2. **Spatial heterogeneity.** There might be a general increase in environmental complexity on the latitudinal gradient toward the tropics. The more heterogeneous and complex the physical environment becomes, the more complex and diverse will be the plant and animal communities supported by that environment. Certainly total diversity due to topographic relief, and consequently the number of habitats, increase toward the tropics. Temperature gradients and moisture gradients (ranges) are much longer in the tropics than in temperate regions. This is seen in Chapter 21 on biogeography when the Holdridge (1947, 1967, Holdridge et al. 1971) system of classifying world plant formations is considered. Unfortunately this diversity of habitats does not explain why there should be so much diversity within habitats in the tropics. Vegetative heterogeneity presumably depends on microhabitat diversity that has not been studied, although Janzen's (1967c) paper refers to this and invokes this as the causative agent in restricting plant dispersal in the tropics, thus increasing diversity. But Janzen's paper is better dealt with under climatic stability. Once plant species diversity increases, then the animal species diversity follows, according to MacArthur and MacArthur's (1961) study (see

Chapter 15), as the structural diversity of the community will increase. So some emphasis should be placed on plant species diversity.

3. **The competition hypothesis.** Dobzhansky (1950) and Williams (1964) have proposed that natural selection in temperate zones is controlled mainly by the physical environment, whereas in the tropics biological competition is more important in evolution. Therefore in the tropics there is a much greater restriction of food types and habitat requirements, and thus more species can coexist in a given habitat. Tropical species will be more finely adapted and have narrower niche exploitation patterns than those in temperate regions. In temperate zones mortality is often catastrophic and indiscriminate, that is, density-independent, such as drought and cold, and r selection for increased fecundity and development rate will be important, rather than selection for competitive ability or K selection seen in tropical species (see Chapter 8).

4. **The predation hypothesis.** Paine (1966) has claimed that there are more predators and parasites in the tropics, and that these suppress prey populations sufficiently to reduce competition between them. The reduced competition then permits the coexistence of additional prey species, which therefore permit additional predators in the system. According to this hypothesis competition among prey organisms is less intense in the tropics than in temperate areas, and this predicts the opposite to the competition hypothesis. However there is evidence to support the predation hypothesis. Grice and Hart (1962) have shown that the proportion of predatory species in the marine zooplankton increases along a latitudinal diversity gradient. Janzen (1970, 1973b) and Harper (1969) also present information suggesting that herbivores, particularly plant predators, are necessary agents in maintaining or permitting high plant species diversity.

5. **Climatic stability.** Klopfer (1959), Klopfer and MacArthur (1960), and others have suggested that regions with stable climates allow the evolution of finer specializations and adaptations than do regions with more changeable climate, because resources remain more constant in the stable conditions. Just as in the competition hypothesis smaller niches are predicted, and therefore closer species packing. Although Janzen (1967c) says that his paper, "Why mountain passes are higher in the tropics," is not an attempt to explain tropical species diversity, his paper clearly relates to the climatic stability hypothesis. Janzen suggests that greater sensitivity to change is promoted by less frequent contact with change. Therefore in a stable environment small changes in environment will be as effective as large changes in temperate regions. Since there are more small changes in a habitat

than large ones this will result in more species being able to colonize that habitat and coexist in it. Sanders (1968, 1969) found more species in deep sea environments where conditions are relatively stable than in shallow waters where physical factors are much more variable. Randolph (1973) showed that snails tended to be generalists in variable environments and more specialized in stable environments. The fact that tropical environments are more predictable than are temperate ones is shown in Costa Rica for example. Although the climate is much more uniform than in temperate regions, eight seasons in the year are recognized, as opposed to four in temperate latitudes. The more precise fitting of population activities to more predictable environmental conditions, the less will be the ability to tolerate different conditions outside the usual habitat. Therefore the smaller will be the change required to form a barrier to colonization which leads to narrow niche requirements and many species per unit area.

6. **The productivity hypothesis.** This states that greater production results in greater diversity; that is, a broader base to the energy pyramid permits more species in that pyramid. However in Chapter 18 on community development, structure, and organization it was seen that increase of any resource that is normally limiting leads to decreased stability and species diversity. If increased production is obtained by increasing the number of species coexisting then this clearly will increase species diversity in the first trophic level and all subsequent trophic levels. But this does not resolve the problem of why more species coexist in lower latitudes. However, Connell and Orias (1964) followed an argument that is conceptually satisfying which correlates high productivity with increased speciation. They considered whole ecosystems that are mature and that are not limited by absolute physical space (see also the hypothesis discussed next, that area is a major factor in biotic diversity). A simplified version of their argument is given in Fig. 19.3 where the comparison is between a stable environment (the climatic stability hypothesis is involved) and an unstable environment.

Three additional hypotheses have been advanced which were not dealt with by Connell and Orias (1964) or Pianka (1966).

7. **Area available as primary source of species diversity.** Terborgh (1973) would agree with Connell and Orias (1964) that existence of a species over a large area increases the chances of isolation between populations with consequent speciation. Terborgh therefore argues that the largest areas of climatic similarity will thus have the great-

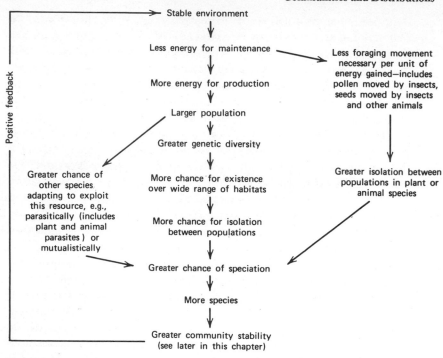

Fig. 19.3 A simplified representation of the hypothesis by Connell and Orias (1964) that greater production in stable environments leads to the evolution of more species.

est species diversity. He notes that there is symmetry of climates on a pole-to-pole gradient but only in the equatorial climatic zone do we see the symmetrically opposite climates adjacent. Therefore in area these contiguous zones must be larger than any other. In addition the temperature gradient between the equator and the poles is nonlinear because cloudiness at the equator reduces mean temperature, and cloud-free areas beyond this zone increase mean temperature relative to insolation (Fig. 19.4). Then by combining the areas with similar climate the amount of habitat available for species to spread into can be estimated. The difference between equatorial and temperate zones is striking (Fig. 19.5), with a correspondingly greater chance for speciation to proceed in the former. This difference can be appreciated also by looking at the Holdridge system of biome classification discussed in Chapter 21 on biogeography, if one remembers that log scales are used in the plot. Terborgh brings together enough supporting evidence to make this hypothesis worthy of detailed consideration. Terborgh's hypothesis is very similar to Dar-

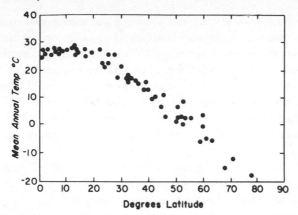

Fig. 19.4 Mean annual temperatures (°C) of low elevation, mesic, continental locations on a latitudinal gradient. Note the wide band of similar temperatures between 20°N and 20°S of the equator. After J. Terborgh. On the notion of favorableness in plant ecology. Amer. Natur. 107:481–501, published by the University of Chicago Press. © 1973 by the University of Chicago. All rights reserved.

lington's (1959) contention that most dominant animals have usually evolved in the largest areas and that species tend to diffuse out from these equatorial zones, thus creating a species diversity gradient.

8. **Resource limitation.** In Chapter 18 we saw that Patrick and Strawbridge (1963) suggested that the high diversity of plants in tropical forests may be due to the inability of species to develop dominance

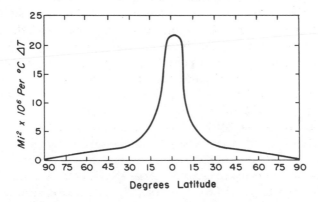

Fig. 19.5 The millions of square miles of earth's surface between 1°C isotherms of mean annual temperature as a function of latitude. Note the much greater area of surface around the equator. Considerations of land masses only would change the pattern little. From J. Terborgh. On the notion of favorableness in plant ecology. Amer. Natur. 107:481–501, published by the University of Chicago Press. © 1973 by the University of Chicago. All rights reserved.

380 Communities and Distributions

in soils of very low nutrient status. Low nutrient status is ensured by high temperatures and high rainfall with consequent rapid recycling or leaching of nutrients. Thus the theory contrasts with the competition theory, since here competition is thought of as being suppressed by lack of sufficient nutrient resources. However Woodwell's (1974) studies suggest that because of nutrient limitation niche specialization is increased, and more species can coexist as a result. The resource limitation and competition hypotheses become closely linked.

9. **Animal pollinators.** In humid parts of the world, particularly the tropics, wind pollination is ineffective and most plants are pollinated by animals—insects, birds, and bats. Even some grasses, that are typically wind pollinated throughout most of the world, are probably pollinated by insects in the tropics (Bogdan 1962, Soderstrom and Calderon 1971, and references therein). Particularly with bee pollination the probability of reproductive isolation between plant populations is greatly increased with a resultant increase in speciation rates (see Grant 1949, Dressler 1968, Dodson et al. 1969, and Chapter 20 on pollination ecology). Increased speciation rates will produce greater species diversity in tropical regions where the proportion of animal pollinated plants is the highest.

No doubt other theories will be proposed and combinations of theories will provide convincing arguments in support of the development of latitudinal gradients. Much more field work must be done before we can determine which hypotheses or combinations of these are the most realistic. But there are many difficulties to be overcome, and the main one is to find the same or similar habitats over a considerable part of the latitudinal gradient so that direct comparisons can be made between the habitats in low and high latitudes. Here the mangrove islands that Wilson and Simberloff have been studying may provide a neat solution to the problem. Mangrove islands extend from about 27°N on the west coast of Florida down to about 23°S on the Brazilian coast. Islands of the same size provide habitats that are more or less identical except for the climatic component. If there is no difference in animal species diversity with latitude, then diversity must depend on plant species diversity and the search for causative agents could be narrowed. Therefore we can hope for some interesting new data on this problem of latitudinal gradients in species diversity which will relate to the time theory, the competition hypothesis, the predation hypothesis, climatic stabliity, and possibly the productivity hypothesis. Recent results indicate that animal species diversity does not seem to change with latitude on mangrove islands (Simberloff, personal communication), which suggests that the causes of plant species diversity alone must be understood. Given this possibility, and Baker's (1970) request for synthesis of hypotheses after he had considered those that relate to plant species diversity, a partial synthesis has been attempted (Fig. 19.6) drawing from the references already cited and from Smith (1973). Connell and Orias' hypothesis should be integrated with the figure but was omitted to avoid congestion. Most interactions have been discussed already in this chapter.

Why has the measurement and causation of diversity occupied a large part of ecological thinking? Primarily it is because of the long-held belief that diversity leads to stability and thus it is related to one of the central themes of ecology: homeostasis or balance in the system. May (1973a) considers that stability can be identified where there is a "tendency for population perturbations to damp out," thus "returning the system to some persistent configuration." Holling (1973) defines stability in the same way.

There is indeed evidence that diversity leads to stability. Pimentel (1961a) tested the concept experimentally by planting collards (*Brassica oleracea*), some in pure stands, and some in the middle of an old field community, so that the collards represented one species in about 300 species present in the mixed community. He sampled the arthropods each week for 15 weeks, so that the species abundance and trophic position in the community were known. Pimentel found that outbreaks of aphids, flea beetles, and Lepidoptera occurred in the single-species planting, but they were not observed in the mixed-species planting. The outbreaks were due to much higher numbers of pests and much longer persistence of populations. Although the actual causes of this difference were impossible to determine (but see Root, 1973, for a detailed analysis and hypotheses on similar systems), it appears that difficulty of host plant finding and the increased efficiency of predators and parasitoids in the mixed-species planting all contributed to the maintenance of population stability. Pimentel concluded that species diversity and complexity of association among species were essential to the stability of the community.

Paine (1966) has suggested that animal diversity is related to the number of predators in the system and their efficiency in preventing single species from monopolizing some important, limiting, requisite. In the marine rocky intertidal zone that he studied at Mukkaw Bay, Washington State, space was the main limiting factor as observed in Connell's

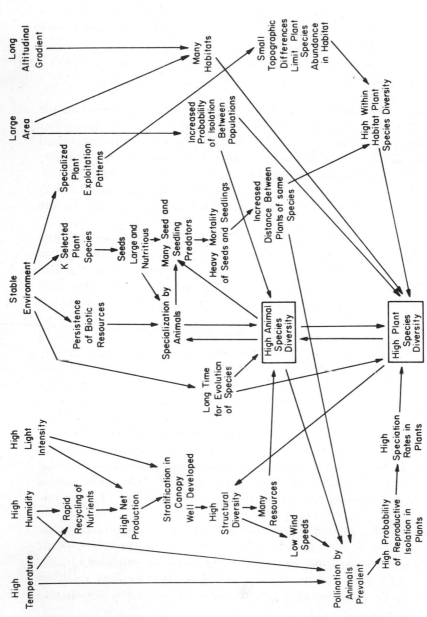

Fig. 19.6 Some factors that interact and possibly result in high plant and animal species diversity in the tropics where the environment is characterized by six physical factors listed at the top of the figure. A composite scheme derived from many sources cited in the text.

study of competition between *Balanus* and *Chthamalus*. Here the top predator was a starfish, *Pisaster*, which fed on chitons, limpets, bivalves, barnacles, and *Mitella* (a goose-necked barnacle). When *Pisaster* was present 15 species actually coexisted in the rocky intertidal zone. Paine set aside a treatment area that he kept free of *Pisaster* and observed the change in the community. The barnacle *Balanus glandula* rapidly became a dominant species, but within a year *Balanus* was being crowded out by the mussel, *Mytilus*, and the goose necked barnacle, *Mitella*. The space became occupied by the most efficient exploiters and the other species were outcompeted as one should predict for competition for a single large resource. After 3 years the community had been reduced in species from 15 to 8 just because of the removal of a single predator species, *Pisaster*, and the simplification process had not run its course. Several of the species that became extinct were not in the *Pisaster* food chain at all, but were crowded out by species released from predation, so that *Pisaster* had an extensive influence on the intertidal community. A species with this sort of control on community structure Paine later called a Keystone species (1969a,b, see later for definition). A top predator can play an important role in maintaning community diversity and stability by preventing overt competition in the trophic level below by always feeding on the most abundant species. However, where interactions between members of a trophic level are not intense, as among protozoa in pitcher plant communities, predators (mosquito larvae) tend to decrease diversity by their activity (Addicott 1974).

MacArthur (1955) attempted to quantify the stability of a hypothetical system by counting the number of possible routes along which energy can travel along the food chain, and by assuming energy flow is equal along each route (Fig. 19.7). For example, there are four routes each carrying 0.25 of the total energy in the food chains represented by Fig. 19.7a and b. Applying the formula for diversity (H') MacArthur calculated the stability of the system, indicating again that diversity and stability have been traditionally closely correlated concepts. In fact in this way MacArthur defined diversity and stability in the same way, whereas May's (1973a) definition of stability is preferable since then the two characteristics can be measured independently. As discussed later diverse communities may not be stable under certain influences so that the two terms should not be equated. The way in which MacArthur regarded stability suggests that the term complexity (cf., May 1973a) might be better substituted for it. However MacArthur's reasoning is

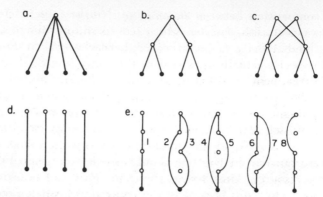

Fig. 19.7 Feeding links in a community between, for example, herbivores (●) and predators (○) where equal amounts of energy pass up each link. Thus arrangements such as in *a*, *b*, and *d* lead to equal stability in the system but stability in *c* is higher. In a five species system maximum stability is achieved as in *e* where all species can feed at all trophic levels below, providing eight routes up which energy can flow. Thus the system in *e* with five species is as stable as the system in *c* with eight species.

intuitively satisfying and will be followed here. Calculating the stability of the food chains in Fig. 19.7*a* and *b*:

$$\text{stability} = -\Sigma p_i \log_e p_i = -(4 \times 0.25 \times \log 0.25) = \log 4 = 1.38$$

By adding another predator that eats all prey (Fig. 19.7*c*), the number of routes doubles to eight, and stability = log 8 = 2.08. A notable result is that the same stability as in examples *a* and *b* can be achieved by four highly specialized predators each feeding on a single species of prey (Fig. 19.7*d*).

There are several properties of food chains that are worthy of note. (1) Stability increases as the number of links increases. (2) If the number of prey species for each predator species remains constant, an increase in number of species in the community will increase the stability. (3) A given stability can be achieved either by a large number of species, each with a fairly restricted diet, or by a smaller number of species each eating a wide variety of other species. (4) The maximum possible stability for *m* species would arise when there are *m* trophic levels with one species on each, eating all species below. If *m* = 5 there are eight possible paths up which energy can travel (Fig. 19.7*e*). Minimum stability would arise with one species eating all the others, these being on the same trophic level. For example, in a five species system there are four possible paths up which energy can travel (Fig. 19.7*a*).

From these properties of stability it is clear that restricted diet lowers stability, but this restriction is essential for efficient exploitation. Also efficiency and stability are the two features required for survival under natural selection. Efficiency enables species to outcompete others but stability in a community enables individual populations to outsurvive populations in less stable ones. Thus there must be an evolutionary compromise between efficiency and stability, which can be solved in two ways. (1) Where there are few species stability is hard to achieve. Species have to eat a wide variety of foods on many trophic levels. This pattern is seen in arctic regions where fox, for example, have an extremely varied diet. Even this variety tends not to compensate for the small number of species present and populations fluctuate considerably. (2) Where there is a large number of species, for example, in the tropics, stability can be achieved with a fairly restricted diet, and species can specialize in their feeding habits, and feed only on one or at the most two trophic levels.

The more complex the food web, the better is the community buffered against environmental change, which causes populations to fluctuate in size, and this buffering leads to increased stability of the system. In fact some species seem to depend for their existence on stability of the system produced by the presence of a top predator. This has been discovered by Paine (1969b). There are many species in the intertidal community that coexist from Alaska down to Baja California, a distribution coincident with the carnivorous starfish *Pisaster ochraceus*. This close relationship between prey and predator led Paine to the hypothesis, "The patterns of species occurrence, distribution and density are disproportionately affected by the activities of a single species of high trophic status—the 'Keystone species.'" A Keystone species can be identified where (1) a primary consumer is capable of monopolizing a basic resource and outcompetes other species; and (2) this primary consumer is itself preferentially consumed by the keystone species.

Thus rank in the food preference hierarchy is important in understanding community organization, diversity, and stability, just as it was important in other predation studies (Chapter 4). The feeding preference hierarchy for *Pisaster* from the most preferred prey is: (1) *Mytilus edulis* and *Mytilus californicus* (Mussels), (2) *Thais emarginata* (a small muricid gastropod predator of bivalves and barnacles), and (3) *Tegula funebralis* (a trochid gastropod).

It was observed in Paine's (1966) study that *Mytilus* dominates the community in the absence of *Pisaster*, but since it is the preferred prey its distribution is likely to be adjacent to that of *Pisaster*, not overlapping. The resultant distributions are seen on an intertidal bench of rock

(Fig. 19.8). *Pisaster* remains in the low intertidal so that it is not exposed above the tide for long. *Tegula* settles high in the intertidal zone above the level exploited by *Pisaster*. After about 6 years *Tegula* migrates down into the range of *Pisaster* as conditions are less crowded and under these circumstances reproduction is much more successful, and growth is improved. However the *Tegula* tend to occur in cobbly areas where grinding action of the cobbles prevents *Pisaster* from becoming too abundant. This factor together with the rank of *Tegula* in the food hierarchy permit the coexistence of *Tegula* with its predator.

Therefore the major characteristics of the intertidal community are explained by three ecologically different processes (Paine 1969b): (1) For *Tegula*, reproductive output (fitness) of mature individuals in a predator-exploited subpopulation was higher than in an adjacent unexploited one. Therefore coexistence of prey and predator is not only possible but selected for. (2) Where direct interaction is completely negative for the prey species, for example, for the mussels (*Mytilus*), the result is contiguous, nonoverlapping arrangement of prey and predator distribution; a vertical zonation with a well defined lower limit to prey distribution. Reproductive prey individuals inhabit a refuge from predation. (3) Living space is kept available for a complex of other species through the activity of the keystone species. The keystone species preferentially removes a prey with which the others cannot coexist, in this case *Mytilus*.

Much more work needs to be completed before the relationships be-

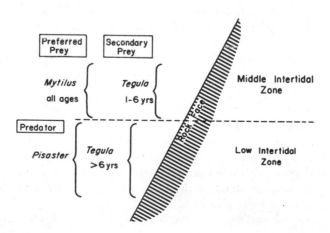

Fig. 19.8   The arrangement of a predator, *Pisaster*, its preferred prey, *Mytilus*, and a secondary prey species, *Tegula*, on an intertidal rock bench. From information in Paine 1969b.

tween diversity and stability are adequately understood. One approach is to use experimental manipulation in the study of communities. For example, our concept derived from MacArthur's (1955) paper, that complexity of the food web buffers the community against change and leads to community stability, must be tempered by more recent evidence from experimental manipulation in the study of stability and diversity. Hurd, Mellinger, Wolf, and McNaughton (1971) found that perturbation of a community in the form of addition of inorganic fertilizer caused greater effects in the simpler plant community than in the more complex one as predicted by MacArthur's concepts. However it appears that at the herbivore and carnivore trophic levels, resistance to perturbation was greatest in the simpler community. This interpretation has been challenged by Harger (1972, but see defense by Hurd et al. 1972), but the experiment is of interest in more carefully defining the concept of stability. Does stability imply resistance to change or merely lack of change? Docs it involve both physical and biotic factors? The term fragile ecosystems has been used more and more recently and applied particularly to arctic tundra and tropical rain forests. In the latter case diversity is unequalled and stability of climate and biotic communities is evident. But the impact man has on this system is catastrophic compared to his influence on temperate systems. High diversity implies a finely adjusted accumulation of coevolved species, perhaps a commonness of mutualistic relationships, and therefore a fragile balance in the community (Futuyma 1973). The biotic relationships in these communities maintain stability, but the impact of abiotic forces may be catastrophic, including man's use of technology. Thus the concepts of stability and resistance to perturbation must be segregated. Diversity will lead to a stable community given stable physical factors; diversity will not necessarily lead to reduced perturbability of a community if physical changes are involved. More experiments are needed where communities are changed by addition and subtraction of biotic components to test the concept of the relation between diversity and stability. At the same time questions posed by Murdoch (1970) concerning the regulation, stability, and inertia of populations may be answered; and Holling's (1973 concepts of stability, resilience, and persistence may be reinforced. Perhaps the necessary lexicon relating to the balance of nature is almost complete.

Greater depth in the understanding of diversity and stability may be obtained by consulting the symposium on the subject edited by Woodwell and Smith (1969), "Stability and complexity in model ecosystems," and May (1973a), May (1973b), Levin (1974), Holling (1973), and of particular interest to insect ecologists, Root's (1973) study of plant-arthropod associations in simple and diverse habitats.

Chapter 20

POLLINATION ECOLOGY

Pollination ecology offers a very good example of how necessary it is to integrate many of the aspects of ecology treated in this book to evaluate ecological processes adequately. Obviously many areas of ecology must be understood: the trophic structure of the community (Chapter 2), the coevolution between plant and pollinator (Chapter 3), energetic relationships (Chapter 6), demography of plant and pollinator (Chapter 7), reproductive strategies (Chapter 8), population dynamics (Chapter 9), niche segregation, competition and species packing (Chapters 13, 14, and 15), sociality since many pollinators are social insects (Chapter 16), community ecology (Chapters 17, 18, and 19), and finally paleoecology and biogeography (Chapter 21), since we deal with isolation of populations and speciation in time and space. Gilbert's (1975) study on *Heliconius* butterflies mentioned in Chapter 18 involves most of these aspects. It should be clear in this chapter how the subject matter relates to all these areas of ecology.

It has long been understood that pollination by animals involves a coevolutionary process, and this has been proceeding perhaps for 225 million years. As opposed to other coevolutionary processes that have been discussed, the fossil record provides a time sequence of events, so that the steps in coevolution may be observed moderately clearly (Fig. 20.1). It provides us with few surprises. Winged insects were abundant in the Carboniferous long before any flower-like structures were available as food sources. Even predatory groups (e.g., Neuroptera) had emerged before the Mesozoic. The first holometabolous insects became abundant in the late Carboniferous, Permian, and Triassic. Thus for the first time in history, many adults were seeking new food sources different from those of their larvae as the larvae became adapted to concealed feeding sites impossible for the adults to occupy. These were mandibulate adults and all were potential "mess-and-soil" pollinators (Smart and Hughes 1973), and the Coleoptera were particularly numerous, although perhaps they preserve better and make better fossils. It is significant then that the first flowers evolved at this time—those of the gymnospermous Bennettitales—about 225 million years ago.

At first the flowers were small (5 mm) and had the appearance of a composite inflorescence (Leppik 1960), which must have been insect-pollinated. Flower size tended to increase with time but rather suddenly about 140 million years ago they became 10–12 cm across and Smart and Hughes (1973) suggest that this large size may be correlated with the emergence of birds at this time. No evolutionary link has been established between the Bennettitales and the angiosperms, but it is most likely that many insects were pollinators before other flying animals were extant.

Although the angiosperms emerged after birds had appeared it is hard

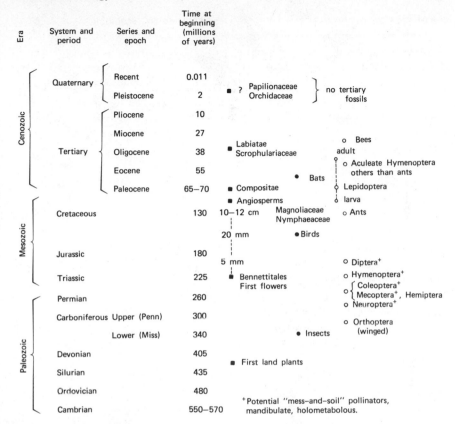

Fig. 20.1   Time of first records of plant taxa and the animals, insects, birds, and bats, that pollinate them. Time is not to scale. After Smart and Hughes 1973.

to imagine the possibility of such rapid and explosive radiation of this group in the absence of insects. Primitive angiosperms such as the Magnoliaceae and the Nymphaeaceae, which are still pollinated by insects today, appeared in the fossil record in the late Mesozoic. By the early Paleocene, Compositae (Fig. 20.2) were present that are evolved in inflorescence structure to provide a landing platform for large insects.

It is also significant that no highly evolved pollinators such as Lepidoptera and bees have been found before the Angiosperms appeared. Although a head capsule of a lepidopteran caterpillar was found from the Cretaceous, adults were not found until the Oligocene, just before bees appeared in the fossil record, but it appears that the Lepidoptera must have evolved at the same time as the early Angiosperms. It is notable also that bees appear at the same time as the families Scrophulariaceae and

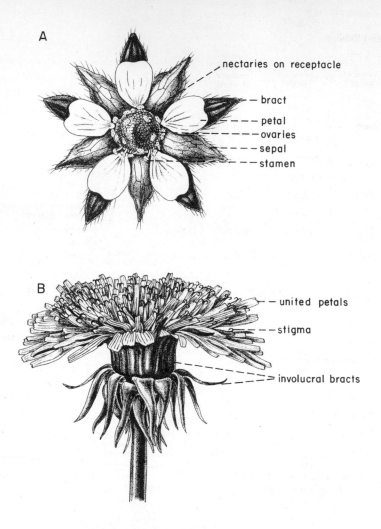

A

nectaries on receptacle

— bract

— — petal
— — — ovaries
— — — sepal
— — stamen

B

— united petals

— — stigma

— — involucral bracts

Fig. 20.2 (*a*) The actinomorphic (symmetrical) flower of the rough cinquefoil, *Potentilla monspeliensis* (Rosaceae). The open, flattish arrangement of the flower permits many insects to reach nectar secreted on the receptacle and unspecialized "mess and soil" pollinators such as beetles and flies are common visitors. Reduction of floral parts has progressed to a certain extent: petals are reduced to five but stamens are still numerous (15–20 per flower). (*b*) An inflorescence of the dandelion, *Taraxacum officinale*, showing how the small flowers are grouped to form a landing platform for insects. Apparently the flowers of the now extinct Bennettitales looked like this. Each flower is composed of five united petals which form a narrow tube, at the base of which nectar is secreted. Only insects with elongated mouthparts can reach nectar, although pollen is more easily obtained as stamens are arranged at the mouth of the tube.

Labiatae with their highly specialized flowers. These families evolved zygomorphic arrangement of flower parts (bilaterally symmetrical as opposed to the actinomorphic or symmetrical flowers of more primitive angiosperms, e.g., Fig. 20.2a), reduced numbers of stamens, and a landing platform—obviously adaptations as bee flowers (Fig. 20.3). Finally, after bees had been evolving and diversifying for some 35 million years, those most beautifully bee-adapted families, the Papilionaceae and the Orchidaceae, left their stamp in the fossil record.

The relationship between plant and flower pollinator is a mutualistic one. However, the extent of this mutualism is not yet fully appreciated. Recently, Baker and Baker (1973a,b) provided evidence for an unsuspected and important aspect of the coevolutionary process. Nectar that may contain sucrose, glucose, and fructose has usually been considered as an energy source while protein-making chemicals (amino acids) had to be found by pollinators elsewhere, by larval feeding in Lepidoptera, from pollen by bees, and from insects by vertebrates. But clearly if the plant could provide amino acids, foraging could be concentrated on the flowers, and both foraging and pollinating efficiency would improve. Therefore, the Bakers surveyed 266 species of flowering plants in California and discovered significant concentrations of amino acids in nectar (Table 20.1). This is no fortuitous array of amino acid sources and these flowers provide an important source. Butterflies (except for *Heliconius*

Table 20.1 The relative amounts of amino acids (estimated on a histidine scale) of various types of flowers. As dependence on nectar as a source of amino acids declines so the amino acid level declines.

	Flower type	Number of species	Mean on histidine scale*
1.	Fly (specialized for carrion flies)	8	9.25
2.	Butterfly	41	6.68
3.	Butterfly and bee	44	6.02
4.	Moth	30	5.60
5.	Bird	49	5.22
6.	Bee	95	4.76
7.	Fly (unspecialized)	34	3.77

SOURCE. From Baker and Baker 1973a.
* $1 \equiv 49\ \mu M$, $2 \equiv 98\ \mu M$, $10 \equiv 25\ mM$.

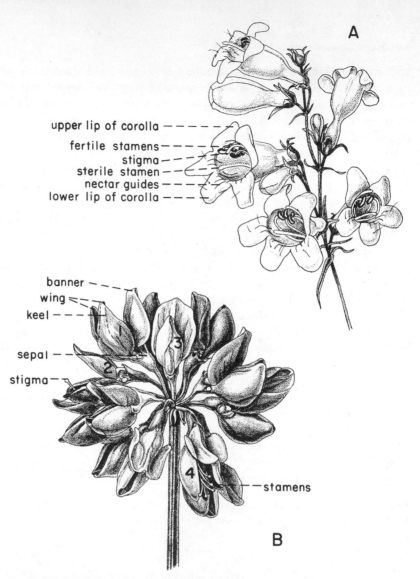

A

upper lip of corolla ------
fertile stamens ------
stigma ------
sterile stamen ------
nectar guides ------
lower lip of corolla ------

banner ------
wing ------
keel ------

sepal ------
stigma ------

stamens

B

Fig. 20.3 (a) Part of an inflorescence of the foxglove beard-tongue, *Penstemon digitalis* (Scrophulariaceae). Flowers are zygomorphic (bilaterally symmetrical). The five petals are fused into a tube which narrows near the receptacle, preventing all but long-tongued insects such as bees from reaching the nectar secreted at the end of the tube. The lips of the three lower petals form a landing platform for bees, and nectar guides act as a visual cue for guiding the bee down the tubular corolla. There are four fertile stamens that dust the dorsum of a visiting bee. The stigma is similarly placed and this receives pollen when a pollen-carrying bee visits. A sterile stamen, the beard-tongue, lies ventrally in the corolla tube. In the Scrophulariaceae there is an evolutionary reduction of stamens from five to two. (b) An inflorescence of the crown vetch, *Coronilla varia* (Papilionaceae). Each flower is strongly zygomorphic with five petals fused at their bases. A banner petal is dorsal, and two wing petals are arranged either side of the two fused petals which form the keel (see flower 1). A heavy insect lands on the wings, depresses the wings and keel and the stamens and stigma spring up in contact with the underside of the insects' abdomen (2). A pollinated flower is shown at 4. Thus nectar and pollen are protected in the closed flower (3) until a heavy bee visits the flower. Mess and soil pollinators are excluded.

butterflies which digest pollen, Gilbert 1972) and moths have few other readily available sources of amino acids and we see fairly high concentrations in the nectar of flowers adapted to pollination by Lepidoptera. However birds use insects as a protein source and bees have a rich source in the form of pollen and we see amino acid concentration reduced in flowers pollinated by these animals. Finally in relatively unspecialized flowers both nectar and pollen are freely available to pollinators so that there is little need for an amino acid "supplement" to the nectar food source. The Bakers found amino acids in primitive angiosperm nectar, but with coevolution more and more has been produced, as can be seen in a comparison between the unspecialized fly flower to the tubular flowers adapted to pollination by butterflies and moths.

The service required for the energy expended in nectar production is pollen transport and outcrossing. Such an important food source to animals as nectar and pollen can be manipulated by the evolutionary process so that the plant receives the best possible service from the pollinator. The promotion of outcrossing can be achieved by several means, which are considered by Heinrich and Raven (1972).

1. Flower evolution can tend to restrict visits by a certain population of pollinators to flowers of a single species. This involves flower constancy which is adaptive for the plant as well as the insect (see later).
2. The pollinator must not confine its visits to a single plant and therefore the amount of nectar secreted per flower and per total plant at any one time must be precisely adjusted. Evolutionarily speaking, the plant must control the caloric and amino acid reward presented synchronously. Agriculturalists and plant breeders select plants that must grow at abnormally high densities. Foraging by bees in alfalfa, clover, and soybeans is extremely easy but may result in low seed set because not many flowers are visited. However, if plants with lower nectar secretion are selected for, the energy gain per unit effort would be balanced, and seed set would be improved. Heinrich and Raven (1972) explain how naturally reduced nectar supply has achieved this end in red clover seed crops. Large numbers of pollinator visits produce greater crop yields. Short-tongued bumblebees take nectar by piercing the corolla without pollinating, but rather than reducing the seed crop, they actually lead to an increase in seed production. This is probably because the real pollinators (long-tongued bumblebees) visited more flowers when less nectar remained per flower after robbing.

3. The plant can only control the caloric reward in relation to a certain organism because each has a very different energy requirement. For example a 100-mg bumblebee lands on a flower and uses about 0.08 cal/min while walking on the flower (see also Heinrich 1973 on bumblebee energetics), but 3-g sphinx moths and hummingbirds use energy at about 11 cal/min while hovering (Heinrich 1971a,b), a 140-fold difference. Hickman (1974) describes the need for secretion of small quantities of nectar in ant-pollinated flowers. He outlines many characteristics in flower design and location on the plant, plant morphology, plant population dispersion, and community characteristics that result in and reinforce this low-energy pollination system.

Therefore plants evolve with flowers that restrict access to all but a few, or even one, pollinator species. Animals that require high levels of energy will not utilize species with low nectar production, and those plants with high nectar production must evolve protection against small organisms that may utilize nectar but not outcross the plants. A common evolutionary device is the development of a longer corolla tube so that only larger organisms (often with prolonged mouthparts such as bees and moths) can reach the reward. Examples include many Scrophulariaceae (Fig. 20.3a), Labiatae, and Solanaceae, and an extreme case where nectar is secreted in the end of a spur 30 cm long in the Christmas Star orchid, *Angraecum sesquipedale*, and is perhaps pollinated by a magnificent moth, *Xanthopan morgani praedicta*, with a 20-cm wing span and a 30-cm proboscis.

Shape, color, and scent of flowers may also be adapted for restricting pollinators. Flowers with much nectar may open and secrete nectar briefly at night, so that the flowers are available to bats and hawk moths, but unavailable to many day flying insects and birds. Bird-pollinated flowers are often scentless, red in color, and open during the day, and thus less conspicuous and less attractive to many insects (which do not perceive red light) and unavailable to nocturnal pollinators. Insect pollinated flowers emit fragrances, while birds are poorly adapted for receiving such chemical stimuli. Bee flowers, and many other insect pollinated blooms responding to the insects' vision which reaches into the ultraviolet, often show ultraviolet reflectance patterns (Eisner et al. 1969), which are presumably not visible to vertebrates. Detailed considerations of insect perception and the evolution of flower shape are provided by Leppik (1972 and references therein) and Meeuse (1973).

Clustering of flowers will also influence the type of organism that can make a net energetic gain while foraging. If large inflorescences of small flowers open flowers synchronously then the energetic gain becomes more profitable for larger alighting pollinators than if flowers tend to open sequentially. We may see an evolutionary trend for greater flowering synchrony with increasing depth of nectar source where large pollinators exist in abundance. Outcrossing may also be promoted by evolution of inflorescences far larger than is optimal for attracting pollinators and achieving adequate pollination (Willson and Rathcke 1974). Here plants may increase fitness by the low cost strategy of being pollen donors, since seed and fruit production are relatively expensive in terms of energy and nutrients required. On a larger scale synchronous blooming of one species in an area would reduce time and energy required by pollinators flying between plants, whereas brief blooming of individuals occurring at random over a long period would increase time and energy required to exploit the nectar source. In the latter case either nectar reward must increase or pollinator size must decrease. Plant density also influences the distance of pollen-mediated gene dispersal in a density-dependent manner (Levin and Kerster 1969a,b). The more clumped the plants are, the shorter is the distance of pollinator movement, and the more probable is local differentiation of types within the plant species.

In any one plant species the frequency of cross-pollination would be inversely related to the number of other species blooming at the same time if foragers visited flowers indiscriminately. Thus cross-pollination will be more effective and competition by plants for pollinators will be reduced if species bloom sequentially so that the same pollinators use a succession of blooming species. For example, Mosquin (1971) studied the activities of pollinating insects in relation to flowering phenology of plants near Banff, Alberta. From snow-melt (early May) to the end of May, pollinating insects were abundant and competed for relatively scarce pollen and nectar. In early June, some "cornucopian species" (e.g., Willows, *Salix* spp., and dandelion, *Taraxacum offinale*) began flowering, offering virtually unlimited supplies of nectar and pollen. Insects left the spring flowers and foraged on the cornucopian species. In the presence of cornucopian species natural selection would therefore favor evolution of earlier or later flowering populations of competing species. The direction of movement in time will also depend on competition with other species. For example, Mosquin suggested that in the spring insects competed for flowers, but after the cornucopian species had completed flowering, flowers competed for pollinating insects.

Cruden's (1972a) data suggest that there may be competitive displacement between hummingbirds and bees on an altitudinal gradient. Cruden found in Mexico that hummingbirds are more effective pollinators at high elevations (2300 m and above) during the rainy season because they remain active during cloudy and rainy weather. Also nearly twice as many hummingbird species are reported in high elevation communities as at midelevations (1000–2300 m). Cruden considered that there was little or no difference in effectiveness between bees and birds as pollinators provided that flight conditions were favorable, as they were more frequently in middle elevations. However, the fitness of plants pollinated by bees at middle elevations was much higher (Table 20.2). Therefore,

Table 20.2 Pollination, seed set, and fecundity in labiates from Chiapas, Oaxaca, Mexico, and Durango.

Flower type	Elevation	Pollination (%) (A)	Seed set (%) (Percent of ovules that develop into seeds) (B)	Fecundity (%) (A×B)
Bee	High	83	58	48
	Middle	93	91	85
Bird	High	92	87	80
	Middle	91	76	69

SOURCE. From Cruden 1972a.

one might argue that bees are better pollinators. Since bees maintain their resources better than hummingbirds at middle elevations, this might be considered as a form of indirect competitive displacement. Of course hummingbirds may occur at higher elevations for many reasons but the possible interactions would be interesting to study.

In deserts, blooming after rain leads to synchrony of many species and divergence is seen in a variety of ways: (a) daily time of blooming as in the *Oenothera* species that Linsley, MacSwain, and Raven (1963a,b, 1964) studied (e.g., see Fig. 13.13), (b) amount of caloric reward provided, (c) type of flower product (nectar, pollen, or both), and (d) structures affecting access to nectar or pollen. Thus many sympatric bee species specialize and diverge in foraging patterns and thus decrease competition for food.

The term flower constancy relates to the foraging pattern of pollinators. Where flower constancy is high, foraging is restricted to one plant species during single trips, during a day, and even over several days. This high constancy may be seen in individuals and in colonies of bees. Flower constancy is adaptive for both the insect (frequently a bee) and the plant, and coevolution is likely to progress toward this end, particularly involving flower evolution to favor a certain type of very efficient pollinator. The adaptiveness for the plant is obvious; cross pollination is ensured and nectar supply and pollen production can be efficiently adjusted to certain pollinating species, and protected by floral parts to conserve this resource for the specialists. An early development in this evolution for constancy was the fusing of petals into a tube around the stamens. Then fewer insects can enter the flower, but those that can experience less competition and flower constancy is reinforced. The result is seen in the alpine flora of Europe, for example, where beetles, wasps, flies, and other unspecialized and inconstant insects that make up 86% of insect species on flowers with exposed nectar, constitute only 37% of visitors to flowers with concealed nectar (Grant 1950). Further evidence of this coevolution for flower constancy is seen in the number of taxonomic characters used to distinguish species in the same genus. Grant (1949) found that the percentage of these characters that were correlated with the pollination mechanism was very high in bird pollinated plants (37%) and bee and long-tongued fly plants (40%) but low in plants that were pollinated indiscriminately (promiscuous) (15%) and wind- and water-pollinated species (4%).

For the bee, flower constancy becomes more efficient as it learns to extract nectar and pollen while visiting the same flower type (Grant 1950) and larvae can specialize metabolic processes for utilizing a constant source of nutrients. Development may become more rapid and utilization more efficient. Bees that visit flowers of a single plant species are called monotropic bees, or those that collect a single species' pollen are monolectic. Those that visit a few related species are oligotropic and oligolectic, and those that visit many species are polytropic and polylectic. The constancy of bees can be estimated from examination of pollen types on the body after foraging and we frequently see a high proportion of bees with a pure pollen load (Grant 1950) (Table 20.3).

But bees in temperate regions (e.g., *Apis mellifera*) tend to forage in small areas 10–20 m^2 and thus considerable inbreeding may result. The bees are constant to a particular species not only in single flights, as indicated by the pure pollen loads, but also over periods up to 10 or 11 days (Grant 1950), and they are quite constant in a colony. We actually see a dynamic interaction between honey bee colonies that must influence the population structure of the plants immensely. This has been studied by Butler (1943, 1945) and Butler et al. (1943). The first flowers to bloom

Table 20.3   The flower constancy in genera of bees indicated by the percent of individuals in a sample that contained pollen from one species of plant. Note the high frequency of pure pollen loads in all genera except Anthophora. If estimates were for pollen loads with 90% or more of one pollen type the percentage would be much higher.

Genus of bee	Percent pure pollen loads (from various sources)
Andrena	44, 64
Apis	62, 88, 93
Anthophora	20
Bombus	59, 49, 57
Halictus	84, 75
Megachile	75, 55

SOURCE.   From Grant 1950.

in the spring will have a colony of bees that utilize flowers in a certain area and will defend this area against intrusion by members of other colonies. Honey bees from other colonies arriving after local patches have been preempted will not be able to forage on a group-defended area and will wander over the field more or less at random and these will cause much more extensive movement of pollen. But as a second plant species comes into bloom, the wanderers will become constant and defend areas. This second source does not attract the older bees and new bees will act as wanderers until new sources become available. As a plant blooming period ends, competition for pollen ensues and a new wave of inconstancy results and equilibrium is finally established when some groups forage in other areas.

This type of foraging dynamics may also be observed in the tropics on species that flower abundantly but intermittently. However, where food plants occur singly and far apart a completely different foraging pattern has been observed among the pollinators, and a different flowering pattern among the plants. For example, Janzen (1971) showed that euglossine bees forage for food over many kilometers of tropical forest and that females may visit the same set of plants each day. They behave as if they remember the location of food plants and act as if they are operating a trapline for food. The same trapline behavior has been observed for the butterfly, *Heliconius ethilla*, by Ehrlich and Gilbert (1973) and Gilbert (1975), one of the species discussed at the end of Chapter 18. Janzen (1971) described the significance of traplining to the host plants: (1) outcrossing occurs at very low host plant densities characteristic of tropical populations; (2) only one or very few flowers need to be produced in any one day; (3) much energy need not be stored for a large synchronized flowering; (4) floral morphology can become specialized to the intelligent, effective pollinators, so that energy is not wasted on feeding species that do not carry pollen of that species over long distances; (5) since only small amounts of energy are required for flowering, a woody plant can reproduce much earlier in its life history, or under conditions of heavy competition for light or nutrients; and (6) floral visibility is less important and pollination can be effective in the heavily shaded forest understory. Gilbert's (1975) studies demonstrate how these factors interact to produce organization of the host plants and the pollinators at the population and community levels (see Chapter 18 for brief description).

Flower constancy and local foraging may lead to isolation of populations and eventually to speciation, with the strong possibility of sympatric speciation. Grant (1949) pointed out that bee plants may speciate more rapidly than do promiscuous species (being pollinated by many types of insect) because of this ethological isolation caused by the bees. Two processes may be involved. First, bees may cause an initial evolutionary divergence of flowers within a population as a result of selective pollination of mutant floral types. Sympatric speciation may be possible (see Straw, 1955, for a supporting example of fixation of *Penstemon* hybrids by bees, wasps, and hummingbirds). Second, in the zone of secondary contact between populations that have been geographically isolated, but have become sympatric, bees may effectively isolate these populations although only small differences in floral characters were acquired during isolation. Evidence for Grant's contention of more rapid speciation in bee plants is seen in the southern California flora where there is an average of 5.94 species per genus in bee plants but only 3.38 species per genus in promiscuous insect pollinated plants.

Dressler (1968), Dodson et al. (1969), and Hills et al. (1972) provide strong reason to believe that sympatric and allopatric speciation are highly likely in orchids pollinated by euglossine bees. Dressler uses the term euglossine pollination for the relationship in which orchid flowers are visited only by male euglossine bees that are attracted by odor and "brush" on the surface of the flower. This brushing action is apparently to obtain the fragrance, which is then transferred to the inflated hind tibiae (Evoy and Jones 1971). It may be used in one of three ways (Dodson et al. 1969): (1) Male bees live longer than normal, but they die if deprived of the compounds. Thus the bees may metabolize the compounds to make up for a natural deficiency of their diet. (2) They may convert the compounds into sex attractants. Males fly in their territory leaving odor on leaves and produce a fine mist which may attract the females. (3) Males may use the compounds to attract other males of the same species so that several males congregate and may thus be more attractive to females, since the buzzing of the bees will be louder and the compounds more concentrated. Thus a lek system may be involved.

Since only odor is involved in attraction, an odor-modifying mutation may lead to pollination by another species of bee. A shift in size of bee may cause severe selection pressure and rapid morphological change, since flower morphology is crucial to pollination success (e.g., see Fig. 20.4), and sympatric speciation may result. Also, as an orchid species disperses, populations may come into contact with preadapted pollinators in new areas after long distance dispersal, and again flower morphology would adapt to increase precision of the pollinating mechanism. Allopatric speciation may result.

In a similar vein Cruden (1972b) discusses two ways in which plants may influence speciation in oligolectic bees. First, the host plant population may be split geographically, which may result in two new species, oligolectic bees modify to the diverging plant populations, and we see

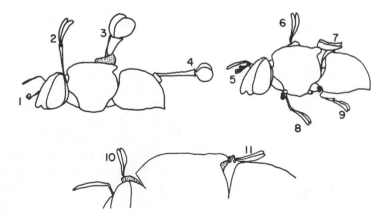

Fig. 20.4   Outlines of male euglossine bees showing how the pollinia of 11 species of orchid are deposited in precise locations on the bee's body. This emphasizes the need for close coevolution between flower and pollinator, and the likely changes in flower morphology with change in bee species and consequent behavioral and morphological changes. From Dressler 1968.

closely related bee-plant pairs as we saw in coevolution of insects with toxic plants (Chapter 3), for example,

Andrena torulosa—Nemophila atomaria (Hydrophyllaceae)

Andrena crudeni—Nemophila menziesii

The second possibility depends on the local extinction of a host plant with a shift in the bee to a new pollen source, and subsequent adaptation of the bee population to this new source. Adaptation will result as a response to changes in flower size, pollen size, and phenology of the new host plant (see Thorp 1969); thus the local populations will diverge from those where the original plant host survived, and speciation may result.

Most energetic studies in pollination ecology have involved hummingbirds (e.g., Pearson 1954, Williamson 1956, Stiles 1971, Wolf, Hainesworth, and Stiles 1972). Flowering time and breeding time of hummingbirds are closely and essentially linked. In the time and energy budget on the male anna hummingbird (*Calypte anna*), Stiles (1971) found that the birds do not increase the energy utilized during breeding but apportion time and energy in a different way, made possible by the relatively rapid foraging for food while blooms were abundant (Table 20.4).

During breeding an area of about 0.1 ha and a buffer zone of 4–6 ha is defended and the "males engage in advertizing flights, display dives, and frequent long chases in defense of their territories." In contrast, feeding territories are only a few square meters, the surrounding area is not defended, and intruders are not extensively chased. Thus the energetic cost of maintaining a breeding territory is much greater than for a feeding territory. This can be seen in Table 20.4. The interesting feature of the bird's energetic relationships is that although during breeding it spends a little (6%) less time on feeding it expends much less energy in gaining enough food (17 vs 30%) because of the presence of nectar-rich flowers, and thus the energy saved in foraging is available for increased energy utilization for territorial aggression.

Temperature also has a profound effect on pollinators, particularly the poikilothermic insects (see Heinrich and Raven 1972). For example, bumblebees can forage at 5°C or less by producing endogenous heat that elevates body temperatures, but the energy cost is two or three times greater than at 26°C (Heinrich and Raven 1972). Therefore flowers pollinated at low temperatures should provide more caloric reward than those blooming at high temperatures, or they should be closer together so that they can be visited in rapid succession. Perhaps the clumping of spring flowers is adaptive in this way. It is not surprising, therefore, to see ecotypic

Table 20.4 **Time and energy budgets of male anna hummingbirds during breeding territoriality and feeding territoriality.** Time and energy not accounted for in these percentages were used for miscellaneous flying activities and during time out of contact with the observer.

	Percent time				Percent energy			
	Feeding at flowers	Insect catching	Territorial aggression	Perching	Feeding at flowers	Insect catching	Territorial aggression	Perching
Breeding territoriality								
Day 1	8.39	1.19	5.94	81.0	17.7	2.57	12.5	59.8
Day 2	8.17	1.13	7.89	79.9	16.4	2.22	15.9	59.7
Feeding territoriality	14.6	0.54	1.80	81.8	30.2	1.15	3.43	63.5

SOURCE.   From Stiles 1971.

404

variation in caloric reward, where more northerly ecotypes secrete' more nectar (Heinrich and Raven 1972). Similar trends may be seen on elevational gradients.

Also, cool temperatures in early morning in temperate regions can be utilized only by large insects capable of temperature regulation, and the flowers are usually large, for example, *Oenothera* spp., and we see a trend in decreasing size of pollinators as temperatures rise. *Bombus edwardsii* (0.12 g) had a thoracic temperature of 37°C while foraging at 2°C from a manzanita, *Arctostaphylos otayensis*, an energetically expensive operation. However each flower contained 1.5 cal of sugar while the maintenance cost was about 0.8 cal/minute, so that the bees could make an energetic gain while foraging at near freezing temperatures. At noon when the flowers were visited by small insects each flower contained only 0.32 cal of sugar. Thus it may be energetically most profitable for bees to forage in the early morning when there is either little competition for nectar, a considerable accumulation of nectar, or the rate of nectar secretion is high (Heinrich and Raven 1972). Conversely low energy sources such as golden rod, *Solidago* spp., are visited by bees at relatively high ambient temperatures.

Heinrich and Raven (1972) have also discussed alternative strategies to the main theme. When temperatures get too cold, for example, during spring in temperate climates, or in northern latitudes, autogamy tends to increase, or nectar production increases for good competitive advantage, or very close clumping may achieve the same end. Where nectar rewards are very small plants must be close and pollen dispersal will be very local, as is the case in Compositae, but wide dispersal of seed ensures constant mixing of gene pools and high genetic variability. In warm humid regions plants that are typically wind pollinated may become dependent on animals for pollen transfer. Grasses in tropical regions are visited by many insects (Bogdan 1962, Soderstrom and Calderon 1971) whereas elsewhere they are anemophilous.

Orchid plants are frequently widely separated, but insure outcrossing by the extreme precision in pollen transfer and reception (e.g., Dressler 1968); pollen is not lost when flowers of different species are visited, and large numbers of seeds are set with a single pollination. Since flowers are widely separated in space and time, the pollinator cannot depend on flowers for its energy supply, no energy balance need be maintained, and thus about half of all orchid species offer no energy reward. Thus attraction is achieved frequently by deception: by mimicry of other flowers with nectar, by mimicking females of the pollinating male insects involving pseudocopulation (e.g., Kullenberg 1950, 1956a,b, 1961, Coleman 1933, van der Pijl and Dodson 1966), by mimicry of potential hosts of parasitoids involving pseudoparasitism (van der Pijl and Dodson 1966, Stoutamire 1974), and by mimicry of other insects, which elicits territorial aggression by a bee and thus results in pollination—called pseudo-antagonism (Dodson and Frymire 1961, van der Pijl and Dodson 1966). In the last case orchid flowers of the genus *Oncidium* mimic insects. The racemes of flowers are arched and the slightest breeze causes the flowers to dance. Male bees of the genus *Centris* attack the flowers as if they were flying insects, and pollination results. Other bizarre methods of pollination involve figs and fig wasps (Galil and Eisikowitch 1968, 1969, Ramirez 1969, 1970, Baker 1961) and yucca and the yucca moths (Riley 1892, 1893, Holland 1903, Powell and Mackie 1966).

The fascination of pollination ecology will never wane. Fortunately an easy access to an extensive literature can be obtained through general books on pollination (Faegri and van der Pijl 1971, Proctor and Yeo 1972) and Free's (1970) book on insect pollination of crops. But there is ample room for further study. Particularly for entomologists the energetics of pollinating insects is a wide-open field (but see important progress by Heinrich 1972a,b,c, 1973), and the adaptive strategies of floral arrangements in response to pollinators and herbivores has hardly been investigated (see Willson and Rathcke, 1974, for references and a contribution). No doubt many biotic interactions concerning pollination remain to be discovered. One glimpse into what the future of pollination ecology has to offer is provided by Colwell (1973) who studied the interactions of four bird species feeding on the nectar of four hummingbird-pollinated plants, and two nectar-feeding mites in the genus *Rhinoseius*, which are phoretic on the birds. Considerations on organization of this small community of ten species included coevolution of flowers and hummingbirds, convergence in flower color and morphology, competition between bird species, competition between mites, probability of mites being transferred between flowers of the same and different species, number of mite species that could coexist, and number of bird species that could coexist. Finally the question of general concepts on the evolution of high species diversity in the tropics could be addressed. Gilbert's (1975) study on *Heliconius* butterflies discussed in Chapter 18 also emphasizes the precision of interspecies links, and the power of interpretation on community organization made possible when the details of species interactions are regarded as central organizing influences.

Chapter 21

PALEOECOLOGY
AND BIOGEOGRAPHY

I n this book it has been taken for granted that organisms are adapted to a certain set of conditions that provide the minimal physiological needs: sufficient moisture, heat, oxygen, food, and such. The requirements of organisms have an important influence on where they live and how they are distributed. Distribution of organisms in relation to each other in the community and in relation to the structural features of the community has been discussed. It therefore seems to be a natural step to examine how the larger features of the environment affect the distribution of organisms. These larger features are those recognized as significant by a geographer: mountain ranges, river valleys, rift valleys, oceans, seas, islands, continents, and the spatial relationships among these geographical features, their formation, and their erosion. All these factors have a strong influence on the distribution of organisms. The most extensive influences on distribution are treated first and then more local influences.

In 1839–1843 Hooker was an assistant surgeon on an antarctic voyage and he was able to study the flora and collect plants in Tasmania, New South Wales, New Zealand, Tierra del Fuego and its archipelago (Feugia), the Falkland islands, and Kerguelen island between South Africa and Australia, due south of India. Thus he had a good look at, and a first-hand experience with, the circumantarctic flora. Hooker was struck by the similarity of the plants in these southern lands separated by vast stretches of ocean, where he found many genera peculiar to the south in common, and even species in common. Hooker felt that these disjunct distribution patterns could not be accounted for by long distance dispersal, and he believed that the circumantarctic flora was the split-off remnant of a once much larger austral vegetation that evolved and flourished under warmer conditions and greater proximity between the southern land masses. These ideas he discussed in the volumes of *The botany of the Antarctic voyage of His Majesties Discovery Ships Erebus and Terror in the years 1839–1843*, published between 1847 and 1860.

Much more recently similar distributions have been seen in insects, for example, in Brundin's (1960, 1967) studies of chironomid midges conducted between 1953 and 1963. These are small, nonbiting, primitive flies (Diptera), the larvae of which are aquatic. Some have a red blood pigment and are known as bloodworms. In the southern hemisphere the larvae occur in cool mountain streams. The world distribution of two tribes is shown in Fig. 21.1. In the Tribe Podonomini many genera occur in the southern temperate regions and only one genus and one species occur in the north. This clearly indicates that the center of evolution for the tribe was in the south. Not only is the tribe represented on three widely separated land masses South America, Australia, and New Zealand,

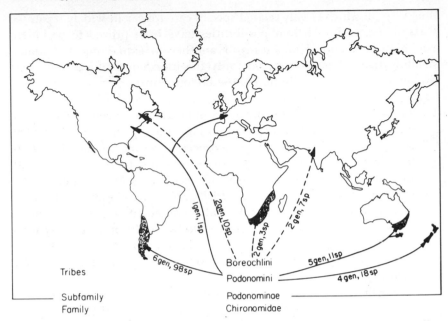

Fig. 21.1 Distribution of chironomid midges of the subfamily Podonominae, tribes Boreochlini and Podonomini. Note that the Boreochlini are distributed mainly in Africa, Eurasia, and North America whereas the Podonomini are most abundant in South America, Australia, and New Zealand. After Brundin 1960, 1967.

Table 21.1 Examples of the close relationships in genera of the tribe Podonomini (Chironomidae).

Genus	Number of species per genus			
	South America	South Africa	Australia	New Zealand
Parochlus	30	0	4	10
Podonomus	38	0	2	3
Podochlus	22	0	2	4

but also each has species of the same genera (Table 21.1), indicating very close phylogenetic lines—so close that it is inconceivable that the evolution in the tribe occurred in anything but a situation that permitted considerable movement of genetic material between these land masses.

The question is how is it possible for such closely related species to occur on such widely disjunct areas of land? There are at least four possible ways in which closely related species can appear in widely separated parts of the world. All four possibilities have been proved to be important for one group of organisms or another in explaining and understanding their biogeography, but only the fourth provides an adequate explanation for the distribution of the Podonomini.

1. The first possibility is remote and can be almost certainly discounted; that is, they were transported by man either purposely or accidentally. While man has had a pronounced effect on the distribution of carabid beetles by transporting them in ship's ballast (see Lindroth 1957, 1963, 1971), and the distribution of pests by transporting the economic crops (e.g., see Elton 1958), there is no way in which the present distribution can be logically explained by invoking man's activities. If man had been responsible we could predict many more species present in North America and Eurasia, and it would be hard to explain why none of the Tribe Podonomini had arrived in South Africa.

2. The second possibility is more plausible, but still most unlikely. That is that there was a migration of populations across the tropics, from South America perhaps, over the Bering Land Bridge and into eastern Eurasia, and down into Australia and New Zealand, and the present distribution is a relic of the much more extensive distribution. There are two strong reasons for rejecting this argument: (*a*) If such a migration had occurred many more species would have remained in the north temperate where suitable conditions for chironomids exist just as they do in the south. (*b*) Movement of populations from south to north and around the Pacific Ocean would provide many opportunities for geographical barriers to reduce gene flow between contiguous populations which would lead to speciation. Many such events would result in species that arrived in Australia and New Zealand which would be very distantly related to those in South America, whereas they are actually closely related species.

3. The third possibility is that these small, highly mobile, flying insects drifted as aerial plankton from one continent to another, or in a series of hops from one oceanic island to another, on the prevailing westerly winds in these temperate latitudes. Johnson (1969) provides much information that shows the importance and commonness of this form of movement. Again at least two reasons prevent acceptance of this suggestion for the chironomids studied by Brundin. First, we would expect South America and Africa to have more closely related species just as Australia and South America have congeneric species. Second, colonization by drift over such a vast area would be a rare

phenomenon. Only one or two specimens are likely to arrive on a new continent and thus they would represent a minute sample of the gene pool of the parent population. This minute sample could not possibly represent the full genetic diversity of the population it left. This principle that the founders of a new colony or population contain only a small fraction of the total genetic variation of the parental population or species is known as the founder principle (see Mayr 1963). Under a new set of environmental conditions there would probably be a rapid divergence of genetic stock between the new and parent population, rapid speciation in a previously uncolonized area, and resultant large differences between species, rather than the small differences actually seen.

4. The fourth possibility is the most reasonable explanation for the chironomids. It is thought that the evolution of the subfamily occurred on a single land mass, which later split up to produce the disjunct austral distribution seen at present. This concept of continental drift has been discussed since 1620 when Bacon suggested that North and South America had been joined to Europe and Africa at one time. Only since about 1965 has sufficient information accumulated to make evidence almost incontrovertable that the earth's crust is formed of numerous plates that are moving relative to each other, thus causing the continents to move. The new theory of plate tectonics goes a long way to explaining the present positions of the continents, the formation of many of the world's mountain ranges, and practically all major earthquakes. Just what is causing movement of the plates is not yet understood. Hurley's (1968) and Hammond's (1971a,b) papers describe many of the important aspects of plate-tectonic theory and show how it is one of those great theories that brings a large and diverse set of observations into an organized concept.

Hurley (1968) discusses the evidence that leads to the conclusion that the present continents were once assembled into two great landmasses, Laurasia in the north and Gondwanaland in the south (together called Pangaea) (Fig. 21.2). These land masses have been split and driven apart by slow upwelling from the earth's mantle, which has resulted in the present upwellings being midway between continents in the middle of the oceans. This is clearly shown in the National Geographic Society maps of the Atlantic and Indian Ocean floors (Fig. 21.3 and 21.4), where a midoceanic ridge is cut longitudinally by a rift valley.

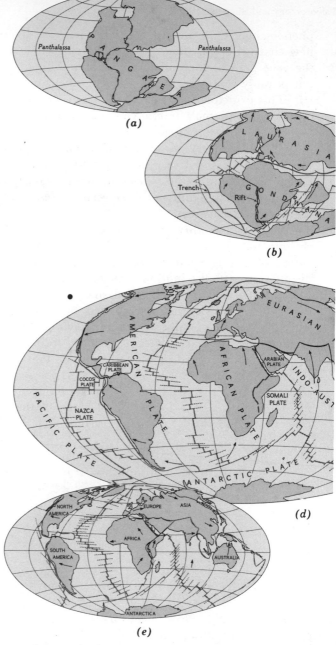

Fig. 21.2 The movement of the earth's land masses due to tectonic forces, top to bot-
rounded by a single ocean Panthalassa; (b) 135 million years ago Laurasia and
moving towards Laurasia; lines indicate edges of plates where upwelling or downward
Africa have split to form the Atlantic Ocean; (d) the present, with plates delineated;
and Indian Oceans will continue to widen, and much of California will have become an

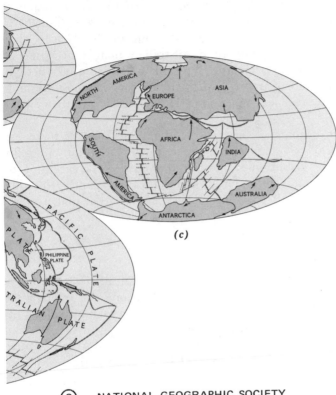

(c)

tom: (*a*) 200 million years ago Pangaea existed as the single land mass on earth sur-
Gondwanaland have divided up Pangaea, and Gondwanaland is splitting up with India
movement of the earth's crust occurs; (*c*) 65 million years ago South America and
(*e*) 50 million years in the future Australia will still be moving northwards, the Atlantic
island. Arrows indicate direction of land movement. From Matthews 1973.

Rocks on the ocean floor become progressively younger as the rift valley is approached indicating that this is the site of the upwelling that causes the plates to move. As the American plate has moved westward, part of the Nazca plate has been forced down into the earth's mantle again and the Peru-Chile trench is the site of subduction. Thus congestion of the earth's crust at this junction of plates has resulted in the formation of the Andes. The complex structure of the Alps in Europe is thought to be the result of repeated crunching and shearing of the African plate against the Eurasian plate. The Indo--Australian plate that crunched against Asia produced the Himalayas. Volcanic and earthquake activity is concentrated at plate margins, which are clearly the most unstable parts of the earth's crust (e.g., Dietz and Holden 1970, Matthews 1973, Wilson et al. 1974).

Thus the plate tectonic theory unites under one concept those elements of the world's geography that are critically important in influencing the present distribution of plants and animals: (1) creation of the continents and oceans, (2) formation of mountain ranges, and (3) production of volcanic islands, all providing geographic isolation that prevents gene flow between populations thus promoting speciation.

To return to the chironomids studied by Brundin all that remains to be known is how Gondwanaland split up before one can explain the present distribution. It appears that the first split in Gondwanaland occurred along what is now the Mid-Indian Ocean Ridge in the Permian about 280 million years ago. In the Triassic the now Mid-Atlantic Ridge split North America from Europe and Africa, a process that was completed in the Cretaceous, 135 million years ago when South America split from Africa. Sea floor spreading has separated these continents more and more and is continuing to do so at about 2 cm/year.

Evidence suggests then that Africa was widely separated from Gondwanaland before South America, Antarctica, and Australia drifted far apart (cf., Fig. 21.2). This explains why South America and Australia have more closely related chironomids than does South Africa. This pattern is also evident in the insect taxa Ephemeroptera (Edmunds 1972), Plecoptera (Illies 1965, 1969), Curculionidae (Kuschel 1962, 1969), Mycetophilidae (Monroe 1974), Formicidae (Brown 1973), and many others (Gressitt 1965, 1970, Mackerras 1970). It is also interesting to note, in the light of the breakup of Gondwanaland, that some primitive insects show affinities between India and Australia (e.g., ledrine leafhoppers, Evans 1959) and India and South America (e.g., termites, Sen-Sarma 1974). By

Fig. 21.3   Relief map of a portion of the Atlantic Ocean floor showing the Mid-Atlantic Ridge divided longitudinally by the Rift Valley. From National Geographic Society, June 1968.

Fig. 21.4   Relief map of part of the Indian Ocean floor showing the Mid-Oceanic Ridge and the longitudinal rift valley. From National Geographic Society, October 1967.

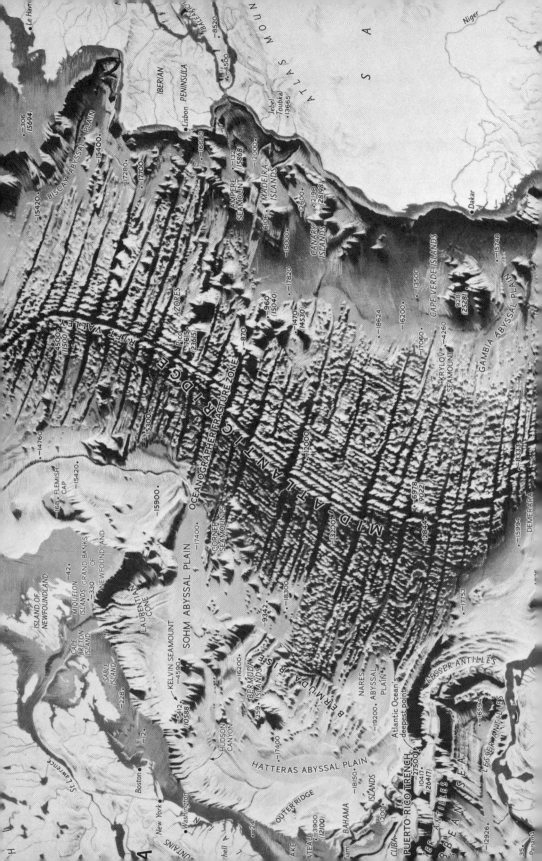

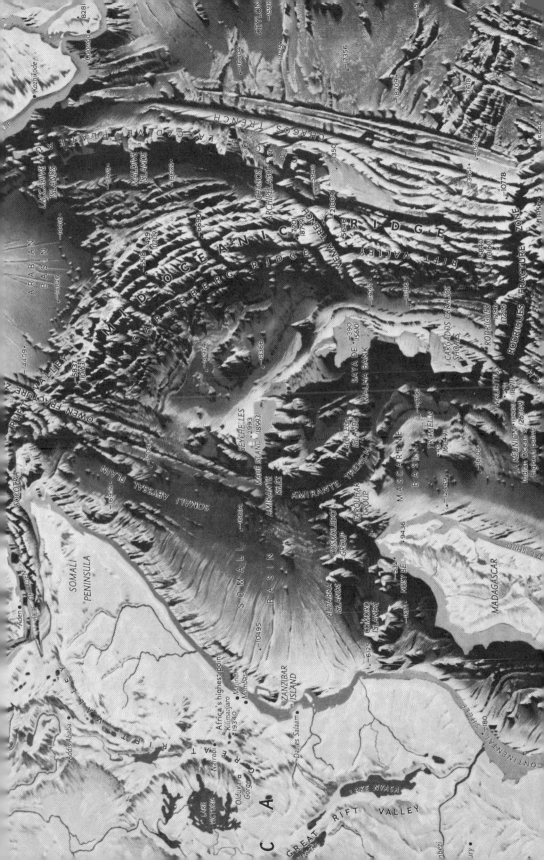

reference to continental drift many other plant and animal distributions have been explained (e.g., Axelrod 1972 and references at end of chapter). Mackerras (1970) states that most orders of insects, from the mayflies to the beetles have closely related species in South America and Australia, but usually the early groups to evolve are representative of this pattern. The distributions of more recently evolved taxa are more easily explained by invoking dispersal over land or sea, sometimes under the influence of wind and ocean currents. Therefore the biogeographic patterns of these taxa differ in many features from the more primitive groups.

Once the continents have drifted apart it is clear that they are effectively isolated, so that continued evolution on these continents will be more or less independent of what is going on elsewhere and endemic faunas and floras will result that are characteristic of that continent. Wallace in his book, *The geographical distribution of animals*, printed in 1876, recognized six basically dissimilar distributions or groupings of the existing animals, which are the six biogeographic realms still recognized today with very little alteration (Fig. 21.5). However the Nearctic

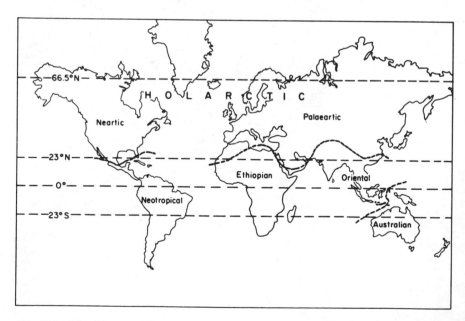

Fig. 21.5   The biogeographic realms of the world delimited by major barriers to dispersal of plants and animals.

and Palearctic regions are more similar than the others and may be considered as one Holarctic Realm. The boundaries fall more or less around the continents, although the changes in fauna reflect response to barriers other than those most obvious to us. For example, the Sahara desert has proved to be as much of a barrier as the Mediterranean Sea between the Holarctic fauna and the Ethiopian fauna. The Sierra Madré have provided the barrier between the Nearctic and Neotropical, and not the isthmus of Panama. The Himalayas and adjoining mountain ranges cut off the Oriental Realm from the Palearctic and not the Indian Ocean and the South China Sea.

It took Wallace 500 pages to describe the faunas of each realm, so that it is hard to characterize briefly the essential components of each, but a grossly abbreviated list of vertebrates is provided (e.g., see Darlington 1957, Kendeigh 1961).

Australian Realm.
Absence of placental mammals and a preponderance of marsupials: parrots, honey eaters, birds of paradise, emu, cassowary, lyre-bird, and kiwi.
Neotropical Realm.
Sloths, armadillos, anteaters, tapirs, rhea, toucans, and hummingbirds.
Ethiopian Realm.
Giraffes, antelopes, zebras, elephant, hippopotamus, rhinocerus, chimpanzee, gorilla, and the cats and dogs: lions, leopards, jackals, foxes, and such.
Oriental Realm.
Tree shrews, orangutan, and gibbon.
Holarctic Realm.
Nearctic vultures, turkeys, mockingbirds, vireos, wood warblers, rattlesnakes, suckers, and catfish.

Most differences between Nearctic and Palearctic regions are at the specific and generic levels.

One feature of distribution that Darlington (1957) pointed out is the complementarity of taxa. He applies this term to "dominant, ecologically equivalent, presumably competing groups of animals that occupy complementary areas." The obvious example is the world distribution of mammals where the placental mammals dominate all biogeographic realms except the Australian, and here the marsupials are dominant. Another case can be seen in the Order Rodentia, which contains among many others, two very large families: Cricetidae (five subfamilies) and the Muridae (six subfamilies). Each family contains a large subfamily, Cricetinae, the New World mice and rats in North and South America, and Murinae, the Old World mice and rats in Africa and temperate and tropical Eurasia. That is, each subfamily has colonized a complementary area, and by being ecologically similar they tend to compete when members of one taxon invade the area of the other.

There is an example among the insects where the ant genus *Crematogaster* is dominant in the Old World while the genus *Iridomyrmex* and closely related genera are dominant in Australia and in South America (Brown 1973, Fig. 21.6). The latter group will be referred to as "*Iridomyrmex.*" Notice again that, as in the chironomid midges that Brundin studied, there is a closer relationship between taxa in South America and Australia than with either of these taxa and that in Africa. Although *Crematogaster* and "*Iridomyrmex*" are not closely related, Brown 1973 states, "they have entered a very similar adaptive zone."

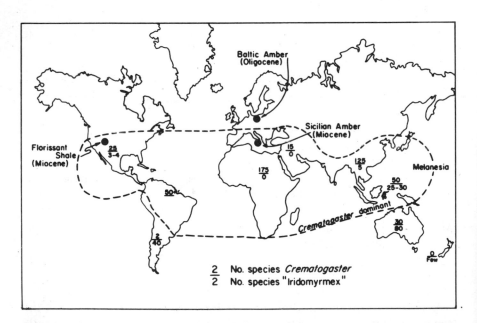

Fig. 21.6 Complementary distributions of two groups of ants, the genus *Crematogaster* and the taxon "*Iridomyrmex.*" Numbers of species are given above a line for the former and below a line for the latter. Sites of fossil records are indicated by solid circles. From W. L. Brown, Jr., 1973, and personal communication.

Crematogaster has a weak sting that is spoon-shaped. It contains the exit of a gland that secretes a repellent viscous poison. The gaster can be brought overhead and pointed forward when defense is necessary. *"Iridomyrmex"* has no sting but a gland at the tip of the abdomen secretes terpenoids that, when exposed to air become gummy, so that enemies can be immobilized. The gaster can also be lifted over the head and aimed forward. These two taxa are ecologically equivalent in many ways (see Brown 1973 for details): colonies are large; they attend Homoptera on stems and foliage; and they form long dense columns from nest to food.

In Baltic Amber (Oligocene), and Florissant Shale in Colorado, one third of all fossil ants found were *"Iridomyrmex."* No *Crematogaster* were discovered in these deposits or in the Sicilian Amber. It looks as if *Crematogaster* has evolved later than *"Iridomyrmex"* and is actually replacing *"Iridomyrmex."* Thus their complementary distributions reflect a dynamic process, and one often involving competitive displacement. These are the sorts of interactions that are going on between realms. There is a continuing movement of animals and plants.

Within each realm more local influences are acting on species distributions; mountain ranges, deserts, prairies, and such. For example, the small winter stoneflies of the genus *Allocapnia* are all restricted to the Eastern United States and as far west as Missouri. Since the majority of the immature stages occupy cold rapid streams it seems that the genus has been unable to spread across the rain shadow of the Rockies. This dry zone acts as a barrier to the dispersal of winter stoneflies (Ross and Ricker 1971). The distribution of subspecies of the bee, *Hoplitis producta*, indicates that the desert of the Great Basin of Nevada (cool desert with sage brush) has acted as a barrier to dispersal (Fig. 21.7). The subspecies *gracilis* occupies California and Oregon, *subgracilis* occupies Washington, and *interior* occupies the Rocky Mountain range down into Arizona and New Mexico (Michener 1947). From Utah, California has been recolonized by individuals that do not interbreed with *gracilis* and in fact three species are living in close proximity in California, *gracilis*, *bernardina*, and *panamintana*. Thus subspecies have encircled the Great Basin and in so doing have overlapped, and the overlapped populations have been sufficiently different; they have accumulated sufficient isolating mechanisms, so that they do not interbreed. That is, a new biological species has been created, and the phenomenon is known as circular overlap (see Mayr 1963 for other examples).

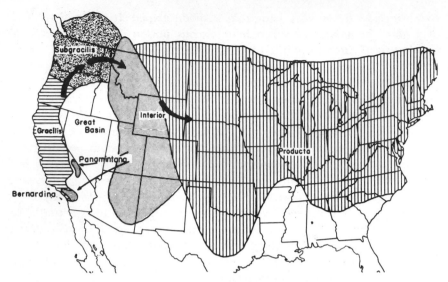

Fig. 21.7 Distribution of subspecies of the megachilid bee, *Hoplitis producta*, in North America showing how the east has been colonized by dispersal around the Great Basin. This eventually led to circular overlap when two subspecies, *panamintana* and *bernardina* derived from *interior* became established in California. From Michener 1947.

Present geographical features cannot provide explanations for all distributions. For example, past glaciations have had a profound influence on speciation of birds (e.g., Mengel 1964), amphibians (e.g., Smith 1957), and insects, and present distributions reflect the strong influence that glaciation has had.

This is shown by the winter stoneflies of the genus *Allocapnia*, so called because all species emerge as adults during the winter or early spring (see Ross 1965, 1967, Ross and Ricker 1971, Ross and Yamamoto 1967 for more details). The center of origin of the genus was the Appalachian Mountain system, which provided an abundance of habitats in the form of cold, rapid, spring-fed, streams that the majority of the species requires. A curious feature of the distribution is that although the Appalachians reach into Maine, many *Allocapnia* species are not distributed beyond Pennsylvania or New York State, and Ross has pointed out that in the Eastern States this limit of distribution is marked by the southern boundary of the most extensive glaciations during the Pleistocene. For example, Nantucket Island, Martha's Vineyard, and Long Island are all composed at least partly of terminal moraines. Thus some distributions of *Allocapnia* species appear as in Fig. 21.8, indicating very

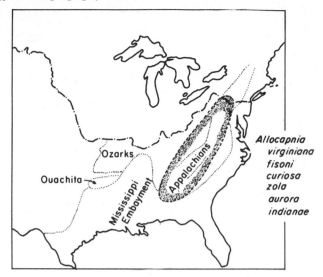

Fig. 21.8 Approximate distributions (shaded outline) of *Allocapnia* species which are restricted to the Appalachian Mountains. The southernmost extent of the Illinoian and Wisconsin glaciations is shown running north of the Ozark Plateau and the Ouachita Mountains up to Long Island. Martha's Vineyard and Nantucket Island are shown to the right of Long Island. The Mississippi Embayment was underwater until the coastal plain was uplifted in the Tertiary. After Ross and Ricker 1971.

little migration since the ice-age. Other species have migrated north as the glaciers have receded, so that several species now exist in Canada.

However, before the ice-age, in the late Pliocene there was considerable tectonic uplifting in central North America. Subsequent erosion produced a series of spring-fed streams that permitted dispersal of *Allocapnia* species around the Mississippi embayment and into the Ozark Plateau and Ouachita Mountains. Thus *Allocapnia rickeri* has a present distribution as in Fig. 21.9. Subsequent glaciation, and particularly the Illinoian glaciation, which reached almost to the southern tip of Illinois, eroded away this central corridor for dispersal leaving only the very narrow belt of uplands in southern Illinois. As the glaciers receded they left what is seen today, flat land with sluggish, muddy rivers, unsuitable for colonization by *Allocapnia*. Thus the species such as *rickeri* that had spread into the Ozarks were more or less cut off into two isolated sets of populations, and speciation occurred in some cases. As a result sister species occur such as *Allocapnia recta* in the Appalachians and *Allocapnia mohri* in the Ozarks and Ouachita mountains (Fig. 21.10).

Occasional dispersal from west to east has produced further speciation, and has increased the diversity of species in the Appalachians. Also, as

Fig. 21.9   Approximate distribution of *Allocapnia rickeri* which occupies the Appalachians, Ozarks, and Ouachita Mountains. After Ross and Ricker 1971.

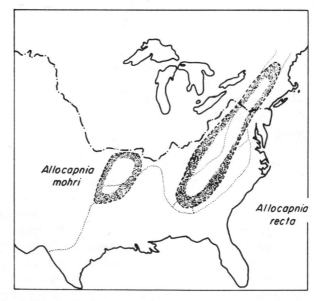

Fig. 21.10   Approximate distributions of the closely related species *Allocapnia mohri*
in the west and *A. recta* in the east indicating how the narrow waist of mountains in
southern Illinois, through which dispersal would be rare, has acted as a barrier to
gene flow with consequent speciation of the isolated populations. After Ross and Ricker
1971.

the glaciations receded, some populations migrated north and others became isolated in the south in the high mountains where cold streams persisted, such as in the Great Smoky Mountains, in spite of the general warming trend. Thus some closely related species pairs occupy southern and northern parts of the Appalachian chain.

Ross' studies clearly show how geographic features such as mountains, lowlands, and rivers, and past geological events, particularly mountain formation and glaciation, and the juxtaposition of all these features, influence speciation and species distribution. Note that whereas mountains are normally thought of as barriers, in the case of the stoneflies, it is the mountains that provided the habitats and corridors for dispersal. Thus it is important to understand the detailed ecological requirements of a group of species before trying to interpret reasons for their present distribution.

Climate is having a continuing influence on distribution of animals and plants. Merriam, who published his ideas in 1894 and 1898, made a long accepted description of animal and plant distributions by defining what he called life zones. After having been on an expedition to the San Francisco Peak area in Arizona he was impressed by the sharp zonation of plants and animals up the mountains, apparently under the sole influence of temperature. He formulated two laws about the control of temperature on the distribution of living things: Law 1: The northward distribution of terrestrial plants and animals is governed by the sum of the positive temperatures (above 6°C) for the entire season of growth and reproduction. Law 2: The southward distribution is governed by the mean temperature of a brief period during the hottest part of the year. Using these criteria he divided the continent into areas, or life zones, with similar temperature characteristics so that the belts up a mountain appeared as in Fig. 21.11. Tilting of the zones results because the south slope is warmer than the north slope, in the northern hemisphere. As pointed out in Chapter 18, Merriam's system worked well in the mountainous west but could not be used effectively in the east. Pitelka's (1941) approach to animal distribution by defining major differences in the structural characters of the vegetation, the biomes, has improved on Merriam's life-zone system.

Holdridge (1947, 1967, Holdridge et al. 1971) has gone one step further than Pitelka by producing a system that shows how biomes can be delimited, particularly plant formations, by using three climatic parameters, temperature, precipitation, and evaporation (Fig. 21.12). Mean tempera-

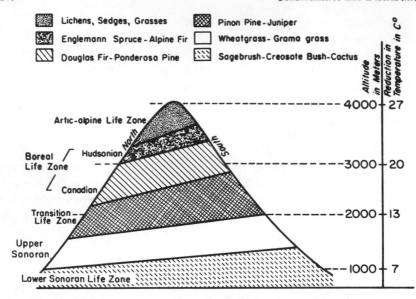

Fig. 21.11 Life zones recognized by Merriam in the Rocky Mountains. South slopes in the Northern Hemisphere receive more insolation and thus ecotones are at slightly higher altitudes than on north slopes. Reprinted with permission of Macmillan Publishing Co., Inc. from Ecology of Populations by A. S. Boughey. Copyright © 1968 by Arthur S. Boughey.

ture above 0°C declines from the equator to the polar regions, so that temperatures can be plotted as parallel lines representing isotherms. The values are plotted on a logarithmic scale. Precipitation is calculated as the average mean annual rainfall in millimeters, and plotted at about 60° to the temperature axis, again on a log scale. The evaporation lines represent the balance between temperature and rainfall and the values represent the number of times the actual rainfall could be evaporated in 1 year at sea-level atmospheric pressure, plotted on a log scale. Holdridge also gives the altitude belts that result from the equivalent effect to latitude and he points out that only in the tropics will all altitudinal belts be encountered. This relates back to the tropical species diversity problem and the environmental diversity in the tropics caused by the longer physical gradients present (Chapter 19). By measuring two parameters one can predict what the vegetation structure will be and from the vegetation structure one can predict what sorts of animals will be present.

So far oceanic islands have almost been ignored in this chapter, and yet they are known to be important in speciation, providing good exam-

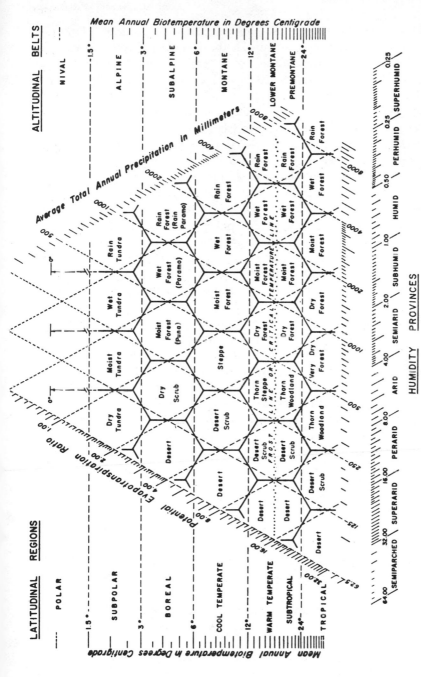

Fig. 21.12 The Holdridge system for classifying life zones using temperature, rainfall, and potential evapotranspiration to delimit each zone. From Holdridge et al. 1971.

427

ples of adaptive radiation. Also the theoretical aspects of island biogeography are much more advanced than those for continents. The
theory of island biogeography was advanced by MacArthur and Wilson
in 1963 and 1967. In Chapter 18 it was stated that it is Wilson and
Simberloff (e.g., Simberloff 1969, Simberloff and Wilson 1969, 1970, Wilson 1969, Wilson and Simberloff 1969) who are testing this theory with
defaunation studies on the mangrove islands off the Florida Keys.

Many people have observed a striking relationship between area of an
island and the number of species of a given taxon it can support, for
example, the number of species of land and fresh-water birds of the
Sunda islands, the Philippines, and New Guinea (Fig. 21.13). These
species-area curves were discussed in relation to community organization
(Chapter 18). These islands and archipelagoes are grouped close to one
another and to the Asian continent, and the areas of the islands explain
at least 90% of the variance about the mean. As a general trend Hamilton, Barth and Rubinoff (1964), and Hamilton and Rubinoff (1967) have
found that in most cases area of the island accounts for 80–90% of the
variation, and elevation for another 2–15%. Actually both these factors
can be interpreted functionally as contributing to the habitat diversity of
an island. By calculating the habitat diversity for each island and relating it to bird species Watson (1964) explained practically all variation
in the Aegean islands between Greece and Turkey in the Mediterranean.

But other groups of islands support fewer species than the number
predicted from size alone. If area and species richness are plotted for
the Moluccas, Melanesia, Micronesia, and Polynesia the slope of the

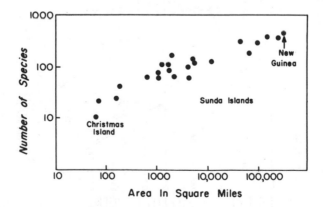

Fig. 21.13 Relationship between area of island in square miles (log scale) and the
number of land and fresh-water bird species in the Sunda Island group, the Philippine
Islands, and New Guinea. The islands are grouped close together and close to the
Asian continent. From MacArthur and Wilson 1967.

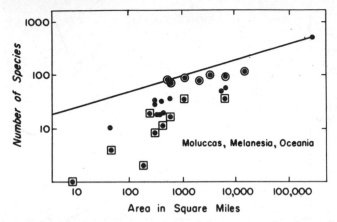

Fig. 21.14 Relationship between area of island in square miles (log scale) and the number of land and fresh-water bird species in the Moluccas, Melanesia, Micronesia, and Polynesia. Circled islands are less than 500 miles from New Guinea and conform to the species-area curve observed for the Sunda Islands. Squared islands are over 2000 miles from New Guinea and the relationship diverges significantly from that expected from the species area curve. From MacArthur and Wilson 1967.

species-area curve is much steeper than for the Sunda Islands (Fig. 21.14). These islands are spread out over the Pacific ocean and clearly some are isolated, so that a good chance exists that all species that could have colonized these islands have not done so; that is, a distance factor is involved. In fact the islands close to New Guinea (less than 500 miles), which has the richest bird fauna, can be grouped, and all are close to the saturation number of species. Islands greater than 2000 miles from New Guinea are those that deviate furthest from the expected species saturation line.

Therefore, MacArthur and Wilson (1963, 1967) proposed the theory of island biogeography to relate the three components, (1) species numbers per island, (2) size of island, and (3) distance of island from source of colonists. MacArthur and Wilson point out that there are two components to the number of species on an island regardless of its distance from the mainland or its area. For each island there will be an immigration rate of animal and plant species arriving on the island per unit time. Not all species that immigrate will survive so that there must also be an extinction rate. These opposing factors will act to produce an equilibrium number of species on any given island (Fig. 21.15). The immigration rate of species will decline as a function of species number because as more species become established, fewer immigrants will belong to new species. The line will be steeper at first as the most rapidly dispersing spe-

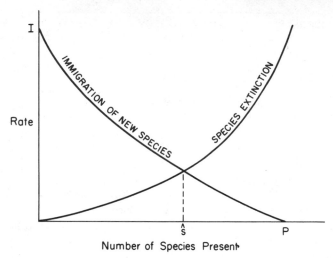

Fig. 21.15 The relationship between the immigration and extinction rates on an island which leads to an equilibrium number of species, $\hat{s}$, on the island. I is the initial immigration rate and P the total number of species in the source of colonizers. From MacArthur and Wilson 1967.

cies will become established first, whereas the late, slowly dispersing arrivals will prolong the time of immigration and cause the rate to decline only slowly as the point P is reached. P is the total possible number that can reach the island because that is all the species the mainland supports. The extinction curve has an exponential shape and a positive slope because as more species arrive there is a greater chance of some going extinct; competition between species will increase and population sizes may be reduced, both accelerating the rate of extinction.

The distance of an island from the source of colonizing species and its size should have considerable impact on the relationship between immigration and extinction. The nearer the island to the source of the species, the more colonists will arrive per unit time and the closer $\hat{s}$, the equilibrium number of species, approaches P, the number of species in the source area (Fig. 21.16). The larger the island is, the higher the carrying capacity will be for each species. More diverse habitats will permit species to exist in suitable enclaves from competition, and the net result will be reduced rates of extinction with increased island size.

This theory has supplied an impressive impetus to ecological research and is rapidly being extended to ecological island situations on continents as described in Chapter 18. Theoretical biogeography will eventually encompass continental regions. The theory also provides a new

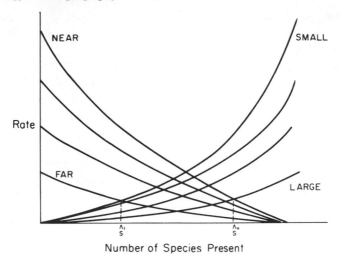

Number of Species Present

Fig. 21.16   The effects of size of island and distance from source of colonizers on the equilibrium number of species. Near, large islands have many more species, $\hat{S}''$, than far, small islands, $\hat{S}'$. From MacArthur and Wilson 1967.

method of looking at ecological islands such as crops and the colonization of crops by insects. Do crop conditions permit equilibrium to develop or is the colonization curve truncated by harvesting the crop? The theory will help in understanding of the community organization of insects on crops, and thus the most ecologically sound methods of managing insect pests (see Price and Waldbauer 1975).

Another theory that relates to continental biogeography is important in relation to competition, and particularly the development of dominance in competitive interactions. It was Darlington (1959) who asked himself the question, "Where do dominant animals evolve?" Do they evolve in large or small areas, warm or cold, stable or less predictable climates? To be dominant an animal must possess adaptations that are general in nature, that will promote its survival in every environment it invades. Brown (1958a) contrasted this general adaptation of dominant species, which might increase an animal's efficiency in food utilization, or rate of development, independently of the local environment, with what he called special adaptations that would promote the welfare of an organism in relation to a particular set of environmental conditions. To occupy a large area, to be competitively superior, to be an effective colonizer, a species must have accumulated a large number of general adaptations. Darlington wanted to know under which conditions are factors likely to be favorable for the accumulation of such a set of general adaptations.

Darlington examined the evidence for the origin of several dominant or potent groups of animals. For example, all clues point to the evolution of *Homo sapiens* in the Old World tropics. In the elephants, mastodonts, and such, the earliest fossils were found in Egypt, and Simpson (1940) has suggested that they radiated from North Africa. The family Bovidae, which includes cattle, antelopes, sheep, and goats, is the most recent family of hoofed animals to evolve, and now they are the most numerous and diverse in Africa. The Old World rats and mice, the murid rodents, are dominant practically wherever they have dispersed, and these are most diverse in the Old World tropics. In fact the evidence shows that many dominant groups have arisen in the Old World tropics and they have spread northward and southward. There has been considerably less movement in the opposite directions (Fig. 21.17). The most

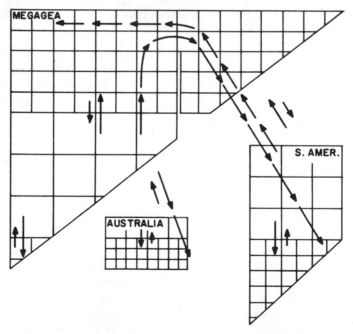

Fig. 21.17   Diagram illustrating Darlington's concept that large land area in a favorable climate will lead to a large number of populations (represented by the large squares) per unit area and consequent evolution of new generally adapted species. These then disperse as indicated by the long arrows, with very little dispersal in the opposite direction as indicated by the short arrows. Megagea is the land mass composed of Eurasia, Africa, and North America. From Darlington 1959.

dominant groups seem to evolve in the largest areas with the most favorable climate. Here species will not have to specialize in tolerating physiological hardships and they are more likely to evolve toward a strong competitive ability because so many other related species coexist. Darlington suggested further that the tropical climate might accelerate reproduction and mutation. A large area will contain many populations, and the larger the area the more numerous and diverse will be the populations of any species. The gene pool will be very diverse making the likelihood of combinations of genes that produce dominance much greater. Thus the theory also relates to the discussion of diversity and stability in Chapter 19.

There is much more to be said that is relevant to an understanding of biogeography and paleoecology, and other works should be consulted. Text books on the subject include Darlington (1957) and Udvardy (1969). Darlington's (1965), *Biogeography of the southern end of the world*, provides a discussion of an area that is of great importance; it includes much more information on insects than his former book; and it will introduce the reader to his major contributions on the biogeography of carabid beetles. Strongly ecological treatments may be found in MacArthur's (1972), *Geographical ecology*, and the section on geographical ecology in Kendeigh (1974). Symposia on regional biogeographies include South America (Fittkau et al. 1968, 1969), India (Mani 1974), Australia (Keast et al. 1959), and Anarctica (van Mieghem et al. 1965).

BIBLIOGRAPHY

Abrahamson, W. G., and M. Gadgil. 1973. Growth form and reproductive effort in goldenrods (*Solidago,* Compositae). *Amer. Natur.* 107:651–661.

Addicott, J. F. 1974. Predation and prey community structure: An experimental study of the effect of mosquito larvae on the protozoan communities of pitcher plants. *Ecology* 55:475–492.

Alcock, J. 1973a. The foraging behavior of seed-caching beetle larvae (Coleoptera: Carabidae). *Bull. Ecol. Soc. Amer.* 54(1):45–46.

Alcock, J. 1973b. Cues used in searching for food by red-winged blackbirds (*Agelaius phoeniceus*). *Behaviour* 46:174–188.

Alexander, R. D. 1961. Aggressiveness, territoriality, and sexual behavior in field crickets (Orthoptera: Gryllidae). *Behaviour* 17:130–223.

Alexander, R. D., and W. L. Brown, Jr. 1963 Mating behavior and the origin of insect wings. *Occas. Pap. Mus. Zool. Univ. Mich.* 628:1–19.

Allee, W. C, A. E. Emerson, O. Park, T. Park, and K. P. Schmidt. 1949. *Principles of animal ecology.* Saunders, Philadelphia, 837 pp.

Amadon, D. 1950. The Hawaiian honeycreepers (Aves, Drepaniidae). *Bull. Amer. Mus. Natur. Hist.* 95:151–262.

Andrewartha, H. G., and L. C. Birch. 1953. The Lotka-Volterra theory of interspecific competition. *Austr. J. Zool.* 1:174–177.

Andrewartha, H.G., and L. C. Birch. 1954. *The distribution and abundance of animals.* Univ. Chicago Press, Chicago. 782 pp.

Andrzejewska, L. 1967. Estimation of the effects of feeding of the sucking insect *Cicadella viridis* L. (Homoptera-Auchenorrhyncha) on plants. In K. Petrusewicz (ed.). *Secondary productivity of terrestial ecosystems.* Inst. Ecol., Polish Acad. Sci, Warsaw, pp. 791–805.

Anonymous. 1971. *Biological control programmes against insects and weeds in Canada. 1959–1968.* Commonwealth Inst. Biol. Control, Tech. Comm. 4. 266 pp.

Applebaum, S. W. 1964. Physiological aspects of host specificity in the Bruchidae. I. General considerations of developmental compatibility. *J. Insect Physiol.* 10:783–788.

Ashmole, N. P., and M. J. Ashmole. 1967. Comparative feeding ecology of sea birds of a tropical oceanic island. *Bull. Peabody Mus. Natur. Hist. Yale Univ.* 24:1–131.

Askew, R. R. 1968. Considerations on speciation in Chalcidoidea (Hymenoptera). *Evolution* 22:642–645.

Askew, R. R. 1971. *Parasitic insects.* American Elsevier, New York. 316 pp.

435

Auer, C. 1961. Ergebnisse zwölfjähriger quantitativer Untersuchungen der Populations-bewegung des Grauen Lärchenwicklers (*Zeiraphera griseana* Hb.) im Oberengadin, 1949–1958. *Mitt. Schweiz. Anst. Forstl. VersWes.* **37**:175–263.

Auer, C. 1968. Erste Ergebnisse einfacher stochastischer Modelluntersuchungen über die Ursachen der Populations bewegung des grauen Lärchenwicklers *Zeiraphera diniana*, Gn. (=*Z. griseana* Hb.) im Oberengadin, 1949/66. *Z. Angew. Entomol.* **62**:202–235.

Axelrod, D. I. 1972. Ocean-floor spreading in relation to ecosystematic problems. In R. T. Allen and F. C. James (eds.). *A symposium on ecosystematics*. Univ. Arkansas Mus., Occ. Paper No. 4, pp 15–68.

Ayala, F. J. 1968. Genotype, environment and population numbers. *Science* **162**:1453–1459.

Ayala, F. J. 1970. Competition, coexistence and evolution. In M. K. Hecht and W. C. Steere (eds.). *Essays in evolution and genetics*. Appleton-Century-Crofts, New York, pp. 121–158.

Ayala, F. J. 1971. Competition between species: Frequency dependence. *Science* **171**: 820–824.

Ayala, F. J., D. Hedgecock, G. S. Zumwalt, and J. W. Valentine. 1973. Genetic variation in *Tridacna maxima*, an ecological analog of some unsuccessful evolutionary lineages. *Evolution* **27**:177–191.

Ayala, F. J., J. R. Powell, and M. L. Tracey. 1972a. Enzyme variability in the *Drosophila willistoni* group. V. Genic variation in natural populations of *Drosophila equinoxalis*. *Genet. Res.* **20**:19–42.

Ayala, F J., J. R. Powell, M. L. Tracey, C. A. Mourão, and S. Pérez-Salas. 1972b. Enzyme variability in the *Drosophila willistoni* group IV. Genic variation in natural populations of *Drosophila willistoni*. *Genetics* **70**:113–139.

Ayala, F. J., M. L. Tracey, L. G. Barr, and J. G. Ehrenfeld. 1974. Genetic and reproductive differentiation of the subspecies, *Drosophila equinoxalis caribbensis*. *Evolution* **28**:24–41.

Bagenal, T. B. 1951. A note on the papers of Elton and Williams on the generic relations of species in small ecological communities. *J. Anim. Ecol.* **20**:242–245.

Baker, H. G. 1961. *Ficus* and *Blastophaga*. *Evolution* **15**:378–379.

Baker, H. G. 1970. Evolution in the tropics. *Biotropica* **2**:101–111.

Baker, H. G., and I. Baker. 1973a. Amino-acids in nectar and their evolutionary significance. *Nature* **241**:543–545.

Baker, H. G., and I. Baker. 1973b. Some anthecological aspects of the evolution of nectar-producing flowers, particularly amino acid production in nectar. In V. H. Heywood (ed.). *Taxonomy and ecology*. Academic Press, New York, pp. 243–264.

Baker, R. R. 1972. Territorial behaviour of the nymphalid butterflies, *Aglais urticae* (L.) and *Inachis io* (L.). *J. Anim. Ecol.* **41**:453–469.

Baltensweiler, W. 1958. Zur Kenntnis der Parasiten des Grauen Lärchenwicklers (*Zeiraphera griseana* Hübner) im Oberengadin. Ihre Biologie und Bedeutung während der Gradation von 1949–1958. *Mitt. Schweiz. Anst. Forstl. VersWes.* **35**:277–315.

Baltensweiler, W. 1964. *Zeiraphera griseana* Hübner (Lepidoptera: Tortricidae) in the European Alps. A contribution to the problem of cycles. *Can. Entomol.* **96**:792–800.

Baltensweiler, W. 1968. The cyclic population dynamics of the grey larch tortrix, *Zeiraphera griseana* Hübner (=*Semasia diniana* Guenée) (Lepidoptera: Tortricidae). In T. R. E. Southwood (ed.). *Insect abundance.* Symp. Roy. Entomol. Soc. London No 4, pp 88–97.

Barr, B. A. 1969. Sound production in Scolytidae (Coleoptera) with emphasis on the genus *Ips. Can. Entomol.* 101:636–672.

Bartholomew, B. 1970. Bare zone between California shrub and grassland communities: The role of animals. *Science* 170:1210–1212.

Bartholomew, B. 1971. Role of. animals in suppression of herbs by shrubs. *Science* 173:463.

Batzli, G. O. 1974. Production, assimilation and accumulation of organic matter in ecosystems. *J. Theor. Biol.* 45:205–217.

Batzli, G. O., and F. A. Pitelka. 1970. Influence of meadow mouse populations on California grassland. *Ecology* 51:1027–1039.

Beaver, R. A. 1966. The development and expression of population tables for the bark beetle *Scolytus scolytus* (F.) *J. Anim. Ecol.* 35:27–41.

Belt, T. 1874. *The naturalist in Nicaragua.* Murray, London.

Bennet-Clark, H. C., and A. W. Ewing. 1968. The wing mechanism involved in the courtship of *Drosophila. J. Exp. Biol.* 49:117–128.

Bennet-Clark, H. C., and A. W. Ewing. 1970. The love song of the fruit fly. *Sci. Amer.* 223(1):84–92.

Berger, E. M. 1970. A comparison of gene-enzyme variation between *Drosophila melanogaster* and *D. simulans. Genetics* 66:677–683.

Bernays, E. A., and R. F. Chapman. 1970. Food selection by *Chorthippus parallelus* (Zetterstedt) (Orthoptera: Acrididae) in the field. *J. Anim. Ecol.* 39:383–394.

Beroza, M. 1972. Attractants and repellents for insect pest control. In *Pest control strategies for the future.* Nat. Acad. Sci., Washington, pp. 226–253.

Berry, R. J., and H. M. Murphy. 1970. The biochemical genetics of an island population of the house mouse. *Proc. Roy. Soc. London Ser. B.* 176:87–103.

Berryman, A. A. 1973. Population dynamics of the fir engraver, *Scolytus ventralis* (Coleoptera: Scolytidae). I. Analysis of population behavior and survival from 1964 to 1971. *Can. Entomol.* 105:1465–1488.

Bess, H. A., and F. H. Haramoto. 1958. Biological control of the oriental fruit fly in Hawaii. *Proc. Int. Congr. Entomol. 10. Montreal 1956* 4:835–840.

Birch, L. C. 1948. The intrinsic rate of natural increase of an insect population. *J. Anim. Ecol.* 17:15–26.

Black, C. C. 1971. Ecological implications of dividing plants into groups with distinct photosynthetic production capacities. *Adv. Ecol. Res.* 7:87–114.

Blackman, M. W., and H. H. Stage. 1924. On the succession of insects living in the bark and wood of dying, dead and decaying hickory. *New York State Col. Forest., Syracuse Univ. Tech. Publ.* 17:1–269.

Blest, A. D. 1957a. The function of eyespot patterns in the Lepidoptera. *Behaviour* 11:209–256.

Blest, A. D. 1957b. The evolution of protective displays in the Saturnioidea and Sphingidae (Lepidoptera). *Behaviour* 11:257–309.

Blest, A. D. 1963. Longevity, palatability and natural selection in five species of new world saturniid moth. *Nature* 197:1183–1186.

Bogdan, A. V., 1962. Grass pollination by bees in Kenya. *Proc. Linn. Soc. London* 173:57–60.

Bohlool, B. B., and E. L. Schmidt. 1974. Lectins: A possible basis for specificity in the *Rhizobium*-legume root nodule symbiosis. *Science* 185:269–271.

Bonnell, M. L., and R. K. Selander. 1974. Elephant seals: Genetic variation and near extinction. *Science* 184:908–909.

Botkin, D. B., and R. S. Miller. 1974. Mortality rates and survival of birds. *Amer. Natur.* 108:181–192.

Brian, A. D. 1957. Differences in the flowers visited by four species of bumble-bees and their causes. *J. Anim. Ecol.* 26:71–98.

Brncic, D. 1962. Chromosomal structure of populations of *Drosophila flavopilosa* studied in larvae collected in their natural breeding sites. *Chromosoma* 13:183–195.

Brncic, D. 1968. The effects of temperature on chromosomal polymorphism of *Drosophila flavopilosa* larvae. *Genetics* 59:427–432.

Broadhead, E. 1958. The psocid fauna of larch trees in northern England—An ecological study of mixed species populations exploiting a common resource. *J. Anim. Ecol.* 27:217–263.

Broadhead, E., and A. J. Wapshere. 1966. *Mesopsocus* populations on larch in England—The distribution and dynamics of two closely related co-existing species of Psocoptera sharing the same food source. *Ecol. Monogr.* 36:327–388.

Brock, M. L., R. G. Wiegert, and T. D. Brock. 1969. Feeding by *Paracoenia* and *Ephydra* (Diptera: Ephydridae) on microorganisms of hot springs. *Ecology* 50:192–200.

Brock, T. D. 1967. Relationship between standing crop and primary productivity along a hot spring thermal gradient. *Ecology* 48:566–571.

Brock, T. D. 1970. High temperature systems. *Annu. Rev. Ecol. Syst.* 1:191–220.

Brock, T. D., and M. L. Brock. 1966. Temperature optima for algal development in Yellowstone and Iceland hot springs. *Nature* 209:733–734.

Brock, T. D., and M. L. Brock. 1968. Measurement of steady state growth rates of a thermophilic alga directly in nature. *J. Bact.* 95:811–815.

Brock, T. D., and M. L. Brock. 1971. *Life in geyser basins.* Yellowstone Library and Museum Assn., Wyoming.

Brody, S. 1952. Facts, fables, and fallacies on feeding the world population. *Fed. Proc.* 11:681–693.

Brower, J. V. Z. 1958a. Experimental studies of mimicry in some North American butterflies. I. The monarch, *Danaus plexippus*, and viceroy, *Limenitis archippus. Evolution* 12:32–47.

Brower, J. V. Z. 1958b. Experimental studies of mimicry in some North American butterflies. III. *Danaus gilippus berenice* and *Limenitis archippus floridensis. Evolution* 12:273–285.

Brower, L. P. 1969. Ecological chemistry. *Sci. Amer.* 220(2):22–29.

Brower, L. P., J. Alcock, and J. V. Z. Brower. 1971. Avian feeding behaviour and the selective advantage of incipient mimicry. In R. Creed (ed.) *Ecological genetics and evolution.* Appleton-Century-Crofts, New York, pp. 261–274.

Brower, L. P., and J. V. Z. Brower. 1964. Birds, butterflies, and plant poisons: A study in ecological chemistry. *Zoologica* 49:137–159.

Brower, L. P., P. B. McEvoy, K. L. Williamson, and M. A. Flannery. 1972. Variation in cardiac glycoside content of monarch butterflies from natural populations in Eastern North America. *Science* 177:426–429.

Brower, L. P., W. N. Ryerson, L. L. Coppinger, and S. C. Glazier. 1968. Ecological chemistry and the palatability spectrum. *Science* 161:1349–1351.

Brown, E. S. 1951. The relation between migration-rate and type of habitat in aquatic insects, with special reference to certain species of Corixidae. *Proc. Zool. Soc. London* 121:539–545.

Brown, J. H. 1971. Mammals on mountaintops: nonequilibrium insular biogeography. *Amer. Natur.* 105:467–478.

Brown, J. L. 1964. The evolution of diversity in avian territorial systems. *Wilson Bull.* 76:160–169.

Brown, J. L. 1966. Types of group selection. *Nature* 211:870.

Brown, W. L., Jr. 1958a. General adaptation and evolution. *Syst. Zool.* 7:157–168.

Brown, W. L., Jr. 1958b. Some zoological concepts applied to problems in evolution of the hominid lineage. *Amer. Sci.* 46:151–158.

Brown, W. L., Jr. 1960. Ants, acacias and browsing mammals. *Ecology* 41:587–592.

Brown, W. L., Jr. 1973. A comparison of the Hylean and Congo-West African rain forest ant faunas. In B. J. Meggers, E. S. Ayensu, and W. D. Duckworth (eds.). *Tropical forest ecosystems in Africa and South America: A comparative review.* Smithsonian Inst. Press, Washington, D.C., pp. 161–185.

Brown, W. L., Jr., and E. O. Wilson. 1956. Character displacement. *Syst. Zool.* 5:49–64.

Brues, C. T. 1924. The specificity of food plants in the evolution of phytophagous insects. *Amer. Natur.* 58:127–144.

Brundin, L. 1960. *Transantarctic relationships and their significance, as evidenced by chironomid midges.* Almquist and Wiksell, Stockholm. 472 pp.

Brundin, L. 1967. Insects and the problem of austral disjunctive distribution. *Annu. Rev. Entomol.* 12:149–168.

Bryant, E. H. 1971. Life history consequences of natural selection: Cole's result. *Amer. Natur.* 105:75–76.

Bryant, E. H. 1974. On the adaptive significance of enzyme polymorphisms in relation to environmental variability. *Amer. Natur.* 108:1–19.

Budnik, M., and D. Brncic. 1974. Preadult competition between *Drosophila pavani* and *Drosophila melanogaster, Drosophila simulans,* and *Drosophila willistoni. Ecology* 55:657–661.

Burbott, A. J., and W. D. Loomis. 1969. Evidence for metabolic turnover of monoterpenes in peppermint. *Plant Physiol.* 44:173–179.

Burges, H. D., and N. W. Hussey (eds.). 1971. *Microbial control of insects and mites.* Academic Press, London. 861 p.

Burnett, T. 1958. A model of host-parasite interaction. *Proc. 10th Int. Cong. Entomol.* Vol. 2 pp. 679–686.

Butler, C. G. 1943. Work on bee repellents. Management of colonies for pollination. *Ann. Appl. Biol.* 30:195–196.

Butler, C. G. 1945. The influence of various physical and biological factors of the environment in honeybee activity. An examination of the relationship between activity and nectar concentration and abundance. *J. Exp. Biol.* 21:5–12.

Butler, C. G. 1967. Insect pheromones. *Biol. Rev.* 42:42–87.

Butler, C. G., E. P. Jeffree, and H. Kalmus. 1943. The behaviour of a population of honeybees on an artificial and on a natural crop. *J. Exp. Biol.* **20**:65–73.

Cade, T. J., and R. Fyfe. 1970. The North American peregrine survey, 1970. *Can. Field Natur.* **84**:231–245.

Cade, T. J., J. L. Lincer, C. M. White, D. G. Roseneau, and L. G. Swartz. 1971. DDE residues and eggshell changes in Alaskan falcons and hawks. *Science* **172**:955–957

Cain, A. J., and P. M. Sheppard. 1950. Selection in the polymorphic land snail *Cepaea nemoralis. Heredity* **4**:275–294.

Cain, A. J., and P. M. Sheppard. 1954a. Natural selection in *Cepaea. Genetics* **39**:89–116.

Cain, A. J., and P. M. Sheppard. 1954b. The theory of adaptive polymorphism. *Amer. Natur.* **88**:321–326.

Cain, S. A. 1938. The species-area curve. *Amer. Midland Natur.* **19**:573–581.

Calhoun, J. B. 1952. The social aspects of population dynamics *J. Mammal.* **33**:139–159.

Campbell, B. (ed.). 1972. *Sexual selection and the descent of man 1871–1971.* Aldine, Chicago. 378 pp.

Carlisle, D. B., and P. E. Ellis. 1968. Bracken and locust ecdysones: Their effect on molting in the desert locust. *Science* **159**:1472–1474.

Carson, H. L. 1958a. The population genetics of *Drosophila robusta. Adv. Genet.* **9**:1–40.

Carson, H. L. 1958b. Response to selection under different conditions of recombination in *Drosophila. Cold Spring Harbor Symp. Quant. Biol.* **23**:291–306.

Carson, H. L. 1968. The population flush and its genetic consequences. In R. C. Lewontin (ed.). *Population biology and evolution.* Syracuse Univ. Press, Syracuse, New York, pp. 123–137.

Carson, H. L., D. E. Hardy, H. T. Spieth, and W. S. Stone. 1970. The evolutionary biology of the Hawaiian Drosophilidae. In M. K. Hecht and W. C. Steere (eds.). *Essays in evolution and genetics in honor of Theodosius Dobzhansky.* Appleton-Century-Crofts, New York, pp. 437–543.

Caswell, H. and F. C. Reed. 1975. Digestibility of C_4 bundle sheath cells. *Ann. Entomol. Soc. Amer.* In press.

Caswell, H., F. Reed, S. N. Stephenson, and P. A. Werner. 1973. Photosynthetic pathways and selective herbivory: A hypothesis. *Amer. Natur.* **107**:465–480.

Cates, R. G. 1975. The interface between slugs and wild ginger: Some evolutionary aspects. *Ecology* **56**:391–400.

Cates, R. G., and G. H. Orians. 1975. Successional status and the palatability of plants to generalized herbivores. *Ecology* **56**:410–418.

Caughley, G. 1970. Eruption of ungulate populations, with emphasis on Himalayan thar in New Zealand. *Ecology* **51**:53–72.

Center, T D., and C. D. Johnson. 1974. Coevolution of some seed beetles (Coleoptera: Bruchidae) and their hosts. *Ecology* **55**:1096–1103.

Chandler, A. E. F. 1967. Oviposition responses of aphidophagous Syrphidae (Diptera). *Nature, London* **213**:736.

Chandler, A. E. F. 1968a. Some host-plant factors affecting oviposition by aphidophagous Syrphidae (Diptera). *Ann. Appl. Biol.* **61**:415–423.

Chandler, A. E. F. 1968b. The relationship between aphid infestations and oviposition by aphidophagous Syrphidae (Diptera). *Ann. Appl. Biol.* **61**:425–434.

Chandler, A. E. F. 1968c. Some factors influencing the occurrence and site of oviposition by aphidophagous Syrphidae (Diptera). *Ann. Appl. Biol.* **61**:435–446.

Chapman, R. N. 1928. The quantitative analysis of environmental factors. *Ecology* **9**:111–122.

Chapman, R. N. 1931. *Animal ecology with especial reference to insects.* McGraw-Hill, New York. 464 pp.

Charnov, E. L., and W. M. Schaffer. 1973. Life-history consequences of natural selection: Cole's result revisited. *Amer. Natur.* **107**:791–793.

Chermock, R. L. 1946. Migration of *Ascia monuste phileta* (Lepidoptera, Pieridae). *Entomol. News* **57**:144–146.

Chevin, H. 1966. Végétation et peuplement entomologique des terrains sablonneux de la côte ouest du Cotentin. *Mem. Soc. Nat. Sci. Natur. Math. Cherbourg* **52**:8–137.

Chew, R. M. 1974. Consumers as regulators of ecosystems: an alternative to energetics. *Ohio J. Sci.* **74**:359–370.

Chitty, D. 1957. Self-regulation of numbers through changes in viability. *Cold Spring Harbor Symp. Quant. Biol.* **22**:277–280.

Chitty, D. 1960. Population processes in the vole and their relevance to general theory. *Can. J. Zool.* **38**:99–113.

Chitty, D. 1967. The natural selection of self-regulatory behaviour in animal populations. *Proc. Ecol. Soc. Australia* **2**:51–78.

Christian, J. J. 1950. The adreno-pituitary system and population cycles in mammals. *J. Mammal.* **31**:247–259.

Christian, J. J. 1959. The roles of endocrine and behavioral factors in the growth of mammalian populations. In A. Gorbman (ed.). *Comparative endocrinology.* Wiley, New York, pp. 71–97.

Christian, J. J., and D. E. Davis. 1964. Endocrines, behavior and population. *Science* **146**:1550–1560.

Clark, L. R., P. W. Geier, R. D. Hughes, and R. F. Morris. 1967. *The ecology of insect populations in theory and practice.* Methuen, London. 232 pp.

Clarke, B. 1960. Divergent effects on natural selection in two closely related polymorphic snails. *Heredity* **14**:423–443.

Clarke, B. 1962a. Balanced polymorphism and the diversity of sympatric species. In D. Nichols (ed.). *Taxonomy and geography.* Syst. Assoc. Publ. 4, pp. 47–70.

Clarke, B. 1962b. Natural selection in mixed populations of two polymorphic snails. *Heredity* **17**:319–345.

Clarke, C. A., and P. M. Sheppard. 1960a. The evolution of mimicry in the butterfly *Papilio dardanus. Heredity* **14**:163–173.

Clarke, C. A., and P. M. Sheppard. 1960b. Super-genes and mimicry. *Heredity* **14**:175–185.

Clarke, C. A , and P. M. Sheppard. 1963. Interactions between major genes and polygenes in the determination of the mimetic patterns of *Papilio dardanus. Evolution* **17**:404–413.

Clarke, G. L. 1954. *Elements of ecology.* Wiley, New York.

Clausen, C. P. 1956. Biological control of insect pests in the continental United States. *U.S. Dep. Agric. Tech. Bull.* **1139**:1–151.

Clements, F. E. 1916. Plant succession, an analysis of the development of vegetation. *Carnegie Inst. Washington Publ.* **242**:1-512.

Clench, H. K. 1967. Temporal dissociation and poplation regulation in certain hesperiine butterflies. *Ecology* **48**:1000–1006.

Cody, M. L. 1966. A general theory of clutch size. *Evolution* **20**:174–184.

Cody, M. L. 1969. Convergent characteristics in sympatric species: A possible relation to interspecific competition and aggression. *Condor* **71**:222–239.

Cody, M. L. 1971. Ecological aspects of reproduction. In D. S. Farner and J. R. King (eds.). *Avian Biology*, Vol. 1. Academic Press, New York, pp. 461–512.

Cole, L. C. 1951. Population cycles and random oscillations. *J. Wildl. Mgt.* **15**:233–252.

Cole, L. C. 1954a. Some features of random population cycles. *J. Wildl. Mgt.* **18**:2–24.

Cole, L. C. 1954b. The population consequences of life history phenomena. *Quart. Rev. Biol.* **29**:103–137.

Cole, L. C. 1960. Competitive exclusion. *Science* **132**:348–349.

Coleman, E. 1933. Pollination of the orchid genus *Prasophyllum*. *Victorian Natur.* **49**:214–221.

Colinvaux, P. A. 1973. *Introduction to ecology*. Wiley, New York. 621 pp.

Colwell, R. K. 1973. Competition and coexistence in a simple tropical community. *Amer. Natur.* **107**:737–760.

Connell, J. H. 1961. The influence of interspecific competition and other factors on the distribution of the barnacle *Chthamalus stellatus*. *Ecology* **42**:710–723.

Connell, J. H., and E. Orias. 1964. The ecological regulation of species diversity. *Amer. Natur.* **98**:399–414.

Cook, A. D., P. R. Atsatt, and C. A. Simon. 1971. Doves and dove weed: Multiple defenses against avian predation. *BioScience* **21**:277–281.

Coombs, C. W., and G. E. Woodroffe. 1973. Evaluation of some factors involved in ecological succession in an insect population breeding in stored wheat. *J. Anim. Ecol.* **42**:305–322.

Cott, H. B. 1940. *Adaptive coloration in animals*. Oxford Univ. Press. New York. 508 pp.

Coulson, J. C., and I. R. Deans. 1970. The effects of drastic population decrease on the subsequent recruitment and breeding biology of shags on the Farne Islands. *Bull. Brit. Ecol. Soc.* **1**(3):9. (Abstract).

Cowles, H. C. 1899. The ecological relations of the vegetation on the sand dunes of Lake Michigan. *Bot. Gaz.* **27**:95–117, 167–202, 281–308, 361–391.

Creed, E. R. (ed.) 1971a. *Ecological genetics and evolution*. Blackwell Sci. Publ., Oxford. 391 pp.

Creed, E. R. 1971b. Melanism in the two-spot ladybird, *Adalia bipunctata*, in Great Britain. In E. R. Creed (ed.). *Ecological genetics and evolution*. Blackwell Sci. Publ., Oxford, pp. 134–151.

Crossley, D. A , Jr., and M. P. Hoglund. 1962. A litter-bag method for the study of microarthropods inhabiting leaf litter. *Ecology* **43**:571–573.

Croteau, R., A. J. Burbott, and W. D. Loomis. 1972. Biosynthesis of mono- and sesquiterpenes in peppermint from glucose-^{14}C and $^{14}CO_2$. *Phytochemistry* **11**:2459–2467.

Crow, J. F., and M. Kimura. 1970. *An introduction to population genetics theory*. Harper and Row, New York, 592 pp.

Crowell, K. L. 1962. Reduced interspecific competition among the birds of Bermuda. *Ecology* **43**:75–88.

Croze, H. 1970. *Searching image in carrion crows*. Parey, Berlin. 86 pp.

Cruden, R. W. 1972a. Pollinators in high-elevation ecosystems: Relative effectiveness of birds and bees. *Science* **176**:1439–1440.

Cruden, R. W. 1972b. Pollination biology of *Nemophila menziesii* (Hydrophyllaceae) with comments on the evolution of oligolectic bees. *Evolution* **26**:373–389.

Crumpacker, D. W., and J. S. Williams. 1974. Rigid and flexible chromosomal polymorphisms in neighboring populations of *Drosophila pseudoobscura*. *Evolution* **28**:57–66.

Culver, D., J. R. Holsinger, and R. Baroody. 1973. Toward a predictive cave biogeography: The Greenbrier Valley as a case study. *Evolution* **27**:689–695.

Cumber, R. A. 1949. The biology of humble-bees, with special reference to the production of the worker caste. *Trans. Roy. Entomol. Soc. London* **100**:1–45.

DaCosta, C. P., and C. M. Jones. 1971. Cucumber beetle resistance and mite susceptibility controlled by the bitter gene in *Cucumis sativus* L. *Science* **172**:1145–1146.

Da Cunha, A. B., and Th. Dobzhansky. 1954. A further study of chromosomal polymorphism in *Drosophila willistoni* in its relation to the environment. *Evolution* **8**:119–134.

Da Cunha, A. B., Th. Dobzhansky, O. Pavlosky, and B. Spassky. 1959. Genetics of natural populations. XXVIII. Supplementary data on the chromosomal polymorphism in *Drosophila willistoni* in its relation to the environment. *Evolution* **13**:389–404.

Darling, F. F. 1937. *A herd of red deer. A study in animal behaviour.* Oxford Univ. Press, New York. 215 pp.

Darlington, P. J., Jr. 1957. *Zoogeography: The geographical distribution of animals.* Wiley, New York. 675 pp.

Darlington, P. J., Jr. 1959. Area, climate, and evolution. *Evolution* **13**:488–510.

Darlington, P. J., Jr. 1965. *Biogeography of the southern end of the world.* Harvard Univ. Press, Cambridge, Mass. 236 pp.

Darnell, R. M. 1961. Trophic spectrum of an estuarine commmunity, based on studies of Lake Pontchartrain, Louisiana. *Ecology* **42**:553–568.

Darwin, C. (and A. Wallace). 1859a. On the tendency of species to form varieties; and on the perpetuation of varieties and species by natural means of selection. *J. Proc. Linnean Soc. London. Zoology* **3**:45–62.

Darwin, C. 1859b. *The origin of species by means of natural selection.* Murray, London.

Darwin, C. 1871. *The descent of man and selection in relation to sex.* 2 vols. Appleton, New York. 409 and 436 pp.

Davidson, J., and H. G. Andrewartha. 1948a. Annual trends in a natural population of *Thrips imaginis* (Thysanoptera). *J. Anim. Ecol.* **17**:193–199.

Davidson, J., and H. G. Andrewartha. 1948b. The influence of rainfall, evaporation and atmospheric temperature on fluctuations in the size of a natural population of *Thrips imaginis* (Thysanoptera). *J. Anim. Ecol.* **17**:200–222.

Davies, R. W., and T. B. Reynoldson. 1971. The incidence and intensity of predation on lake dwelling triclads in the field. *J. Anim. Ecol.* **40**:191–214.

Davis, D. E. 1953. The characteristics of rat populations. *Quart. Rev. Biol.* **28**:373–401.

Dawkins, M. 1971a. Perceptual changes in chicks: Another look at the "search image" concept. *Anim. Behav.* **19**:566–574.

Dawkins, M. 1971b. Shifts of "attention" in chicks during feeding. *Anim. Behav.* **19**:575–582.

Day, P. R. 1972. Crop resistance to pests and pathogens. In *Pest control strategies for the future*. Nat. Acad. Sci., Washington, pp. 257–271.

DeBach, P. (ed.). 1964a. *Biological control of insect pests and weeds*. Reinhold, New York. 844 pp.

DeBach, P. 1964b. Successes, trends, and future possibilities. In P. DeBach (ed.). *Biological control of insect pests and weeds*. Reinhold, New York, pp. 673–713.

DeBach, P. 1966. The competitive displacement and coexistence principles. *Annu. Rev. Entomol.* 11:183–212.

DeBach, P. 1974. *Biological control by natural enemies*. Cambridge Univ. Press, New York. 323 pp.

DeBach, P., and H. S. Smith. 1941. Are population oscillations inherent in the host-parasite relation? *Ecology* 22:363–369.

DeBach, P., and R. A. Sundby. 1963. Competitive displacement between ecological homologues. *Hilgardia* 34:105–166.

Deevey, E. S., Jr. 1947. Life tables for natural populations of animals. *Quart. Rev. Biol.* 22:283–314.

Deevey, E. S., Jr. 1960. The human population. *Sci. Amer.* 203(3):195–204.

Dempster, J. P. 1960. A quantitative study of the predators on the eggs and larvae of the broom beetle, *Phytodecta olivacea* Forster, using the precipitin test. *J. Anim. Ecol.* 29:149–167.

Dempster, J. P. 1968. Intra-specific competition and dispersal: As examplified by a psyllid and its anthocorid predator. In T. R. E. Southwood (ed.). *Insect abundance*. Symp. Royal Entomol. Soc. London. No. 4, pp. 8–17.

den Boer, P. J., and G. R. Gradwell (eds.). 1970. *Dynamics of populations*. Proc. Advanced Study Inst. *Dynamics of numbers in populations*. Osterbeek, Netherlands. Centre Agri. Publ. and Documentation (Pudoc). Wageningen. 611 pp.

Dethier, V. G. 1954. Evolution of feeding preferences in phytophagous insects. *Evolution* 8:33–54.

Detwyler, T. R. (ed.). 1971. *Man's impact on environment*. McGraw-Hill, New York. 731 pp.

de Wilde, J., and L. M. Schoonhoven (eds). 1969. *Insect and host plant*. North-Holland, Amsterdam. pp. 471–810. Reprinted from *Ent. Exp. Appl.* 12:471–810.

deWit, C. T. 1960. *On competition*. Versl. Landbouwk. Onderzoek. No. 66, 8. Wageningen, Netherlands. 82 pp.

deWit, C. T. 1961. Space relationships within populations of one or more species. In F. L. Milthorpe (ed.). *Mechanisms in biological competition*. Symp. Soc. Exp. Biol. 15, pp. 314–329.

Dietz, R. S., and J. C. Holden. 1970. Reconstruction of Pangea: Breakup and dispersion of continents, Permian to present. *J. Geophys. Res.* 75:4939–4956.

Dingle, H. 1972. Migration strategies of insects. *Science* 175:1327–1335.

Dixon, A. F. G. 1970a. Quality and availability of food for a sycamore aphid population. In A. Watson (ed). *Animal populations in relation to their food resources*. Brit. Ecol. Soc. Symp. 10, pp. 271–286.

Dixon, A. F. G. 1970b. Factors limiting the effectiveness of the coccinellid beetle, *Adalia bipunctata* (L.) as a predator of the sycamore aphid, *Drepanosiphum platanoides* (Schr.). *J. Anim. Ecol.* 39:739–751.

Dixon, A. F. G. 1972. Control and significance of the seasonal development of colour forms in the sycamore aphid, *Drepanosiphum platanoides* (Schr.). *J. Anim. Ecol.* 41:689–697.

Dixon, A. F. G., and M. Logan. 1972. Population density and spacing in the sycamore aphid, *Drepanosiphum platanoides* (Schr.), and its relevance to the regulation of population growth. *J. Anim. Ecol.* 41:751–759.

Dobzhansky, Th. 1947. Genetics· of natural populations. XIV. A response of certain gene arrangements in the third chromosome of *Drosophila pseudoobscura* to natural selection. *Genetics* 32:142–160.

Dobzhansky, Th. 1948. Genetics of natural populations. XVI. Altitudinal and seasonal changes produced by natural selection in certain populations of *Drosophila pseudoobscura* and *Drosophila persimilis*. *Genetics* 33:158–176.

Dobzhansky, Th. 1950. Evolution in the tropics. *Amer. Sci.* 38:209–221.

Dobzhansky, Th. 1970. *Genetics of the evolutionary process.* Columbia Univ. Press, New York. 505 pp.

Dobzhansky, Th., H. Burla, and A. B. da Cunha. 1950. A comparative study of chromosomal polymorphism in sibling species of the *willistoni* group of *Drosophila*. *Amer. Natur.* 84:229–246.

Dodd, A. P. 1940. *The biological campaign against prickly pear.* Commonwealth Prickly Pear Board, Brisbane, Australia. 177 pp.

Dodson, C. H., R. L. Dressler, H. G. Hills, R. H. Adams, and N. H. Williams. 1969. Biologically active compounds in orchid fragrances. *Science* 164:1243–1249.

Dodson, C. H., and G. P. Frymire. 1961. Natural pollination of orchids. *Bull. Missouri Bot. Gdn.* 49:133–152.

Doutt, R. L. 1958. Vice, virtue and the vedalia. *Bull. Entomol. Soc. Amer.* 4:119–123.

Doutt, R. L. 1964. The historical development of biological control. In P. DeBach (ed.). *Biological control of insect pests and weeds.* Reinhold, New York, pp. 21–42.

Doutt, R. L., and P. DeBach. 1964. Some biological control concepts and questions. In P. DeBach (ed.). *Biological control of insect pests and weeds.* Reinhold, New York, pp. 118–142.

Doutt, R. L., and J. Nakata. 1973. The *Rubus* leafhopper and its egg parasitoid: An endemic biotic system useful in grape-pest management. *Environ. Entomol.* 2:381–386.

Dressler, R. L. 1968. Pollination in euglossine bees. *Evolution* 22:202–210.

Drooz, A. T. 1971. The elm spanworm (Lepidoptera: Geometridae): Natural diets and their effect on the F_2 generation. *Ann. Entomol. Soc. Amer.* 64:331–333.

Duffey, E., and A. S. Watt (eds.). 1971. *The scientific management of animal and plant communities for conservation.* Brit. Ecol. Symp. 11. Blackwell Sci. Publ., Oxford, 652 pp.

Duffey, S. S. 1970. Cardiac glycosides and distastefulness: Some observations on the palatability spectrum of butterflies. *Science* 169:78–79.

Duffey, S. S., and G. G. E. Scudder. 1972. Cardiac glycosides in North American Asclepiadaceae, a basis for unpalatability in brightly coloured Hemiptera and Coleoptera. *J. Insect Physiol.* 18:63–78.

Durand, J. D. 1967. The modern expansion of world population. *Proc. Amer. Phil. Soc.* 111:136–145.

Eberhardt, L. L. 1970. Correlation, regression, and density dependence. *Ecology* 51:306–310.

Edington, J. M., and M. A. Edington. 1972. Spatial patterns and habitat partition in the breeding birds of an upland wood. *J. Anim. Ecol.* 41:331–357.

Edmunds, G. F., Jr. 1972. Biogeography and evolution of Ephemeroptera. *Annu. Rev. Entomol.* 17:21–42.

Edwards, C. A., and G. W. Heath. 1963. The role of soil animals in breakdown of leaf material. In J. Doeksen and J. van der Drift (eds.). *Soil organisms.* North-Holland, Amsterdam, pp. 76–84.

Edwards, C. A., D. E. Reichle, and D. A. Crossley, Jr. 1970. The role of soil invertebrates in turnover of organic matter and nutrients. In D. E. Reichle (ed.). *Analysis of temperate forest ecosystems.* Springer-Verlag, Berlin, pp. 147–172.

Ehrlich, P. R., and L. C. Birch. 1967. The "balance of nature" and "population control." *Amer. Natur.* 101:97–107.

Ehrlich, P. R., and A. H. Ehrlich. 1970. *Population, resources, environment. Issues in human ecology.* W. H. Freeman, San Francisco. 383 pp.

Ehrlich, P. R., and L. E. Gilbert. 1973. Population structure and dynamics of the tropical butterfly *Heliconius ethilla. Biotropica* 5:69–82.

Ehrlich, P. R., and P. H. Raven. 1964. Butterflies and plants: A study in coevolution. *Evolution* 18:586–608.

Ehrlich, P. R., and P. H. Raven. 1967. Butterflies and plants. *Sci. Amer.* 216(6):104–113.

Ehrman, L. 1972. Genetics and sexual selection. In B. Campbell (ed.). *Sexual selection and the descent of man, 1871–1971.* Aldine, Chicago, pp. 105–135.

Eickwort, K. R. 1973. Cannibalism and kin selection in *Labidomera clivicollis* (Coleoptera: Chrysomelidae). *Amer. Natur.* 107:452–453.

Eisner, T. 1970. Chemical defense against predation in arthropods. In E. Sondheimer and J. B. Simeone (eds.). *Chemical ecology.* Academic Press, New York, pp. 157–217.

Eisner, T., L. B. Hendry, D. B. Peakall, and J. Meinwald. 1971. 2,5-Dichlorophenol (from ingested herbicide?) in defensive secretion of grasshopper. *Science* 171:277–278.

Eisner, T., J. S. Johnessee, J. Carrel, L. B. Hendry and J. Meinwald. 1974. Defensive use by an insect of a plant resin. *Science* 184:996–999.

Eisner, T., F. C. Kafatos, and E. G. Linsley. 1962. Lycid predation by mimetic adult Cerambycidae (Coleoptera). *Evolution* 16:316–324.

Eisner, T., R. E. Silberglied, D. Aneshansley, J. E. Carrel, and H. C. Howland. 1969. Ultraviolet video-viewing: The television camera as an insect eye. *Science* 166:1172–1174.

Elton, C. 1927. *Animal ecology.* Macmillan, New York. 207 pp.

Elton, C. 1942. *Voles, mice and lemmings; problems in population dynamics.* Oxford Univ. Press, Oxford. 496 pp.

Elton, C. 1946. Competition and the structure of ecological communities. *J. Anim. Ecol.* 15:54–68.

Elton, C. S. 1958. *The ecology of invasions by animals and plants.* Methuen, London. 181 pp.

Elton, C. S. 1966. *The pattern of animal communities.* Methuen, London. 432 pp.

Embree, D. G. 1965. The population dynamics of the winter moth in Nova Scotia, 1954–1962. *Mem. Entomol. Soc. Can.* 46:1–57.

Emlen, J. M. 1973. *Ecology: An evolutionary approach.* Addison-Wesley, Reading, Mass. 493 pp.

Emlen, J. T., Jr., A. W. Stokes, and C. P. Winsor. 1948. The rate of recovery of decimated populations of brown rats in nature. *Ecology* 29:133–145.

Enders, F. 1974. Vertical stratification in orb-web spiders (Araneidae, Araneae) and a consideration of other methods of coexistence. *Ecology* 55:317–328.

Engelmann, M. D. 1966. Energetics, terrestrial field studies, and animal productivity. *Adv. Ecol. Res.* 3:73–115.

Erickson, J. M., and P. Feeny. 1974. Sinigrin: A chemical barrier to the black swallowtail butterfly, *Papilio polyxenes. Ecology* 55:103–111.

Errington, P. L. 1946. Predation and vertebrate populations. *Quart. Rev. Biol.* 21:144–177, 221–245.

Errington, P. L. 1967. *Of predation and life.* Iowa State Univ. Press, Ames, Iowa. 277 pp.

Evans, G. R., and E. W. Tisdale. 1972. Ecological characteristics of *Aristida longiseta* and *Agropyron spicatum* in west-central Idaho. *Ecology* 53:137–142.

Evans, H. E., and M. J. W. Eberhard. 1970. *The wasps.* Univ. Michigan Press, Ann Arbor. 265 pp.

Evans, J. W. 1959. The zoogeography of some Australian insects. In A. Keast, R. L. Crocker, and C. S. Christian (eds.). *Biogeography and ecology in Australia.* Monogr. Biol. 8, pp. 150–163.

Evoy, W. H., and B. P. Jones. 1971. Motor patterns of male euglossine bees evoked by floral fragrances. *Anim. Behav.* 19:583–588.

Ewing, A. W., and H. C. Bennet-Clark. 1968. The courtship songs of *Drosophila. Behaviour* 31:288–301.

Faegri, K., and L. van der Pijl. 1971. *The principles of pollination ecology.* 2nd ed. Rev. Pergamon, New York. 291 pp.

Falcon, L. A. 1971. Microbial control as a tool in integrated control programs. In C. B. Huffaker (ed.). *Biological control.* Plenum Press, New York, pp. 346–364.

Feeny, P. P. 1968. Effect of oak leaf tannins on larval growth of the winter moth *Operophtera brumata. J. Insect Physiol.* 14:805–817.

Feeny, P. P. 1970. Seasonal changes in oak leaf tannins and nutrients as a cause of spring feeding by winter moth caterpillars. *Ecology* 51:565–581.

Feeny, P. P., K. L. Paauwe, and N. J. Demong. 1970. Flea beetles and mustard oils: Host plant specificity of *Phyllotreta cruciferae* and *P. striolata* adults (Coleoptera: Chrysomelidae). *Ann. Entomol. Soc. Amer.* 63:832–841.

Feir, D., and J-S. Suen. 1971. Cardenolides in the milkweed plant and feeding by the milkweed bug. *Ann. Entomol. Soc. Amer.* 64:1173–1174.

Fellows, D. P., and W. B. Heed. 1972. Factors affecting host plant selection in desert-adapted cactiphilic *Drosophila. Ecology* 53:850–858.

Fischer, A. G. 1960. Latitudinal variations in organic diversity. *Evolution* 14:64–81.

Fisher, R. A., A. S. Corbet, and C. B. Williams. 1943. The relation between the number of species and the number of individuals in a random sample from an animal population. *J. Anim. Ecol.* 12:42–58.

Fittkau, E. J., J. Illies, H. Klinge, G. H. Schwabe, and H. Sioli (eds.). 1968, 1969. Biogeography and ecology in South America. Vols. 1 and 2. *Monogr. Biol.* 18-19:1–946.

Fitzgerald, T. D. 1973. Coexistence of three species of bark-mining *Marmara* (Lepidoptera: Gracillariidae) on green ash and descriptions of new species. *Ann. Entomol. Soc. Amer.* **66**:457–464.

Fleschner, C. A. 1950. Studies on searching capacity of the larvae of three predators of the citrus red mite. *Hilgardia* **20**:233–265.

Force, D. C. 1972. *r*- and *K*-strategists in endemic host-parasitoid communities. *Bull. Entomol. Soc. Amer.* **18**:135–137.

Ford, E. B. 1940. Polymorphism and taxonomy. In J. Huxley (ed.). *The new systematics.* Clarendon Press, Oxford, pp. 493–513.

Ford, E. B. 1957. *Butterflies.* 3rd ed. Collins, London. 368 pp.

Ford, E. B. 1964. *Ecological genetics.* 2nd ed. Methuen, London, 335 pp.

Ford, H. D., and E. B. Ford. 1930. Fluctuation in numbers and its influence on variation in *Melitaea aurinia*, Rott. (Lepidoptera). *Trans. Roy. Entomol. Soc. London* **78**:345–351.

Fordham, R. A. 1971. Field populations of deermice with supplemental food. *Ecology* **52**:138–146.

Foster, M. S. 1974. A model to explain molt-breeding overlap and clutch size in some tropical birds. *Evolution* **28**:182–190.

Fox, L. R. 1975. Factors influencing cannibalism, a mechanism of population limitation in the predator *Notonecta hoffmanni*. *Ecology*. In press.

Fraenkel, G. 1959. The raison d'être of secondary plant substances. *Science* **129**:1466–1470.

Fraenkel, G. 1969. Evaluation of our thoughts on secondary plant substances. *Entomol. Exp. Appl.* **12**:473–486.

Frank, F. 1957. The causality of microtine cycles in Germany. *J. Wildl. Mgt.* **21**:113–121.

Frank, J. H. 1967. The insect predators of the pupal stage of the winter moth, *Operophtera brumata* (L.) (Lepidoptera: Hydriomenidae). *J. Anim. Ecol.* **36**:375–389.

Frank, P. W. 1952. A laboratory study of intraspecies and interspecies competition in *Daphnia pulicaria* (Forbes) and *Simocephalus vetulus* O. F. Müller. *Physiol. Zool.* **25**:178–204.

Frank, P. W. 1957. Coactions in laboratory populations of two species of *Daphnia*. *Ecology* **38**:510–519.

Frank, P. W. 1968. Life histories and community stability. *Ecology* **49**:355–357.

Franz, J. M. 1961. Biological control of pest insects in Europe. *Annu. Rev. Entomol.* **6**:183–200.

Franz, J. M., and A. Krieg. 1972. *Biologische Schädlingsbekämpfung.* Parey, Berlin. 208 pp.

Free, J. B. 1970. *Insect pollination of crops.* Academic Press, New York. 544 pp.

Freeland, W J., and D. H. Janzen. 1974. Strategies in herbivory by mammals: the role of plant secondary compounds. *Amer. Natur.* **108**:269–289.

Fretwell, S. D. 1969. The adjustment of birth rate to morality in birds. *Ibis* **111**:624–627.

Frings, H., E. Goldberg, and J. C. Arentzen. 1948. Antibacterial action of the blood of the large milkweed bug. *Science* **108**:689–690.

Futuyma, D. J. 1973. Community structure and stability in constant environments. *Amer. Natur.* **107**:443–446.

Gadgil, M. 1971. Dispersal: Population consequences and evolution. *Ecology* 52:253–261.

Gadgil, M., and W. H. Bossert. 1970. Life historical consequences of natural selection. *Amer. Natur.* 104:1–24.

Galil, J., and D. Eisikowitch. 1968. On the pollination ecology of *Ficus sycomorus* in East Africa. *Ecology* 49:259–269.

Galil, J., and D. Eisikowitch. 1969. Further studies on the pollination ecology of *Ficus sycomorus* L. (Hymenoptera, Chalcidoidea, Agaonidae). *Tijdsch. Entomol.* 112:1–13.

Gause, G. F. 1934. *The struggle for existence.* Williams & Wilkins, Baltimore. Reprinted 1964. Hafner Publ. Co., New York. 163 pp.

Gause, G. F., and A. A. Witt. 1935. Behavior of mixed populations and the problem of natural selection. *Amer. Natur.* 69:596–609.

Geier, P. W., L. R. Clark, D. J. Anderson, and H. A. Nix (eds.). 1973. Insects: Studies in population management. *Mem. Ecol. Soc. Australia* 1:1–295.

Gilbert, L. E. 1971. Butterfly-plant coevolution: Has *Passiflora adenopoda* won the selectional race with heliconiine butterflies? *Science* 172:585–586.

Gilbert, L. E. 1972. Pollen feeding and reproductive biology of *Heliconius* butterflies. *Proc. Nat. Acad. Sci.* 69:1403–1407.

Gilbert, L. E. 1975. Ecological consequences of a coevolved mutualism between butterflies and plants. In L. E. Gilbert and P. H. Raven (eds.). *Coevolution of animals and plants.* Univ. Texas Press, Austin, pp. 210–240.

Gilbert, L. E., and P. H. Raven (eds.). 1975. *Coevolution of animals and plants.* Univ. Texas Press, Austin. 246 pp.

Gill, D. E. 1974. Intrinsic rate of increase, saturation density, and competitive ability. II. The evolution of competitive ability. *Amer. Natur.* 108:103–116.

Gillespie, J. H., and K. Kojima. 1968. The degree of polymorphisms in enzymes involved in energy production compared to that in nonspecific enzymes in two *Drosophila ananassae* populations. *Proc. Nat. Acad. Sci.* 61:582–585.

Gillett, J. B. 1962. Pest pressure, an underestimated factor in evolution. In D. Nichols (ed.). *Taxonomy and geography.* Syst. Assoc. Publ. No. 4, pp. 37–46.

Gilpin, M. E. 1974. Intraspecific competition between *Drosophila* larvae in serial transfer systems. *Ecology* 55:1154–1159.

Glas, P. 1960. Factors governing density in the chaffinch (*Fringilla coelebs*) in different types of wood. *Arch. Neerl. Zool.* 13:466–472.

Gleason, H. A. 1922. On the relation between species and area. *Ecology* 3:158–162.

Gleason, H. A. 1925. Species and area. *Ecology* 6:66–74.

Gleason, H. A. 1926. The individualistic concept of the plant association. *Bull. Torrey Bot. Club* 53:7–26.

Gleason, H. A. 1939. The individualistic concept of the plant association. *Amer. Midland Natur.* 21:92–110.

Golley, F. B. 1960. Energy dynamics of a food chain of an old-field community. *Ecol. Monogr.* 30:187–206.

Golley, F. B. 1972. Energy flux in ecosystems. In J. A. Wiens (ed.). *Ecosystem structure and function.* Oregon State Univ. Press, Corvallis, pp. 69–88.

Golley, F. B., and J. B. Gentry. 1964. Bioenergetics of the southern harvester ant, *Pogonomyrmex badius. Ecology* 45:217–225.

Goodman, D. 1974. Natural selection and a cost ceiling on reproductive effort. *Amer. Natur.* **108**:247–268.

Goudriaan, J., and C. T. de Wit. 1973. A re-interpretation of Gause's population experiments by means of simulation. *J. Anim. Ecol.* **42**:521–530.

Grant, B., G. A. Snyder, and S. F. Glessner. 1974. Frequency-dependent mate selection in *Mormoniella vitripennis*. *Evolution* **28**:259–264.

Grant, P. R. 1966a. Ecological compatibility of bird species on islands. *Amer. Natur.* **100**:451–462.

Grant, P. R. 1966b. The density of land birds on the Tres Marías Islands in Mexico, II: Distribution of abundances in the community. *Can. J. Zool.* **44**:1023–1030.

Grant, V. 1949. Pollination systems as isolating mechanisms in angiosperms. *Evolution* **3**:82–97.

Grant, V. 1950. The flower constancy of bees. *Bot. Rev.* **16**:379–398.

Green, R. G., and C. A. Evans. 1940. Studies on a population cycle of snowshoe hares on the Lake Alexander area. *J. Wild. Manage.* **4**:220–238, 267–278, 347–358.

Green, R. G., and C. L. Larson. 1938. A description of shock disease in the snowshoe hare. *Amer. J. Hyg.* **28**:190–212.

Greenbank, D. O. 1956. The role of climate and dispersal in the initiation of outbreaks of the spruce budworm in New Brunswick. I. The role of climate. *Can. J. Zool.* **34**:453–476.

Greenslade, P. J. M. 1968. Island patterns in the Solomon Islands bird fauna. *Evolution* **22**:751–761.

Greenslade, P. J. M. 1969. Land fauna: Insect distribution patterns in the Solomon Islands. *Phil. Trans. Roy Soc. B.* **255**:271–284.

Gressitt, J. L. 1965. Biogeography and ecology of land arthropods of Antarctica. In J. van Mieghem, P. van Oye, and J. Schell. *Biogeography and ecology in Antarctica.* Monogr. Biol. 15, pp. 431–490.

Gressitt, J. L. 1970. Subantarctic entomology and biogeography. *Pac. Insects Monogr.* **23**:295–374.

Grice, G. D., and A. D. Hart. 1962. The abundance, seasonal occurrence and distribution of the epizooplankton between New York and Bermuda. *Ecol. Monogr.* **32**:287–309.

Griffiths, D. 1973. The structure of an acid moorland pond community. *J. Anim. Ecol.* **42**:263–283.

Grinnell, J. 1904. The origin and distribution of the chestnut-backed chickadee. *Auk.* **21**:364–382.

Grinnell, J. 1917. The niche-relationships of the California thrasher. *Auk* **34**:427–433.

Guillot, F. S., and S. B. Vinson. 1972. The rôle of the calyx and poison gland of *Cardiochiles nigriceps* in the host-parasitoid relationship. *J. Insect Physiol.* **18**:1315–1321.

Hadley, M. 1972. Perspectives in productivity studies, with special reference to some social insect populations. *Ekol. Pol.* **20**:173–184.

Haeckel, E. 1870. Uber Entwickelungsgang und Aufgabe der Zoologie. *Jenaische Z.* **5**:353–370.

Hairston, N. G. 1959. Species abundance and community organization. *Ecology* **40**:404–416.

Hairston, N. G., F. E. Smith, and L. B. Slobodkin. 1960. Community structure, population control, and competition. *Amer. Natur.* **94**:421–425.

Hagen, K. S., and J. M. Franz. 1973. A history of biological control. In T. E. Mittler, C. N. Smith and R. F. Smith, (eds.). *History of entomology*. Annual Reviews, Inc., Palo Alto, CA., pp. 433–476.

Haldane, J B. S. 1932. *The causes of evolution*. Harper, London, 235 pp.

Haldane, J. B. S. 1955. Population genetics. *New Biol.* **18**:34–51.

Hamilton, T. H. 1967. *Process and pattern in evolution*. Macmillan, New York. 118 pp.

Hamilton, T. H., R. H. Barth, Jr., and I. Rubinoff. 1964. The environmental control of insular variation in bird species abundance. *Proc. Nat. Acad. Sci.* **52**:132–140.

Hamilton, T. H., and I. Rubinoff. 1967. On predicting insular variation in endemism and sympatry for the Darwin finches in the Galapagos archipelago. *Amer. Natur.* **101**:161–171.

Hamilton, W. D. 1964a. The genetical evolution of social behaviour. I. *J. Theoret. Biol.* **7**:1–16.

Hamilton, W. D. 1964b. The genetical evolution of social behaviour. II. *J. Theoret. Biol.* **7**:17–52.

Hamilton, W. D. 1971. The genetical evolution of social behavior. I and II. In G. C. Williams (ed.). *Group selection*. Aldine-Atherton, Chicago, pp. 23–89.

Hamilton, W. D. 1972. Altruism and related phenomena, mainly in social insects. *Annu. Rev. Ecol. Syst.* **3**:193–232.

Hammond, A. L. 1971a. Plate tectonics: The geophysics of the earth's surface. *Science* **173**:40–41.

Hammond, A. L. 1971b. Plate tectonics II: Mountain building and continental geology. *Science* **173**:133–134.

Hansson, L. 1970. Methods of morphological diet micro-analysis in rodents. *Oikos* **21**:255–266.

Harborne, J. B. (ed.), 1972. *Phytochemical ecology*. Academic Press, New York. 272 pp.

Harcourt, D. G. 1963. Major mortality factors in the population dynamics of the diamondback moth, *Plutella maculipennis* (Curt) (Lepidoptera: Plutellidae). *Mem. Entomol. Soc. Can.* **32**:55–66.

Harcourt, D. G. 1966. Major factors in survival of the immature stages of *Pieris rapae* (L.). *Can Entomol.* **98**:653–662.

Harcourt, D. G. 1969. The development and use of life tables in the study of natural insect populations. *Annu. Rev. Entomol.* **14**:175–196.

Hardin, G. (ed.). 1969. *Population, evolution and birth control*. W. H. Freeman, San Francisco. 386 pp.

Harger, R. 1972. Relative consumer species diversity with respect to producer diversity and net productivity. *Science* **176**:544–545.

Harman, W. N. 1972. Benthic substrates: Their effect on fresh-water Mollusca. *Ecology* **53**:271–277.

Harper, J. L. 1968. The regulation of numbers and mass in plant populations. In R. C. Lewontin (ed.). *Population biology and evolution*. Syracuse Univ. Press, New York, pp. 139–158.

Harper, J. L. 1969. The role of predation in vegetational diversity. In *Diversity and stability in ecological systems*. Brookhaven Symp. Biol. 22, pp. 48–61.

Harper, J. L., P. H. Lovell, and K. G. Moore. 1970. The shapes and sizes of seeds. *Annu. Rev. Ecol. Syst.* 1:327–356

Harper, J. L., and J. Ogden. 1970. The reproductive strategy of higher plants. 1. The concept of strategy with special reference to *Senecio vulgaris* L. *J. Ecol.* 58:681–698.

Harris, H. 1970. *The principles of human biochemical genetics.* American Elsevier, New York. 328 pp.

Harris, H. 1971. Protein polymorphism in man. *Can. J. Genet. Cytol.* 13:381–396.

Harris, H., and D. A. Hopkinson. 1972. Average heterozygosity per locus in man: An estimate based on the incidence of enzyme polymorphisms. *Ann. Hum. Genet.* 36:9–20.

Harvey, H. W. 1950. On the production of living matter in the sea off Plymouth. *J. Marine Biol. Assoc. U.K. n.s.* 29:97–137.

Harville, J. P. 1955. Ecology and population dynamics of the California oak moth *Phryganidia californica* Packard (Lepidoptera: Dioptidae). *Microentomology* 20:83–166.

Hassell, M. P. 1970. Parasite behaviour as a factor contributing to the stability of insect host-parasite interactions. In P. J. den Boer and G. R. Gradwell. *Dynamics of populations.* Centre Agr. Publ. and Documentation, Wageningen, pp. 366–378.

Hassell, M. P., and R. M. May. 1973. Stability in insect host-parasite models. *J. Anim. Ecol.* 42:693–726.

Hassell, M. P., and D. J. Rogers. 1972. Insect parasite responses in the development of population models. *J. Anim. Ecol.* 41:661–676.

Hassell, M. P., and G. C. Varley. 1969. New inductive population model for insect parasites and its bearing on biological control. *Nature* 223:1133–1137.

Heatwole, H., and D. M. Davis. 1965. Ecology of three sympatric species of parasitic insects of the genus *Megarhyssa* (Hymenoptera: Ichneumonidae). *Ecology* 46:140–150.

Heatwole, H., and R. Levins. 1972a. Biogeography of the Puerto Rican Bank: Flotsam transport of terrestrial animals. *Ecology* 53:112–117.

Heatwole, H., and R. Levins. 1972b. Trophic structure stability and faunal change during recolonization. *Ecology* 53:531–534.

Heatwole, H., and R. Levins. 1973. Biogeography of Puerto Rican Bank: Species turnover on a small cay, Cayo Ahogado. *Ecology* 54:1042–1055.

Heimpel, A. M. 1972. Insect control by microbial agents. In *Pest control strategies for the future.* Nat. Acad. Sci., Washington, pp. 298–316.

Heinrich, B. 1971a. Temperature regulation of the sphinx moth, *Manduca sexta.* 1. Flight energetics and body temperature during free and tethered flight. *J. Exp. Biol.* 54:141–152.

Heinrich, B. 1971b. Temperature regulation of the sphinx moth, *Manduca sexta.* II. Regulation of heat loss by control of blood circulation. *J. Exp. Biol.* 54:153–166.

Heinrich, B. 1972a. Energetics of temperature regulation and foraging in a bumblebee, *Bombus terricola* Kirby. *J. Comp. Physiol.* 77:49–64.

Heinrich, B. 1972b. Patterns of endothermy in bumblebee queens, drones and workers. *J. Comp. Physiol.* 77:65–79.

Heinrich, B. 1972c. Temperature regulation in the bumblebee *Bombus vagans*: A field study. *Science* 175:185–187.

Heinrich, B. 1973. The energetics of the bumblebee. *Sci. Amer.* 228(4):96–102.

Heinrich, B., and P. H. Raven. 1972. Energetics and pollination ecology. *Science* **176**:597–602.

Hellmers, H. 1964. An evaluation of the photosynthetic efficiency of forests. *Quart. Rev. Biol.* **39**:249–257.

Hewitt, O. H. (ed.) 1954. A symposium on cycles in animal populations. *J. Wildl. Manage.* **18**:1–112.

Hickman, J. C. 1974. Pollination by ants: A low energy system. *Science* **184**:1290–1292.

Hikino, H., and T. Takemoto. 1972. Arthropod moulting hormones from plants, *Achyranthes* and *Cyathula*. *Naturwissenschaften* **59**:91–98.

Hills, H. G., N. H. Williams, and C. H. Dodson. 1972. Floral fragrances and isolating mechanisms in the genus *Catasetum* (Orchidaceae). *Biotropica* **4**:61–76.

Hinde, R. A. 1956. The biological significance of the territories of birds. *Ibis* **98**:340–369.

Hinton, H. E. 1955. Protective devices of endopterygote pupae. *Trans. Soc. Brit. Entomol.* **12**:49–92.

Ho, F. K., and P. S. Dawson. 1966. Egg cannibalism by *Tribolium* larvae. Ecology **47**:318–322.

Holdridge, L. R. 1947. Determination of world plant formations from simple climatic data. *Science* **105**:367–368.

Holdridge, L. R. 1967. *Life zone ecology.* 2nd ed. Trop. Res. Center, San José, Costa Rica. 206 pp.

Holdridge, L. R., W. C. Grenke, W. H. Hatheway, T. Liang, and J. A. Tosi, Jr. 1971. *Forest environments in tropical life zones: A pilot study.* Pergamon, Oxford, 747 pp.

Holland, W. J. 1903. *The moth book. A guide to the moths of North America.* Doubleday, Page. New York. Reprinted 1968, Dover, New York. 479 pp.

Holling, C. S. 1959a. Some characteristics of simple types of predation and parasitism. *Can. Entomol.* **91**:385–398.

Holling, C. S. 1959b. The components of predation as revealed by a study of small mammal predation of the European pine sawfly. *Can. Entomol.* **91**:293–320.

Holling, C. S. 1961. Principles of insect predation. *Annu. Rev. Entomol.* **6**:163–182.

Holling, C. S. 1965. The functional response of predators to prey density and its role in mimicry and population regulation. *Mem. Entomol. Soc. Can.* **45**:1–60.

Holling, C. S. 1966. The functional response of invertebrate predators to prey density. *Mem. Entomol. Soc. Can.* **48**:1–86.

Holling, C. S. 1968. The tactics of a predator. In T. R. E. Southwood (ed.). *Insect abundance.* Symp. Roy. Entomol. Soc. London. No. 4, pp. 47–58.

Holling, C. S. 1973. Resilience and stability of ecological systems. *Annu. Rev. Ecol. Syst.* **4**:1–23.

Holling, C. S., and S. Ewing. 1971. Blind man's buff: Exploring the response space generated by realistic ecological simulation models. In G. P. Patil, E. C. Pielou, and W. E. Waters (eds.). *Statistical ecology,* Vol. 2. Pennsylvania State Univ. Press, University Park, pp. 207–223.

Hooker, J. D. 1847–1860. *The botany of the Antarctic voyage of H. M. Discovery ships Erebus and Terror in the years 1839–1843, under the command of Captain Sir James Clark Ross.* Reeve, London.

Hauffaker, C. B. 1958. Experimental studies on predation: dispersion factors and predator-prey oscillations. *Hilgardia* **27**:343–383.

Huffaker, C. B. 1967. A comparison of the status of biological control of St. Johnswort in California and Australia. *Mushi* (Suppl.) **39**:51–73.

Haffaker, C. B. (ed.). 1971. *Biological control.* Plenum, New York, 511 pp.

Huffaker, C. B., and C. E. Kennett. 1969. Some aspects of assessing efficiency of natural enemies. *Can. Entomol.* **101**:425–447.

Huffaker, C. B., and J. E. Laing. 1972. "Competitive displacement" without a shortage of resources? *Res. Popul. Ecol.* **14**:1–17.

Humphries, D. A., and P. M. Driver. 1970. Protean defense by prey animals. *Oecologia* **5**:285–302.

Hunt, E. G., and A. I. Bischoff. 1960. Inimical effects on wildlife of periodic DDD applications to Clear Lake. *Calif. Fish Game* **46**(1):91–106.

Hurd, L. E., M. V. Mellinger, L. L. Wolf, and S. J. McNaughton. 1971. Stability and diversity at three trophic levels in terrestrial successional ecosystems. *Science* **173**:1134–1136.

Hurd, L. E., M. V. Mellinger, L. L. Wolf, and S. J. McNaughton. 1972. *Science* **176**:545.

Hurley, P. M., 1968. The confirmation of continental drift. *Sci. Amer.* **218**(4):52–64.

Hutchinson, G. E. 1953. The concept of pattern in ecology. *Proc. Acad. Natur. Sci. Philadelphia.* **105**:1–12.

Hutchinson, G. E. 1957. Concluding remarks. *Cold Spring Harbor Symp. Quant. Biol.* **22**:415–427.

Hutchinson, G. E. 1959. Homage to Santa Rosalia or why are there so many kinds of animals? *Amer. Natur.* **93**:145–159.

Hutchinson, G. E., 1965. *The ecological theater and the evolutionary play.* Yale Univ. Press, New Haven, Conn. 139 pp.

Hutchinson, G. E. 1968. When are species necessary? In R. C. Lewontin (ed.). *Population biology and evolution.* Syracuse Univ. Press, Syracuse, New York, pp. 177–186.

Hutchinson, G. E., and E. S. Deevey. 1949. Ecological studies on populations. *Surv. Biol. Progr.* **1**:325–359.

Illies, J. 1965. Phylogeny and zoogeography of the Plecoptera. *Annu. Rev. Entomol.* **10**:117–140.

Illies, J. 1969. Biogeography and ecology of neotropical freshwater insects, especially those from running waters. In E. J. Fittkau, J. Illies, H. Klinge, G. H. Schwabe, and H. Sioli (eds.). *Biogeography and ecology in South America.* Vol. 2. Monogr. Biol. 19, pp. 685–708.

Istock, C. A. 1967. Transient competitive displacement in natural populations of whirligig beetles. *Ecology* **48**:929–937.

Istock, C. A. 1973. Population characteristics of a species ensemble of waterboatmen Corixidae). *Behaviour* **46**:1–36.

Jacobs, M. E. 1955. Studies on territorialism and sexual selection in dragonflies. *Ecology* **36**:566–586.

Jansson, A. 1973. Stridulation and its significance in the genus *Cenocorixa* (Hemiptera, Corixidae). *Behaviour* **46**:1–36.

Janzen, D. H. 1966. Coevolution of mutualism between ants and acacias in Central America. *Evolution* **20**:249–275.

Janzen, D. H. 1967a. Fire, vegetation structure, and the ant x acacia interaction in Central America. *Ecology* **48**:26–35.

Janzen, D. H. 1967b. Interaction of the bull's horn acacia (*Acacia cornigera* L.) with an ant inhabitant (*Pseudomyrmex ferruginea* F. Smith) in eastern Mexico. *Univ. Kans. Sci. Bull.* **47**:315–558.

Janzen, D. H. 1967c. Why mountain passes are higher in the tropics. *Amer. Natur.* **101**:233–249.

Janzen, D. H. 1968. Host plants as islands in evolutionary and contemporary time. *Amer. Natur.* **102**:592–595.

Janzen, D. H. 1969a. Seed-eaters versus seed size, number, toxicity and dispersal. *Evolution* **23**:1–27.

Janzen, D. H. 1969b. Allelopathy by myrmecophytes: The ant *Azteca* as an allelopathic agent of *Cecropia. Ecology* **50**:147–153.

Janzen, D. H. 1970. Herbivores and the number of tree species in tropical forests. *Amer. Natur.* **104**:501–528.

Janzen, D. H. 1971. Euglossine bees as long-distance pollinators of tropical plants. *Science* **171**:203–205.

Janzen, D. H. 1973a. Host plants as islands. II. Competition in evolutionary and contemporary time. *Amer. Natur.* **107**:786–790.

Janzen, D. H. 1973b. Comments on host-specificity of tropical herbivores and its relevance to species richness. In V. H. Heywood (ed.). *Taxonomy and ecology.* Academic Press, New York, pp. 201–211.

Johnson, C. G. 1966. A functional system of adaptive dispersal by flight. *Annu. Rev. Entomol.* **11**:233–260.

Johnson, C. G. 1969. *Migration and dispersal of insects by flight.* Methuen, London. 764 pp.

Johnson, C. G. 1971. Entomology department. In *Rothamsted Exp. Sta. Rep. 1970,* Part 1, pp. 183–200, 330–337.

Johnson, G. B. 1971. Metabolic implications of polymorphism as an adaptive strategy. *Nature* **232**:347–349.

Johnson, G. B. 1973. Enzyme polymorphism and biosystematics: The hypothesis of selective neutrality. *Annu. Rev. Ecol. Syst.* **4**:93–116.

Johnson, G. B. 1974. Enzyme polymorphism and metabolism. *Science* **184**:28–37.

Jones, J. S. 1973. Ecological genetics and natural selection in molluscs. *Science* **182**:546–552.

Jordan, D. S. 1905. The origin of species through isolation. *Science* **22**:545–562.

Juday, C. 1940. The annual energy budget of an inland lake. *Ecology* **21**:438–450.

Kaneshiro, K. Y., H. L. Carson, F. E. Clayton, and W. B. Heed. 1973. Niche separation in a pair of homosequential *Drosophila* species from the island of Hawaii. *Amer. Natur.* **107**:766–774.

Kato, M., and K. Hayasaka. 1958. Notes on the dominance order in the experimental populations of crickets. *Ecol. Rev.* **14**:311–315. (In Japanese).

Keast, A., R. L. Crocker, and C. S. Christian (eds.). 1959. Biogeography and ecology in Australia. *Monogr. Biol.* **8**:1–640.

Keiper, R. R. 1969. Behavioral adaptations of cryptic moths. IV. Preliminary studies on species resembling dead leaves. *J. Lepidop. Soc.* **23**:205–210.

Keith, L. B. 1963. *Wildlife's ten-year cycle.* Univ. Wisconsin Press, Madison. 201 pp.

Kemp, G. A., and L. B. Keith. 1970. Dynamics and regulation of red squirrel (*Tamiasciurus hudsonicus*) populations. *Ecology* **51**:763–779.

Kendeigh, S. C. 1961. *Animal ecology.* Prentice-Hall, Englewood Cliffs, N.J. 468 pp.

Kendeigh, S. C. 1974. *Ecology with special reference to animals and man.* Prentice-Hall, Englewood Cliffs, N.J. 474 pp.

Kettlewell, H. B. D. 1955. Selection experiments on industrial melanism in the Lepidoptera. *Heredity* **9**:323–342.

Kettlewell, H. B. D. 1956. Further selection experiments on industrial melanism in the Lepidoptera. *Heredity* **10**:287–301.

Kettlewell, H. B. D. 1959. Darwin's missing evidence. *Sci. Amer.* **200**(3):48–53.

Kettlewell, H. B. D. 1961. The phenomenon of industrial melanism in Lepidoptera, *Annu. Rev. Entomol.* **6**:245–262.

Kilpatrick, J. W., and H. F. Schoof. 1959. Interrelationship of water and *Hermetia illucens* breeding to *Musca domestica* production in human excrement. *Amer. J. Trop. Med. Hygiene* **8**:597–602.

Kimura, M., and T. Ohta. 1971. *Theoretical aspects of population genetics.* Princeton Univ. Press, Princeton, N.J. 219 pp.

King, P. E., R. R. Askew, and C. Sanger. 1969. The detection of parasitised hosts by males of *Nasonia vitripennis* (Walker) (Hymenoptera: Pteromalidae) and some possible implications. *Proc. Roy. Entomol. Soc. London. A.* **44**:85–90.

Kiritani, K., S. Kawahara, T. Sasaba, and F. Nakasuji. 1972. Quantitative evaluation of predation by spiders on the green rice leafhopper, *Nephotettix cincticeps* Uhler, by a sight-count method. *Res. Pop. Ecol.* **13**:187–200.

Kirk, V. M. 1972. Seed-caching by larvae of two ground beetles, *Harpalus pensylvanicus* and *H. erraticus. Ann. Entomol. Soc. Amer.* **65**:1426–1428.

Kirk, V. M. 1973. Biology of a ground beetle, *Harpalus pensylvanicus. Ann. Entomol. Soc. Amer.* **66**:513–518.

Kloet, G. S., and W. D. Hincks. 1945. *A check list of British insects.* Published by the authors. Stockport. 483 pp.

Klomp, H. 1966. The dynamics of a field population of the pine looper, *Bupalus piniarius* L. *Adv. Ecol. Res.* **3**:207–305.

Klomp, H. 1968. A seventeen-year study of the abundance of the pine looper, *Bupalus piniarius* L. (Lepidoptera: Geometridae). In T. R. E. Southwood (ed.). *Insect abundance.* Symp. Roy. Entomol. Soc. London. No. 4, pp. 98–108.

Klopfer, P. H. 1959. Environmental determinants of faunal diversity. *Amer. Natur.* **93**:337–342.

Klopfer, P. H. 1962. *Behavioral aspects of ecology.* Prentice-Hall, Englewood Cliffs, N.J. 173 pp.

Klopfer, P. H., and R. H. MacArthur. 1960. Niche size and faunal diversity. *Amer. Natur.* **94**:293–300.

Klots, A. B. 1951. *A field guide to the butterflies of North America, east of the Great Plains.* Houghton Mifflin, Boston, Mass. 349 pp.

Knipling, E. F. 1972. Sterilization and other genetic techniques. In *Pest control strategies for the future*. Nat. Acad. Sci., Washington, pp. 272–287.

Kojima, K., J. H. Gillespie, and Y. N. Tobari. 1970. A profile of *Drosophila* species' enzymes assayed by electrophoresis. I. Number of alleles, heterozygosities, and linkage disequilibrium in glucose-metabolizing systems and some other enzymes. Biochem. Genet. 4:627–637.

Konishi, M. 1973. Locatable and nonlocatable acoustic signals for barn owls. *Amer. Natur.* 107:775–785.

Kontkanen, P. 1950. Quantitative and seasonal studies on the leafhopper fauna of the field stratum on open areas in North Karelia. *Ann. Zool. Soc. Zool. Bot. Fennicae Vanamo*, 13(8):1–91.

Kormondy, E. J. 1961. Territoriality and dispersal in dragonflies (Odonata). *J. N. Y. Entomol. Soc.* 69:42–52.

Kozlovsky, D. G. 1968. A critical evaluation of the trophic level concept. I. Ecological efficiencies. *Ecology* 49:48–60.

Krebs, C. J. 1964. *The lemming cycle in Baker Lake, Northwest Territories, during 1959–1962*. Arctic Inst. N. Amer. Tech. Paper No. 15. pp. 1–104.

Krebs, C. J. 1970. *Microtus* population biology: Behavioral changes associated with the population cycle in *M. ochrogaster* and *M. pennsylvanicus*. *Ecology* 51:34–52.

Krefting, L. W., and E. I. Roe. 1949. The role of some birds and mammals in seed germination. *Ecol. Monogr.* 19:269–286.

Krieger, R. I., P. P. Feeny, and C. F. Wilkinson. 1971. Detoxication enzymes in the guts of caterpillars: An evolutionary answer to plant defenses? *Science* 172:579–581.

Kullenberg, B. 1950. Investigations on the pollination of *Ophrys* species. *Oikos* 2:1–19.

Kullenberg, B. 1956a. On the scents and colours of *Ophrys* flowers and their specific pollinators among the aculeate Hymenoptera. *Svensk. Bot. Tidskr.* 50:25–46.

Kullenberg, B. 1956b. Field experiments with chemical sexual attractants on aculeate Hymenoptera males. I. *Zool. Bidr. Upps.* 31:253–354.

Kullenberg, B. 1961. Studies in *Ophrys* pollination. *Zool. Bidr. Upps.* 34:1–340.

Kuschel, G. 1962. The Curculionidae of Gough island and the relationships of the weevil fauna of the Tristan da Cunha group. *Proc. Linn. Soc. London* 173:69–78.

Kuschel, G. 1969. Biogeography and ecology of South American Coleoptera. In E. J. Fittkau, J. Illies, H. Klinge, G. H. Schwabe, and H. Sioli (eds.). *Biogeography and ecology in South America*. Vol. 2. Monogr. Biol. 19, pp. 709–722.

Labine, P. A. 1968. The population biology of the butterfly, *Euphydryas editha*. VIII. Oviposition and its relation to patterns of oviposition in other butterflies. *Evolution* 22:799–805.

Lack, D. 1947a. The significance of clutch size. Parts I and II. *Ibis* 89:302–352.

Lack, D. 1947b. *Darwin's finches*. Cambridge Univ. Press, Cambridge, England.

Lack, D. 1949. Comments on Mr. Skutch's paper on clutch size. *Ibis* 91:455–458.

Lack, D. 1954. *The natural regulation of animal numbers*. Clarendon Press, Oxford. 343 pp.

Lack, D. 1966. *Population studies of birds*. Oxford Univ. Press, London. 341 pp.

Lack, D. 1971. *Ecological isolation in birds*. Blackwell Sci. Publ., Oxford. 404 pp.

Laing, J. 1937. Host-finding by insect parasites. 1. Observations on the finding of hosts by *Alysia manducator, Mormoniella vitripennis* and *Trichogramma evanescens*. *J. Anim. Ecol.* **6**:298–317.

Landahl, J. T., and R. B. Root. 1969. Differences in the life tables of tropical and temperate milkweed bugs, genus *Oncopeltus* (Hemiptera: Lygaeidae). *Ecology* **50**:734–737.

LeCam, L. M., J. Neyman, and E. L. Scott (eds.) 1972. *Darwinian, neo-Darwinian and non-Darwinian evolution*. Proc. 6th Berkeley Symp. Math. Stat. Probability. Vol. 5. Univ. California Press, Berkeley, 369 pp.

Leius, K. 1967. Influence of wild flowers on parasitism of tent caterpillar and codling moth. *Can. Entomol.* **99**:444–446.

Leonard, D. E. 1970a. Intrinsic factors causing qualitative changes in populations of *Porthetria dispar* (Lepidoptera: Lymantriidae). Can. Entomol. **102**:239–249.

Leonard, D. E. 1970b. Intrinsic factors causing qualitative changes in populations of the gypsy moth. *Proc. Entomol. Soc. Ontario* **100**:195–199.

Leopold, A. 1943. Deer irruptions. *Wisconsin Conserv. Bull.* Aug. 1943. Reprinted in *Wisconsin Conserv. Dept. Publ.* **321**:3–11.

Leppik, E. E. 1960. Early evolution of flower types. *Lloydia* **23**:72–92.

Leppik, E. E. 1972. Origin and evolution of bilateral symmetry in flowers. In T. Dobzhansky, M. K. Hecht, and W. C. Steere (eds.). *Evolutionary biology*. Vol. 5. Appleton-Century-Crofts, New York, pp. 49–85.

LeRoux, E. J., R. O. Paradis, and M. Hudon. 1963. Major mortality factors in the population dynamics of the eye-spotted bud moth, the pistol casebearer, the fruit-tree leaf roller, and the European corn borer in Quebec. *Mem. Entomol. Soc. Can.* **32**:67–82.

LeRoux, E. J., and others. 1963. Population dynamics of agricultural and forest insect pests. *Mem. Entomol. Soc. Can.* **32**:1–103.

Leslie, P. H. 1959. The properties of a certain lag type of population growth and the influence of an external random factor on a number of such populations. *Physiol. Zool.* **32**:151–159.

Leslie, P. H., and J. C. Gower. 1960. The properties of a stochastic model for the predator-prey type of interaction between two species. *Biometrika* **47**:219–234.

Levin, D. A. 1974. The oil content of seeds: An ecological perspective. *Amer. Natur.* **108**:193–206.

Levin, D. A., and H. Kerster. 1969a. Density-dependent gene dispersal in *Liatris. Amer. Natur.* **103**:61–74.

Levin, D. A., and H. W. Kerster. 1969b. The dependence of bee-mediated pollen and gene dispersal upon plant density. *Evolution* **23**:560–571.

Levin, S. A. 1974. Dispersion and population interactions. *Amer. Natur.* **108**:207–228.

Levins, R. 1968. Evolution in changing environments. Princeton Univ. Press, Princeton, N.J. 120 pp.

Levins, R., and H. Heatwole. 1973. Biogeography of the Puerto Rican Bank: Introduction of species onto Palominitos Island. *Ecology* **54**:1056–1064.

Lewis, T., and L. R. Taylor. 1967. *Introduction to experimental ecology*. Academic Press, London. 401 pp.

Lewis, W. H. P. 1971. Polymorphism of human enzyme proteins. *Nature* **230**:215–218.

Lewis, W. J., and R. L. Jones. 1971. Substance that stimulates host-seeking by *Microplitis croceipes* (Hymenoptera: Braconidae), a parasite of *Heliothis* species. *Ann. Entomol. Soc. Amer.* **64**:471–473.

Lewis, W. J., A. N. Sparks, and L. M. Redlinger. 1971. Moth odor: A method of host-finding by *Trichogramma evanescens*. *J. Econ. Entomol.* **64**:557–558.

Lewontin, R. C. 1965. Selection for colonizing ability. In H. G. Baker and G. L. Stebbins (eds.). *The genetics of colonizing species.* Academic Press, New York, pp. 77–91.

Lewontin, R. C. 1968. The concept of evolution. In D. L. Sills (ed.). *International encyclopedia of the social sciences.* Vol. 5. Macmillan, New York, pp. 202–210.

Lewontin, R. C. 1970. The units of selection. *Annu. Rev. Ecol. Syst.* **1**:1–18.

Lewontin, R. C. 1974. *The genetic basis of evolutionary change.* Columbia Univ. Press, New York. 346 pp.

Lewontin, R. C., and J. L. Hubby. 1966. A molecular approach to the study of genic heterozygosity in natural populations. II. Amount of variation and degree of heterozygosity in natural populations of *Drosophila pseudoobscura*. *Genetics* **54**:595–609.

Lidicker, W. Z. 1962. Emigration as a possible mechanism permitting the regulation of population density below carrying capacity. *Amer. Natur.* **96**:29–33.

Liebig, J. 1840. *Chemistry in its application to agriculture and physiology.* Taylor and Walton, London.

Lindeman, R. L. 1942. The trophic-dynamic aspect of ecology. *Ecology* **23**:399–418.

Lindroth, C. H. 1957. *The faunal connections between Europe and North America.* Wiley, New York. 344 pp.

Lindroth, C. H. 1963. The fauna history of Newfoundland, illustrated by carabid beetles. *Opusc. Entomol., Suppl.,* **23**:1–112.

Lindroth, C. H. 1971. On the occurrence of the continental element in the ground-beetle fauna of eastern Canada (Coleoptera: Carabidae). *Can. Entomol.* **103**:1455–1462.

Linhart, Y. B. 1974. Intra-population differentiation in annual plants. I. *Veronica peregrina* L. raised under non-competitive conditions. *Evolution* **28**:232–243.

Linsdale, J. M. 1946. *The California ground squirrel.* Univ. Calif. Press, Berkeley. 475 pp.

Linsley, E. G., J. W. MacSwain, and P. H. Raven. 1963a. Comparative behavior of bees and Onagraceae. I. *Oenothera* bees of the Colorado Desert. *Univ. Calif. Publ. Entomol.* **33**:1–24.

Linsley, E. G., J. W. MacSwain, and P. H. Raven. 1963b. Comparative behavior of bees and Onagraceae. II. *Oenothera* bees of the Great Basin. *Univ. Calif. Publ. Entomol.* **33**:25–58.

Linsley, E. G., J. W. MacSwain, and P. H. Raven. 1964. Comparative behavior of bees and Onagraceae. III. *Oenothera* bees of the Mohave Desert, California. *Univ. Calif. Publ. Entomol.* **33**:59–98.

Llewellyn, M. 1972. The effects of the lime aphid, *Eucalypterus tiliae* L. (Aphididae) on the growth of the lime, *Tilia x vulgaris* Hayne. I. Energy requirements of the aphid population. *J. Appl. Ecol.* **9**:261–282.

Lloyd, M., and H. S. Dybas. 1966. The periodical cicada problem. I. Population ecology. *Evolution* **20**:133–149.

Lloyd, M., and R. J. Ghelardi. 1964. A table for calculating the "equitability" component of species diversity. *J. Anim. Ecol.* **33**:217–225.

Lloyd, M., J. H. Zar, and J. R. Karr. 1968. On the calculation of information-theoretical measures of diversity. *Amer. Midl. Natur.* **79**:257–272.

Loomis, W. D. 1967. Biosynthesis and metabolism of monoterpenes. In J. B. Pridham (ed.). *Terpenoids in plants.* Academic Press, London, pp. 59–82.

Lotka, A. J. 1925 *Elements of physical biology.* Williams and Wilkins, Baltimore. Reprinted as *Elements of mathematical biology.* 1956. Dover, New York. 465 pp.

Luckinbill, L. S. 1973. Coexistence in laboratory populations of *Paramecium aurelia* and its predator *Didinium nasutum. Ecology* **54**:1320–1327.

Lugo, A. E., E. G. Farnworth, D. Pool, P. Jerez, and G. Kaufman. 1973. The impact of the leaf cutter ant *Atta colombica* on the energy flow of a tropical wet forest. *Ecology* **54**:1292–1301.

MacArthur, R. H. 1955. Fluctuations of animal populations, and a measure of community stability. *Ecology* **36**:533–536.

MacArthur, R. H. 1957. On the relative abundance of bird species. *Proc. Nat. Acad. Sci. U.S.* **43**:293–295.

MacArthur, R. H. 1958. Population ecology of some warblers of northeastern coniferous forests. *Ecology* **39**:599–619.

MacArthur, R. H. 1962. Some generalized theorems of natural selection. *Proc. Nat. Acad. Sci.* **48**:1893–1897.

MacArthur, R. H. 1972. *Geographical ecology: Patterns in the distribution of species.* Harper and Row, New York. 269 pp.

MacArthur, R. H., and R. Levins. 1964. Competition, habitat selection, and character displacement in a patchy environment. *Proc. Nat. Acad. Sci.* **51**:1207–1210.

MacArthur, R. H., and R. Levins. 1967. The limiting similarity, convergence and divergence of coexisting species. *Amer. Natur.* **101**:377–385.

MacArthur, R. H., and J. W. MacArthur. 1961. On bird species diversity. *Ecology* **42**: 594–598.

MacArthur, R. H., and E. O. Wilson. 1963. An equilibrium theory of insular zoogeography. *Evolution* **17**:373–387.

MacArthur, R. H., and E. O. Wilson. 1967. *The theory of island biogeography.* Princeton Univ. Press, Princeton, N.J. 203 pp.

MacDonald, D. R., and F. E. Webb. 1963. Insecticides and the spruce budworm. In R. F. Morris ed. *The dynamics of epidemic spruce budworm populations.* Mem. Entomol. Soc. Can 31, pp. 288–310.

Macfadyen, A. 1957. *Animal ecology: Aims and methods.* Pitman, London. 264 pp.

Macfadyen, A. 1963. *Animal ecology: Aims and methods.* 2nd ed. Pitman, London. 344 pp.

MacKay, R. J., and J. Kalff. 1973. Ecology of two related species of caddis fly larvae in the organic substrates of a woodland stream. *Ecology* **54**:499–511.

Mackerras, I. M. 1970. Composition and distribution of the fauna. In *The Insects of Australia.* Melbourne Univ. Press, Melbourne, pp. 187–203.

MacNab, B. K. 1963. Bioenergetics and the determination of home range size. *Amer. Natur.* **97**:133–140.

Malthus, T. R. 1798. *An essay on the principle of population as it affects the future improvement of society.* Johnson, London.

Mani, M. S. 1968. *Ecology and biogeography of high altitude insects.* Series Entomologica. Vol. 4. W. Junk. The Hague. 527 pp.

Mani, M. S. (ed.). 1974. Ecology and biogeography in India. *Monogr. Biol.* 23:1–773.

Manley, G. V. 1971. A seed-cacheing carabid (Coleoptera). *Ann. Entomol. Soc. Amer.* 64:1474–1475.

Marler, P. 1955. Characteristics of some animal calls. *Nature* 176:6–8.

Marshall, D. R., and S. K. Jain. 1969. Interference in pure and mixed populations of *Avena fatua* and *A. barbata. J. Ecol.* 57:251–270.

Martin, J. L. 1966. The insect ecology of red pine plantations in central Ontario. IV. The crown fauna. *Can. Entomol.* 98:10–27.

Matthews, S. W. 1973. This changing earth. *Nat. Geog. Mag.* 143:1–37.

May, R. M. 1973a. *Stability and complexity in model ecosystems.* Princeton Univ. Press, Princeton, N.J. 235 pp.

May, R. M. 1973b. Stability in randomly fluctuating versus deterministic environments. *Amer. Natur.* 107:621–650.

Mayhew, S. H., S. K. Kato, F. M. Ball, and C. Epling. 1966. Comparative studies of arrangements within and between populations of *Drosophila pseudoobscura. Evolution* 20:646–662.

Maynard Smith, J. 1964. Group selection and kin selection. *Nature* 201:1145–1147.

Mayr, E. 1963. *Animal species and evolution.* Belknap Press of Harvard Univ. Press. Cambridge, Mass. 797 pp.

McClure, M. S. 1974. Biology of *Erythroneura lawsoni* (Homoptera: Cicadellidae) and coexistence in the sycamore leaf-feeding guild. *Environ. Entomol.* 3:59–68.

McKey, D. 1974. Adaptive patterns in alkaloid physiology. *Amer. Natur.* 108:305–320.

McLeod, J. H., B. M. McGugan, and H. C. Coppel. 1962. *A review of the biological control attempts against insects and weeds in Canada.* Commonwealth Inst. Biol. Control. Tech. Comm. 2. 216 pp.

McLeod, J. M. 1972. The Swaine jack pine sawfly, *Neodiprion swainei,* life system: Evaluating the long-term effects of insecticide applications in Quebec. *Environ. Entomol.* 1:371–381.

McNeill, S. 1971. The energetics of a population of *Leptopterna dolabrata* (Heteroptera: Miridae). *J. Anim. Ecol.* 40:127–140.

McNeill, S. 1973. The dynamics of a population of *Leptopterna dolabrata* (Heteroptera: Miridae) in relation to its food resources. *J. Anim. Ecol.* 42:495–507.

Medawar, P. B. 1960. *The future of man.* Basic books, New York. 128 pp.

Meeuse, A. D. J. 1973. Anthecology, floral morphology and angiosperm evolution. In V. H. Heywood (ed.). *Taxonomy and ecology.* Academic Press, New York, pp. 189–200.

Mengel, R. M. 1964. The probable history of species formation in some northern wood warblers (Parulidae). *Living Bird* 3:9–43.

Merriam, C. H. 1894. Laws of temperature control of the geographic distribution of terrestrial animals and plants. *Nat. Geog. Mag.* 6:229–238.

Merriam, C. H. 1898. Life zones and crop zones. *U.S. Dep. Agric. Div. Biol. Surv. Bull.* 10:9–79.

Mertz, D. B. 1970. Notes on methods used in life-history studies. In J. H. Connell, D. B. Mertz, and W. W. Murdoch (eds.). *Readings in ecology and ecological genetics.* Harper and Row, New York, pp. 4–17.

Mertz, D. B., and R. B. Davies. 1968. Cannibalism of the pupal stage by adult flour beetles: An experiment and a stochastic model. *Biometrics* 24:247–275.

Mertz, D. B., and J. R. Robertson. 1970. Some developmental consequences of handling, egg-eating, and population density for flour beetle larvae. *Ecology* 51:989–998.

Metcalf, R. L., and W. H. Luckmann. 1975. *Introduction to insect pest management.* Wiley, New York.

Michener, C. D. 1947. A revision of the American species of *Hoplitis* (Hymenoptera, Megachilidae). *Bull. Amer. Mus. Natur. Hist.* 89:257–318.

Michener, C. D. 1969. Comparative social behavior of bees. *Annu. Rev. Entomol.* 14:299–342.

Miller, C. A. 1957. A technique for estimating the fecundity of natural populations of the spruce budworm. *Can. J. Zool.* 35:1–13.

Miller, R. S. 1967. Pattern and process in competition. *Adv. Ecol. Res.* 4:1–74.

Miller, W. E. 1967. The European pine shoot moth—Ecology and control in the Lake States. *For. Sci. Monogr.* 14:1–72.

Milne, A. 1957a. The natural control of insect populations. *Can. Entomol.* 89:193–213.

Milne, A. 1957b. Theories of natural control of insect populations. *Cold Spring Harbor Symp. Quant. Biol.* 22:253–267.

Milne, A. 1962. On a theory of natural control of insect population. *J. Theoret. Biol.* 3:19–50.

Mitchell, R. 1968. Site selection by larval water mites parasitic on the damselfly *Cercion hieroglyphicum* Brauer. *Ecology* 49:40–47.

Mitchell, R. 1970. An analysis of dispersal in mites. *Amer. Natur.* 104:425–431.

Mitchell, R. 1973. Growth and population dynamics of a spider mite (*Tetranychus urticae* K., Acarina: Tetranychidae). *Ecology* 54:1349–1355.

Monroe, D. D. 1974. The systematics, phylogeny, and zoogeography of *Symmerus* Walker and *Australosymmerus* Freeman (Diptera: Mycetophilidae: Ditomyiinae). *Mem. Entomol. Soc. Can.* 92:1–183.

Mook, L. J. 1963. Birds and the spruce budworm. In R. F. Morris (ed.). *The dynamics of epidemic spruce budworm populations.* Mem. Entomol. Soc. Can. 31, pp. 268–271.

Moore, N. W. 1957. Territory in dragonflies and birds. *Bird Study* 4:125–130.

Moore, N. W. 1960. The behaviour of the adult dragonfly. Dispersal. In P. S. Corbet, C. Longfield, and N. W. Moore (eds.). *Dragonflies.* Collins, London, pp. 108–126, 127–137.

Moore, N. W. 1964. Intra- and interspecific competition among dragonflies (Odonata). *J. Anim. Ecol.* 33:49–71.

Moore, N. W. 1967. A synopsis of the pesticide problem. *Adv. Ecol. Res.* 4:75–129.

Moran, P. A. P. 1954. The logic of the mathematical theory of animal populations. *J. Wildl. Manage.* 18:60–66.

Moreton, B. D. 1969. *Beneficial insects and mites.* 6th ed. Ministry Agr. Fish. Food Bull. 20 H. M. S. O., London. 118 pp.

Morris, G. K. 1971. Aggression in male conocephaline grasshoppers (Tettigoniidae). *Anim Behav.* **19**:132–137.

Morris, G. K. 1972. Phonotaxis of male meadow grasshoppers (Orthoptera: Tettigoniidae). *J. N. Y. Entomol. Soc.* **80**:5–6.

Morris, R. F. 1955. The development of sampling techniques for forest insect defoliators, with particular reference to the spruce budworm. *Can. J. Zool.* **33**:225–294.

Morris, R. F. 1959. Single-factor analysis in population dynamics. *Ecology* **40**:580–588.

Morris, R. F. (ed.). 1963. The dynamics of epidemic spruce budworm populations. *Mem. Entomol. Soc. Can.* **31**:1–332.

Morris, R. F. 1971a. Observed and simulated changes in genetic quality in natural populations of *Hyphantria cunea*. *Can. Entomol.* **103**:893–906.

Morris, R. F. 1971b. The influence of land use and vegetation on the population density of *Hyphantria cunea*. *Can. Entomol.* **103**:1525–1536.

Morris, R. F. 1972. Predation by wasps, birds, and mammals on *Hyphantria cunea*. *Can. Entomol.* **104**:1581–1591.

Morris, R. F., and C. W. Bennett. 1967. Seasonal population trends and extensive census methods for *Hyphantria cunea*. *Can. Entomol.* **99**:9–17.

Morris, R. F., and W. C. Fulton. 1970a. Models for the development and survival of *Hyphantria cunea* in relation to temperature and humidity. *Mem. Entomol. Soc. Can.* **70**:1–60.

Morris, R. F., and W. C. Fulton. 1970b. Heritability of diapause intensity in *Hyphantria cunea* and correlated fitness responses. *Can. Entomol.* **102**:927–938.

Morris, R. F., and C. A. Miller. 1954. The development of life tables for the spruce budworm. *Can. J. Zool.* **32**:283–301.

Mosquin, T. 1971. Competition for pollinators as a stimulus for the evolution of flowering time. *Oikos* **22**:398–402.

Motomura, I. 1932. A statistical treatment of associations (in Japanese). *Japan. J. Zool.* **44**:379–383.

Muller, C. H. 1966. The role of chemical inhibition (allelopathy) in vegetational composition. *Bull. Torrey Botan. Club* **93**:332–351.

Muller, C. H., and R. del Moral. 1971. Role of animals in supression of herbs by shrubs. *Science* **173**:462–463.

Murdoch, W. W. 1966a. Aspects of the population dynamics of some marsh carabidae. *J. Anim. Ecol.* **35**:127–156.

Murdoch, W. W. 1966b. Population stability and life history phenomena. *Amer. Natur.* **100**:5–11.

Murdoch, W. W. 1966c. "Community structure, population control, and competition" —a critique. *Amer. Natur.* **100**:219–226.

Murdoch, W. W. 1969. Switching in general predators: Experiments on predator specificity and stability of prey populations. *Ecol. Monogr.* **39**:335–354.

Murdoch, W. W. 1970. Population regulation and population inertia. *Ecology* **51**:497–502.

Murdoch, W. W. 1971. The developmental response of predators to changes in prey density. *Ecology* **52**:132–137.

Murdoch, W. W. 1973. The functional response of predators. *J. Appl. Ecol.* **10**:335–342.

Murdoch, W. W., F. C. Evans, and C. H. Peterson. 1972. Diversity and pattern in plants and insects. *Ecology* 53:819–829.

Murdoch, W. W., and J. R. Marks. 1973. Predation by coccinellid beetles: experiments on switching. *Ecology* 54:160–167.

Murie, A. 1944. *Wolves of Mount McKinley.* Fauna of Nat. Parks U.S. Fauna Ser. No. 5. Washington, D.C. 238 pp.

Myers, J. H., and C. J. Krebs. 1971. Genetic, behavioral, and reproductive attributes of dispersing field voles *Microtus pennsylvanicus* and *Microtus ochrogaster*. *Ecol. Monogr.* 41:53–78.

Nassar, R., H. J. Muhs, and R. D. Cook. 1973. Frequency-dependent selection at the Payne inversion in *Drosophila melanogaster*. *Evolution* 27:558–564.

National Academy of Sciences. 1969. *Insect-pest management and control. Principles of plant and animal pest control.* Vol. 3. Washington. 508 pp.

National Academy of Sciences. 1972. *Pest control strategies for the future.* Washington. 376 pp.

Neumann, U. 1971. Die Sukzession der Bodenfauna (Carabidae [Coleoptera], Diplopoda und Isopoda) in den forstlich rekultivierten Gebietendes Rheinischen Braunkohlen-reviers. *Pedobiologia* 11:193–226.

Nice, M. M. 1941. The role of territory in bird life. *Amer. Midl. Natur.* 26: 441–487.

Nicholson, A. J. 1933. The balance of animal populations. *J. Anim. Ecol.* 2(Suppl):132–178.

Nicholson, A. J. 1954a. Compensatory reactions of populations to stress, and their evolutionary significance. *Austr. J. Zool.* 2:1–8.

Nicholson, A. J. 1954b. An outline of the dynamics of animal populations. *Austr. J. Zool.* 2:9–65.

Nicholson, A. J. 1957. The self-adjustment of populations to change. *Cold Springs Harbor Symp. Quant. Biol.* 22:153–172.

Nicholson, A. J. 1958. Dynamics of insect populations. *Annu. Rev. Entomol.* 3:107–136.

Nicholson, A. J., and V. A. Bailey. 1935. The balance of animal populations. Part I. *Proc. Zool. Soc. London*, pp. 551–598.

Nickerson, R. P., and M. Druger. 1973. Maintenance of chromosomal polymorphism in a population of *Drosophila pseudoobscura*. II. Fecundity, longevity, viability and competitive fitness. *Evolution* 27:125–133.

Nielsen, E. T. 1961. On the habits of the migratory butterfly *Ascia monuste* L. *Biol. Meddr.* 23:1–81.

Odum, E. P. 1957. The ecosystem approach in the teaching of ecology illustrated with simple class data. *Ecology* 38:531–535.

Odum, E. P. 1969. The strategy of ecosystem development. *Science* 164:262–270.

Odum, E. P. 1971. *Fundamentals of ecology.* 3rd ed. Saunders, Philadelphia. 574 pp.

Odum, E. P., C. E. Connell, and L. B. Davenport. 1962. Population energy flow of three primary consumer components of old-field ecosystems. *Ecology* 43:88–96.

Odum, E. P., and A. E. Smalley. 1959. Comparison of population energy flow of a herbivorous and a deposit-feeding invertebrate in a salt marsh ecosystem. *Proc. Nat. Acad. Sci. Washington* 45:617–622.

Odum, H. T. 1956. Efficiencies, size of organisms and community structure. *Ecology* 37:592–597.

Odum, H. T., and R. C. Pinkerton. 1955. Time's speed regulator: The optimum efficiency for maximum power output in physical and biological systems. *Amer. Sci.* 43:331–343.

Ogden, J. 1974. The reproductive strategy of higher plants. II. The reproductive strategy of *Tussilago farfara* L. *J. Ecol.* 62:291–324.

Ohno, S. C. Stenius, L. Christian, and G. Schipmann. 1969. *De novo* mutation-like events observed at the 6PGD locus of the Japanese quail, and the principle of polymorphism breeding more polymorphism. *Biochem. Genet.* 3:417–428.

O'Neill, R. V. 1967. Niche segregation in seven species of diplopods. *Ecology* 48:983.

Opler, P. A. 1974. Oaks as evolutionary islands for leaf-mining insects. *Amer. Sci.* 62:67–73.

Oshima, K., H. Honda, and I. Yamamoto. 1973. Isolation of an oviposition marker from azuki bean weevil. *Callosobruchus chinensis* (L.). Agr. Biol. Chem. 37:2679–2680.

Ovington, J. D. 1962. Quantitative ecology and the woodland ecosystem concept. *Adv. Ecol. Res.* 1:103–192.

Ovington, J. D., D. Heitkamp, and D. B. Lawrence. 1963. Plant biomass and productivity of prairie, savanna, oakwood, and maize field ecosystems in central Minnesota. *Ecology* 44:52–63.

Paine, R. T. 1962. Ecological diversification in sympatric gastropods of the genus *Busycon. Evolution* 16:515–523.

Paine, R. T. 1964. Ash and calorie determinations of sponge and opisthobranch tissues. *Ecology* 45:384–387.

Paine, R. T. 1966. Food web complexity and species diversity. *Amer. Natur.* 100:65–75.

Paine, R. T. 1969a. A note on trophic complexity and community stability. *Amer. Natur.* 103:91–93.

Paine, R. T. 1969b. The *Pisaster-Tegula* interaction: Prey patches, predator food preference, and intertidal community structure. *Ecology* 50:950–961.

Paine, R. T. 1971. The measurement and application of the calorie to ecological problems. *Annu. Rev. Ecol. Syst.* 2:145–164.

Pajunen, V. I. 1966. The influence of population density on the territorial behaviour of *Leucorrhinia rubicunda* L. (Odon., Libellulidae). *Ann. Zool. Fenn.* 3:40–52.

Park, T. 1932. Studies in population physiology: The relation of numbers to initial population growth in the flour beetle, *Tribolium confusum* Duval. *Ecology* 13:172–181.

Park, T. 1948. Experimental studies of interspecies competition. I. Competition between populations of the flour beetles, *Tribolium confusum* Duval and *Tribolium castaneum* Herbst. *Ecol. Monogr.* 18:265–308.

Park, T. 1954a. Experimental studies of interspecies competition. II. Temperature, humidity, and competition in two species of *Tribolium. Physiol. Zool.* 27:177–238.

Park, T. 1954b. Competition: an experimental and statistical study. In O. Kempthorne, T. A. Bancroft, J. W. Gowen, and J. L. Lush (eds.). *Statistics and mathematics in biology*. State College Press, Ames, Iowa, pp. 175–195.

Park, T., P. H. Leslie, and D. B. Mertz. 1964. Genetic strains and competition in populations of *Tribolium. Physiol. Zool.* 37:97–162.

Parker, F. D. 1971. Management of pest populations by manipulating densities of both hosts and parasites through periodic releases. In C. B. Huffaker (ed.). *Biological control*. Plenum Press. New York, pp. 365–376.

Parker, G. A. 1971. The reproductive behaviour and the nature of sexual selection in *Scatophaga stercoraria* L. (Diptera: Scatophagidae). VI. The adaptive significance of emigration from the oviposition site during the phase of genital contact. *J. Anim. Ecol.* **40**:215–233.

Parker, G. A. 1974. The reproductive behaviour and the nature of sexual selection in *Scatophaga stercoraria* L. (Diptera: Scatophagidae). IX. Spatial distribution of fertilization rates and evolution of male search strategy within the reproductive area. *Evolution* **28**:93–108.

Parnell, J. R. 1966. Observations on the population fluctuations and life histories of the beetles *Bruchidius ater* (Bruchidae) and *Apion fuscirostre* (Curculionidae) on broom (*Sarothamnus scoparius*). *J. Anim. Ecol.* **35**:157–188.

Parsons, P. A., and J. A. McKenzie. 1972. The ecological genetics of *Drosophila*. *Evol. Biol.* **5**:87–132.

Pathak, M. D. 1970. Genetics of plants in pest management. In R. L. Rabb and F. E. Guthrie (eds.). *Concepts of pest management*. North Carolina State Univ. Press, Raleigh, N.C., pp. 138–157.

Patrick, R., and D. Strawbridge. 1963. Variation in the structure of natural diatom communities. *Amer. Natur.* **97**:51–57.

Paulson, D. R. 1973. Predator polymorphism and apostatic selection. *Evolution* **27**:269–277.

Payne, R. 1968. Among wild whales. *New York Zool. Soc. Newsletter, Nov.* 1968:1–6.

Pearl, R., and J. R. Miner. 1935. Experimental studies on the duration of life. XIV. The comparative mortality of certain lower organisms. *Quart. Rev. Biol.* **10**:60–79.

Pearl, R., and S. L. Parker. 1921. Experimental studies on the duration of life. I. Introductory discussion of the duration of life in *Drosophila*. *Amer. Natur.* **55**:481–509.

Pearl, R., and L. J. Reed. 1920. On the rate of growth of the population of the United States since 1790 and its mathematical representation. *Proc. Nat. Acad. Sci.* **6**:275–288.

Pearson, O. P. 1954. The daily energy requirements of a wild anna hummingbird. *Condor* **56**:317–322.

Pearson, O. P. 1964. Carnivore-mouse predation: An example of its intensity and bioenergetics. *J. Mammal.* **45**:177–188.

Pechuman, L. L. 1967. Observations on the behavior of the bee *Anthidium manicatum* (L.). *J. N. Y. Entomol. Soc.* **75**:68–73.

Pemberton, C. E., and H. F. Willard. 1918. A contribution to the biology of fruit-fly parasites in Hawaii. *J. Agric. Res.* **15**:419–465.

Perrins, C. M. 1964. Survival of young swifts in relation to brood-size. *Nature* **201**:1147–1148.

Peschken, D. P. 1972. *Chrysolina quadrigemina* (Coleoptera: Chrysomelidae) introduced from California to British Columbia against the weed *Hypericum perforatum*: Comparison of behaviour, physiology, and colour in association with post-colonization adaptation. *Can. Entomol.* **104**:1689–1698.

Petit, C., and L. Ehrman. 1969. Sexual selection in *Drosophila*. *Evol. Biol.* **3**:177–223.

Petras, M. L., J. D. Reimer, F. G. Biddle, J. E. Martin, and R. S. Linton. 1969. Studies of natural populations of *Mus*. V. A survey of nine loci for polymorphisms. *Can. J. Genet. Cytol.* 11:497–513.

Philip, J. R. 1955. Note on the mathematical theory of population dynamics and a recent fallacy. *Austr. J. Zool.* 3:287–294.

Phillipson, J. 1966. Ecological energetics. Arnold, London. 57 pp.

Pianka, E. R. 1966. Latitudinal gradients in species diversity: A review of concepts. *Amer. Natur.* 100:33–46.

Pianka, E. R. 1969. Sympatry of desert lizards (*Ctenotus*) in Western Australia. *Ecology* 50:1012–1030.

Pianka, E. R. 1970. On *r*- and *K*- selection. *Amer. Natur.* 104:592–597.

Pickett, S. T., and J. M. Baskin. 1973. Allelopathy and its role in the ecology of higher plants. *Biologist* 55:49–73.

Pielou, E. C. 1969. *An introduction to mathematical ecology*. Wiley-Interscience, New York. 286 pp.

Pimentel, D. 1961a. Species diversity and insect population outbreaks. *Ann. Entomol. Soc. Amer.* 54:76–86.

Pimentel, D. 1961b. Animal population regulation by the genetic feed-back mechanism. *Amer. Natur.* 95:65–79.

Pimentel, D. 1968. Population regulation and genetic feedback. *Science* 159:1432–1437.

Pimlott, D. H. 1967. Wolf predation and ungulate populations. *Amer. Zool.* 7:267–278.

Pitelka, F. A. 1941. Distribution of birds in relation to major biotic communities. *Amer. Midl. Natur.* 25:113–137.

Pitelka, F. A. 1959. Population studies of lemmings and lemming predators in northern Alaska. *Proc. Int. Congr. Zool.* 15:757–759.

Pitelka, F. A. 1964. The nutrient-recovery hypothesis for arctic microtine cycles. I. Introduction. In D. Crisp (ed.). *Grazing in terrestrial and marine environments*. Blackwell, Oxford, pp. 55–56.

Pitelka, F. A., P. Q. Tomich, and G. W. Treichel. 1955. Ecological relations of jaegers and owls as lemming predators near Barrow, Alaska. *Ecol. Monogr.* 25:85–117.

Platt, A. P., and L. P. Brower. 1968. Mimetic versus disruptive coloration in integrading populations of *Limenitis arthemis* and *astyanax* butterflies. *Evolution* 22:699–718.

Platt, A. P., R. P. Coppinger, and L. P. Brower. 1971. Demonstration of the selective advantage of mimetic *Limenitis* butterflies presented to caged avian predators. *Evolution* 25:692–701.

Poole, R. W. 1974. *An introduction to quantitative ecology*. McGraw-Hill. New York. 432 pp.

Portmann, A. 1959. *Animal camouflage*. Univ. Michigan Press, Ann Arbor. 111 pp.

Pottinger, R. P., and E. J. LeRoux. 1971. The biology and dynamics of *Lithocolletis blancardella* (Lepidoptera: Gracillariidae) on apple in Quebec. *Mem. Entomol. Soc. Can.* 77:1–437.

Powell, J. A., and R. A. Mackie. 1966. Biological interrelationships of moths and *Yucca whipplei*. *Univ. Calif. Publ. Entomol.* 42:1–59.

Prakash, S. 1969. Genic variation in a natural population of *Drosophila persimilis*. *Proc. Nat. Acad. Sci.* 62:778–784.

Prakash, S., R. C. Lewontin, and J. L. Hubby. 1969. A molecular approach to the study of genic heterozygosity in natural populations. IV. Patterns of genic variation in central, marginal and isolated populations of *Drosophila pseudoobscura*. *Genetics* **61**:841–858.

Preston, F. W. 1948. The commonness, and rarity, of species. *Ecology* **29**:254–283.

Preston, F. W. 1962. The canonical distribution of commonness and rarity. Parts I and II. *Ecology* **43**:182–215, 410–432.

Price, P. W. 1970a. A loosestrife sawfly, *Monostegia abdominalis* (Hymenoptera: Tenthredinidae). *Can. Entomol.* **102**:491–495.

Price, P. W. 1970b. Biology of and host exploitation by *Pleolophus indistinctus* (Hymenoptera: Ichneumonidae). *Ann. Amer. Entomol. Soc.* **63**:1502–1509.

Price, P. W. 1970c. Characteristics permitting coexistence among parasitoids of a sawfly in Quebec. *Ecology* **51**:445–454.

Price, P. W. 1970d. Trail odors: Recognition by insects parasitic on cocoons. *Science* **170**:546–547.

Price, P. W. 1971a. Niche breadth and dominance of parasitic insects sharing the same host species. *Ecology* **52**:587–596.

Price, P. W. 1971b. Toward a holistic approach to insect population studies. *Ann. Entomol. Soc. Amer.* **64**:1399–1406.

Price, P. W. 1972a. Methods of sampling and analysis for predictive results in the introduction of entomophagous insects. *Entomophaga* **17**:211–222.

Price, P. W. 1972b. Behavior of the parasitoid *Pleolophus basizonus* (Hymenoptera: Ichneumonidae) in response to changes in host and parasitoid density. *Can. Entomol.* **104**:129–140.

Price, P. W. 1972c. Parasitoids utilizing the same host: Adaptive nature of differences in size and form. *Ecology* **53**:190–195.

Price, P. W. 1973a. Reproductive strategies in parasitoid wasps. *Amer. Natur.* **107**:684–693.

Price, P. W. 1973b. Parasitoid strategies and community organization. *Environ. Entomol.* **2**:623–626.

Price, P. W. 1973c. The development of parasitoid communities. *Proc. Northeastern Forest Insect Work Conf.* **5**:29–41.

Price, P. W. 1974a. Strategies for egg production. *Evolution* **28**:76–84.

Price, P. W. 1974b. Energy allocation in ephemeral adult insects. *Ohio J. Sci.* **74**:380–387.

Price, P. W. 1975. Reproductive strategies of parasitoids. In P. W. Price (ed.). *Evolutionary strategies of parasitic insects and mites.* Plenum, New York, pp. 87–111.

Price, P. W., and H. A. Tripp. 1972. Activity patterns of parasitoids on the Swaine jack pine sawfly, *Neodiprion swainei* (Hymenoptera: Diprionidae), and parasitoid impact on the host. *Can. Entomol.* **104**:1003–1016.

Price, P. W. and G. P. Waldbauer. 1975. Ecological aspects of insect pest management. In R. L. Metcalf and W. H. Luckmann (eds.). *Introduction to insect pest management.* Wiley, New York. pp. 36–73.

Pritchard, G. 1969. The ecology of a natural population of Queensland fruit fly, *Dacus tryoni*. II. The distribution of eggs and its relation to behaviour. *Aust. J. Zool.* **17**:293–311.

Proctor, M., and P. Yeo. 1972. *The pollination of flowers*. Taplinger, New York. 418 pp.

Prokopy, R. J. 1972. Evidence for a marking pheromone deterring repeated oviposition in apple maggot flies. *Environ. Entomol.* 1:326–332.

Prop, N. 1960. Protection against birds and parasites in some species of tenthredinid larvae. *Arch. Neerl. Zool.* 13:380–447.

Pukowski, E. 1933. Ökologische Untersuchungen an *Necrophorus* F. *Z. Morph. Ökol. Tiere* 27:518–586.

Putnam, A. R., and W. B. Duke. 1974. Biological suppression of weeds: Evidence for allelopathy in accessions of cucumber. *Science* 185:370–372.

Quednau, F. W. 1970. Competition and co-operation between *Chrysocharis laricinellae* and *Agathis pumila* on larch casebearer in Quebec. *Can. Entomol.* 102:602–612.

Rabb, R. L., and F. E. Guthrie (eds.). 1970. *Concepts of pest management*. North Carolina State Univ., Raleigh. 242 pp.

Ramensky, L. G. 1926. Die Grundgesetzmässigkeiten im Aufbau der Vegetationsdecke. *Bot. Centralblatt. N.F.* 7:453–455.

Ramirez, B. W. 1969. Fig wasps: Mechanism of pollen transfer. *Science* 163:580–581.

Ramirez, B. W. 1970. Host specificity of fig wasps (Agaonidae). *Evolution* 24:680–691.

Randolph, P. A. 1973. Influence of environmental variability on land snail population properties. *Ecology* 54:933–955.

Read, D. P., P. P. Feeny, and R. B. Root. 1970. Habitat selection by the aphid parasite *Diaeretiella rapae* (Hymenoptera: Braconidae) and hyperparasite *Charips brassicae* (Hymenoptera: Cynipidae). *Can. Entomol.* 102:1567–1578.

Readshaw, J. L., 1965. A theory of phasmatid outbreak release. *Austr. J. Zool.* 13:475–490

Reddingius, J. 1971. Gambling for existence. A discussion of some theoretical problems in animal population ecology. *Bibl. Biotheor.* 12:1–208.

Rees, C. J. C. 1969. Chemoreceptor specificity associated with choice of feeding site by the beetle, *Chrysolina brunsvicensis* on its foodplant, *Hypericum hirsutum*. In J. de Wilde and L. M. Schoonhoven (eds.). *Insect and host plant*. North-Holland, Amsterdam, pp. 565–583.

Rehr, S. S., P. P. Feeny, and D. H. Janzen. 1973. Chemical defense in Central American non-ant-acacias. *J. Anim. Ecol.* 42:405–416.

Reichle, D. E., R. A. Goldstein, R. I. Van Hook, Jr., and G. J. Dodson. 1973. Analysis of insect consumption in a forest canopy. *Ecology* 54:1076–1084.

Reichstein, T., J. von Euw, J. A. Parsons, and M. Rothschild. 1968. Heart poisons in the monarch butterfly. *Science* 161:861–866.

Remington, C. L. 1963. Historical backgrounds of mimicry. *Proc. XVI Int. Congr. Zool.* 4:145–149.

Rensch, B. 1938. Einwirkung des Klimas bie der Ausprägung von Vogelrassen, mit besonderer Berücksichtigung der Flügelform und der Eizahl. *Proc. 8th Int. Orn. Cong. 1934*:305–311.

Rettenmeyer, C. W. 1970. Insect mimicry. *Annu. Rev. Entomol.* 15:43–74.

Reuter, O. M. 1913. *Lebensgewohnheiten und Instinkte der Insekten bis zum Erwachen der sozialen Instinkte*. Friedländer, Berlin. 448 pp.

Reynoldson, T. B. 1957. Population fluctuations in *Urceolaria mitra* (Peritricha) and *Enchytraeus albidus* (Oligochaeta) and their bearing on regulation. *Cold Spring Harbor Symp. Quant. Biol.* 22:313–324.

Reynoldson, T. B. 1964. Evidence for intra-specific competition in field populations of triclads. *J. Anim. Ecol.* **33** Suppl:187–201.

Reynoldson, T. B. 1966. The distribution and abundance of lake-dwelling triclads— Towards a hypothesis. *Adv. Ecol. Res.* **3**:1–71.

Reynoldson, T. B., and R. W. Davies. 1970. Food niche and co-existence in lake-dwelling triclads. *J. Anim. Ecol.* **39**:599–617.

Richards, O. W. 1961. The theoretical and practical study of natural insect populations. *Annu. Rev. Entomol.* **6**:147–162.

Richards, O. W. 1927. Sexual selection and allied problems in the insects. *Biol. Rev.* **2**:298–364.

Richards, O. W., and N. Waloff. 1961. A study of a natural population of *Phytodecta olivacea* (Forster) (Coleoptera: Chrysomelidae). *Phil. Trans. Roy. Soc. London B.* **244**:205–257.

Richmond, R. C. 1972. Enzyme variability in the *Drosophila willistoni* group. III. Amounts of variability in the superspecies, *D. paulistorum. Genetics* **70**:87–112.

Ricklefs, R. E. 1970a. Clutch size in birds: Outcome of opposing predator and prey adaptations. *Science* **168**:599–600.

Ricklefs, R. E. 1970b. Stage of taxon cycle and distribution of birds on Jamaica, Greater Antilles. *Evolution* **24**:475–477.

Ricklefs, R. E. 1973. *Ecology.* Chiron, Newton, Mass. 861 pp.

Ricklefs, R. E., and G. W. Cox. 1972. Taxon cycles in the West Indian avifauna. *Amer. Natur.* **106**:195–219.

Rickson, F. R. 1971. Glycogen plastids in Müllerian body cells of *Cecropia peltata*—A higher green plant. *Science* **173**:344–347.

Riebesell, J. F. 1974. Paradox of enrichment in competitive systems. *Ecology* **55**:183–187.

Riley, C. V. 1892. *The yucca moth and yucca pollination.* Missouri Bot. Gdn. 3rd Annu. Rep. pp. 99–159.

Riley, C. V. 1893. Further notes on yucca insects and yucca pollination. *Proc. Biol. Soc. Wash.* **8**:41–54.

Ripper, W. E. 1956. Effect of pesticides on balance of arthropod populations. *Annu. Rev. Entomol.* **1**:403–438.

Robbins, W. E. 1972. Hormonal chemicals for invertebrate pest control. In *Pest control strategies for the future.* Nat. Acad. Sci. Washington, pp. 172–196.

Robinson, I. 1953. On the fauna of a brown flux of an elm tree, *Ulmus procera* Salisb. *J. Anim. Ecol.* **22**:149–153.

Robinson, M. H. 1969. Defenses against visually hunting predators. *Evol. Biol.* **3**:225–259.

Robinson, T. 1973. The metabolism and function of alkaloids in plants. *Phytochem. Bull.* **6**(4):5–11.

Roeder, K. D., and A. E. Treat. 1961. The detection and evasion of bats by moths. *Amer. Sci.* **49**:135–148.

Roelofs, W. L., E. H. Glass, J. Tette, and A. Comeau. 1970. Sex pheromone trapping for red-banded leaf roller control: Theoretical and actual. *J. Econ. Entomol.* **63**:1162–1167.

Rogers, D. J., and M. P. Hassell. 1974. General models for insect parasite and predator searching behaviour: Interference. *J. Anim. Ecol.* **43**:239–253.

Root, R. B. 1967. The niche exploitation pattern of the blue-gray gnatcatcher. *Ecol. Monogr.* **37**:317–350.

Root, R. B. 1973. Organization of a plant-arthropod association in simple and diverse habitats: The fauna of collards (*Brassica oleracea*). *Ecol. Monogr.* **43**:95–124.

Rosenzweig, M. L. 1971. Paradox of enrichment: Destabilization of exploitation ecosystems in ecological time. *Science* **171**:385–387.

Ross, H. H. 1957. Principles of natural coexistence indicated by leafhopper populations. *Evolution* **11**:113–129.

Ross, H. H. 1958. Further comments on niches and natural coexistence. *Evolution* **12**:112–113.

Ross, H. H. 1965. Pleistocene events and insects. In H. E. Wright, Jr., and D. G. Frey (eds.). *The quaternary of the United States.* Princeton Univ. Press, Princeton, N.J. pp. 583–596.

Ross, H. H. 1967. The evolution and past dispersal of the Trichoptera. *Annu. Rev. Entomol.* **12**:169–206.

Ross, H. H., and W. E. Ricker. 1971. The classification, evolution, and dispersal of the winter stonefly genus *Allocapnia*. *Illinois Biol. Monogr.* **45**:1–166.

Ross, H. H., and T. Yamamoto. 1967. Variations in the winter stonefly *Allocapnia granulata* as indicators of Pleistocene faunal movements. *Ann. Entomol. Soc. Amer.* **60**:447–458.

Royama, T. 1970. Factors governing the hunting behaviour and selection of food by the great tit (*Parus major* L.). *J. Anim. Ecol.* **39**:619–668.

Royama, T. 1971. A comparative study of models for predation and parasitism. *Res. Pop. Ecol.* **13** (Suppl. 1):1–91.

Ruiter, L. de. 1952. Some experiments on the camouflage of stick caterpillars. *Behaviour* **4**:222–232.

Ruiter, L. de. 1956. Countershading in caterpillars. *Arch. Neerl. Zool.* **11**:285–342.

Salt, G. 1934a. Experimental studies in insect parasitism. I. Introduction and technique. *Proc. Roy. Soc. London. Ser. B.* **114**:450–454.

Salt, G. 1934b. Experimental studies in insect parasitism. II. Superparasitism. *Proc. Roy. Soc. London. Ser. B.* **114**:455–476.

Salt, G. 1935. Experimental studies in insect parasitism. III. Host selection. *Proc. Roy. Soc. London. Ser. B.* **117**:413–435.

Salt, G. 1936. Experimental studies in insect parasitism. IV. The effect of superparasitism on populations of *Trichogramma evanescens*. *J. Exp. Biol.* **13**:363–375.

Salt, G. 1937. The sense used by *Trichogramma* to distinguish between parasitized and unparasitized hosts. *Proc. Roy. Soc. London. Ser. B.* **122**:57–75.

Salt, G. 1963. The defense reactions of insects to metazoan parasites. *Parasitology* **53**:527–642.

Salt, G. 1968. The resistance of insect parasitoids to the defense reactions of their hosts. *Biol. Rev.* **43**:200–232.

Salt, G. 1970. *The cellular defense reactions of insects.* Cambridge Univ. Press, New York. 118 pp.

Salt, G. W. 1967. Predation in an experimental protozoan population (*Woodruffia-Paramecium*). *Ecol. Monogr.* **37**:113–144.

Samarasinghe, S., and E. J. LeRoux. 1966. The biology and dynamics of the oystershell scale, *Lepidosaphes ulmi* (L.) (Homoptera: Coccidae) on apple in Quebec. *Ann. Entomol. Soc. Quebec* 11:206–292.

Sanders, H. L. 1968. Marine benthic diversity: A comparative study. *Amer. Natur.* 102:243–282.

Sanders, H. L. 1969. Benthic marine diversity and the stability-time hypothesis. In G. M. Woodwell and H. H. Smith (eds.). *Diversity and stability in ecological systems.* Brookhaven Symp. Biol. 22, pp. 71–81.

Sargent, T. D., and R. R. Keiper. 1969. Behavioral adaptations of cryptic moths. 1. Preliminary studies on bark-like species. *J. Lepidop. Soc.* 23:1–9.

Sarukhán, J. 1974. Studies on plant demography: *Ranunculus repens* L., *R. bulbosus* L. and *R. acris* L. II. Reproductive strategies and seed population dynamics. *J. Ecol.* 62:151–177.

Sarukhán, J., and J. L. Harper. 1973. Studies on plant demography: *Ranunculus repens* L., *R. bulbosus* L., and *R. acris* L. I. Population flux and survivorship. *J. Ecol.* 61:675–716.

Savage, J. M. 1958. The concept of ecologic niche, with reference to the theory of natural coexistence. *Evolution* 12:111–112.

Schedl, K. E. 1958. Breeding habits of arboricole insects in Central Africa. *Proc. 10th Int. Cong. Entomol. Montreal.* 1:183–197.

Schmidt-Nielsen, K. 1972. Locomotion: Energy cost of swimming, flying, and running. *Science* 177:222–228.

Schoener, T. W. 1965. The evolution of bill size differences among sympatric congeneric species of birds. *Evolution* 19:189–213.

Schoener, T. W. 1967. The ecological significance of sexual dimorphism in the lizard *Anolis conspersus*. *Science* 155:474–477.

Schoener, T. W. 1968. Sizes of feeding territories among birds. *Ecology* 49:123–141.

Schoener, T. W. 1969. Optimal size and specialization in constant and fluctuating environments: An energy-time approach. In G. M. Woodwell and H. H. Smith (eds.). *Diversity and stability in ecological systems.* Brookhaven Symp. Biol. 22, pp. 103–114.

Schoener, T. W. 1971. Theory of feeding strategies. *Annu. Rev. Ecol. Syst.* 2:369–404.

Schoener, T. W. 1974. Resource partitioning in ecological communities. *Science* 185:27–39.

Schultz, A. M. 1964. The nutrient-recovery hypothesis for arctic microtine cycles. II. Ecosystem variables in relation to the arctic microtine cycles. In D. J. Crisp (ed.). *Grazing in terrestrial and marine environments.* Blackwell, Oxford, pp. 57–68.

Schuster, M. F., J. C. Boling, and J. J. Marony, Jr. 1971. Biological control of Rhodesgrass scale by airplane releases of an introduced parasite of limited dispersing ability. In C. B. Huffaker (ed.). *Biological control.* Plenum Press, New York, pp. 227–250.

Schwerdtfeger, F., 1941. Über die Ursachen des Massenwechsels der Insekten. *Z. Angew. Entomol.* 28:254–303.

Scudder, G. G. E., and S. S. Duffey. 1972. Cardiac glycosides in the Lygaeinae (Hemiptera: Lygaeidae). *Can. J. Zool.* 50:35–42.

Selander, R. K. 1966. Sexual dimorphism and differential utilization in birds. Condor 68:113–151.

Selander, R. K., and W. E. Johnson. 1973. Genetic variation among vertebrate species. *Annu. Rev. Ecol. Syst.* **4**:75–91.

Selander, R. K., S. Y. Yang, R. C. Lewontin, and W. E. Johnson. 1970. Genetic variation in the horseshoe crab (*Limulus polyphemus*), a phylogenetic "relic." *Evolution* **24**:402–414.

Sen-Sarma, P. K. 1974. Ecology and biogeography of the termites of India. In M. S. Mani (ed.). *Ecology and biogeography in India.* Monogr. Biol. 23, pp. 421–472.

Shapiro, A. M. 1970. The role of sexual behavior in density-related dispersal of pierid butterflies. *Amer. Natur.* **104**:367–372.

Shelford, V. E. 1907. Preliminary note on the distribution of the tiger beetles (*Cicindela*) and its relation to plant succession. *Biol. Bull.* **14**:9–14.

Shelford, V. E. 1913. *Animal communities in temperate America.* Univ. Chicago Press, Chicago. 362 pp.

Shepard, P., and D. McKinley. 1969. *The subversive science. Essays toward an ecology of man.* Houghton Mifflin, Boston. 453 pp.

Sheppard, P. M. 1952. Natural selection in two colonies of the polymorphic land snail *Cepaea nemoralis. Heredity* **6**:233–238.

Sheppard, P. M. 1956. Ecology and its bearing on population genetics. *Proc. Roy. Soc. London, Ser. B.* **145**:308–315.

Sheppard, P. M. 1958. *Natural selection and heredity.* Hutchinson, London. 212 pp.

Sheppard, P. M. 1961. Recent genetical work on polymorphic mimetic Papilios. In *Insect polymorphism.* J. S. Kennedy (ed.). Roy. Entomol. Soc. London. 1, pp. 20–29.

Sheppard, P. M. 1962. Some aspects of the geography, genetics and taxonomy of a butterfly. In D. Nichols (ed.). *Taxonomy and geography.* Syst. Assoc. Publ. 4, pp. 135–152.

Shure, D. J. 1970. Limitations in radiotracer determination of consumer trophic positions. *Ecology* **51**:899–901.

Shure, D. J. 1973. Radionuclide tracer analysis of trophic relationships in an old-field ecosystem. *Ecol. Monogr.* **43**:1–19.

Silliman, R. P., and J. S. Gutsell. 1958. Experimental exploitation of fish populations. *U.S. Fish and Wild. Serv., Fish. Bull.* **58**:215–252.

Simberloff, D. S. 1969. Experimental zoogeography of islands: A model for insular colonization. *Ecology* **50**:296–314.

Simberloff, D. S., and E. O. Wilson. 1969. Experimental zoogeography of islands: the colonization of empty islands. *Ecology* **50**:278–296.

Simberloff, D S., and E. O. Wilson 1970. Experimental zoogeography of islands. A two-year record of colonization. *Ecology* **51**:934–937.

Simpson, G. G. 1940. Mammals and land bridges. *J. Wash. Acad. Sci.* **30**:137–163.

Simpson, G. G. 1964a. *This view of life. The world of an evolutionist.* Harcourt, Brace and World, New York. 308 pp.

Simpson, G. G. 1964b. Species density of North American recent mammals. *Syst Zool.* **13**:57–73.

Singer, M. C., P. R. Ehrlich, and L E. Gilbert. 1971 Butterfly feeding on lycopsid. *Science* **172**:1341–1342.

Skellam, J. G. 1951. Random dispersal in theoretical populations. *Biometrika* **38**:196–218.

Skutch, A. F. 1949. Do tropical birds rear as many young as they can nourish? *Ibis* 91:430–455.

Skutch, A. F. 1967. Adaptive limitation of the reproductive rate of birds. *Ibis* 109:579–599.

Sláma, K. 1969. Plants as a source of materials with insect hormone activity. *Entomol. Exp. Appl.* 12:721–728.

Sláma, K., and C. M. Williams. 1965. Juvenile hormone activity for the bug *Pyrrhocoris apterus. Proc. Nat. Acad. Sci.* 54:411–414.

Sláma, K., and C. M. Williams. 1966. The juvenile hormone. V. The sensitivity of the bug, *Pyrrhocoris apterus*, to a hormonally active factor in American paper-pulp. *Biol. Bull.* 130:235–246.

Slatkin, M. 1974. Competition and regional coexistence. *Ecology* 55:128–134.

Slobodkin, L. B. 1961. *Growth and regulation of animal populations.* Holt, Rinehart and Winston, New York. 184 pp.

Slobodkin, L. B. 1962. Energy in animal ecology. *Adv. Ecol. Res.* 1:69–101.

Slobodkin, L. B., F. E. Smith, and N. G. Hairston. 1967. Regulation in terrestrial ecosystems, and the implied balance of nature. *Amer. Natur.* 101:109–124.

Smart, J., and N. F. Hughes. 1973. The insect and the plant: progressive palaeoecological integration. In H. F. van Emden (ed.). *Insect/plant relationships.* Roy. Entomol. Soc. London. Symp. 6, pp. 143–155.

Smith, A. P. 1973. Stratification of temperate and tropical forests. *Amer. Natur.* 107:671–683.

Smith, C. C. 1970. The coevolution of pine squirrels (*Tamiasciurus*) and conifers. *Ecol. Monogr.* 40:349–371.

Smith, F. E. 1954. Quantitative aspects of population growth. In E. J. Boell (ed.). *Dynamics of growth processes.* Princeton Univ. Press, Princeton, N.J., pp. 277–294.

Smith, F. E. 1961. Density dependence in the Australian thrips. *Ecology* 42:403–407.

Smith, H. S. 1929. Multiple parasitism: Its relation to the biological control of insect pests. *Bull. Entomol. Res.* 20:141–149.

Smith, J. N. M. 1974. The food searching behaviour of two European thrushes. II: The adaptiveness of the search patterns. *Behaviour* 49:1-61.

Smith, P. H. 1972. The energy relations of defoliating insects in a hazel coppice. *J Anim. Ecol.* 41:567–587.

Smith, P. W. 1957. An analysis of post-Wisconsin biogeography of the prairie peninsula region based on distributional phenomena among terrestrial vertebrate populations. *Ecology* 38:205–218.

Snodgrass, R. E. 1925. *Insect musicians, their music, and their instruments.* Smiths' Inst. Annu. Rep. 1923, pp. 405–452.

Soderstrom, T. R., and C. E. Calderon. 1971. Insect pollination in tropical rain forest grasses. *Biotropica* 3:1–16.

Solomon, M. E. 1949. The natural control of animal populations. *J. Anim. Ecol.* 18:1–35.

Solomon, M. E. 1964. Analysis of processes involved in the natural control of insects. *Adv. Ecol. Res.* 2:1-58.

Solomon, M. E. 1969. *Population dynamics.* St. Martin's Press, New York. 60 pp. Reprinted 1973.

Sondheimer, E., and J. B. Simeone (eds.). 1970. *Chemical ecology.* Academic Press, New York. 336 pp.

Southwood, T. R. E. 1961. The number of species of insect associated with various trees. *J. Anim. Ecol.* **30**:1–8.

Southwood, T. R. E. 1966. *Ecological methods with particular reference to the study of insect populations.* Methuen, London. 391 pp.

Southwood, T. R. E. (ed.). 1968. *Insect abundance.* Symp. Royal Entomol. Soc. London. 4. 160 pp.

Spanner, D. C. 1963. The green leaf as a heat engine. *Nature* **198**:934–937.

Spieth, H. T. 1968. Evolutionary implications of sexual behavior in *Drosophila. Evol. Biol.* **2**:157–193.

Springett, B. P. 1968. Aspects of the relationship between burying beetles, *Necrophorus* spp. and the mite, *Poecilochirus necrophori* Vitz. *J. Anim. Ecol.* **37**:417–424.

Stark, R. W. 1959. Population dynamics of the lodgepole needle miner, *Recurvaria starki* Freeman, in Canadian Rocky Mountain parks. *Can. J. Zool.* **37**:917–943.

Stehr, F. W. 1975. Parasitoids and predators in pest management. In R. L. Metcalf and W. H. Luckmann (eds.). *Introduction to insect pest management.* Wiley, New York. pp. 147–188.

Stephenson, S. N. 1973. Fertilization responses in six southern Michigan oldfied communities. *Bull. Ecol. Soc. Amer.* **54**(1):33. (Abstract).

Stiles, F. G. 1971. Time, energy, and territoriality of the anna hummingbird (*Calypte anna*). *Science* **173**:818–821.

Stockner, J. G. 1971. Ecological energetics and natural history of *Hedriodiscus truquii* (Diptera) in two thermal spring communities. *J. Fish. Res. Bd. Can.* **28**:73–94.

Stoutamire, W. P. 1974. Australian terrestrial orchids, thynnid wasps, and pseudocopulation. *Amer. Orchid Soc. Bull.* **43**:13–18.

Straw, R. M. 1955. Hybridization, homogamy, and sympatric speciation. *Evolution* **9**:441–444.

Stuart, A. M. 1972. Behavioral regulatory mechanisms in the social homeostasis of termites (Isoptera). *Amer. Zool.* **12**:589–594.

Sudd, J. H. 1967. *An introduction to the behavior of ants.* St. Martin's Press, New York. 200 pp.

Swaine, J. M. 1918. Canadian bark-beetles. Part II. A preliminary classification, with an account of the habits and means of control. *Dom. Can. Dept. Agr. Tech. Bull.* **14**:1–143.

Sweetman, H. L. 1936. *The biological control of insects.* Comstock, Ithaca, N.Y. 461 pp.

Tahvanainen, J. O. 1972. Phenology and microhabitat selection of some flea beetles (Coleoptera: Chrysomelidae) on wild and cultivated crucifers in central New York. *Entomol. Scand.* **3**:130–138.

Tahvanainen, J. O., and R. B. Root. 1970. The invasion and population outbreak of *Psylloides napi* (Coleoptera: Chrysomelidae) on yellow rocket (*Barbarea vulgaris*) in New York. *Ann. Entomol. Soc. Amer.* **63**:1479–1480.

Takahashi, F. 1968. Functional response to host density in a parasitic wasp, with reference to population regulation. *Res. Pop. Ecol.* **10**:54–68.

Tatton, J. O'G., and J. H. A. Ruzicka. 1967. Organochlorine pesticides in Antarctica. *Nature* **215**:346–348.

Taylor, R. J. 1974. Role of learning in insect parasitism. *Ecol. Monogr.* **44**:89–104.

Terborgh, J. 1971. Distribution on environmental gradients: Theory and a preliminary interpretation of distributional patterns in the avifauna of the Cordillera Vilcabamba, Peru. *Ecology* **52**:23–40.

Terborgh, J. 1973. On the notion of favorableness in plant ecology. *Amer. Natur.* **107**:481–501.

Tetley, J. 1947. Increased variability accompanying an increase in population in a colony of *Argynnis selene* (Lep. Nymphalidae). *Entomologist* **80**:177–179.

Thayer, G. H. 1909. *Concealing-coloration in the animal kingdom: An exposition of the laws of disguise through color and pattern.* Macmillan, New York. 260 pp.

Thompson, W. R. 1939. Biological control and the theories of the interactions of populations. *Parasitology* **31**:299–388.

Thorp, R. W. 1969. Systematics and ecology of bees of the subgenus *Diandrena* (Hymenoptera: Andrenidae). *Univ. Calif. Pub. Entomol.* **52**:1–146.

Tinbergen, L. 1960. The natural control of insects in pinewoods. I. Factors influencing the intensity of predation by songbirds. *Arch. Neerl. Zool.* **13**:265–343.

Tinbergen, L., and H. Klomp. 1960. The natural control of insects in pinewoods. II. Conditions for damping of Nicholson oscillations in parasite-host systems. *Arch. Neerl. Zool.* **13**:344–379.

Tinkle, D. W. 1969. The concept of reproductive effort and its relation to the evolution of life histories of lizards. *Amer. Natur.* **103**:501–516.

Tomoff, C. S. 1974. Avian species diversity in desert scrub. *Ecology* **55**:396–403.

Tonzetich, J., and C. L. Ward. 1973a. Adapative chromosomal polymorphism in *Drosophila melanica. Evolution* **27**:486–494.

Tonzetich, J., and C. L. Ward. 1973b. Interaction effects of temperature and humidity on pupal survival in *Drosophila melanica. Evolution* **27**:495–504.

Tostowaryk, W. 1972. The effect of prey defense on the functional response of *Podisus modestus* (Hemiptera: Pentatomidae) to densities of the sawflies *Neodiprion swainei* and *N. pratti banksianae* (Hymenoptera: Neodiprionidae). *Can. Entomol.* **104**:61–69.

Townes, H. 1962. Host selection patterns in some nearctic ichneumonids (Hymenoptera). *11th Int. Congr. Entomol. Vienna* **2**:738–741.

Townes, H. 1969. *The genera of Ichneumonidae.* Part 2. Mem. Amer. Entomol. Inst. **12**. 537 pp.

Trivers, R. L. and H. Hare. 1975. Haplodiploidy and the evolution of the social insects. *Science.* In press.

Tso, T. C., and R. N. Jeffrey. 1959. Biochemical studies on tobacco alkaloids. I. The fate of labeled tobacco alkaloids supplied to *Nicotiana* plants. *Arch. Biochem. Biophys.* **80**:46–56.

Tso, T. C., and R. N. Jeffrey. 1961. Biochemical studies on tobacco alkaloids. IV. The dynamic state of nicotine supplied to *N. rustica. Arch. Biochem. Biophys.* **92**:253–256.

Tucker, V. A. 1969. The energetics of bird flight. *Sci. Amer.* **220**(5):70–78.

Turnbull. A. L. 1966. A population of spiders and their potential prey in an overgrazed pasture in eastern Ontario. *Can. J. Zool.* **44**:557–583.

Turnbull, A. L. 1967. Population dynamics of exotic insects. *Bull. Entomol. Soc. Amer.* **13**:333–337.

Turnbull, A. L., and D. A. Chant. 1961. The practice and theory of biological control of insects in Canada. *Can. J. Zool.* 39:697–753.

Turesson, G. 1922. The genotypical response of the plant species to the habitat. *Hereditas* 3:211–350.

Udvardy, M. D. F. 1969. *Dynamic zoogeography with special reference to land animals.* Van Nostrand Reinhold, New York. 445 pp.

Van den Bosch, R. 1968. Comments on population dynamics of exotic insects. *Bull. Entomol. Soc. Amer.* 14:112–115.

Van den Bosch, R. 1971. Biological control of insects. *Annu. Rev. Ecol. Syst.* 2:45–66.

Van den Bosch, R., and P. S. Messenger. 1973. *Biological Control.* Intext Press, New York. 180 pp.

Van den Bosch, R., E. I. Schlinger, E. J. Dietrick, J. C. Hall, and B. Puttler. 1964. Studies on succession, distribution, and phenology of imported parasites of *Therioaphis trifolii* (Monell) in Southern California. *Ecology* 45:602–621.

Van der Drift, J., and M. Witkamp. 1960. The significance of the break-down of oak litter by *Enoicyla pusilla* Burm. *Arch. Neerl. Zool.* 13:486–492.

Van der Pijl, L., and C. H. Dodson. 1966. *Orchid flowers, their pollination and evolution.* Univ. Miami Press, Coral Gables, Florida. 214 pp.

Van Emden, H. F. (ed.). 1972a. *Insect/plant relationships.* Symp. Royal Entomol. Soc. London 6. 215 pp.

Van Emden, H. F. (ed.). 1972b. *Aphid technology.* Academic Press, London. 344 pp.

Van Hook, R. I., Jr., and G. L. Dodson. 1974. Food energy budget for the yellow-poplar weevil, *Odontopus calceatus* (Say). *Ecology* 55:205–207.

Van Mieghem, J., P. van Oye, and J. Schell. (eds.). 1965. Biogeography and ecology in Antarctica. *Monogr. Biol.* 15:1–762.

Van Valen, L. 1973. Body size and numbers of plants and animals. *Evolution* 27:27–35.

Varley, G. C. 1947. The natural control of population balance in the knapweed gall-fly (*Urophora jaceana*). *J. Anim. Ecol.* 16:139–187.

Varley, G. C. 1959. The biological control of agricultural pests. *J. Roy. Soc. Arts.* 107:475–490.

Varley, G. C. 1970. The concept of energy flow applied to a woodland community. In A. Watson (ed.). *Animal populations in relation to their food resources.* Brit. Ecol. Soc. Symp. 10, pp. 389–404.

Varley, G. C., and G. R. Gradwell. 1960. Key factors in population studies. *J. Anim. Ecol.* 29:399–401.

Varley, G. C., and G. R. Gradwell. 1968. Population models for the winter moth. In T. R. E. Southwood (ed.). *Insect abundance.* Symp. Royal Entomol. Soc. London 4, pp. 132–142.

Varley, G. C., and G. R. Gradwell. 1970. Recent advances in insect population dynamics. *Annu. Rev. Entomol.* 15:1–24.

Varley, G. C., and G. R. Gradwell. 1971. The use of models and life tables in assessing the role of natural enemies. In C. B. Huffaker (ed.). *Biological control.* Plenum, New York, pp. 93–112.

Varley, G. C., G. R. Gradwell, and M P. Hassell. 1973. *Insect population ecology: An analytical approach.* Blackwell Sci. Publ., Oxford. 212 pp.

Vaurie, C. 1951. Adaptive differences between two sympatric species of nuthatches (*Sitta*). *Proc. 10th. Int. Orn. Cong.* pp. 163–166.

Verhulst, P. F. 1838. Notice sur la loi que la population suit dans son accroissement. *Correspond. Math. Phys.* 10:113–121.

Vinson, S. B. 1968. Source of a substance in *Heliothis virescens* (Lepidoptera: Noctuidae) that elicits a searching response in its habitual parasite *Cardiochiles nigriceps* (Hymenoptera: Braconidae). *Ann. Entomol. Soc. Amer.* 61:8–10.

Vinson, S. B. 1969. General morphology of the digestive and internal reproductive systems of adult *Cardiochiles nigriceps* (Hymenoptera: Braconidae). *Ann. Entomol. Soc. Amer.* 62:1414–1419.

Vinson, S. B. 1971. Defense reaction and hemocytic changes in *Heliothis virescens* in response to its habitual parasitoid *Cardiochiles nigriceps*. *J. Invert. Path.* 18:94–100.

Vinson, S. B. 1972. Effect of the parasitoid, *Campoletis sonorensis*, on the growth of its host, *Heliothis virescens*. *J. Insect Physiol.* 18:1509–1514.

Vinson, S. B., and F. S. Guillot. 1972. Host marking: Source of a substance that results in host discrimination in insect parasitoids. *Entomophaga* 17:241–245.

Volterra, V. 1926. Variazioni e fluttuazioni del numero d'individui in specie animali conviventi. *Mem. Acad. Lincei Roma* 2:31–113.

Vuilleumier, F. 1970. Insular biogeography in continental regions. I. The northern Andes of South America. *Amer. Natur.* 104:373–388.

Waldbauer, G. P. 1968. The consumption and utilization of food by insects. *Adv. Insect Physiol.* 5:229–288.

Waldbauer, G. P., and J. K. Sheldon. 1971. Phenological relationships of some aculeate Hymenoptera, their dipteran mimics, and insectivorous birds. *Evolution* 25:371–382.

Wallace, A. R. 1876. *The geographical distribution of animals.* 2 vols. Harper, New York. 503 and 607 pp.

Wallwork, J. A. 1958. Notes on the feeding behaviour of some forest soil Acarina. *Oikos* 9:260–271.

Wallwork, J. A. 1970. *Ecology of soil animals.* McGraw-Hill, London. 283 pp.

Waloff, N. 1968a. A comparison of factors affecting different insect species on the same host plant. In T. R. E. Southwood (ed.). *Insect abundance.* Symp. Royal Entomol. Soc. London. 4, pp. 76–87

Waloff, N. 1968b. Studies on the insect fauna on scotch broom *Sarothamnus scoparius* (L.) Wimmer. *Adv. Ecol. Res.* 5:87–208.

Wangersky, P. J., and W. J. Cunningham. 1957. Time lag in prey-predator population models. *Ecology* 38:136–139.

Watson, A. (ed.), 1970. Animal populations in relation to their food resources. *Brit. Ecol. Soc. Symp.* 10. 477 pp.

Watson, A., and R. Moss. 1970. Dominance, spacing behaviour and aggression in relation to population limitation in vertebrates. *Brit. Ecol. Soc. Symp.* 10:167–220.

Watson, G. 1964. Ecology and evolution of passerine birds on the islands of the Aegean Sea. Ph.D. Thesis, Department of Biology, Yale University.

Watt, K. E. F. 1963a. Mathematical population models for five agricultural crop pests. *Mem. Entomol. Soc. Can.* 32:83–91.

Watt, K. E. F. 1963b. The analysis of the survival of large larvae in the unsprayed area. In R. F. Morris (ed.). *The dynamics of epidemic spruce budworm populations*. Mem. Entomol. Soc. Can. 31, pp. 52–63.

Way, M. J., and M. Cammell. 1970. Aggregation behaviour in relation to food utilization by aphids. In A. Watson (ed.). *Animal populations in relation to their food resources*. Symp. Brit. Ecol. Soc. 10, pp. 229–246.

Webb, F. E., J. R. Blais, and R. W. Nash. 1961. A cartographic history of spruce budworm outbreaks and aerial forest spraying in the Atlantic Region of North America, 1949–1959. Can. Entomol. 93:360–379.

Wellington, W. G. 1954a. Atmospheric circulation processes and insect ecology. *Can. Entomol.* 86:312–333.

Wellington, W. G. 1954b. Weather and climate in forest entomology. *Meteorol. Monogr.* 2(8):11–18.

Wellington, W. G. 1957. Individual differences as a factor in population dynamics: The development of a problem. *Can. J. Zool.* 35:293–323.

Wellington, W. G. 1960. Qualitative changes in natural populations during changes in abundance. *Can. J. Zool.* 38:289–314.

Wellington, W. G. 1964. Qualitative changes in unstable environments. *Can. Entomol.* 96:436–451.

Westlake, D. F. 1963. Comparisons of plant productivity. *Biol. Rev.* 38:385–425.

Weygoldt, P. 1969. *The biology of pseudoscorpions*. Harvard Univ. Press, Cambridge, Mass. 145 pp.

Whitaker, J. O., Jr. 1972. Food habits of bats from Indiana. *Can. J. Zool.* 50:877–883.

Whittaker, J. B. 1971. Population changes in *Neophilaenus lineatus* (L.) (Homoptera: Cercopidae) in different parts of its range. *J. Anim. Ecol.* 40:425–443.

Whittaker, R. H. 1952. A study of summer foliage insect communities in the Great Smoky Mountains. *Ecol. Monogr.* 22:1–44.

Whittaker, R. H. 1956. Vegetation of the Great Smoky Mountains. *Ecol. Monogr.* 26:1–80.

Whittaker, R. H. 1962. Classification of natural communities. *Bot. Rev.* 28:1–239.

Whittaker, R. H. 1965. Dominance and diversity in land plant communities. *Science* 147:250–260.

Whittaker, R. H. 1967. Gradient analysis of vegetation. *Biol. Rev.* 42:207–264.

Whittaker, R. H. 1969. Evolution of diversity in plant communities. In G. M. Woodwell and H. H. Smith (eds.). *Diversity and stability in ecological systems*. Brookhaven Symp. Biol. 22, pp. 178–195.

Whittaker, R. H. 1970a. The biochemical ecology of higher plants. In E. Sondheimer and J. B. Simeone (eds.). *Chemical ecology*. Academic Press, N.Y., pp. 43–70.

Whittaker, R. H. 1970b. *Communities and ecosystems*. Macmillan, New York. 162 pp.

Whittaker, R. H. 1972. Evolution and the measurement of species diversity. *Taxon*. 21:213–251.

Whittaker, R. H., and P. P. Feeny. 1971. Allelochemics: Chemical interactions between species. *Science* 171:757–770.

Whittaker, R. H., S. A. Levin, and R. B. Root. 1973. Niche, habitat, and ecotope. *Amer. Natur.* 107:321–338.

Whittaker, R. H., and G. M. Woodwell. 1968. Dimension and production relations of trees and shrubs in the Brookhaven Forest, New York. *J. Ecol.* **56**:1–25.

Whittaker, R. H., and G. M. Woodwell. 1969. Structure, production and diversity of the oak-pine forest at Brookhaven, New York. *J. Ecol.* **57**:155–174.

Whitten, M. J. 1970. Genetics of pests in their management. In R. L. Rabb and F. E. Guthrie (eds.). *Concepts of pest management.* North Carolina State University Press, Raleigh, N.C., pp. 119–135.

Wiegert, R. G. 1964a. The ingestion of xylem sap by meadow spittlebugs, *Philaenus spumarius* (L.). *Amer. Midland Natur.* **71**:422–428.

Wiegert, R. G. 1964b. Population energetics of meadow spittlebugs (*Philaenus spumarius* L.) as affected by migration and habitat. *Ecol. Monogr.* **34**:217–241.

Wiegert, R. G. 1965. Energy dynamics of the grasshopper populations in old field and alfalfa field ecosystems. *Oikos* **16**:161–176.

Wiegert, R. G., and F. C. Evans. 1967. Investigations of secondary productivity in grasslands. In K. Petrusewicz (ed.). *Secondary productivity in terrestrial ecosystems.* Inst. Ecol., Polish Acad. Sci , Warsaw, pp. 499–518.

Wiegert, R. G., and R. Mitchell. 1973. Ecology of Yellowstone thermal effluent systems: Intersects of blue-green algae, grazing flies (*Paracoenia*, Ephydridae) and water mites (*Partnuniella*, Hydrachnellae). *Hydrobiologia* **41**:251–271.

Wiegert, R. G., and D. F. Owen. 1971. Trophic structure, available resources and population density in terrestrial vs. aquatic ecosystems. *J. Theoret. Biol.* **30**:69–81.

Wiens, J. A. 1966. On group selection and Wynne-Edwards' hypothesis. *Amer. Sci.* **54**:273–287.

Williams, C. B. 1944. Some applications of the logarithmic series and the index of diversity to ecological problems. *J. Ecol.* **32**:1–44.

Williams, C. B. 1947a. The logarithmic series and its application to biological problems. *J. Ecol.* **34**:253–272.

Williams, C. B. 1947b. The generic relations of species in small ecological communities. *J. Anim. Ecol.* **16**:11–18.

Williams, C. B. 1951. Intra-generic competition as illustrated by Moreau's records of East African bird communities. *J. Anim. Ecol.* **20**:246–253.

Williams, C. B. 1964. *Patterns in the balance of nature and related problems in quantitative ecology.* Academic Press, London. 324 pp.

Williams, C. M., and W. E. Robbins. 1968. Conference on insect-plant interactions. *BioScience* **18**:791–799.

Williams, E. C., Jr. 1941. An ecological study of the floor fauna of the Panama rain forest. *Bull. Chicago Acad. Sci.* **6**:63–124.

Williams, G. C. 1966a. *Adaptation and natural selection.* Princeton Univ. Press, Princeton, N.J. 307 pp.

Williams, G. C. 1966b. Natural selection, the costs of reproduction, and a refinement of Lack's principle. *Amer. Natur.* **100**:687–690.

Williams, G. C. (ed.). 1971. *Group selection.* Aldine-Atherton, Chicago. 210 pp.

Williamson, F. S. L. 1956. The molt and testis cycles of the anna hummingbird. *Condor* **58**:342–366.

Williamson, P. 1971. Feeding ecology of the red-eyed vireo (*Vireo olivaceus*) and associated foliage-gleaning birds. *Ecol. Monogr.* **41**:129–152.

Willson, M. F. 1971. Life history consequences of death rates. *Biologist* **53**:49–56.

Willson, M. F., and B. J. Rathcke. 1974. Adaptive design of the floral display in *Asclepias syriaca* L. *Amer. Midl. Natur.* **92**:47–57.

Wilson, E. O. 1955. A monographic revision of the ant genus *Lasius. Bull. Mus. Comp. Zool. Harvard* **113**:1–201.

Wilson, E. O. 1961. The nature of the taxon cycle in the Melanesian ant fauna. *Amer. Natur.* **95**:169–193.

Wilson, E. O. 1969. The species equilibrium. In G. M. Woodwell and H. H. Smith (eds.). *Diversity and stability in ecological systems*. Brookhaven Symp. Biol. 22, pp. 38–47.

Wilson, E. O. 1971a. *The insect societies*. Belknap Press, Cambridge, Mass. 548 pp.

Wilson, E. O. 1971b. Competitive and aggressive behavior. In J. F. Eisenberg and W. Dillon (eds.). *Man and beast: Comparative social behavior*. Smithsonian Inst. Press. pp. 182–217.

Wilson, E. O. 1973. Group selection and its significance for ecology. *BioScience* **23**:631–638.

Wilson, E. O., and W. H. Bossert. 1971. *A primer of population biology*. Sinauer, Stamford. Conn. 192 pp.

Wilson, E. O., and D. S. Simberloff. 1969. Experimental zoogeography of islands. Defaunation and monitoring techniques. *Ecology* **50**:267–278.

Wilson, F. 1960a. *A review of the biological control of insects and weeds in Australia and Australian New Guinea*. Commonwealth Inst. Biol. Control. Tech. Comm. 1. 102 pp.

Wilson, F. 1960b. The future of biological control. *Commonwealth Entomol. Conf. Rept. London* **7**:72–79.

Wilson, F. 1961. Adult reproductive behaviour in *Asoecus basalis* (Hymenoptera: Scelionidae). *Aust. J. Zool.* **9**:739–751.

Wilson, J. W. 1974. Analytical zoogeography of North American mammals. *Evolution* **28**:124–140.

Wilson, R. D., P. H. Monaghan, A. Osanik, L. C. Price, and M. A. Rogers. 1974. Natural marine oil seepage. *Science* **184**:857–865

Witkamp, M. 1971. Soils as components of ecosystems. *Annu. Rev. Ecol. Syst.* **2**:85–110.

Wolf, L. L., F. R. Hainsworth, and F. G. Stiles. 1972. Energetics of foraging: Rate and efficiency of nectar extraction by hummingbirds. *Science* **176**:1351–1352.

Woodwell, G. M. 1967. Toxic substances and ecological cycles. *Sci. Amer.* **216**(3):24–31.

Woodwell, G. M. 1974. Variation in the nutrient content of leaves of *Quercus alba*, *Quercus coccinea*, and *Pinus rigida* in the Brookhaven Forest from bud-break to abscission. *Amer. J. Bot.* **61**:749–753.

Woodwell, G. M., and H. H. Smith, eds. 1969. *Diversity and stability in ecological systems*. Brookhaven National Laboratory. Brookhaven Symp. Biol. 22.

Woodwell, G. M., C. F. Wurster, Jr., and P. A. Isaacson. 1967. DDT residues in an east coast estuary: A case of biological concentration of a persistent insecticide. *Science* **156**:821–824.

Wright, S. 1968. *Evolution and the genetics of populations*. Vol. 1. *Genetic and biometric foundations*. Univ. Chicago Press. Chicago. 469 pp.

Wright, S. 1969. *Evolution and the genetics of populations*. Vol. 2. *The theory of gene frequencies*. Univ. Chicago Press, Chicago. 511 pp.

Wright, S., and Th. Dobzhansky. 1946. Genetics of natural populations. XII. Experimental reproduction of some of the changes caused by natural selection in certain populations of *Drosophila pseudoobscura. Genetics* 31:125–156.

Wynne-Edwards, V. C. 1959. The control of population-density through social behaviour: A hypothesis. *Ibis* 101:436–441.

Wynne-Edwards. V. C. 1962. *Animal dispersion in relation to social behaviour.* Hafner, New York. 653 pp.

Wynne-Edwards, V. C. 1963. Intergroup selection and the evolution of social systems. *Nature* 200:623–626.

Wynne-Edwards, V. C. 1964a. (Responses to J. Maynard Smith 1964 and C. M. Perrins 1964) *Nature* 201:1147, 1148–1149.

Wynne-Edwards, V. C. 1964b. Population control in animals. *Sci. Amer.* 211(2):68–74.

Wynne-Edwards, V. C. 1965. Self-regulating systems in populations of animals. *Science* 147:1543–1548.

Yang, S., M. Wheeler, and I. Bock. 1972. Isozyme variations and phylogenetic relationships in the *Drosophila bipectinata* species complex. Studies in genetics. VII. *Texas Univ. Publ.* 7213:213–227.

Yoda, K., T. Kira, H. Ogawa, and K. Hozumi. 1963. Self-thinning in overcrowded pure stands under cultivated and natural conditions (Intraspecific competition among higher plants XI). *J. Biol. Osaka City Univ.* 14:107–129.

Young, J. O., I. G. Morris, and T. B. Reynoldson. 1964. A serological study of *Asellus* in the diet of lake-dwelling triclads. *Arch. Hydrobiol.* 60:366–373.

Zeikus, J. G., and T. D. Brock. 1972. Effects of thermal additions from the Yellowstone geyser basins on the bacteriology of the Firehole River. *Ecology* 53:283–290.

Zimmerman, E. C. 1948. *Insects of Hawaii.* Vol. 1. Univ. Hawaii Press, Honolulu. 206 pp.

Zimmerman, E. C. 1960. Possible evidence of rapid evolution in Hawaiian moths. *Evolution* 14:137–138.

TAXONOMIC INDEX

AUTHOR INDEX

Numbers in *italics* give the page in the bibliography on which the author's name appears.

SUBJECT INDEX

Pages on which definitions occur are in **bold face**; pages on which figures occur are in *italics*.